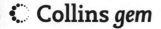

Collins *gem*

World
Atlas

D0591938

HarperCollins*Publishers*
Westerhill Road, Bishopbriggs, Glasgow, G64 2QT

www.collins.co.uk

First Published 2001
This edition published 2005
Reprint 10 9 8 7 6 5 4 3 2 1 0

ISBN 0 00 720561 9

Printed in Italy by Amadeus S.p.A.

All mapping in this atlas is generated from Collins Bartholomew
digital databases. Collins Bartholomew, the UK's leading independent
geographical information supplier, can provide a digital, custom, and
premium mapping service to a variety of markets.
For further information:
Tel: +44 (0) 141 306 3752
e-mail: collinsbartholomew@harpercollins.co.uk

Visit our website at: www.collinsbartholomew.com

World Atlas

world

states and territories		8-23
countries		24-25
physical features		26-27
climate		28-29
population and cities		30-31

europe

countries	1:46 500 000	32-33
western russian federation	1:26 500 000	34-35
baltic states and moscow region	1:10 500 000	36-37
ukraine and moldova	1:10 500 000	38-39
scandinavia and iceland	1:13 000 000	40-41
british isles	1:10 500 000	42-43
scotland	1:5 500 000	44
ireland	1:5 500 000	45
england and wales	1:5 500 000	46-47
northwest europe	1:5 500 000	48-49
central europe	1:10 500 000	50-51
france and switzerland	1:10 500 000	52-53
spain and portugal	1:10 500 000	54-55
italy and the balkans	1:10 500 000	56-57
southeast europe	1:10 500 000	58-59

asia

countries	1:103 000 000	60-61
southeast asia	1:40 000 000	62-63
malaysia and western indonesia	1:20 000 000	64-65
myanmar, thailand and indo-china	1:20 000 000	66-67
philippines	1:20 000 000	68
north korea and south korea	1:12 000 000	69
japan	1:13 000 000	70-71
china and mongolia	1:40 000 000	72-73
central china	1:20 000 000	74-75
southern asia	1:26 500 000	76-77
pakistan, northern india, nepal and bangladesh	1:20 000 000	78-79
central asia	1:26 500 000	80-81
arabian peninsula	1:20 000 000	82-83
eastern mediterranean	1:20 000 000	84-85
russian federation	1:55 500 000	86-87

africa

countries	1:79 500 000	88-89
northwest africa	1:34 500 000	90-91
northeast africa	1:34 500 000	92-93
central africa	1:26 500 000	94-95
southern africa	1:26 500 000	96-97
republic of south africa	1:13 000 000	98-99

oceania

countries	1:86 000 000	100-101
australia	1:33 000 000	102-103
southeast australia	1:13 000 000	104-105
new zealand	1:13 000 000	106
antarctica	1:79 500 000	107

north america

countries	1:86 000 000	108-109
canada	1:40 000 000	110-111
western canada	1:20 000 000	112-113
eastern canada	1:20 000 000	114-115
united states of america	1:33 000 000	116-117
western united states	1:14 500 000	118-119
north central united states	1:14 500 000	120-121
northeast united states	1:14 500 000	122-123
southeast united states	1:14 500 000	124-125
south central united states	1:14 500 000	126-127
mexico	1:20 000 000	128-129
the caribbean	1:26 500 000	130-131

south america

countries	1:66 000 000	132-133
northern south america	1:33 000 000	134-135
southern south america	1:33 000 000	136-137
southeast brazil	1:13 000 000	138-139

oceans

features		140-141
pacific ocean	1:123 500 000	142-143
atlantic ocean and indian ocean	1:123 500 000	144-145
arctic ocean	1:79 500 000	146

index   147-255

INTRODUCTION

The atlas is introduced by details of the world's states and territories and by maps and information on major geographical themes. The reference maps which follow this world section have been compiled to provide the best coverage for each part of the world through careful selection of scales and map projections. Maps are arranged on a continental basis, with each continent being introduced by maps and statistics on the continent's physical features and countries. Maps of Antarctica and the world's oceans complete the worldwide coverage.

Map symbolization

Maps show information by using symbols which are designed to reflect the features on the earth that they represent. Map symbols can be in the form of points – such as those used to show towns and airports; lines – used to represent roads and rivers; or areas – such as lakes. Variation in size, shape and colour of these types of symbol allow a great range of information to be shown. The symbols used in this atlas are explained here. Not all details can be shown at the small map scales used in this atlas, so information is generalized to allow easy interpretation. This generalization takes the form of selection – the inclusion of some features and the omission of others of less importance; and simplification – where lines are smoothed, areas combined, or symbols displaced slightly to add clarity. This is done in such a way that the overall character of the area mapped is retained. The degree of generalization varies, and is determined largely by the scale at which the map is drawn.

Scale

Scale is the relationship between the size of an area shown on the map and the actual size of the area on the ground. It determines the amount of detail shown on a map – larger scales show more, smaller scales show less – and can be used to measure the distance between two points, although the projection of the map must also be taken into account when measuring distances.

Geographical names

The spelling of place names on maps is a complex problem for the cartographer. There is no single standard way of converting them from one alphabet, or symbol set, to another. Changes in official languages also have to be taken into account when creating maps and policies need to be established for the spelling of names on individual atlases and maps. Such policies must take account of the local official position, international conventions or traditions, as well as the purpose of the atlas or map. The policy in this atlas is to use local name forms which are officially recognized by the governments of the countries concerned, but with English conventional name forms being used for the most well-known places. In these cases, the local form is often included in brackets on the map and also appears as a cross-reference in the index. All country names and those for international features appear in their English forms.

Boundaries

The status of nations and their boundaries are shown in this atlas as they are in reality at the time of going to press, as far as can be ascertained. Where international boundaries are the subject of disputes the aim is to take a strictly neutral viewpoint, based on advice from expert consultants.

MAP SYMBOLS

Settlements

Population	National Capital		Administrative Capital		City or Town	
over 5 million	⊡	BEIJING	⊙	Tianjin	⊙	New York
1 million – 5 million	☐	MADRID	○	Sydney	⊙	Madurai
500 000 – 1 million	☐	BANGUI	○	Douala	○	Barranquilla
100 000 – 500 000	☐	WELLINGTON	○	Mansa	○	Yong'an
50 000 – 100 000	☐	PORT OF SPAIN	○	Lubango	○	Puruliya
under 50 000	☐	MALABO	○	Chinhoyi	○	El Tigre

Styles of lettering

Country name	**FRANCE**	Island	*Gran Canaria*
Overseas territory / Dependency	**Guadaloupe**	Lake	*Lake Erie*
Administrative name	SCOTLAND	Mountain	*Mt Blanc*
Area name	PATAGONIA	River	*Thames*

Physical features

	Freshwater lake
	Seasonal freshwater lake
	Salt lake
	Seasonal salt lake
	Dry salt lake
	Ice cap
—	River
⚬ 2188	Mountain pass
△ 6960	Summit

Communications

══════	Motorway
───────	Main road
– – – – –	Track
– – – – –	Railway
✈	Main airport
···········	Canal

Other features

∴	Site of special interest
∿∿∿	Wall

Boundaries

───────	International
– – – – –	International disputed
───────	Administrative (selected countries only)
···········	Ceasefire line

EUROPE COUNTRIES		area sq km	area sq miles	population	capital
ALBANIA		28 748	11 100	3 166 000	Tirana
ANDORRA		465	180	71 000	Andorra la Vella
AUSTRIA		83 855	32 377	8 116 000	Vienna
BELARUS		207 600	80 155	9 895 000	Minsk
BELGIUM		30 520	11 784	10 318 000	Brussels
BOSNIA-HERZEGOVINA		51 130	19 741	4 161 000	Sarajevo
BULGARIA		110 994	42 855	7 897 000	Sofia
CROATIA		56 538	21 829	4 428 000	Zagreb
CZECH REPUBLIC		78 864	30 450	10 236 000	Prague
DENMARK		43 075	16 631	5 364 000	Copenhagen
ESTONIA		45 200	17 452	1 323 000	Tallinn
FINLAND		338 145	130 559	5 207 000	Helsinki
FRANCE		543 965	210 026	60 144 000	Paris
GERMANY		357 022	137 849	82 476 000	Berlin
GREECE		131 957	50 949	10 976 000	Athens
HUNGARY		93 030	35 919	9 877 000	Budapest
ICELAND		102 820	39 699	290 000	Reykjavík
IRELAND, REPUBLIC OF		70 282	27 136	3 956 000	Dublin
ITALY		301 245	116 311	57 423 000	Rome
LATVIA		63 700	24 595	2 307 000	Riga
LIECHTENSTEIN		160	62	34 000	Vaduz
LITHUANIA		65 200	25 174	3 444 000	Vilnius
LUXEMBOURG		2 586	998	453 000	Luxembourg
MACEDONIA (F.Y.R.O.M.)		25 713	9 928	2 056 000	Skopje
MALTA		316	122	394 000	Valletta
MOLDOVA		33 700	13 012	4 267 000	Chişinău
MONACO		2	1	34 000	Monaco-Ville
NETHERLANDS		41 526	16 033	16 149 000	Amsterdam/The Hag
NORWAY		323 878	125 050	4 533 000	Oslo
POLAND		312 683	120 728	38 587 000	Warsaw
PORTUGAL		88 940	34 340	10 062 000	Lisbon
ROMANIA		237 500	91 699	22 334 000	Bucharest
RUSSIAN FEDERATION		17 075 400	6 592 849	143 246 000	Moscow

uages	religions	currency
nian, Greek	Sunni Muslim, Albanian Orthodox, Roman Catholic	Lek
nish, Catalan, French	Roman Catholic	Euro
ian, Croatian, Turkish	Roman Catholic, Protestant	Euro
russian, Russian	Belorussian Orthodox, Roman Catholic	Belarus rouble
h (Flemish), French (Walloon), German	Roman Catholic, Protestant	Euro
ian, Serbian, Croatian	Sunni Muslim, Serbian Orthodox, Rom. Catholic, Protestant	Marka
arian, Turkish, Romany, Macedonian	Bulgarian Orthodox, Sunni Muslim	Lev
atian, Serbian	Roman Catholic, Serbian Orthodox, Sunni Muslim	Kuna
ch, Moravian, Slovak	Roman Catholic, Protestant	Czech koruna
sh	Protestant	Danish krone
nian, Russian	Protestant, Estonian and Russian Orthodox	Kroon
sh, Swedish	Protestant, Greek Orthodox	Euro
ch, Arabic	Roman Catholic, Protestant, Sunni Muslim	Euro
nan, Turkish	Protestant, Roman Catholic	Euro
k	Greek Orthodox, Sunni Muslim	Euro
garian	Roman Catholic, Protestant	Forint
ndic	Protestant	Icelandic króna
ish, Irish	Roman Catholic, Protestant	Euro
n	Roman Catholic	Euro
an, Russian	Protestant, Roman Catholic, Russian Orthodox	Lats
nan	Roman Catholic, Protestant	Swiss franc
anian, Russian, Polish	Roman Catholic, Protestant, Russian Orthodox	Litas
mburgish, German, French	Roman Catholic	Euro
edonian, Albanian, Turkish	Macedonian Orthodox, Sunni Muslim	Macedonian denar
ese, English	Roman Catholic	Maltese lira
anian, Ukrainian, Gagauz, Russian	Romanian Orthodox, Russian Orthodox	Moldovan leu
h, Monegasque, Italian	Roman Catholic	Euro
n, Frisian	Roman Catholic, Protestant, Sunni Muslim	Euro
egian	Protestant, Roman Catholic	Norwegian krone
n, German	Roman Catholic, Polish Orthodox	Zloty
guese	Roman Catholic, Protestant	Euro
anian, Hungarian	Romanian Orthodox, Protestant, Roman Catholic	Romanian leu
an, Tatar, Ukrainian, local languages	Russian Orthodox, Sunni Muslim, Protestant	Russian rouble

EUROPE COUNTRIES (continued)		area sq km	area sq miles	population	capital
SAN MARINO		61	24	28 000	San Marino
SERBIA AND MONTENEGRO		102 173	39 449	10 527 000	Belgrade
SLOVAKIA		49 035	18 933	5 402 000	Bratislava
SLOVENIA		20 251	7 819	1 984 000	Ljubljana
SPAIN		504 782	194 897	41 060 000	Madrid
SWEDEN		449 964	173 732	8 876 000	Stockholm
SWITZERLAND		41 293	15 943	7 169 000	Bern
UKRAINE		603 700	233 090	48 523 000	Kiev
UNITED KINGDOM		243 609	94 058	58 789 194	London
VATICAN CITY		0.5	0.2	472	Vatican City

EUROPE DEPENDENT TERRITORIES			area sq km	area sq miles	popul
Azores		Autonomous Region of Portugal	2 300	888	242
Faroe Islands		Self-governing Danish Territory	1 399	540	47
Gibraltar		United Kingdom Overseas Territory	7	3	2
Guernsey		United Kingdom Crown Dependency	78	30	62
Isle of Man		United Kingdom Crown Dependency	572	221	78
Jersey		United Kingdom Crown Dependency	116	45	8

ASIA COUNTRIES		area sq km	area sq miles	population	capital
AFGHANISTAN		652 225	251 825	23 897 000	Kābul
ARMENIA		29 800	11 506	3 061 000	Yerevan
AZERBAIJAN		86 600	33 436	8 370 000	Baku
BAHRAIN		691	267	724 000	Manama
BANGLADESH		143 998	55 598	146 736 000	Dhaka
BHUTAN		46 620	18 000	2 257 000	Thimphu
BRUNEI		5 765	2 226	358 000	Bandar Seri Begawa
CAMBODIA		181 000	69 884	14 144 000	Phnom Penh
CHINA		9 584 492	3 700 593	1 289 161 000	Beijing
CYPRUS		9 251	3 572	802 000	Nicosia
EAST TIMOR		14 874	5 743	778 000	Dili
GEORGIA		69 700	26 911	5 126 000	T'bilisi

guages	religions	currency
an	Roman Catholic	Euro
bian, Albanian, Hungarian	Serbian Orthodox, Montenegrin Orthodox, Sunni Muslim	Serbian dinar, Euro
vak, Hungarian, Czech	Roman Catholic, Protestant, Orthodox	Slovakian koruna
vene, Croatian, Serbian	Roman Catholic	Tólar
stilian, Catalan, Galician, Basque	Roman Catholic	Euro
edish	Protestant, Roman Catholic	Swedish krona
rman, French, Italian, Romansch	Roman Catholic, Protestant	Swiss franc
rainian, Russian	Ukrainian Orthodox, Ukrainian Catholic, Roman Catholic	Hryvnia
glish, Welsh, Gaelic	Protestant, Roman Catholic, Muslim	Pound sterling
an	Roman Catholic	Euro

ital	languages	religions	currency
ta Delgada	Portuguese	Roman Catholic, Protestant	Euro
shavn	Faroese, Danish	Protestant	Danish krone
altar	English, Spanish	Roman Catholic, Protestant, Sunni Muslim	Gibraltar pound
Peter Port	English, French	Protestant, Roman Catholic	Pound sterling
glas	English	Protestant, Roman Catholic	Pound sterling
Helier	English, French	Protestant, Roman Catholic	Pound sterling

guages	religions	currency
, Pushtu, Uzbek, Turkmen	Sunni Muslim, Shi'a Muslim	Afghani
enian, Azeri	Armenian Orthodox	Dram
ri, Armenian, Russian, Lezgian	Shi'a Muslim, Sunni Muslim, Russ. and Armenian Orthodox	Azerbaijani manat
bic, English	Shi'a Muslim, Sunni Muslim Christian	Bahrain dinar
gali, English	Sunni Muslim, Hindu	Taka
ingkha, Nepali, Assamese	Buddhist, Hindu	Ngultrum, Indian rupee
ay, English, Chinese	Sunni Muslim, Buddhist, Christian	Brunei dollar
er, Vietnamese	Buddhist, Roman Catholic, Sunni Muslim	Riel
darin, Wu, Cantonese, Hsiang, reg. lang.	Confucian, Taoist, Buddhist, Christian, Sunni Muslim	Yuan, Hong Kong dollar, Macau pataca
ek, Turkish, English	Greek Orthodox, Sunni Muslim	Cyprus pound
uguese, Tetun, English	Roman Catholic	US dollar
rg., Russ., Armen., Azeri, Osset., Abkhaz	Georgian Orthodox, Russian Orthodox, Sunni Muslim	Lari

ASIA COUNTRIES (continued)	area sq km	area sq miles	population	capital
INDIA	3 064 898	1 183 364	1 065 462 000	New Delhi
INDONESIA	1 919 445	741 102	219 883 000	Jakarta
IRAN	1 648 000	636 296	68 920 000	Tehrān
IRAQ	438 317	169 235	25 175 000	Baghdād
ISRAEL	20 770	8 019	6 433 000	Jerusalem (De facto c Disputed)
JAPAN	377 727	145 841	127 654 000	Tōkyō
JORDAN	89 206	34 443	5 473 000	'Ammān
KAZAKHSTAN	2 717 300	1 049 155	15 433 000	Astana
KUWAIT	17 818	6 880	2 521 000	Kuwait
KYRGYZSTAN	198 500	76 641	5 138 000	Bishkek
LAOS	236 800	91 429	5 657 000	Vientiane
LEBANON	10 452	4 036	3 653 000	Beirut
MALAYSIA	332 965	128 559	24 425 000	Kuala Lumpur/Putraja
MALDIVES	298	115	318 000	Male
MONGOLIA	1 565 000	604 250	2 594 000	Ulan Bator
MYANMAR	676 577	261 228	49 485 000	Rangoon
NEPAL	147 181	56 827	25 164 000	Kathmandu
NORTH KOREA	120 538	46 540	22 664 000	P'yŏngyang
OMAN	309 500	119 499	2 851 000	Muscat
PAKISTAN	803 940	310 403	153 578 000	Islamabad
PALAU	497	192	20 000	Koror
PHILIPPINES	300 000	115 831	79 999 000	Manila
QATAR	11 437	4 416	610 000	Doha
RUSSIAN FEDERATION	17 075 400	6 592 849	143 246 000	Moscow
SAUDI ARABIA	2 200 000	849 425	24 217 000	Riyadh
SINGAPORE	639	247	4 253 000	Singapore
SOUTH KOREA	99 274	38 330	47 700 000	Seoul
SRI LANKA	65 610	25 332	19 065 000	Sri Jayewardenepur
SYRIA	185 180	71 498	17 800 000	Damascus
TAIWAN	36 179	13 969	22 548 000	T'aipei
TAJIKISTAN	143 100	55 251	6 245 000	Dushanbe
THAILAND	513 115	198 115	62 833 000	Bangkok
TURKEY	779 452	300 948	71 325 000	Ankara

languages	religions	currency
...ndi, English, many regional languages	Hindu, Sunni Muslim, Shi'a Muslim, Sikh, Christian	Indian rupee
...donesian, local languages	Sunni Muslim, Protestant, Rom. Catholic, Hindu, Buddhist	Rupiah
...rsi, Azeri, Kurdish, regional languages	Shi'a Muslim, Sunni Muslim, Christian	Iranian rial
...abic, Kurdish, Turkmen	Shi'a Muslim, Sunni Muslim, Christian	Iraqi dinar
...ebrew, Arabic	Jewish, Sunni Muslim, Christian, Druze	Shekel
...panese	Shintoist, Buddhist, Christian	Yen
...abic	Sunni Muslim, Christian	Jordanian dinar
...azakh, Russian, Ukr., Ger., Uzbek, Tatar	Sunni Muslim, Russian Orthodox, Protestant	Tenge
...abic	Sunni Muslim, Shi'a Muslim, Christian, Hindu	Kuwaiti dinar
...rgyz, Russian, Uzbek	Sunni Muslim, Russian Orthodox	Kyrgyz som
...o, local languages	Buddhist, traditional beliefs	Kip
...abic, Armenian, French	Shi'a Muslim, Sunni Muslim, Christian	Lebanese pound
...alay, English, Chinese, Tamil, local lang.	Sunni Muslim, Buddhist, Hindu, Christian, traditional beliefs	Ringgit
...vehi (Maldivian)	Sunni Muslim	Rufiyaa
...alka (Mongolian), Kazakh, local languages	Buddhist, Sunni Muslim	Tugrik (tögrög)
...rmese, Shan, Karen, local languages	Buddhist, Christian, Sunni Muslim	Kyat
...epali, Maithili, Bhojpuri, English, local lang.	Hindu, Buddhist, Sunni Muslim	Nepalese rupee
...orean	Traditional beliefs, Chondoist, Buddhist	North Korean won
...abic, Baluchi, Indian languages	Ibadhi Muslim, Sunni Muslim	Omani riyal
...du, Punjabi, Sindhi, Pushtu, English	Sunni Muslim, Shi'a Muslim, Christian, Hindu	Pakistani rupee
...alauan, English	Roman Catholic, Protestant, traditional beliefs	US dollar
...nglish, Pilipino, Cebuano, local languages	Roman Catholic, Protestant, Sunni Muslim, Aglipayan	Philippine peso
...abic	Sunni Muslim	Qatari riyal
...ussian, Tatar, Ukrainian, local languages	Russian Orthodox, Sunni Muslim, Protestant	Russian rouble
...abic	Sunni Muslim, Shi'a Muslim	Saudi Arabian riyal
...inese, English, Malay, Tamil	Buddhist, Taoist, Sunni Muslim, Christian, Hindu	Singapore dollar
...orean	Buddhist, Protestant, Roman Catholic	South Korean won
...nhalese, Tamil, English	Buddhist, Hindu, Sunni Muslim, Roman Catholic	Sri Lankan rupee
...abic, Kurdish, Armenian	Sunni Muslim, Shi'a Muslim, Christian	Syrian pound
...andarin, Min, Hakka, local languages	Buddhist, Taoist, Confucian, Christian	Taiwan dollar
...jik, Uzbek, Russian		Somoni
...ai, Lao, Chinese, Malay, Mon-Khmer lang.	Buddhist, Sunni Muslim	Baht
...rkish, Kurdish	Sunni Muslim, Shi'a Muslim	Turkish lira

world states and territories
asia

ASIA COUNTRIES (continued)

ASIA COUNTRIES (continued)	area sq km	area sq miles	population	capital
TURKMENISTAN	488 100	188 456	4 867 000	Ashgabat
UNITED ARAB EMIRATES	77 700	30 000	2 995 000	Abu Dhabi
UZBEKISTAN	447 400	172 742	26 093 000	Tashkent
VIETNAM	329 565	127 246	81 377 000	Ha Nôi
YEMEN	527 968	203 850	20 010 000	Şan'ā'

ASIA DEPENDENT AND DISPUTED TERRITORIES		area sq km	area sq miles	populati
Christmas Island	Australian External Territory	135	52	1 5
Cocos Islands	Australian External Territory	14	5	6
Gaza	Semi-autonomous region	363	140	1 203 5
Jammu and Kashmir	Disputed territory (India/Pakistan)	222 236	85 806	13 000 C
West Bank	Disputed territory	5 860	2 263	2 303 6

AFRICA COUNTRIES		area sq km	area sq miles	population	capital
ALGERIA		2 381 741	919 595	31 800 000	Algiers
ANGOLA		1 246 700	481 354	13 625 000	Luanda
BENIN		112 620	43 483	6 736 000	Porto-Novo
BOTSWANA		581 370	224 468	1 785 000	Gaborone
BURKINA		274 200	105 869	13 002 000	Ouagadougou
BURUNDI		27 835	10 747	6 825 000	Bujumbura
CAMEROON		475 442	183 569	16 018 000	Yaoundé
CAPE VERDE		4 033	1 557	463 000	Praia
CENTRAL AFRICAN REPUBLIC		622 436	240 324	3 865 000	Bangui
CHAD		1 284 000	495 755	8 598 000	Ndjamena
COMOROS		1 862	719	768 000	Moroni
CONGO		342 000	132 047	3 724 000	Brazzaville
CONGO, DEMOCRATIC REP. OF		2 345 410	905 568	52 771 000	Kinshasa
CÔTE D'IVOIRE		322 463	124 504	16 631 000	Yamoussoukro
DJIBOUTI		23 200	8 958	703 000	Djibouti
EGYPT		1 000 250	386 199	71 931 000	Cairo
EQUATORIAL GUINEA		28 051	10 831	494 000	Malabo
ERITREA		117 400	45 328	4 141 000	Asmara

languages	religions	currency
Turkmen, Uzbek, Russian	Sunni Muslim, Russian Orthodox	Turkmen manat
Arabic, English	Sunni Muslim, Shi'a Muslim	United Arab Emirates dirham
Uzbek, Russian, Tajik, Kazakh	Sunni Muslim, Russian Orthodox	Uzbek som
Vietnamese, Thai, Khmer, Chinese, local lang.	Buddhist, Taoist, Roman Catholic, Cao Dai, Hoa Hao	Dong
Arabic	Sunni Muslim, Shi'a Muslim	Yemeni rial

capital	languages	religions	currency
The Settlement	English	Buddhist, Sunni Muslim, Protestant, Rom. Cath.	Australian dollar
West Island	English	Sunni Muslim, Christian	Australian dollar
Gaza	Arabic	Sunni Muslim, Shi'a Muslim	Israeli shekel
Srinagar			
	Arabic, Hebrew	Sunni Muslim, Jewish, Shi'a Muslim, Christian	Jordanian dinar, Israeli shekel

languages	religions	currency
Arabic, French, Berber	Sunni Muslim	Algerian dinar
Portuguese, Bantu, local languages	Roman Catholic, Protestant, traditional beliefs	Kwanza
French, Fon, Yoruba, Adja, local languages	Traditional beliefs, Roman Catholic, Sunni Muslim	CFA franc*
English, Setswana, Shona, local languages	Traditional beliefs, Protestant, Roman Catholic	Pula
French, Moore (Mossi), Fulani, local lang.	Sunni Muslim, traditional beliefs, Roman Catholic	CFA franc*
Kirundi (Hutu, Tutsi), French	Roman Catholic, traditional beliefs, Protestant	Burundian franc
French, English, Fang, Bamileke, local lang.	Rom. Catholic, traditional beliefs, Sunni Muslim, Protestant	CFA franc*
Portuguese, creole	Roman Catholic, Protestant	Cape Verde escudo
French, Sango, Banda, Baya, local languages	Protestant, Rom. Catholic, traditional beliefs, Sunni Muslim	CFA franc*
Arabic, French, Sara, local languages	Sunni Muslim, Rom. Catholic, Protestant, traditional beliefs	CFA franc*
Comorian, French, Arabic	Sunni Muslim, Roman Catholic	Comoros franc
French, Kongo, Monokutuba, local lang.	Rom. Catholic, Protestant, traditional beliefs, Sunni Muslim	CFA franc*
French, Lingala, Swahili, Kongo, local lang.	Christian, Sunni Muslim	Congolese franc
French, creole, Akan, local languages	Sunni Muslim, Rom. Catholic, traditional beliefs, Protestant	CFA franc*
Somali, Afar, French, Arabic	Sunni Muslim, Christian	Djibouti franc
Arabic	Sunni Muslim, Coptic Christian	Egyptian pound
Spanish, French, Fang	Roman Catholic, traditional beliefs	CFA franc*
Tigrinya, Tigre	Sunni Muslim, Coptic Christian	Nakfa

world states and territories
asia, africa

AFRICA COUNTRIES (continued)	area sq km	area sq miles	population	capital
ETHIOPIA	1 133 880	437 794	70 678 000	Addis Ababa
GABON	267 667	103 347	1 329 000	Libreville
THE GAMBIA	11 295	4 361	1 426 000	Banjul
GHANA	238 537	92 100	20 922 000	Accra
GUINEA	245 857	94 926	8 480 000	Conakry
GUINEA-BISSAU	36 125	13 948	1 493 000	Bissau
KENYA	582 646	224 961	31 987 000	Nairobi
LESOTHO	30 355	11 720	1 802 000	Maseru
LIBERIA	111 369	43 000	3 367 000	Monrovia
LIBYA	1 759 540	679 362	5 551 000	Tripoli
MADAGASCAR	587 041	226 658	17 404 000	Antananarivo
MALAWI	118 484	45 747	12 105 000	Lilongwe
MALI	1 240 140	478 821	13 007 000	Bamako
MAURITANIA	1 030 700	397 955	2 893 000	Nouakchott
MAURITIUS	2 040	788	1 221 000	Port Louis
MOROCCO	446 550	172 414	30 566 000	Rabat
MOZAMBIQUE	799 380	308 642	18 863 000	Maputo
NAMIBIA	824 292	318 261	1 987 000	Windhoek
NIGER	1 267 000	489 191	11 972 000	Niamey
NIGERIA	923 768	356 669	124 009 000	Abuja
RWANDA	26 338	10 169	8 387 000	Kigali
SÃO TOMÉ AND PRÍNCIPE	964	372	161 000	São Tomé
SENEGAL	196 720	75 954	10 095 000	Dakar
SEYCHELLES	455	176	81 000	Victoria
SIERRA LEONE	71 740	27 699	4 971 000	Freetown
SOMALIA	637 657	246 201	9 890 000	Mogadishu
SOUTH AFRICA, REPUBLIC OF	1 219 090	470 693	45 026 000	Pretoria/Cape Town
SUDAN	2 505 813	967 500	33 610 000	Khartoum
SWAZILAND	17 364	6 704	1 077 000	Mbabane
TANZANIA	945 087	364 900	36 977 000	Dodoma
TOGO	56 785	21 925	4 909 000	Lomé
TUNISIA	164 150	63 379	9 832 000	Tunis
UGANDA	241 038	93 065	25 827 000	Kampala

languages	religions	currency
Oromo, Amharic, Tigrinya, local languages	Ethiopian Orthodox, Sunni Muslim, traditional beliefs	Birr
French, Fang, local languages	Roman Catholic, Protestant, traditional beliefs	CFA franc*
English, Malinke, Fulani, Wolof	Sunni Muslim, Protestant	Dalasi
English, Hausa, Akan, local languages	Christian, Sunni Muslim, traditional beliefs	Cedi
French, Fulani, Malinke, local languages	Sunni Muslim, traditional beliefs, Christian	Guinea franc
Portuguese, crioulo, local languages	Traditional beliefs, Sunni Muslim, Christian	CFA franc*
Swahili, English, local languages	Christian, traditional beliefs	Kenyan shilling
Sesotho, English, Zulu	Christian, traditional beliefs	Loti, S. African rand
English, creole, local languages	Traditional beliefs, Christian, Sunni Muslim	Liberian dollar
Arabic, Berber	Sunni Muslim	Libyan dinar
Malagasy, French	Traditional beliefs, Christian, Sunni Muslim	Malagasy franc
Chichewa, English, local languages	Christian, traditional beliefs, Sunni Muslim	Malawian kwacha
French, Bambara, local languages	Sunni Muslim, traditional beliefs, Christian	CFA franc*
Arabic, French, local languages	Sunni Muslim	Ouguiya
English, creole, Hindi, Bhojpuri, French	Hindu, Roman Catholic, Sunni Muslim	Mauritius rupee
Arabic, Berber, French	Sunni Muslim	Moroccan dirham
Portuguese, Makua, Tsonga, local languages	Traditional beliefs, Roman Catholic, Sunni Muslim	Metical
English, Afrikaans, Germ., Ovambo, loc. lang.	Protestant, Roman Catholic	Namibian dollar
French, Hausa, Fulani, local languages	Sunni Muslim, traditional beliefs	CFA franc*
English, Hausa, Yoruba, Ibo, Fulani, local lang.	Sunni Muslim, Christian, traditional beliefs	Naira
Kinyarwanda, French, English	Roman Catholic, traditional beliefs, Protestant	Rwandan franc
Portuguese, creole	Roman Catholic, Protestant	Dobra
French, Wolof, Fulani, local languages	Sunni Muslim, Roman Catholic, traditional beliefs	CFA franc*
English, French, creole	Roman Catholic, Protestant	Seychelles rupee
English, creole, Mende, Temne, local lang.	Sunni Muslim, traditional beliefs	Leone
Somali, Arabic	Sunni Muslim	Somali shilling
Afrikaans, English, nine official local languages	Protestant, Roman Catholic, Sunni Muslim, Hindu	Rand
Arabic, Dinka, Nubian, Beja, Nuer, local lang.	Sunni Muslim, traditional beliefs, Christian	Sudanese dinar
Swazi, English	Christian, traditional beliefs	Emalangeni, S. African rand
Swahili, English, Nyamwezi, local languages	Shi'a Muslim, Sunni Muslim, traditional beliefs, Christian	Tanzanian shilling
French, Ewe, Kabre, local languages	Traditional beliefs, Christian, Sunni Muslim	CFA franc*
Arabic, French	Sunni Muslim	Tunisian dinar
English, Swahili, Luganda, local languages	Rom. Catholic, Protestant, Sunni Muslim, traditional beliefs	Ugandan shilling

world states and territories
africa

AFRICA COUNTRIES (continued)		area sq km	area sq miles	population	capital
ZAMBIA		752 614	290 586	10 812 000	Lusaka
ZIMBABWE		390 759	150 873	12 891 000	Harare

AFRICA DEPENDENT AND DISPUTED TERRITORIES			area sq km	area sq miles	populatic
Canary Islands		Autonomous Community of Spain	7 447	2 875	1 694 47
Madeira		Autonomous Region of Portugal	779	301	242 60
Mayotte		French Territorial Collectivity	373	144	171 00
Réunion		French Overseas Department	2 551	985	756 00
St Helena and Dependencies		United Kingdom Overseas Territory	121	47	5 64
Western Sahara		Disputed territory (Morocco)	266 000	102 703	308 00

OCEANIA COUNTRIES		area sq km	area sq miles	population	capital
AUSTRALIA		7 692 024	2 969 907	19 731 000	Canberra
FIJI		18 330	7 077	839 000	Suva
KIRIBATI		717	277	88 000	Bairiki
MARSHALL ISLANDS		181	70	53 000	Delap-Uliga-Djarrit
MICRONESIA, FED. STATES OF		701	271	109 000	Palikir
NAURU		21	8	13 000	Yaren
NEW ZEALAND		270 534	104 454	3 875 000	Wellington
PAPUA NEW GUINEA		462 840	178 704	5 711 000	Port Moresby
SAMOA		2 831	1 093	178 000	Apia
SOLOMON ISLANDS		28 370	10 954	477 000	Honiara
TONGA		748	289	104 000	Nuku'alofa
TUVALU		25	10	11 000	Vaiaku
VANUATU		12 190	4 707	212 000	Port Vila

OCEANIA DEPENDENT TERRITORIES			area sq km	area sq miles	populatic
American Samoa		United States Unincorporated Territory	197	76	67 00
Cook Islands		Self-governing New Zealand Territory	293	113	18 00
French Polynesia		French Overseas Territory	3 265	1 261	244 00
Guam		United States Unincorporated Territory	541	209	163 00
New Caledonia		French Overseas Territory	19 058	7 358	228 00

languages	religions	currency
English, Bemba, Nyanja, Tonga, local lang.	Christian, traditional beliefs	Zambian kwacha
English, Shona, Ndebele	Christian, traditional beliefs	Zimbabwean dollar

capital	languages	religions	currency
S. Cruz de Tenerife, Las Palmas	Spanish	Roman Catholic	Euro
Funchal	Portuguese	Roman Catholic, Protestant	Euro
Dzaoudzi	French, Mahorian	Sunni Muslim, Christian	Euro
St-Denis	French, creole	Roman Catholic	Euro
Jamestown	English	Protestant, Roman Catholic	St Helena pound
Laâyoune	Arabic	Sunni Muslim	Moroccan dirham

*Communauté Financière Africaine franc

languages	religions	currency
English, Italian, Greek	Protestant, Roman Catholic, Orthodox	Australian dollar
English, Fijian, Hindi	Christian, Hindu, Sunni Muslim	Fiji dollar
Gilbertese, English	Roman Catholic, Protestant	Australian dollar
English, Marshallese	Protestant, Roman Catholic	US dollar
English, Chuukese, Pohnpeian, local lang.	Roman Catholic, Protestant	US dollar
Nauruan, English	Protestant, Roman Catholic	Australian dollar
English, Maori	Protestant, Roman Catholic	New Zealand dollar
English, Tok Pisin (creole), local languages	Protestant, Roman Catholic, traditional beliefs	Kina
Samoan, English	Protestant, Roman Catholic	Tala
English, creole, local languages	Protestant, Roman Catholic	Solomon Islands dollar
Tongan, English	Protestant, Roman Catholic	Pa'anga
Tuvaluan, English	Protestant	Australian dollar
English, Bislama (creole), French	Protestant, Roman Catholic, traditional beliefs	Vatu

capital	languages	religions	currency
Pagotogo	Samoan, English	Protestant, Roman Catholic	US dollar
Avarua	English, Maori	Protestant, Roman Catholic	New Zealand dollar
Papeete	French, Tahitian, Polynesian lang.	Protestant, Roman Catholic	CFP franc*
Hagåtña	Chamorro, English, Tagalog	Roman Catholic	US dollar
Nouméa	French, local languages	Roman Catholic, Protestant, Sunni Muslim	CFP franc*

OCEANIA DEPENDENT TERRITORIES (continued)		area sq km	area sq miles	population
Niue	Self-governing New Zealand Territory	258	100	2 000
Norfolk Island	Australian External Territory	35	14	2 037
Northern Mariana Islands	United States Commonwealth	477	184	79 000
Pitcairn Islands	United Kingdom Overseas Territory	45	17	5
Tokelau	New Zealand Overseas Territory	10	4	2 000
Wallis and Futuna Islands	French Overseas Territory	274	106	15 000

NORTH AMERICA COUNTRIES		area sq km	area sq miles	population	capital
ANTIGUA AND BARBUDA		442	171	73 000	St John's
THE BAHAMAS		13 939	5 382	314 000	Nassau
BARBADOS		430	166	270 000	Bridgetown
BELIZE		22 965	8 867	256 000	Belmopan
CANADA		9 984 670	3 855 103	31 510 000	Ottawa
COSTA RICA		51 100	19 730	4 173 000	San José
CUBA		110 860	42 803	11 300 000	Havana
DOMINICA		750	290	79 000	Roseau
DOMINICAN REPUBLIC		48 442	18 704	8 745 000	Santo Domingo
EL SALVADOR		21 041	8 124	6 515 000	San Salvador
GRENADA		378	146	80 000	St George's
GUATEMALA		108 890	42 043	12 347 000	Guatemala City
HAITI		27 750	10 714	8 326 000	Port-au-Prince
HONDURAS		112 088	43 277	6 941 000	Tegucigalpa
JAMAICA		10 991	4 244	2 651 000	Kingston
MEXICO		1 972 545	761 604	103 457 000	Mexico City
NICARAGUA		130 000	50 193	5 466 000	Managua
PANAMA		77 082	29 762	3 120 000	Panama City
ST KITTS AND NEVIS		261	101	42 000	Basseterre
ST LUCIA		616	238	149 000	Castries
ST VINCENT AND THE GRENADINES		389	150	120 000	Kingstown
TRINIDAD AND TOBAGO		5 130	1 981	1 303 000	Port of Spain
UNITED STATES OF AMERICA		9 826 635	3 794 085	294 043 000	Washington DC

capital	languages	religions	currency
Alofi	English, Polynesian	Christian	New Zealand dollar
Kingston	English	Protestant, Roman Catholic	Australian dollar
Capitol Hill	English, Chamorro, local lang.	Roman Catholic	US dollar
Adamstown	English	Protestant	New Zealand dollar
	English, Tokelauan	Christian	New Zealand dollar
Matā'utu	French, Wallisian, Futunian	Roman Catholic	CFP franc*

*Franc des Comptoirs Français du Pacifique

languages	religions	currency
English, creole	Protestant, Roman Catholic	East Caribbean dollar
English, creole	Protestant, Roman Catholic	Bahamian dollar
English, creole	Protestant, Roman Catholic	Barbados dollar
English, Spanish, Mayan, creole	Roman Catholic, Protestant	Belize dollar
English, French	Roman Catholic, Protestant, Eastern Orthodox, Jewish	Canadian dollar
Spanish	Roman Catholic, Protestant	Costa Rican colón
Spanish	Roman Catholic, Protestant	Cuban peso
English, creole	Roman Catholic, Protestant	East Caribbean dollar
Spanish, creole	Roman Catholic, Protestant	Dominican peso
Spanish	Roman Catholic, Protestant	El Sal. colón, US dollar
English, creole	Roman Catholic, Protestant	East Caribbean dollar
Spanish, Mayan languages	Roman Catholic, Protestant	Quetzal, US dollar
French, creole	Roman Catholic, Protestant, Voodoo	Gourde
Spanish, Amerindian languages	Roman Catholic, Protestant	Lempira
English, creole	Protestant, Roman Catholic	Jamaican dollar
Spanish, Amerindian languages	Roman Catholic, Protestant	Mexican peso
Spanish, Amerindian languages	Roman Catholic, Protestant	Córdoba
Spanish, English, Amerindian languages	Roman Catholic, Protestant, Sunni Muslim	Balboa
English, creole	Protestant, Roman Catholic	East Caribbean dollar
English, creole	Roman Catholic, Protestant	East Caribbean dollar
English, creole	Protestant, Roman Catholic	East Caribbean dollar
English, creole, Hindi	Roman Catholic, Hindu, Protestant, Sunni Muslim	Trinidad and Tob. dollar
English, Spanish	Protestant, Roman Catholic, Sunni Muslim, Jewish	US dollar

world states and territories
oceania, north america

NORTH AMERICA DEPENDENT TERRITORIES			area sq km	area sq miles	population
Anguilla		United Kingdom Overseas Territory	155	60	12 000
Aruba		Self-governing Netherlands Territory	193	75	100 000
Bermuda		United Kingdom Overseas Territory	54	21	82 000
Cayman Islands		United Kingdom Overseas Territory	259	100	40 000
Greenland		Self-governing Danish Territory	2 175 600	840 004	57 000
Guadeloupe		French Overseas Department	1 780	687	440 000
Martinique		French Overseas Department	1 079	417	393 000
Montserrat		United Kingdom Overseas Territory	100	39	4 000
Netherlands Antilles		Self-governing Netherlands Territory	800	309	221 000
Puerto Rico		United States Commonwealth	9 104	3 515	3 879 000
St Pierre and Miquelon		French Territorial Collectivity	242	93	6 000
Turks and Caicos Islands		United Kingdom Overseas Territory	430	166	21 000
Virgin Islands (U.K.)		United Kingdom Overseas Territory	153	59	21 000
Virgin Islands (U.S.A.)		United States Unincorporated Territory	352	136	111 000

SOUTH AMERICA COUNTRIES		area sq km	area sq miles	population	capital
ARGENTINA		2 766 889	1 068 302	38 428 000	Buenos Aires
BOLIVIA		1 098 581	424 164	8 808 000	La Paz/Sucre
BRAZIL		8 514 879	3 287 613	178 470 000	Brasília
CHILE		756 945	292 258	15 805 000	Santiago
COLOMBIA		1 141 748	440 831	44 222 000	Bogotá
ECUADOR		272 045	105 037	13 003 000	Quito
GUYANA		214 969	83 000	765 000	Georgetown
PARAGUAY		406 752	157 048	5 878 000	Asunción
PERU		1 285 216	496 225	27 167 000	Lima
SURINAME		163 820	63 251	436 000	Paramaribo
URUGUAY		176 215	68 037	3 415 000	Montevideo
VENEZUELA		912 050	352 144	25 699 000	Caracas

SOUTH AMERICA DEPENDENT TERRITORIES			area sq km	area sq miles	population
Falkland Islands		United Kingdom Overseas Territory	12 170	4 699	3 000
French Guiana		French Overseas Department	90 000	34 749	178 000

capital	languages	religions	currency
The Valley	English	Protestant, Roman Catholic	East Caribbean dollar
Oranjestad	Papiamento, Dutch, English	Roman Catholic, Protestant	Aruban florin
Hamilton	English	Protestant, Roman Catholic	Bermuda dollar
George Town	English	Protestant, Roman Catholic	Cayman Islands dollar
Nuuk	Greenlandic, Danish	Protestant	Danish krone
Basse-Terre	French, creole	Roman Catholic	Euro
Fort-de-France	French, creole	Roman Catholic, traditional beliefs	Euro
Plymouth	English	Protestant, Roman Catholic	East Caribbean dollar
Willemstad	Dutch, Papiamento, English	Roman Catholic, Protestant	Netherlands guilder
San Juan	Spanish, English	Roman Catholic, Protestant	US dollar
St-Pierre	French	Roman Catholic	Euro
Grand Turk	English	Protestant	US dollar
Road Town	English	Protestant, Roman Catholic	US dollar
Charlotte Amalie	English, Spanish	Protestant, Roman Catholic	US dollar

languages	religions	currency
Spanish, Italian, Amerindian languages	Roman Catholic, Protestant	Argentinian peso
Spanish, Quechua, Aymara	Roman Catholic, Protestant, Baha'i	Boliviano
Portuguese	Roman Catholic, Protestant	Real
Spanish, Amerindian languages	Roman Catholic, Protestant	Chilean peso
Spanish, Amerindian languages	Roman Catholic, Protestant	Colombian peso
Spanish, Quechua, other Amerindian lang.	Roman Catholic	US dollar
English, creole, Amerindian languages	Protestant, Hindu, Roman Catholic, Sunni Muslim	Guyana dollar
Spanish, Guarani	Roman Catholic, Protestant	Guarani
Spanish, Quechua, Aymara	Roman Catholic, Protestant	Sol
Dutch, Surinamese, English, Hindi	Hindu, Roman Catholic, Protestant, Sunni Muslim	Suriname guilder
Spanish	Roman Catholic, Protestant, Jewish	Uruguayan peso
Spanish, Amerindian languages	Roman Catholic, Protestant	Bolivar

capital	languages	religions	currency
Stanley	English	Protestant, Roman Catholic	Falkland Islands pound
Cayenne	French, creole	Roman Catholic	Euro

World extremes – capitals

Largest national capital (population)	Tōkyō, Japan	26 849 000
Smallest national capital (population)	Vatican City	472
Most northerly national capital	Reykjavík, Iceland	64° 08'N
Most southerly national capital	Wellington, New Zealand	41° 18'S
Highest capital	La Paz, Bolivia	3 630 m 11 909 ft

AL.   ALBANIA
A.   ANDORRA
ARM.   ARMENIA
AUS.   AUSTRIA
AZ.   AZERBAIJAN
B.   BURUNDI
BE.   BENIN
BEL.   BELGIUM
B.H.   BOSNIA-HERZEGOVINA
BN.   BAHRAIN
BUR.   BURKINA
CAM.   CAMEROON
C.A.R.   CENTRAL AFRICAN REPUBLIC
C.D'I.   CÔTE D'IVOIRE
CR.   CROATIA
CYP.   CYPRUS
CZ.R.   CZECH REPUBLIC
DEN.   DENMARK
EQ.G.   EQUATORIAL GUINEA
FR.G.   FRENCH GUIANA
GEOR.   GEORGIA
GER.   GERMANY
GH.   GHANA
GUY.   GUYANA
HUN.   HUNGARY
ISR.   ISRAEL

JOR.   JORDAN
K.   KUWAIT
KYR.   KYRGYZSTAN
LEB.   LEBANON
LITH.   LITHUANIA
LUX.   LUXEMBOURG
M.   MACEDONIA
MO.   MOLDOVA
NETH.   NETHERLANDS
NI.   NIGERIA
POL.   POLAND
Q.   QATAR
R.   RWANDA
SLA.   SLOVAKIA
SL.   SLOVENIA
S.M.   SERBIA AND
           MONTENEGRO
SUR.   SURINAME
SW.   SWITZERLAND
T.   TOGO
TAJIK.   TAJIKISTAN
TURKM.   TURKMENISTAN
U.A.E.   UNITED ARAB
           EMIRATES
UZBEK.   UZBEKISTAN

0   1000   2000   3000 miles
0   2000   4000 km

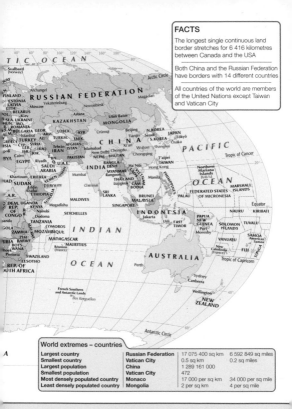

World extremes – countries			
Largest country	Russian Federation	17 075 400 sq km	6 592 849 sq miles
Smallest country	Vatican City	0.5 sq km	0.2 sq miles
Largest population	China	1 289 161 000	
Smallest population	Vatican City	472	
Most densely populated country	Monaco	17 000 per sq km	34 000 per sq mile
Least densely populated country	Mongolia	2 per sq km	4 per sq mile

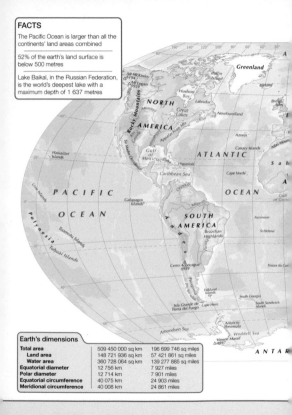

FACTS

The Pacific Ocean is larger than all the continents' land areas combined

52% of the earth's land surface is below 500 metres

Lake Baikal, in the Russian Federation, is the world's deepest lake with a maximum depth of 1 637 metres

Earth's dimensions

Total area	509 450 000 sq km	196 699 746 sq miles
Land area	148 721 936 sq km	57 421 861 sq miles
Water area	360 728 064 sq km	139 277 885 sq miles
Equatorial diameter	12 756 km	7 927 miles
Polar diameter	12 714 km	7 901 miles
Equatorial circumference	40 075 km	24 903 miles
Meridional circumference	40 008 km	24 861 miles

1:238 000 000

World extremes

Highest mountain	**Mt Everest**, China/Nepal	8 848 metres	29 028 feet
Longest river	**Nile**, Africa	6 695 km	4 160 miles
Largest lake	**Caspian Sea**, Asia/Europe	371 000 sq km	143 244 sq miles
Largest island	**Greenland**, North America	2 175 600 sq km	840 004 sq miles
Largest drainage basin	**Amazon**, South America	7 050 000 sq km	2 722 005 sq miles
Lowest point	**Dead Sea**, Asia	-398 miles	-1 306 feet
Deepest water	**Challenger Deep**, Pacific Ocean	10 920 metres	35 826 feet

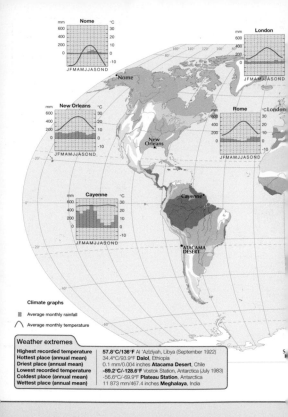

Nome

mm / °C

London

mm / °C

New Orleans

mm / °C

Rome

mm / °C

Cayenne

mm / °C

ATACAMA DESERT

Climate graphs

■ Average monthly rainfall

⋀ Average monthly temperature

Weather extremes

Highest recorded temperature	**57.8°C/136°F** Al 'Aziziyah, Libya (September 1922)
Hottest place (annual mean)	34.4°C/93.9°F **Dalol**, Ethiopia
Driest place (annual mean)	0.1 mm/0.004 inches **Atacama Desert**, Chile
Lowest recorded temperature	**-89.2°C/-128.6°F** Vostok Station, Antarctica (July 1983)
Coldest place (annual mean)	-56.6°C/-69.9°F **Plateau Station**, Antarctica
Wettest place (annual mean)	11 873 mm/467.4 inches **Meghalaya**, India

1:238 000 000

0   1000   2000   3000 miles

0   2000   4000 km

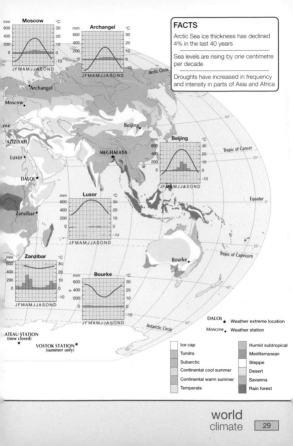

FACTS

Arctic Sea ice thickness has declined 4% in the last 40 years

Sea levels are rising by one centimetre per decade

Droughts have increased in frequency and intensity in parts of Asia and Africa

Moscow

Archangel

Beijing

Luxor

Zanzibar

Bourke

DALOL ★ Weather extreme location

Moscow • Weather station

Ice cap	Humid subtropical
Tundra	Mediterranean
Subarctic	Steppe
Continental cool summer	Desert
Continental warm summer	Savanna
Temperate	Rain forest

world
climate

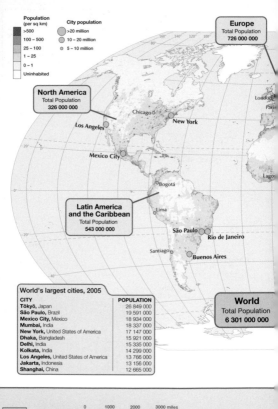

Population (per sq km)

- >500
- 100 – 500
- 25 – 100
- 1 – 25
- 0 – 1
- Uninhabited

City population

- >20 million
- 10 – 20 million
- 5 – 10 million

Europe
Total Population
726 000 000

North America
Total Population
326 000 000

Chicago
New York
Los Angeles
Mexico City

London
Paris

Lagos

Bogotá
Lima

Latin America and the Caribbean
Total Population
543 000 000

São Paulo
Rio de Janeiro
Santiago
Buenos Aires

World
Total Population
6 301 000 000

World's largest cities, 2005

CITY	POPULATION
Tōkyō, Japan	26 849 000
São Paulo, Brazil	19 591 000
Mexico City, Mexico	18 934 000
Mumbai, India	18 337 000
New York, United States of America	17 147 000
Dhaka, Bangladesh	15 921 000
Delhi, India	15 335 000
Kolkata, India	14 299 000
Los Angeles, United States of America	13 766 000
Jakarta, Indonesia	13 156 000
Shanghai, China	12 665 000

1:238 000 000

0   1000   2000   3000 miles
0   2000   4000 km

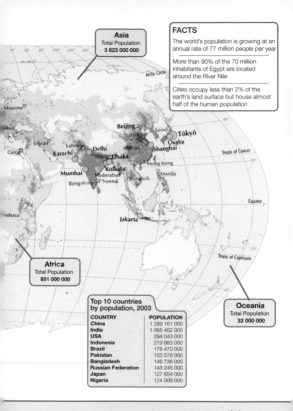

Asia
Total Population
3 823 000 000

FACTS

The world's population is growing at an annual rate of 77 million people per year

More than 90% of the 70 million inhabitants of Egypt are located around the River Nile

Cities occupy less than 2% of the earth's land surface but house almost half of the human population

Africa
Total Population
851 000 000

Oceania
Total Population
32 000 000

Top 10 countries by population, 2003

COUNTRY	POPULATION
China	1 289 161 000
India	1 065 462 000
USA	294 043 000
Indonesia	219 883 000
Brazil	178 470 000
Pakistan	153 578 000
Bangladesh	146 736 000
Russian Federation	143 246 000
Japan	127 654 000
Nigeria	124 009 000

Map labels: Moscow, Istanbul, Tehran, Cairo, Kinshasa, Beijing, Tianjin, Seoul, Tōkyō, Ōsaka, Shanghai, Wuhan, Lahore, Delhi, Karachi, Dhaka, Kolkata, Mumbai, Hyderabad, Bangalore, Chennai, Bangkok, Hong Kong, Manila, Jakarta, Arctic Circle, Tropic of Cancer, Equator, Tropic of Capricorn

Largest country	Russian Federation	17 075 400 sq km	6 592 812 sq miles
Smallest country	Vatican City	0.5 sq km	0.2 sq miles
Largest population	Russian Federation	143 246 000	
Smallest population	Vatican City	472	
Most densely populated country	Monaco	17 000 per sq km	34 000 per sq mile
Least densely populated country	Iceland	3 per sq km	7 per sq mile

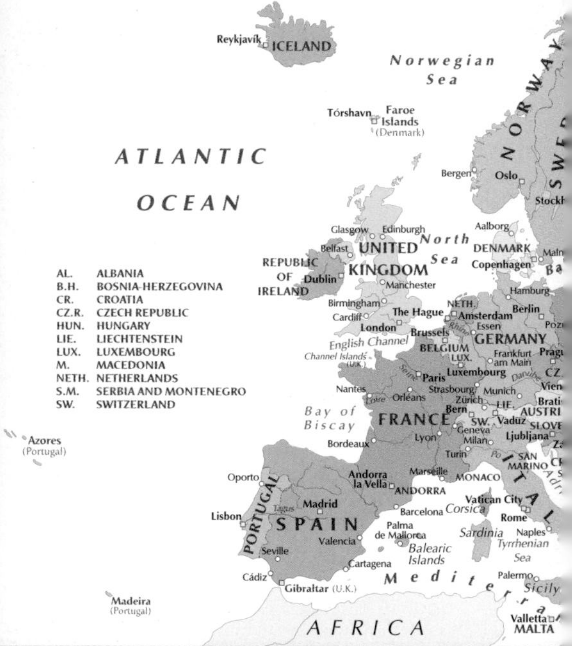

Reykjavik ICELAND

Norwegian Sea

Tórshavn Faroe Islands (Denmark)

ATLANTIC OCEAN

NORWAY SWE

Bergen Oslo Stockl

Glasgow Edinburgh

Belfast North Sea

REPUBLIC OF IRELAND Dublin UNITED KINGDOM DENMARK Aalborg Copenhagen Malmö Ba

Manchester Hamburg

AL.	ALBANIA
B.H.	BOSNIA-HERZEGOVINA
CR.	CROATIA
CZ.R.	CZECH REPUBLIC
HUN.	HUNGARY
LIE.	LIECHTENSTEIN
LUX.	LUXEMBOURG
M.	MACEDONIA
NETH.	NETHERLANDS
S.M.	SERBIA AND MONTENEGRO
SW.	SWITZERLAND

Birmingham The Hague NETH. Berlin Poze

Cardiff Amsterdam Essen

London Brussels GERMANY Praga

English Channel BELGIUM Frankfurt am Main

Channel Islands (U.K.) Paris LUX. Luxembourg Munich Brati

Nantes Loire Orléans Strasbourg Zürich LIE. AUSTR

Azores (Portugal)

Bay of Biscay FRANCE Bern SW. Vaduz SLOVE

Geneva Ljubljana CF

Bordeaux Lyon Turin Milan SAN MARINO

Oporto Marseille MONACO ITA

Andorra la Vella ANDORRA Corsica Rome

Lisbon PORTUGAL Madrid Barcelona Vatican City

Tagus SPAIN Valencia Palma de Mallorca Sardinia Naples

Seville Balearic Islands Tyrrhenian Sea

Cartagena Palermo

Madeira (Portugal) Cádiz Gibraltar (U.K.) *Mediterra* Sicily

Valletta MALTA

AFRICA

1: 46 500 000

| 0 | 150 | 300 | 450 miles |
| 0 | 300 | 600 km | |

Barents
Sea

*Novaya
Zemlya*

Vorkuta

*Ostrov
Kolguyev*

pland

*White
Sea*

Archangel

Severnaya Dvina

R U S S I A N

FINLAND

*Lake
Ladoga*

F E D E R A T I O N

Helsinki
Gulf of Finland

St Petersburg

Perm'

ESTONIA

Tallinn

Yaroslavl'

Izhevsk

Volga

Nizhniy
Novgorod

Kazan'

Ufa

LATVIA

Riga

Moscow

Ul'yanovsk

Samara

A S I A

THUANIA

Vilnius

Tula

Saratov

Orenburg

liningrad

Minsk

BELARUS

rsaw

Brest

Homyel'

Voronezh

Volgograd

ND

owice

Rivne

Kiev

Kharkiv

Don

Astrakhan'

L'viv

U K R A I N E

Dnipropetrovs'k

Donets'k

Rostov-
na-Donu

Caspian Sea

KIA

dapest

MOLDOVA

Chişinău

Krasnodar

Grozny

ROMANIA

Odesa

Caucasus

elgrade

Bucharest

Constanța

Black Sea

jevo

M.

BULGARIA

Sofia

Istanbul

Skopje

T U R K E Y

Thessaloníki

Aegean

GREECE

Athens

Sea

an

Crete

Europe's capitals		
Largest capital (population)	**Paris**, France	9 753 000
Smallest capital (population)	**Vatican City**	472
Most northerly capital	**Reykjavík**, Iceland	64° 39'N
Most southerly capital	**Valletta**, Malta	35° 54'N
Highest capital	**Andorra la Vella**, Andorra	1 029 metres 3 376 feet

europe
countries

1:26 500 000

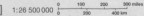

1:10 500 000

| 0 | 50 | 100 | 150 miles |

| 0 | 100 | 200 km |

europe
baltic states and moscow region

38 1:10 500 000

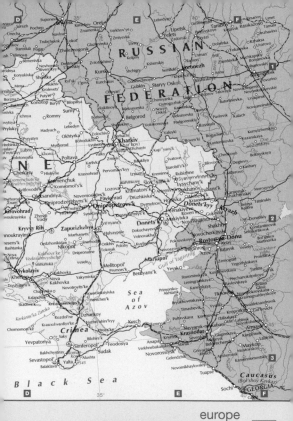

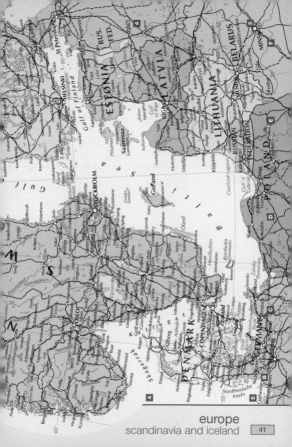

europe
ireland

45

North
Sea

NETHERLANDS
AMSTERDAM

THE HAGUE
Rotterdam

BELGIUM
BRUSSELS

LUXEMBOURG

FRANCE

48   1:5 500 000

1:10 500 000

europe
france and switzerland

1:10 500 000

0   50   100   150 miles

0   100   200 km

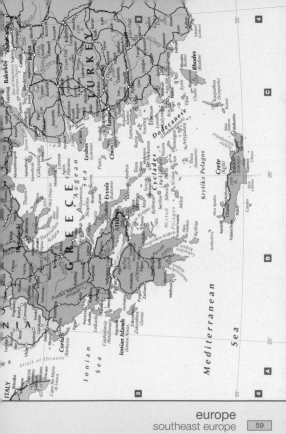

Asia's countries

Largest country	Russian Federation	17 075 400 sq km	6 592 812 sq miles
Smallest country	Maldives	298 sq km	115 sq miles
Largest population	China	1 289 161 000	
Smallest population	Palau	20 000	
Most densely populated country	Singapore	6 656 per sq km	17 219 per sq mile
Least densely populated country	Mongolia	2 per sq km	4 per sq mile

Asia's capitals

Largest capital (population)	Tōkyō, Japan	26 849 000	
Smallest capital (population)	Koror, Palau	14 000	
Most northerly capital	Astana, Kazakhstan	51° 10'N	
Most southerly capital	Dili, East Timor	8° 35'S	
Highest capital	Thimphu, Bhutan	2 423 metres	7 949 feet

1:103 000 000

CTIC OCEAN

Bering
Sea

Magadan

Petropavlovak-
Kamchatskiy

Sea
of
Okhotsk

DERATION

Irkutsk

Lake
Baikal

Ulan Bator

MONGOLIA

Harbin

Vladivostock

Sapporo

Hakodate

Shenyang

NORTH
KOREA (East Sea)

Sea
of
Japan

JAPAN

Beijing Dalian

P'yŏngyang

Tōkyō

Tianjin

SOUTH
KOREA

Seoul

Osaka

Hiroshima

Fukuoka

Yellow River

Lanzhou

Xi'an

Nanjing

Yellow
Sea

Shanghai

CHINA

Chengdu

Yangtze

Hangzhou

Wuhan

East
China
Sea

PACIFIC
OCEAN

Chongqing

Kunming

Liuzhou

T'aipei

Nanning

Guangzhou

Kaohsiung

TAIWAN

Ha Nôi

Hong Kong

Luzon Strait

Hai Phong

MAR   LAOS

VIETNAM

Quezon City

PHILIPPINES

vientiane

THAILAND

South
China
Sea

Manila

PALAU

on

Bangkok

Koror

Phnom
Penh

CAMBODIA

Hồ Chí Minh

Davao

Bandar Seri
Begawan

Kota
Kinabalu

Celebes
Sea

Jayapura

MALAYSIA

BRUNEI

Kuala Lumpur

Kuching

Borneo

New
Guinea

Putrajaya

SINGAPORE

Pontianak

Sumatra

Singapore

I N D O N E S I A

OCEANIA

Palembang

Banjarmasin

Laut Banda

Jakarta

Laut Jawa

Makassar

Bandung

Surabaya

Semarang

Dili

EAST TIMOR

Java

asia
countries

1:40 000 000

1:20 000 000

asia
philippines

1:20 000 000

asia
north korea and south korea

69

E | **1**
D | **2**
C
B
A | **1**

Chukotka

Schmidta
mikasa

Shiretoko-misaki
Abashiri
Mombetsu
Kitami
Shiretoko 1503
Shikotan-tō
Shibetsu
Kushiro
Asahikawa
Wakkanai
Iwamizawa
Hidaka-sammyaku
Nemuro-zaki

Kholmsk
La Pérouse Strait
Rumoi
Teshio-dake
Obihiro
Nemuro

Sakhalin
Ostrov
Moneron
Rebun-tō
Rishiri-tō
Soya-misaki

Hokkaidō

Otaru
Sapporo
Chitose
Tomakomai
Shakotan-misaki
Ishikari-wan
Iwanai
Date
Muroran
Erimo-zaki
Hakodate
Samani

Dal'nerechensk

RUSSIAN

Svetlaya

Sikhote-Alin'

Bikin

Vostok

Tsugaru-kaikyō
Oshima-tō
Shiriya-zaki
Mutsu
Ōma
Ōhata
Esashi
Ōminato
Aomori
Hachinohe
Odate
Towada-ko
Misawa
Noshiro
Hirosaki
Towada
Ōga-hantō
Kitakami-gawa
Iwate-san
Takata
Miyako
Hachimantai
Kamaishi
Ōfunato

FEDERATION

Dunaye
Spassk-Dal'niy
Iman
Ussuriysk
Iturup
Tobol'skaya
Chuguyevka

Akita
Gojōme
Kesennuma
Honjō
Iwaki-san
Ōmagari
Hanamaki
Ishinomaki
Sakata
Yokote
Kitakami
Shinjō

Lake
Khanka
Arsen'yev
Kamen'-Rybolov

JILIN

Jiamusi ▲Shuangyashan
HEILONGJIANG
Baoqing
Qitaihe
Hulin
Boli

Sandao Xing

Mishan
Mudanjiang
Dongning
Ussuri

Wangqing

Suifenhe
Partizansk
Nakhodka
Vladivostok
Dunhua
Artëm

Zarubino
Pos'yet
Slavyanka

CHINA

Sea
of
Japan
(East Sea)

Mudan Jiang

Tumen
Namyang
Tuman-gang
Onsōng
Unggi
Najin
NORTH
Ch'ŏngjin
KOREA

Mishan

140°
145°
135°
130°

45°
40°

70 | 1:13 000 000

0 | 50 | 100 | 150 miles
0 | 100 | 200 km

1:40 000 000

| | 150 | 300 | 450 miles |
| 300 | | 600 km |

asia
china and mongolia

1:26 500 000

0   100   200   300 miles

0   200   400 km

asia
southern asia

1:26 500 000

100   200   300 miles

200   400 km

1:20 000 000

asia
arabian peninsula

83

1:20 000 000

Grid references (right and top margins): A, B, C, D, E, F, G (along right side); 1, 2, 3, 4 (numbered markers on the map)

Major labels visible on the map:

Greenland (Denmark)
Iceland
REYKJAVÍK
Denmark Strait
Arctic Circle
Norwegian Sea
Faroe Islands (Denmark)
Shetland Islands
UNITED KINGDOM
Edinburgh
Greenland Sea
Spitsbergen
Svalbard (Norway)
Jan Mayen (Norway)
ARCTIC
Zemlya Aleksandry
Ostrov Greem-Bell
Zemlya Frantsa-Iosifa
Barents Sea
Severnaya Zemlya
Ostrov Bell
Mys Zhelaniya
Ostrov Belyy
Kara Sea (Karskoye More)
NORWAY
Trondheim
Lofoten
Murmansk
Novaya Zemlya
Ostrov Kolguyev
Ostrov Vaygach
Dikson
SWEDEN
Gulf of Bothnia
FINLAND
White Sea
Kanin
Nar'yan Mar
Pechora
Yamal Peninsula
Obskaya Guba
Gydanskiy Poluostrov
Dudinka
Noril'sk
DENMARK
COPENHAGEN
Baltic Sea
ESTONIA
LATVIA
LITHUANIA
MOSCOW
Arkhangel'sk
Syktyvkar
Vorkuta
Ural Mountains
Salekhard
Nadym
Novyy Urengoy
RUSSIA
POLAND
BELARUS
Yaroslavl'
Kirov
Perm'
Solikamsk
Berezniki
Serov
Nizhnevartovsk
UKRAINE
Nizhniy Novgorod
Kazan'
Izhevsk
Yekaterinburg
Nyagan'
Khanty-Mansiysk
Surgut
Ryazan'
Ufa
Chelyabinsk
Tobol'sk
Kolpashevo
Voronezh
Samara
Orenburg
Magnitogorsk
Kurgan
Petropavlovsk
Omsk
Tomsk
Novosibirsk
Kemerovo
MOLDOVA
Rostov-na-Donu
Volgograd
Saratov
Astrakhan'
Aktobe
Kokshetau
ASTANA
Pavlodar
Semipalatinsk
Barnaul
Sevastopol'
Black Sea
GEORGIA
TBILISI
ARMENIA
AZERBAIJAN
BAKU
Caspian Sea
Atyrau
KAZAKHSTAN
Karaganda
Balkhash
Lake Balkhash
Ayagoz
Tacheng
IRAQ
BAGHDAD
IRAN
Tabriz
Rasht
TURKMENISTAN
UZBEKISTAN
Kyzyl-Orda
Betpak-Dala Desert
Shalkar
Taldykorgan
CHINA
Kyzylkum Desert
Aşgabat
Türkmenbaşy

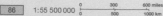

1:55 500 000

0   300   600 miles

0   500   1000 km

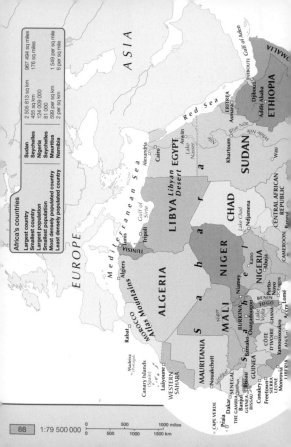

ASIA

Africa's countries			
Largest country	Sudan	2 505 813 sq km	967 494 sq miles
Smallest country	Seychelles	455 sq km	176 sq miles
Largest population	Nigeria	124 009 000	
Smallest population	Seychelles	81 000	
Most densely populated country	Mauritius	599 per sq km	1 549 per sq mile
Least densely populated country	Namibia	2 per sq km	6 per sq mile

EUROPE

Madeira (Portugal)

Canary Islands (Spain)

Mediterranean Sea

Atlas Mountains

MOROCCO

Rabat □

Algiers

Tunis □ TUNISIA

Tripoli

Gulf of Sirte

Libyan Desert

Red Sea

Gulf of Aden

SOMALIA

Djibouti □ Gulf of Aden

ERITREA

Asmara □

Addis Ababa □

ETHIOPIA

Alexandria

Cairo □

Lake Nasser

Aswan

Nile

Blue Nile

White Nile

Khartoum □

SUDAN

Wau

WESTERN SAHARA

Laâyoune □

ALGERIA

S a h a r a

LIBYA

EGYPT

MAURITANIA

Nouakchott □

Niger

MALI

Bamako □

S a h e l

NIGER

Niamey □

CHAD

Lake Chad

Ndjamena □

CENTRAL AFRICAN REPUBLIC

Bangui □

CAPE VERDE

Praia □

SENEGAL

Dakar □

THE GAMBIA

Banjul □

GUINEA-BISSAU

Bissau □

GUINEA

Conakry □

SIERRA LEONE

Freetown □

LIBERIA

Monrovia □

BURKINA

Ouagadougou □

Lake Volta

CÔTE D'IVOIRE

Yamoussoukro □

GHANA

Accra □

TOGO

Lomé □

BENIN

Porto-Novo □

Lagos

Abuja □

NIGERIA

Kano

CAMEROON

Yaoundé □

1:79 500 000   0   500   1000 miles

0   500   1000   1500 km

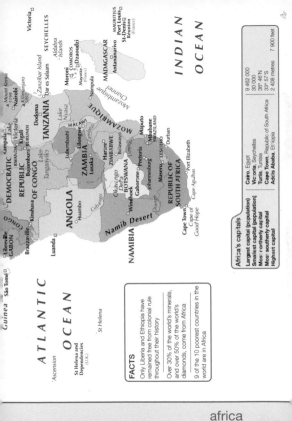

FACTS

Only Liberia and Ethiopia have remained free from colonial rule throughout their history

Over 30% of the world's minerals, and over 50% of the world's diamonds, come from Africa

9 of the 10 poorest countries in the world are in Africa

Africa's capitals		
Largest capital (population)	Cairo, Egypt	9,462,000
Smallest capital (population)	Victoria, Seychelles	30,000
Most northerly capital	Tunis, Tunisia	36° 46'N
Most southerly capital	Cape Town, Republic of South Africa	33° 57'S
Highest capital	Addis Ababa, Ethiopia	2,408 metres	7,900 feet

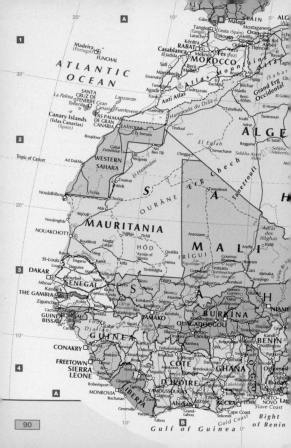

africa
northwest africa

91

1:26 500 000

0 100 200 300 miles

0 200 400 km

africa
southern africa

Wake Island
(U.S.A.)

Pagan
Northern
Mariana Islands
(U.S.A.)
Saipan • Capitol Hill

MARSHALL
ISLANDS

Guam • Hagåtña
(U.S.A.)

Yap

Gaferut

Chuuk

Pohnpei • Palikir

Delap-Uli •
Majuro Djarrit

Caroline Islands

Kosrae

FEDERATED STATES
OF MICRONESIA

Gilbert
Islands

Tarawa
Bairiki

ASIA

Kingsmill
Group

Yaren • NAURU

TUV

Rabaul

New Ireland

Mount
Wilhelm
4509

PAPUA
NEW
GUINEA

Bougainville I.

New
Britain

SOLOMON ISLANDS

New
Guinea

Solomon
Sea

Honiara • Malaita

Santa Cruz
Islands

Fun

Rotum

Arafura
Sea

Torres Strait

Port
Moresby

VANUATU

Banks
Islands

Espíritu Santo

Malakula

Éfaté

FIJ

Darwin

Timor Sea

Gulf
of
Carpentaria

Cairns

Coral Sea
Islands Territory
(Australia)

Coral

Sea

Port Vila

New
Caledonia
(France)

Nouméa •

Viti Le

Îles
Loyauté

INDIAN
OCEAN

North West
Cape

Broome

Lake
Argyle

AUSTRALIA

Uluru
867

Townsville

Alice Springs

Brisbane

Norfolk
Island
(Australia)

Lake Eyre

Darling

Lord Howe
Island
(Australia)

North Cape

Kalgoorlie

Lake
Torrens

Great
Australian Bight

Adelaide

Canberra
Murray

Kangaroo
Island

Sydney

Mount
Kosciuszko
2229

Auckland
North
Island

Wellington

Perth

Cape Leeuwin

Melbourne

Bass Strait

Tasman

Sea

South Island

Aoraki
3754

Christch

NEW
ZEALA

Cape Lévêque

Tasmania

Hobart

Stewart Island

Auckland Islands
(N.Z.)

Campbell Island
(N.Z.)

Macquarie Island
(Australia)

Oceania's capitals		
Largest capital (population)	Canberra, Australia	387 000
Smallest capital (population)	Vaiaku, Tuvalu	5 100
Most northerly capital	Delap-Uliga-Djarrit, Marshall Islands	7° 7'N
Most southerly capital	Wellington, New Zealand	41° 18'S
Highest capital	Canberra, Australia	581 metres 1 906 feet

100   1:86 000 000

500   1000   1500 miles

1000   2000 km

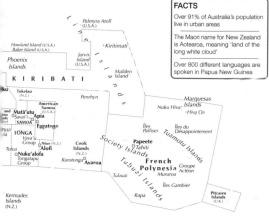

Hawaiian Islands (U.S.A.)

PACIFIC OCEAN

Line Islands

Palmyra Atoll (U.S.A.)

Kiritimati

Howland Island (U.S.A.)
Baker Island (U.S.A.)

Jarvis Island (U.S.A.)

Phoenix Islands

Malden Island

KIRIBATI

Tokelau (N.Z.)

Penrhyn

Marquesas Islands

Nuku Hiva *Hiva Oa*

American Samoa (U.S.A.)

Matāʻutu (U.S.A.)

SAMOA Apia

Savaiʻi

Fagatoge

Îles Palliser

Îles du Désappointement

TONGA

Vavaʻu Group

Niue (N.Z.)

Alofi

Papeete Tahiti

Society Islands

Tuamotu Islands

Cook Islands (N.Z.)

Rarotonga (N.Z.)

Avarua

French Polynesia

Groupe Actéon

Nukuʻalofa

Tongatapu Group

Tubuai Islands

Mururoa

Îles Gambier

Tofua

Tubuai

Rapa

Kermadec Islands (N.Z.)

Pitcairn Islands (U.K.)

Chatham Islands (N.Z.)

Oceania's countries

Largest country	Australia	7 692 024 sq km	2 969 907 sq miles
Smallest country	Nauru	21 sq km	8 sq miles
Largest population	Australia	19 731 000	
Smallest population	Tuvalu	11 000	
Most densely populated country	Nauru	619 per sq km	1 625 per sq mile
Least densely populated country	Australia	3 per sq km	7 per sq mile

INDIAN

OCEAN

Timor
Sea

A   120°   B

Melville
Island
Bathurst Island   Darwin
Joseph   Beagle Gulf   Batchelor
Bonaparte   Adelaide River
Gulf   Timber
Wyndham   Creek
Cape Londonderry
Bonaparte
Archipelago
Collier   Kimberley
Bay   Plateau
Cape Lévêque   King Leopold Range   Mount Ord
916   Lake
Broome   Fitzroy   Argyle
Roebuck Bay   Fitzroy   NOR
Lagrange   Halls   TERRI
Creek
Eighty Mile Beach   TANAMI
Lake Gregory   Desert
Port Hedland   Shay Gap   Great Sandy   Lake White
Barrow Island Karratha   Marble   Desert   Tennant
North West Cape Onslow   Bar   Lake Willis   Creek
Hamersley Range Pannawonica   Nullagine   Lake Mackay   Yuendumu
Coral Bay   Tom Price   Mount Mchany   Liebig   Alice
Parabardoo   1250   Newman   Lake Disappointment   Springs
Minilya   Lake MacLeod   Gibson Desert   Lake Neale   Uluru
Dorre   Mount Augustus   Lake   Warburton   (Ayers Rock)
Island   1106   Robinson Range   Carnegie   867   Erldunda
Dirk   Gascoyne   Petermann Range
Hartog   Lake   Lake   Mount Musgrave Range
Island   Wilmut   Wells   Woodroffe 1440
Kalbarri   Meekatharra   Great Victoria   Lake
Mount   Desert   Maurice   S
Magnet
Northampton   Leinster   AUS
Geraldton   Leonora   Forrest   Hughes
Dongara   Lake   Gunbarrel   Rawlinna   Tar
Moore   Lake Carey   Kalgoorlie   Nullarbor Plain   Penc
Lake Ballard   Coolgardie   Forrest   Eucla   Ceduna
Kalinbin   Kambalda   Mundrabilla   Fowlers Bay   Streaky Ba
Yanchep   Southern   Norseman   Great
Perth   Cross   Balladonia   Australian
Fremantle   Merredin   Bight
Rockingham   York   Hyden
Mandurah   Bonnie Rock   Esperance
Bunbury   Katanning   Archipelago of
Margaret River   Hood Point   the Recherche
Cape Leeuwin Busselton   Denmark
Flinders Bay   Albany
Point d'Entrecasteaux

WESTERN

AUSTRALIA

130°

1

20°

2

30°

3

110°   40° A   120°   B   130°

1:33 000 000   0   150   300   450 miles
0   200   400   600 km

104   1:13 000 000

oceania
southeast australia

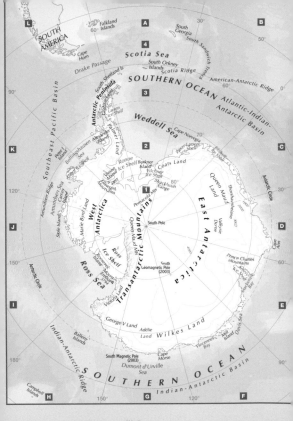

SOUTH AMERICA

Falkland Islands

South Georgia

South Sandwich Trench

Scotia Sea

Cape Horn

Drake Passage

South Orkney Islands

South Shetland Is

Scotia Ridge

American-Antarctic Ridge

SOUTHERN OCEAN

Atlantic-Indian-Antarctic Basin

Antarctic Peninsula

Larsen Ice Shelf

Palmer Land

Alexander Island

Weddell Sea

Cape Norvegia

Bellingshausen Sea

Ronne Ice Shelf

Filchner Ice Shelf

Berkner Island

Coats Land

Rockham

Queen Maud Land

Thurston Island

Pensacola Mts

South Pole

East Antarctica

Valkyrie Dome

Antarctic Circle

Southeast Pacific Basin

Amundsen Ridge

West Antarctica

Ellsworth Mountains

Queen Maud Mts

Transantarctic Mountains

Prince Charles Mountains

Marie Byrd Land

Siple Island

Ross Ice Shelf

South Geomagnetic Pole (2003)

Amery Ice Shelf

Ross Sea

Victoria Land

George V Land

Adélie Land

Wilkes Land

Mill Island

Amundsen Sea

Balleny Islands

Indian-Antarctic Ridge

South Magnetic Pole (2003)

Cape Morse

Vincennes Bay

Dumont d'Urville Sea

SOUTHERN OCEAN

Indian-Antarctic Basin

Campbell Islands

1:79 500 000

500   1000 miles

500   1000   1500 km

antarctica

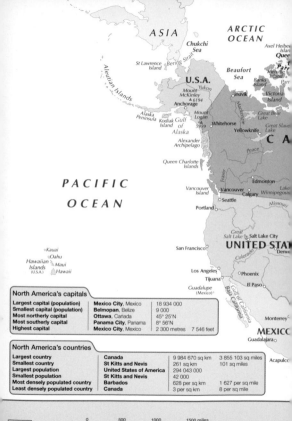

ASIA

ARCTIC OCEAN

Chukchi Sea

Bering Strait

St Lawrence Island

Axel Heiberg Island

Queen

Melville Island

Parr

Banks Island

Beaufort Sea

Victoria Island

U.S.A.

Yukon

Mount McKinley ▲ 6194

Inuvik

Anchorage

Mount Logan ▲ 5959

Great Bear Lake

Alaska Peninsula

Kodiak Island

Gulf of Alaska

Whitehorse

Yellowknife

Great Slave Lake

C A

Aleutian Islands

Alexander Archipelago

Peace

Queen Charlotte Islands

Fraser

Edmonton

Lake Winnipegosis

PACIFIC OCEAN

Vancouver Island

Vancouver

Calgary

Seattle

Portland

Missouri

Great Salt Lake

Salt Lake City

Kauai

Oahu

Hawaiian Islands (U.S.A.)

Maui

Hawaii

San Francisco

UNITED STAT

Colorado

Denve

Los Angeles

Phoenix

Tijuana

El Paso

Guadalupe (Mexico)

Gulf of California

Monterrey

Baja California

MEXICC

Guadalajara

Acapulco

North America's capitals

Largest capital (population)	Mexico City, Mexico	18 934 000
Smallest capital (population)	Belmopan, Belize	9 000
Most northerly capital	Ottawa, Canada	45° 25'N
Most southerly capital	Panama City, Panama	8° 56'N
Highest capital	Mexico City, Mexico	2 300 metres 7 546 feet

North America's countries

Largest country	Canada	9 984 670 sq km	3 855 103 sq miles
Smallest country	St Kitts and Nevis	261 sq km	101 sq miles
Largest population	United States of America	294 043 000	
Smallest population	St Kitts and Nevis	42 000	
Most densely populated country	Barbados	628 per sq km	1 627 per sq mile
Least densely populated country	Canada	3 per sq km	8 per sq mile

1:86 000 000

0 500 1000 1500 miles

0 1000 2000 km

Greenland Sea

Greenland

Denmark Strait

esmere
Island
abeth
ds
on Island
anni

Baffin
Bay

Davis Strait

Nuuk

Cape Farewell

Baffin Island

Foxe
Basin

Southampton
Island

Hudson Strait

Labrador
Sea

FACTS

Mexico City is the highest city in North America and houses approximately 18% of Mexico's population

The Panama Canal, opened in 1914, cut the journey between the Atlantic and the Pacific by over 14 000 km

The territory of Nunavut is Canada's newest administrative division, created in 1999

A D A

Hudson
Bay

Belcher
Islands

James
Bay

Newfoundland

St John's

Île
d'Anticosti

Gulf of
St Lawrence

St-Pierre

St Pierre and Miquelon
(France)

ke
Winnipeg

Winnipeg

Lake
Nipigon

Québec

Halifax

Thunder
Bay

Ottawa

Montréal

Cape Sable

Minnesota

Great Lakes

Minneapolis

Detroit

Toronto

Portland

Boston

Chicago

Columbus

Cleveland

New York

S OF AMERICA

St Louis

Ohio

Pittsburgh

Philadelphia

Washington

ATLANTIC

OCEAN

Memphis

Cape Hatteras

Bermuda
(U.K.)

Kansas

Dallas

Atlanta

Houston

Jacksonville

Orlando

New Orleans

Gulf
of Mexico

THE BAHAMAS

Miami

Nassau

Turks and
Caicos Islands
(U.K.)

Virgin Islands
(U.S.A.)

Virgin Islands
(U.K.)

San
Juan

ST KITTS AND NEVIS

ANTIGUA AND BARBUDA

Mérida

Yucatán

Havana

CUBA

Cayman
Islands
(U.K.)

JAMAICA

Kingston

HAITI

Santo
Domingo

Puerto Rico
(U.S.A.)

DOMINICAN
REPUBLIC

Guadeloupe (France)

DOMINICA

Martinique (France)

Port-
au-Prince

ST LUCIA

BARBADOS

ST VINCENT AND THE GRENADINES

xico City

Veracruz

Pico
de Orizaba

uatemala City

GUATEMALA

San Salvador

EL SALVADOR

BELIZE

Belmopan

HONDURAS

Tegucigalpa

Caribbean Sea

GRENADA

Aruba
(Neth.)

Netherlands
Antilles

TRINIDAD
AND TOBAGO

Lake Nicaragua

NICARAGUA

Managua

San José

COSTA RICA

Panama

Panama City

PANAMA

SOUTH AMERICA

north america
canada

north america
western canada

114   1:20 000 000

0   100   200   300 miles

0   150   300   450 km

1:33 000 000

0	150	300	450 miles
0	200	400	600 km

1:14 500 000

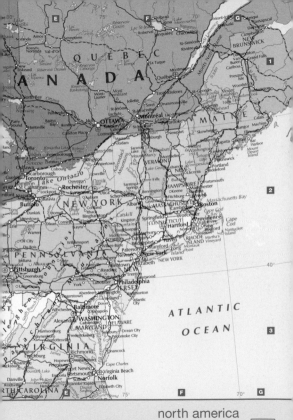

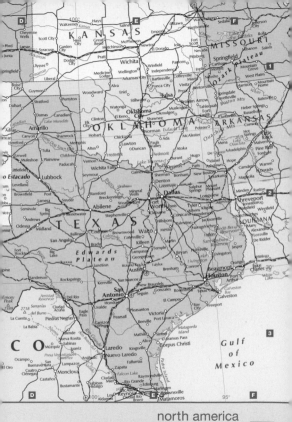

north america
south central united states

C · 70° · D · 60° · E · 30°

ATLANTIC

OCEAN

Tropic of Cancer

2

THE BAHAMAS

Great
Abaco

Eleuthera

NASSAU

Cat Island

Long Island

Exuma Cays

Acklins
Island

Great
Inagua

s Tunas

Holguín

Mayaguana

Turks and
Caicos Islands (U.K.)

GRAND TURK (Cockburn Town)

West Indies

Bayamo

Guantánamo

Caicos
Islands

20°

Hispaniola

Leeward Islands

Santiago

Port-de-
Paix

Puerto Rico
(U.S.A.)

Anguilla
(U.K.)

Gonaïves

DOMINICAN
REPUBLIC

SAN JUAN

Virgin Is
(U.K.)

St-Martin
(France)

ANTIGUA AND
BARBUDA

HAITI

La Romana

Virgin Is (U.S.A.)

St Maarten
(Netherlands)

BASSETERRE

ST JOHN'S

Jérémie

PORT-
AU-PRINCE

SANTO
DOMINGO

Ponce

ST KITTS AND NEVIS

Montserrat
(U.K.)

PLYMOUTH

Guadeloupe
(France)

Les Cayes

Jacmel

BASSE-TERRE

KINGSTON

A n t i l l e s

DOMINICA

ROSEAU

3

Martinique
(France)

FORT-DE-
FRANCE

e a n   S e a

ST LUCIA

CASTRIES

KINGSTOWN

BRIDGETOWN

Windward Islands

ST VINCENT AND THE
GRENADINES

BARBADOS

L e s s e r

GRENADA

ST GEORGE'S

Scarborough Tobago

Netherlands
Antilles

Aruba
(Neth.)

Punta Gallinas
Península
de la Guajira

Curaçao

La Asunción

Isla de
Margarita

TRINIDAD
AND
TOBAGO

Riohacha

WILLEMSTAD

Bonaire

Golfo de
Venezuela

Islas
Los Roques

PORT OF
SPAIN

Barranquilla

Santa
Marta

Coro

Maiquetía

Cumaná

San Fernando

Cartagena

Cabimas

Maracaibo

Barquisimeto

Maracay

CARACAS

Los Teques

Barcelona

San Trinidad

Orinoco
Delta

Valledupar

Sincelejo

Maicao

Machiques

Lago de
Maracaibo

Valencia

Acarigua

Zaraza

El Tigre

Maturín

Tucupita

Montería

Magangué

Mérida

Valera

Barinas

VENEZUELA

COLOMBIA

Turbo

Cúcuta

San Cristóbal

San Fernando de Apure

Llanos

Ciudad Bolívar

Ciudad Guayana

GUYANA

4

Bucaramanga

Pamplona

Arauca

70°

La Paragua

Embalse
de Guri

Orinoco

El Callao

60°

South America's capitals

Largest capital (population)	Buenos Aires, Argentina	12 439 000
Smallest capital (population)	Sucre, Bolivia	183 000
Most northerly capital	Caracas, Venezuela	10° 28'N
Most southerly capital	Montevideo, Uruguay	34° 52'S
Highest capital	La Paz, Bolivia	3 630 metres 11 909 feet

NORTH AMERICA

Caribbean Sea

Galapagos Islands (Ecuador)

Barranquilla
Maracaibo
Caracas
VENEZUELA
Puerto Ayacucho
Medellín
Bogotá
COLOMBIA
Cali
Quito
ECUADOR
Guayaquil
Georgetown
Paramaribo
Cayenne
GUYANA
SURINAME
French Guiana

Orinoco
Negro
Japurá
Amazon Basin
Manaus
Madeira
Purus

BRAZIL

Belém
Fortaleza
Recife
Salvador
São Francisco
Tocantins
Xingu
Araguaia
Tapajós

Brasília
Cuiabá
Porto Velho
La Paz
BOLIVIA

PERU
Iquitos
Cusco
Lake Titicaca
Arequipa
Trujillo
Lima
Ucayali

1:66 000 000

0	300	600	900 miles
0	400	800	1200 km

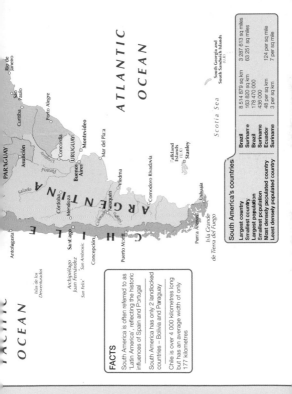

FACTS

South America is often referred to as 'Latin America', reflecting the historic influences of Spain and Portugal

South America has only 2 landlocked countries – Bolivia and Paraguay

Chile is over 4 000 kilometres long but has an average width of only 177 kilometres

South America's countries			
Largest country	Brazil	8 514 879 sq km	3 287 613 sq miles
Smallest country	Suriname	163 820 sq km	63 251 sq miles
Largest population	Brazil	178 470 000	
Smallest population	Suriname	436 000	
Most densely populated country	Ecuador	48 per sq km	124 per sq mile
Least densely populated country	Suriname	3 per sq km	7 per sq mile

PACIFIC OCEAN

COLOMBIA

VENEZUELA

GUIANA HIGHLAND

ECUADOR

PERU

BOLIVIA

1:33 000 000

150   300   450 miles
200   400   600 km

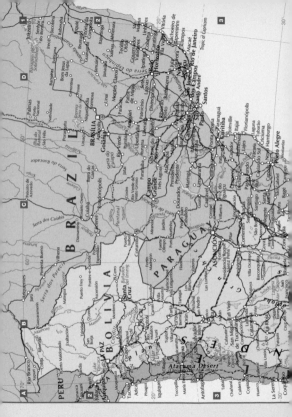

1:33 000 000

ATLANTIC

OCEAN

ARGENTINA

PATAGONIA

Falkland Islands
(U.K.)
East Falkland
West Falkland
STANLEY

MONTEVIDEO
BUENOS AIRES
La Plata
Mar del Plata

Comodoro Rivadavia
Golfo San Jorge
Península Valdés
Golfo San Matías
Bahía Blanca
Bahía Grande

Isla de los Estados
Cape Horn
Tierra del Fuego
Río Grande

South Georgia
(U.K.)
Cape Disappointment

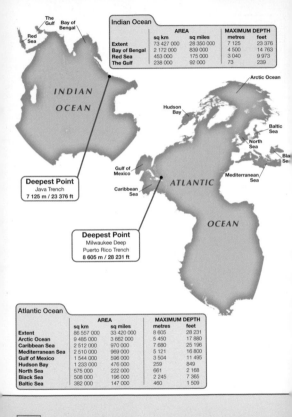

The Gulf

Bay of Bengal

Red Sea

INDIAN OCEAN

Indian Ocean

	AREA		MAXIMUM DEPTH	
	sq km	sq miles	metres	feet
Extent	73 427 000	28 350 000	7 125	23 376
Bay of Bengal	2 172 000	839 000	4 500	14 763
Red Sea	453 000	175 000	3 040	9 973
The Gulf	238 000	92 000	73	239

Arctic Ocean

Hudson Bay

Baltic Sea

North Sea

Black Sea

Gulf of Mexico

ATLANTIC

Mediterranean Sea

Caribbean Sea

OCEAN

Deepest Point
Java Trench
7 125 m / 23 376 ft

Deepest Point
Milwaukee Deep
Puerto Rico Trench
8 605 m / 28 231 ft

Atlantic Ocean

	AREA		MAXIMUM DEPTH	
	sq km	sq miles	metres	feet
Extent	86 557 000	33 420 000	8 605	28 231
Arctic Ocean	9 485 000	3 662 000	5 450	17 880
Caribbean Sea	2 512 000	970 000	7 680	25 196
Mediterranean Sea	2 510 000	969 000	5 121	16 800
Gulf of Mexico	1 544 000	596 000	3 504	11 495
Hudson Bay	1 233 000	476 000	259	849
North Sea	575 000	222 000	661	2 168
Black Sea	508 000	196 000	2 245	7 365
Baltic Sea	382 000	147 000	460	1 509

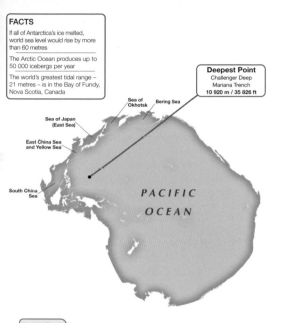

Deepest Point
Challenger Deep
Mariana Trench
10 920 m / 35 826 ft

Sea of Okhotsk

Bering Sea

Sea of Japan (East Sea)

East China Sea and Yellow Sea

South China Sea

PACIFIC OCEAN

Pacific Ocean

	AREA		MAXIMUM DEPTH	
	sq km	sq miles	metres	feet
Extent	166 241 000	64 186 000	10 920	35 826
Bering Sea	2 261 000	873 000	4 150	13 615
Sea of Okhotsk	1 392 000	537 000	3 363	11 033
Sea of Japan (East Sea)	1 013 000	391 000	3 743	12 280
East China Sea and Yellow Sea	1 202 000	464 000	2 717	8 913
South China Sea	2 590 000	1 000 000	5 514	18 090

pacific ocean

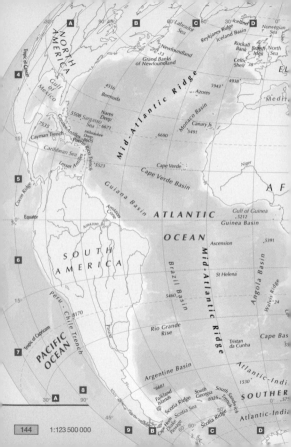

NORTH AMERICA

Tropic of Cancer

Gulf of Mexico

.4556
Bermuda

Nares Deep

5508 Sargasso
Sea
.5335
.6671

Central America
Cayman Trench
Cayman Trench
Caribbean Sea
Lesser Antilles
Puerto Rico
Milwaukee
Deep
.5523

.6690

Labrador Sea

Newfoundland
.13
Grand Banks
of Newfoundland

Reykjanes Ridge
Iceland
Iceland Basin

Rockall
Bank
Rockall
British
Isles
North
Sea

Celtic
Shelf .38

.5943
Azores

.4938

Medit

Monaco Basin

Canary Is.
.3491

Cape Verde

Niger

Mid-Atlantic Ridge

Cape Verde Basin

Guiana Basin

Equator

Amazon
Cone

ATLANTIC

OCEAN

Gulf of Guinea
.5212
Guinea Basin

AF

Cocos Ridge

SOUTH
AMERICA

Ascension

.5391

Angola Basin

St Helena

Brazil Basin

Mid-Atlantic Ridge

Walvis Ridge

Peru - Chile Trench
.8170

Parana

.5460

Rio Grande
Rise

Tristan
da Cunha

Cape Bas

Tropic of Capricorn

PACIFIC
OCEAN

Argentine Basin

Atlantic-Ind

SOUTHER

.1530

Falkland
Islands

Scotia Ridge

Cape Horn Drake
Passage

Scotia Sea

South
Georgia

.8325

South Sandwich
Trench

South
Sandwich Is.

.57

Scotia Ridge

Atlantic-Indi

Irtysh

A S I A

4

Black Sea

Aral Sea

Caspian Sea

Yellow River

Yellow Sea

5996

·916

an Sea

21

The Gulf

Indus

Ganges

East China Sea

·7460

Red Sea

Gulf of Aden

Congo

Arabian Sea

Ganges Cone

Bay of Bengal

Andaman Islands

South China Sea

15

Andaman Basin ·4267

5

C A

·5060

Somali Basin

Carlsberg Ridge

Chagos-Laccadive Ridge

Chagos Trench

Vema Trench ·6402

Mid-Indian Basin

Sumatra

Borneo

Laut Jawa

Java

6

Comoros

Mascarene Ridge

INDIAN

·7125

Java Trench (Sunda Trench)

Zambezi

Mozambique Channel

Madagascar

Mascarene Basin

Mid-Indian Ridge

OCEAN

West Australian Basin

North Australian Basin

nge

Natal Basin

1207

Madagascar Basin ·6400

Ninetyeast Ridge

·1924

·2067

·549

Perth

7

Agulhas Plateau

·6195

Mozambique Ridge

Southwest Indian Ridge

Broken Plateau Basin

·7102

Diamantina Deep ·6602

AUSTRALIA

gulhas asin

dge

Southeast Indian Ridge

Iles Kerguélen

McDonald Islands Heard Island

·230

neast Australian-Antarctic

·186

Kerguelen-Gaussberg

South Australian Basin

Great Australian Bight

I

30

·6972

·6195

arctic Basin

Davis Sea

60

·90

9

N T A R C T I C A

atlantic and indian oceans

PACIFIC OCEAN

Bering Sea

Sea of Okhotsk

Gulf of Alaska

Arctic Circle

Chukchi Sea

NORTH AMERICA

East Siberian Sea

ASIA

Mackenzie

Beaufort Sea

Lena

Canada Basin

Laptev Sea

ARCTIC OCEAN

Mendeleyev Ridge

North Magnetic Pole (2003)

Lomonosov Ridge

Alpha Ridge

North Pole

Amundsen Basin

Victoria Island

Arctic Mid-Ocean Ridge

Nansen Basin

Parry Islands

North Geomagnetic Pole (2003)

Ellesmere Island

Yenisey

Baffin Island

Baffin Bay

Kara Sea

Novaya Zemlya

Franz Josef Land

Barents Sea

Davis Strait

Greenland

Greenland Sea

Spitsbergen

EUROPE

Denmark Strait

Greenland Basin

Jan Mayen

Norwegian Basin

Iceland

Arctic Circle

Norwegian Sea

ATLANTIC OCEAN

Faroe Islands

North Sea

Baltic Sea

British Isles

arctic ocean

1:79 500 000

0   500   1000 m
0   500   1000   1500 km

INTRODUCTION TO THE INDEX

The index includes all names shown on the reference maps in the atlas. Names are referenced by page number and by a grid reference. The grid reference correlates to the alphanumeric values along the edges of each map which reflect the lines of latitude and longitude. Names are generally referenced to the largest scale map on which they appear. Each entry also includes the country or geographical area in which the feature is located. Where relevant, the index clearly indicates (inset) if a feature appears on an inset map.

Name forms are as they appear on the maps, with additional alternative names or name forms included as cross-references which refer the user to the entry for the map form of the name. Names beginning with Mc or Mac are alphabetized exactly as they appear. The terms Saint, Sainte, etc. are abbreviated to St, Ste, etc. but alphabetized as if in the full form.

Names of physical features beginning with generic geographical terms are permuted – the descriptive term is placed after the main part of the name. For example, Lake Superior is indexed as Superior, Lake; Mount Everest as Everest, Mount. This policy is applied to all languages.

Entries, other than those for towns and cities, include a descriptor indicating the type of geographical feature. Descriptors are not included where the type of feature is implicit in the name itself.

Administrative divisions are included to differentiate entries of the same name and feature type within one country. In such cases duplicate names are alphabetized in order of administrative division. Additional qualifiers are also included for names within selected geographical areas.

INDEX ABBREVIATIONS

admin. div.	administrative division	Ger.	Germany	Port.	Portugal
Afgh.	Afghanistan	Guat.	Guatemala	prov.	province
Alg.	Algeria	h.	hill	pt.	point
Arg.	Argentina	hd	headland	r.	river
Austr.	Australia	Hond.	Honduras	reg.	region
aut. reg.	autonomous region	i.	island	Rep.	Republic
aut. rep.	autonomous republic	imp. l.	impermanent lake	resr	reservoir
Azer.	Azerbaijan	Indon.	Indonesia	rf	reef
b.	bay	is	islands	Rus. Fed.	Russian Federation
Bangl.	Bangladesh	isth.	isthmus	S.	South
B.I.O.T.	British Indian Ocean Territory	Kazakh.	Kazakhstan	Serb. and Mont.	Serbia and Montenegro
Bol.	Bolivia	Kyrg.	Kyrgyzstan	str.	strait
Bos.-Herz.	Bosnia Herzegovina	l.	lake	Switz.	Switzerland
Bulg.	Bulgaria	lag.	lagoon	Tajik.	Tajikistan
c.	cape	Lith.	Lithuania	Tanz.	Tanzania
Can.	Canada	Lux.	Luxembourg	terr.	territory
C.A.R.	Central African Republic	Madag.	Madagascar	Thai.	Thailand
Col.	Colombia	Maur.	Mauritania	Trin. and Tob.	Trinidad and Tobago
Czech Rep.	Czech Republic	Mex.	Mexico	Turkm.	Turkmenistan
Dem. Rep. Congo	Democratic Republic of Congo	Moz.	Mozambique	U.A.E.	United Arab Emirates
depr.	depression	mt.	mountain	U.K.	United Kingdom
des.	desert	mts	mountains	Ukr.	Ukraine
Dom. Rep.	Dominican Republic	mun.	municipality	Uru.	Uruguay
esc.	escarpment	N.	North	U.S.A.	United States of America
est.	estuary	Neth.	Netherlands	Uzbek.	Uzbekistan
Eth.	Ethiopia	Nic.	Nicaragua	val.	valley
Fin.	Finland	N.Z.	New Zealand	Venez.	Venezuela
for.	forest	Pak.	Pakistan	vol.	volcano
g.	gulf	Para.	Paraguay		
		pen.	peninsula		
		Phil.	Philippines		
		plat.	plateau		
		P.N.G.	Papua New Guinea		
		Pol.	Poland		

A

Aabenraa Denmark **41** B4
Aachen Ger. **48** C2
Aalborg Denmark **41** B4
Aalst Belgium **48** B2
Aarschot Belgium **48** B2
Aba China **72** C2
Aba Nigeria **91** C4
Ābādān Iran **85** C2
Ābādeh Iran **85** D2
Abadla Alg. **90** B1
Abakaliki Nigeria **91** C4
Abakan Rus. Fed. **87** I3
Abakanskiy Khrebet *mts* Rus. Fed. **81** F1
Abancay Peru **134** B4
Abarqū Iran **85** D2
Abashiri Japan **70** D2
Ābay Wenz *r.* Eth./Sudan *see* **Blue Nile**
Abaza Rus. Fed. **81** G1
Abbasanta Italy **56** A2
Abbeville France **52** C1
Abbeville U.S.A. **124** B3
Abbot Ice Shelf Antarctica **107** J2
Abbottabad Pak. **78** B1
Abéché Chad **91** E3
Abengourou Côte d'Ivoire **90** B4
Abeokuta Nigeria **90** C4
Aberaeron U.K. **47** A3
Aberdare U.K. **47** B4
Aberdaron U.K. **46** A3
Aberdeen S. Africa **98** B3
Aberdeen U.K. **44** C2
Aberdeen *MD* U.S.A. **123** E3
Aberdeen *SD* U.S.A. **121** D1
Aberdeen *WA* U.S.A. **118** B1
Aberdeen Lake Can. **113** F1
Aberystwyth U.K. **47** A3
Abez' Rus. Fed. **34** F2
Abhā Saudi Arabia **82** B3
Abiad, Bahr el *r.* Sudan/Uganda *see* **White Nile**
Abidjan Côte d'Ivoire **90** B4
Abilene *TX* U.S.A. **127** E2
Abingdon U.K. **47** C4
Abinsk Rus. Fed. **39** E3
Abitibi, Lake Can. **114** B2
Abohar India **78** B1
Abomey Benin **90** C4
Aborlan Phil. **68** A3
Absaroka Range *mts* U.S.A. **120** A2
Abşeron Yarımadası *pen.* Azer. **85** C1
Abū 'Arīsh Saudi Arabia **82** B3
Abu Deleiq Sudan **82** A3
Abu Dhabi U.A.E. **83** C2
Abu Hamed Sudan **92** B3
Abuja Nigeria **91** C4
Abū Kamāl Syria **85** C2
Abunā *r.* Bol. **136** B1
Abunā Brazil **134** C3
Abu Road India **78** B2
Abū Sunbul Egypt **92** B2
Abū Ẓabī U.A.E. *see* **Abu Dhabi**
Abyei Sudan **93** A4
Acambaro Mex. **129** B2
Acaponeta Mex. **128** B2
Acapulco Mex. **129** C3
Acará Brazil **135** E3
Acaray, Represa de *resr* Para. **138** A3
Acarigua Venez. **134** C2
Acatlan Mex. **129** C3
Acayucán Mex. **129** C3
Accra Ghana **90** B4
Accrington U.K. **46** B3
Achalpur India **78** B2
Achicourt France **48** A2
Achill Island Rep. of Ireland **45** A2
Achim Ger. **49** D1
Achuyevo Rus. Fed. **39** E2
Acıpayam Turkey **59** C3
Acireale Italy **56** C3
Acklins Island Bahamas **131** C2
Aconcagua, Cerro *mt.* Arg. **136** A4
A Coruña Spain **54** B1
Acqui Terme Italy **56** A2
Ács Hungary **51** D3
Actéon, Groupe *is* Fr. Polynesia **111**
Actopán Mex. **129** C2
Ada U.S.A. **127** E2
Adam Oman **83** C2
'Adan Yemen *see* **Aden**
Adana Turkey **84** B2
Adapazarı Turkey **59** D2
Ad Dafīnah Saudi Arabia **82** B2
Ad Dahnā' *des.* Saudi Arabia **83** B2
Ad Dakhla Western Sahara **90** A2
Ad Dammām Saudi Arabia *see* Dammam
Ad Dār al Ḥamrā' Saudi Arabia **82** A2
Ad Darb Saudi Arabia **82** B3
Ad Dawādimī Saudi Arabia **82** B2
Ad Dawḥah Qatar *see* **Doha**
Aḍ Ḍiffah *plat.* Egypt *see* **Libyan Plateau**
Addis Ababa Eth. **93** B4
Ad Dīwānīyah Iraq **85** C2
Adelaide Austr. **104** B2
Adelaide River Austr. **102** C1
Adélie Land *reg.* Antarctica **107** G3
Aden Yemen **82** B3
Aden, Gulf of Somalia/Yemen **83** B3
Ādīgrat Eth. **92** B3
Adilabad India **79** B3
Adirondack Mountains U.S.A. **123** F2
Adjud Romania **38** C2
Admiralty Island U.S.A. **112** B2
Admiralty Islands P.N.G. **63** D3
Adour *r.* France **52** B3
Adra Spain **54** C2
Adrar Alg. **90** B2
Adrian *TX* U.S.A. **127** D1
Adriatic Sea Europe **56** B2
Ādwa Eth. **92** B3
Adygeysk Rus. Fed. **39** E3
Adzopé Côte d'Ivoire **90** B4
Aegean Sea Greece/Turkey **59** B3
A Estrada Spain **54** B1
Afghanistan *country* Asia **78** A1
'Afīf Saudi Arabia **82** B2
Africa **66**
Afyon Turkey **84** B2
Agadez Niger **91** C3
Agadir Morocco **90** B1
Agadyr' Kazakh. **81** E2
Agar India **78** B2
Agartala India **79** D2
Ağdam Azer. **85** C2
Agde France **53** C3
Agen France **52** C3
Aggeneys S. Africa **98** A2
Agios Dimitrios Greece **59** B3
Agios Efstratios *i.* Greece **59** C3
Agios Konstantinos Greece **84** A2
Agios Nikolaos Greece **59** C3
Agirwat Hills Sudan **82** A3
Agnita Romania **38** B2
Agra India **79** B2
Ağrı Turkey **85** C2
Agrigento Italy **56** B3
Agrinio Greece **59** B3
Agropoli Italy **56** B2
Água Clara Brazil **138** B2
Aguadulce Panama **130** B4
Aguanaval *r.* Mex. **128** B2
Agua Prieta Mex. **128** B1
Aguascalientes Mex. **128** B2
Águas Formosas Brazil **139** D1
Aguilar de Campóo Spain **54** C1
Águilas Spain **55** C2
Agulhas, Cape S. Africa **98** B3
Agulhas Negras *mt.* Brazil **139** D2
Ağva Turkey **59** C2
Ahar Iran **85** C2
Ahaus Ger. **48** C1
Ahlat Turkey **85** C2
Ahlen Ger. **48** C2
Ahmadabad India **78** B2
Ahmadnagar India **77** B3
Ahmadpur East Pak. **78** B2
Ahome Mex. **128** B2
Ahram Iran **85** D3
Ahrensburg Ger. **49** E1
Ahvāz Iran **85** C2
Ai-Ais Namibia **98** A2

Aigio Greece 59 B3
Aiken U.S.A. 125 D2
Aimorés Brazil 139 D1
Aimorés, Serra dos hills Brazil 139 D1
Ain r. France 52 B3
Aïn Azel Alg. 55 E2
Aïn Ben Tili Maur. 90 B2
Aïn Defla Alg. 55 D2
Aïn Oulmene Alg. 55 E2
Aïn Sefra Alg. 90 B1
Ainsworth U.S.A. 120 D2
Aintab Turkey see Gaziantep
Aïn Taya Alg. 55 D2
Aïn Tédélès Alg. 55 D2
Aïn Temouchent Alg. 55 C2
Air, Massif de l' mts Niger 91 C3
Airbangis Indon. 64 A1
Airdrie Can. 112 D2
Aire r. France 48 A3
Aisne r. France 48 A3
Aisne r. France 52 C3
Aix-en-Provence France 53 D3
Aix-les-Bains France 53 D2
Aizawl India 66 A1
Aizkraukle Latvia 36 C2
Aizu-wakamatsu Japan 71 C3
Ajaccio France 53 D3
Ajdābiyā Libya 91 E1
Ajmer India 78 B2
Ajo U.S.A. 126 B2
Akçakale Turkey 84 D2
Akchār reg. Maur. 96
Akdağmadeni Turkey 84 B2
Akersberga Sweden 36 A2
Aketi Dem. Rep. Congo 94 C2
Akhalk'alak'i Georgia 35 D4
Akhdar, Jabal mts Oman 83 C2
Akhisar Turkey 59 C3
Akhtubinsk Rus. Fed. 35 D4
Akita Japan 70 D3
Akjoujt Maur. 90 A3
Akkol' Kazakh. 81 E1
Akmenrags pt Latvia 36 B2
Akmola Kazakh. see Astana
Akobo Sudan 93 B4
Akola India 78 B2
Akordat Eritrea 82 A3
Akpatok Island Can. 111 H2
Akranes Iceland 40 [inset]
Åkrehamn Norway 42 E2
Akron U.S.A. 122 D2
Aksai Chin terr. Asia 79 B1
Aksaray Turkey 84 B2
Aksehir Turkey 84 B2
Aksu China 81 F2
Aktau Kazakh. 80 C1
Aktobe Kazakh. 80 C1
Aktsyabrski Belarus 36 C3
Akure Nigeria 91 C4

Akureyri Iceland 40 [inset]
Akyab Myanmar see Sittwe
Alabama r. U.S.A. 125 C2
Alabama state U.S.A. 124 C2
Alacant Spain see Alicante
Alagoinhas Brazil 135 F4
Alagón Spain 55 C1
Al Aḥmadī Kuwait 83 C2
Alakol', Ozero salt l. Kazakh. 81 F2
Alakurtti Rus. Fed. 40 G2
Al 'Alayyah Saudi Arabia 82 B3
Al 'Amirīyah Egypt 84 A2
Alamo U.S.A. 119 C3
Alamogordo U.S.A. 126 C2
Alamos Sonora Mex. 128 B2
Alamos Sonora Mex. 128 B2
Alamos r. Mex. 128 B2
Alamosa U.S.A. 120 D0
Alarcón, Embalse de resr Spain 55 C2
Al 'Arīsh Egypt 84 A2
Al Arṭāwīyah Saudi Arabia 82 B2
Alas Indon. 65 C2
Alaşehir Turkey 59 C3
Alaska state U.S.A. 110 C2
Alaska, Gulf of U.S.A. 110 C3
Alaska Peninsula U.S.A. 120
Alaska Range mts U.S.A. 110 C2
Älät Azer. 85 C2
Alatyr' Rus. Fed. 35 D3
Alausí Ecuador 134 B3
Alavus Fin. 41 E3
Alba Italy 56 A2
Albacete Spain 55 C2
Alba Iulia Romania 38 B2
Albania country Europe 58 A2
Albany Austr. 102 A3
Albany r. Can. 114 B1
Albany GA U.S.A. 125 D2
Albany NY U.S.A. 123 F2
Albany OR U.S.A. 118 B2
Albatross Bay Austr. 103 D1
Al Bayḍā' Libya 91 E1
Al Bayḍā' Yemen 82 B3
Albemarle U.S.A. 125 D1
Albemarle Sound sea chan. U.S.A. 125 E1
Albenga Italy 56 A2
Alberga watercourse Austr. 104 B1
Albert France 48 A3
Albert, Lake Dem. Rep. Congo/Uganda 95 D2
Alberta prov. Can. 112 D2
Albert Kanaal canal Belgium 48 B2
Albert Lea U.S.A. 121 E2
Albi France 52 C3
Al Bi'r Saudi Arabia 82 A2

Al Birk Saudi Arabia 82 B3
Al Biyāḍh reg. Saudi Arabia 82 B2
Alborz, Reshteh-ye mts Iran see Elburz Mountains
Albufeira Port. 54 B2
Albuquerque U.S.A. 126 C1
Al Buraymī Oman 83 C2
Albury Austr. 105 D3
Alcalá de Henares Spain 54 C1
Alcalá la Real Spain 54 C2
Alcamo Italy 56 B3
Alcañiz Spain 55 C1
Alcántara Spain 54 B2
Alcaraz, Sierra de mts Spain 54 C2
Alcázar de San Juan Spain 54 C2
Alchevs'k Ukr. 39 E2
Alcobaça Brazil 139 E1
Alcoy-Alcoi Spain 55 C2
Alcúdia Spain 55 D2
Aldabra Islands Seychelles 93 C5
Aldan Rus. Fed. 87 K3
Aldan r. Rus. Fed. 87 K2
Alderney i. Channel Is 47 B5
Aleg Maur. 90 A3
Alegrete Brazil 136 C3
Aleksandrovsk-Sakhalinskiy Rus. Fed. 87 L3
Aleksandry, Zemlya i. Rus. Fed. 86 F1
Alekseyevka Belgorodskaya Oblast' Rus. Fed. 39 E1
Alekseyevka Belgorodskaya Oblast' Rus. Fed. 09 E1
Aleksin Rus. Fed. 37 E3
Aleksinac Serbia 58 B2
Alèmbé Gabon 94 B3
Além Paraíba Brazil 139 D2
Alençon France 52 C2
Aleppo Syria 84 B2
Alerta Peru 134 B4
Ales France 53 C3
Alès France 53 C3
Aleşd Romania 38 B2
Alessandria Italy 56 A2
Ålesund Norway 40 F3
Aleutian Islands U.S.A. 142 E1
Aleutian Range mts U.S.A. 120
Alevina, Mys c. Rus. Fed. 87 M3
Alexander Archipelago is U.S.A. 112 B2
Alexander Bay S. Africa 98 A2
Alexander City U.S.A. 125 C2
Alexander Island Antarctica 107 K2
Alexandra Austr. 105 D3
Alexandra N.Z. 106 A4
Alexandria Egypt 92 A1
Alexandria Romania 38 C3
Alexandria LA U.S.A. 124 B2
Alexandria MN U.S.A. 121 D1
Alexandria VA U.S.A. 123 E3

Alexandrina, Lake Austr. 104 B3
Alexandroupoli Greece 59 C2
Alexis r. Can. 115 E3
Aleysk Rus. Fed. 81 F1
Alfaro Spain 55 C1
Al Fayyūm Egypt 84 B3
Alfeld (Leine) Ger. 49 D2
Alfenas Brazil 139 C2
Al Fujayrah U.A.E. see Fujairah
Algeciras Spain 54 B2
Algemesí Spain 55 C2
Algena Eritrea 82 A3
Alger Alg. see Algiers
Algeria country Africa 90 C2
Al Ghaydah Yemen 83 C3
Alghero Italy 56 A2
Al Ghurdaqah Egypt 92 B2
Al Ghwaybiyah Saudi Arabia
83 B2
Algiers Alg. 90 C1
Algoa Bay S. Africa 99 C4
Algona U.S.A. 121 E2
Algorta Spain 54 C1
Al Hadīthah Iraq 85 C2
Al Hajar al Gharbi mts Oman
83 C2
Al Hamādah al Hamrā' plat.
Libya 91 D2
Alhama de Murcia Spain 55 C2
Al Hammām Egypt 84 A2
Al Hanākīyah Saudi Arabia 82 B2
Al Hasakah Syria 85 C2
Al Hayy Iraq 85 C2
Al Hazm al Jawf Yemen 82 B3
Al Hibāk des. Saudi Arabia 83 C3
Al Hillah Saudi Arabia 82 B2
Al Hoceima Morocco 54 C2
Al Hudaydah Yemen see
Hodeidah
Al Hufūf Saudi Arabia 83 B2
Al Hulayq al Kabir hills Libya
91 D2
'Alīābād Iran 85 C3
Aliaga Turkey 59 C3
Alicante Spain 55 C2
Alice U.S.A. 127 E3
Alice Springs Austr. 102 C2
Aligarh India 79 B2
Aligūdarz Iran 85 C2
Alihe China 73 E1
Alima r. Congo 94 B3
Aliova r. Turkey 59 C3
Ali Sabieh Djibouti 93 C3
Al Iskandariyah Egypt see
Alexandria
Al Jaghbūb Libya 91 E2
Al Jahrah Kuwait 83 B2
Al Jawf Libya 91 E2
Al Jawf Saudi Arabia 82 A2
Aljezur Port. 54 B2
Al Jubayl Saudi Arabia 83 B2
Al Junaynah Saudi Arabia 82 A2
Aljustrel Port. 54 B2
Al Kahfah Saudi Arabia 82 B2

Al Kāmil Oman 83 C2
Al Karak Jordan 84 B2
Al Khābūrah Oman 83 C2
Al Khamāsīn Saudi Arabia 82 B2
Al Khārijah Egypt 92 B2
Al Khaşab Oman 83 C2
Al Khawr Qatar 83 C2
Al Khufrah Libya 92 A2
Al Khums Libya 91 D1
Al Khunn Saudi Arabia 83 B2
Alkmaar Neth. 48 B1
Al Kūt Iraq 85 C2
Al Kuwayt Kuwait see Kuwait
Al Lādhiqīyah Syria see Latakia
Allahabad India 79 C2
Allakh-Yun' Rus. Fed. 87 L2
'Allāqi, Wādī al watercourse
Egypt 82 A2
Allegheny r. U.S.A. 123 E2
Allegheny Mountains U.S.A.
123 D3
Allen, Lough l. Rep. of Ireland
45 B1
Allende Coahuila Mex. 129 B2
Allende Nuevo León Mex. 129 B2
Allentown U.S.A. 123 E2
Alleppey India 77 B4
Aller r. Ger. 49 D1
Alliance NE U.S.A. 120 C2
Al Lith Saudi Arabia 82 B2
Alloa U.K. 44 C2
Almada Port. 54 B2
Almadén Spain 54 C2
Al Madīnah Saudi Arabia see
Medina
Al Majma'ah Saudi Arabia 82 B2
Almanor, Lake U.S.A. 118 B2
Almansa Spain 55 C2
Al Mansūrah Egypt 84 B2
Al Mariyyah U.A.E. 83 C2
Al Marj Libya 91 E1
Almaty Kazakh. 81 E2
Almazán Spain 54 C1
Almeirim Brazil 135 D3
Almelo Neth. 48 C1
Almenara Brazil 139 D1
Almendra, Embalse de resr
Spain 54 B1
Almendralejo Spain 54 B2
Almería Spain 54 C2
Almería, Golfo de b. Spain 55 C2
Al'met'yevsk Rus. Fed. 35 E3
Al Mindak Saudi Arabia 82 B2
Al Minyā Egypt 84 B2
Al Mish'āb Saudi Arabia 83 B2
Almonte Spain 54 B2
Al Mubarraz Saudi Arabia 83 B2
Al Mudawwarah Jordan 84 B3
Al Mukallā Yemen see Mukalla
Al Mukhā Yemen see Mocha
Almuñécar Spain 54 C2
Al Muwaylih Saudi Arabia 82 A2
Almyros Greece 59 B3
Alness U.K. 44 B2

Alnwick U.K. 46 C2
Alofi Niue 101
Along India 66 A1
Alonnisos i. Greece 59 B3
Alor, Kepulauan is Indon. 63 C3
Alor Setar Malaysia 64 B1
Alozero Rus. Fed. 40 G2
Alpena U.S.A. 122 D1
Alpine U.S.A. 127 D2
Alps mts Europe 53 D2
Al Qa'āmīyāt reg. Saudi Arabia
83 B3
Al Qaddāhīyah Libya 91 D1
Al Qāhirah Egypt see Cairo
Al Qā'iyah Saudi Arabia 82 B2
Al Qāmishlī Syria 85 C2
Al Qatn Yemen 83 B3
Al Qunfidhah Saudi Arabia 82 B3
Al Quwayīyah Saudi Arabia 82 B2
Alsfeld Ger. 49 D2
Alta Norway 40 F2
Altaelva r. Norway 40 F2
Altai Mountains Asia 81 F2
Altamaha r. U.S.A. 125 D2
Altamira Brazil 135 D3
Altamura Italy 57 C2
Altay China 81 F2
Altay Mongolia 72 C1
Altdorf Switz. 53 D2
Altenburg Ger. 49 F2
Altntaş Turkey 59 D3
Altiplano plain Bol. 136 B2
Alto Araguaia Brazil 138 B1
Alto del Moncayo mt. Spain
55 C1
Alto Garças Brazil 138 B1
Altoona U.S.A. 123 E2
Alto Taquari Brazil 138 B1
Altötting Ger. 50 C3
Altun Shan mts China 81 F3
Alturas U.S.A. 118 B2
Altus U.S.A. 127 E2
Alūksne Latvia 36 C2
Al 'Ulā Saudi Arabia 82 A2
Al 'Uqaylah Libya 91 D1
Al Uqsur Egypt see Luxor
Alushta Ukr. 39 D3
Alva U.S.A. 127 E1
Alvarado Mex. 129 C3
Alvdalen val. Sweden 41 C3
Älvik Norway 42 E1
Älvsbyn Sweden 40 E2
Al Wajh Saudi Arabia 82 A2
Alwar India 78 B2
Al Widyān plat. Iraq/Saudi Arabia
85 C2
Alxa Youqi China see Ehen Hudag
Alyangula Austr. 103 C1
Alytus Lith. 36 B3
Alzada U.S.A. 120 C1
Alzey Ger. 48 D3
Amadeus, Lake salt flat Austr.
102 C2
Amadora Port. 54 B2

Amâ'ir Saudi Arabia **82** B2
Åmål Sweden **41** C4
Amaliada Greece **59** B3
Amamapare Indon. **63** D3
Amambai Brazil **138** A2
Amambai r. Brazil **138** A2
Amambai, Serra de hills Brazil/Para. **138** A2
Amami-shotō is Japan **73** E3
Amapá Brazil **135** D2
Amareleja Port. **54** B2
Amarillo U.S.A. **127** D1
Amasya Turkey **84** B1
Amazon r. S. America **134** D2
Amazon, Mouths of the Brazil **135** E2
Amazonas r. S. America see Amazon
Ambala India **78** N1
Ambato Ecuador **134** B3
Ambato Boeny Madag. **97** [inset] D1
Ambato Finandrahana Madag. **97** [inset] D2
Ambatolampy Madag. **97** [inset] D1
Ambatondrazaka Madag. **97** [inset] D1
Amberg Ger. **49** E3
Ambergris Cay i. Belize **130** B3
Ambikapur India **79** C2
Ambilobe Madag. **97** [inset] D1
Ambleside U.K. **46** B2
Amboasary Madag. **97** [inset] D2
Ambon Indon. **63** C3
Ambon i. Indon. **63** C3
Ambovombe Madag. **97** [inset] D2
Ambriz Angola **94** B3
Amdo China **72** C2
Ameca Mex. **128** B2
Ameland i. Neth. **48** B1
American Falls U.S.A. **118** D2
American Falls Reservoir U.S.A. **118** D2
American Fork U.S.A. **118** D2
American Samoa terr. S. Pacific Ocean **101**
Americus U.S.A. **128** D2
Amersfoort Neth. **48** B1
Amery Ice Shelf Antarctica **107** B3
Ames U.S.A. **126** E2
Amga Rus. Fed. **87** K2
Amguid Alg. **91** C2
Amgun' r. Rus. Fed. **87** L3
Amherst Can. **115** D2
Amiens France **52** C2
Amindivi Islands India **77** B3
Amirun Namibia **98** A1
Amisk Lake Can. **117** E2
Amistad Reservoir Mex./U.S.A. **127** D3
'Ammān Jordan **84** B2

Ammassalik Greenland **111** J2
Amol Iran **85** D2
Amorgos i. Greece **59** C3
Amory U.S.A. **124** C2
Amos Can. **114** C2
Amoy China see Xiamen
Amparo Brazil **139** C2
Amposta Spain **55** D1
Amqui Can. **123** G1
Amravati India **79** B2
Amritsar India **78** B1
Amstelveen Neth. **48** B1
Amsterdam Neth. **48** B1
Amstetten Austria **56** F3
Am Timan Chad **91** E3
Amudar'ya r. Asia **80** C2
Amundsen Gulf Can. **110** D2
Amuntai Indon. **65** C2
Amur r. China see Heilong Jiang
'Amur, Wadi watercourse Sudan **82** A3
Anabanua Indon. **65** D2
Anabarskiy Zaliv b. Rus. Fed. **87** J2
Anaconda U.S.A. **118** D1
Anadolu Dağları mts Turkey **84** B1
Anadyr' r. Rus. Fed. **87** N2
'Ānah Iraq **85** C2
Anáhuac Mex. **129** B2
Anambas, Kepulauan is Indon. **64** B1
Anamur Turkey **84** B2
Anan Japan **71** B4
Anantapur India **77** B3
Anan'yiv Ukr. **38** C2
Anapa Rus. Fed. **39** E3
Anápolis Brazil **139** C1
Anatolia reg. Turkey **66**
Añatuya Arg. **136** B3
Ancenis France **52** B2
Ancona Italy **56** B2
Ancud Chile **137** A5
Åndalsnes Norway **40** B3
Andalucía aut. comm. Spain **54** C2
Andalusia U.S.A. **124** C2
Andaman Islands India **77** D3
Andaman Sea Indian Ocean **67** A2
Andapa Madag. **97** [inset] D1
Andenes Norway **40** D2
Andenne Belgium **48** B2
Anderlecht Belgium **48** B2
Anderson r. Can. **110** D2
Anderson AK U.S.A. **110** C2
Anderson IN U.S.A. **122** C2
Anderson SC U.S.A. **125** D2
Andes mts S. America **136** A1
Andijon Uzbek. **81** C2
Andilamena Madag. **97** [inset] D1
Andilanatoby Madag. **97** [inset] D1

Andizhan Uzbek. see Andijon
Andoany Madag. **97** [inset] D1
Andong S. Korea **69** B2
Andorra country Europe **52** C3
Andorra la Vella Andorra **52** C3
Andover U.K. **47** C4
Andradina Brazil **138** B2
Andrews U.S.A. **127** D2
Andria Italy **57** C2
Androka Madag. **97** [inset] D2
Andros i. Bahamas **130** C2
Andros i. Greece **59** B3
Andros Town Bahamas **125** E4
Andrott i. India **77** B3
Andrushivka Ukr. **38** C1
Andselv Norway **40** D2
Andújar Spain **54** C2
Anduo Angola **96** A1
Anéfis Mali **90** C3
Aneto mt. Spain **36**
Aney Niger **91** D3
Angarsk Rus. Fed. **72** C1
Änge Sweden **41** D3
Ángel de la Guarda, Isla i. Mex. **128** A2
Angeles Phil. **68** B2
Ängelholm Sweden **41** C4
Ångermanälven r. Sweden **40** D3
Angermünde Ger. **49** G1
Angers France **52** B2
Angikuni Lake Can. **113** F1
Anglesey i. U.K. **46** A3
Angoche Moz. **97** C1
Angola country Africa **94** B4
Angoon U.S.A. **112** B2
Angoulême France **52** C2
Angren Uzbek. **80** C2
Anguilla terr. West Indies **131** D3
Angul India **79** C2
Anholt i. Denmark **44** B2
Anhui prov. China **74** B2
Anicuns Brazil **138** C1
Aniva, Mys c. Rus. Fed. **70** D1
Aniva, Zaliv b. Rus. Fed. **70** D1
Ankang China **74** B2
Ankara Turkey **35** C5
Anlu China **74** B2
Anna Rus. Fed. **37** F3
Annaba Alg. **91** C1
Annaberg-Buchholtz Ger. **49** F2
An Nafūd des. Saudi Arabia **82** B2
An Najaf Iraq **85** C2
Annan U.K. **44** C3
Annapolis U.S.A. **123** E3
Annapurna I mt. Nepal **79** C2
Ann Arbor U.S.A. **122** D2
Anna Regina Guyana **134** D2
An Nāşiriyah Iraq **85** C2
Annecy France **53** D2
Anniston U.S.A. **125** C2
An Nu'ayriyah Saudi Arabia **83** B2
Anorontany, Tanjona hd Madag. **97** [inset] D1

151

Ano Viannos Greece 59 C3
Anqing China 75 B2
Ansan S. Korea 69 B2
Ansbach Ger. 49 E3
Anshan China 74 C1
Anshun China 75 A3
An Sirhān, Wādī *watercourse* Saudi Arabia 82 A1
Ansongo Mali 90 C3
Antakya Turkey 84 B2
Antalaha Madag. 97 [inset] E1
Antalya Turkey 84 B2
Antalya Körfezi *g.* Turkey 84 B2
Antananarivo Madag. 97 [inset] D1
Antarctica 107
Antarctic Peninsula Antarctica 107 K3
An Teallach *mt.* U.K. 44 B2
Antequera Spain 54 C3
Anthony U.S.A. 126 C2
Anti Atlas *mts* Morocco 90 B2
Antibes France 53 D3
Anticosti, Île d' *i.* Can. 115 D2
Antigonish Can. 115 D2
Antigua and Barbuda *country* West Indies 131 B3
Antiguo-Morelos Mex. 129 C2
Antikythira *i.* Greece 59 B3
Antipodes Islands N.Z. 110
Antofagasta Chile 136 A3
Antrim U.K. 45 C1
Antrim Hills U.K. 45 C1
Antsalova Madag. 97 [inset] D1
Antsirabe Madag. 97 [inset] D1
Antsiranana Madag. 97 [inset] D1
Antsohihy Madag. 97 [inset] D1
Antwerp Belgium 48 B2
Anuradhapura Sri Lanka 77 C4
Anxi China 72 C2
Anxious Bay Austr. 104 A3
Anyang China 74 B2
Anzio Italy 56 A1
Aomori Japan 70 D2
Aosta Italy 56 A1
Aoukâr *reg.* Mali/Maur. 96
Apalachee Bay U.S.A. 125 D3
Apaporis *r.* Col. 134 C3
Aparecida do Tabuado Brazil 138 B2
Aparri Phil. 68 B2
Apatity Rus. Fed. 34 C2
Apatzingán Mex. 128 B3
Apeldoorn Neth. 48 B1
Apen Ger. 48 C1
Apennines *mts* Italy 56 A2
Apia Samoa 101
Apiaí Brazil 138 C2
Apo, Mount *vol.* Phil. 68 B3
Apolda Ger. 49 E2
Apollo Bay Austr. 104 C3
Apopka, Lake U.S.A. 125 D3
Aporé *r.* Brazil 138 B3

Appalachian Mountains U.S.A. 117 E3
Appleton U.S.A. 122 C2
Apsheronsk Rus. Fed. 39 E3
Apucarana Brazil 138 B2
Apucarana, Serra da *hills* Brazil 138 B2
Aqaba, Gulf of Asia 82 A2
Aqqikkol Hu *salt l.* China 79 C1
Aquidauana Brazil 138 A2
Aquidauana *r.* Brazil 138 A2
Ara India 79 C2
Arab, Bahr el *watercourse* Sudan 93 A4
Arabian Peninsula Asia 92 C5
Arabian Sea Indian Ocean 145 C4
Aracaju Brazil 135 F4
Aracati Brazil 135 F3
Araçatuba Brazil 138 B2
Aracruz Brazil 139 D1
Araçuaí Brazil 139 D1
Arad Romania 38 B2
Arada Chad 91 E3
Arafura Sea Austr./Indon. 63 C3
Aragarças Brazil 135 E3
Aragón *r.* Spain 55 C1
Araguaia *r.* Brazil 135 E3
Araguaína Brazil 135 E3
Araguari Brazil 138 C1
Arak Alg. 90 C2
Arāk Iran 85 C2
Arakan Yoma *mts* Myanmar 66 A1
Arak's *r.* Armenia 85 C2
Aral Sea *salt l.* Kazakh./Uzbek. 80 D2
Aral'sk Kazakh. 80 D2
Aranda de Duero Spain 54 C1
Arandelovac S.M. 58 B2
Aran Islands Rep. of Ireland 45 B2
Aranjuez Spain 54 C1
Aranos Namibia 98 A1
Aransas Pass U.S.A. 127 E3
Araouane Mali 90 C3
Arapiraca Brazil 135 F3
Arapongas Brazil 138 B2
Araquari Brazil 138 C3
'Ar'ar Saudi Arabia 82 B1
Araraquara Brazil 138 C2
Araras Brazil 138 C2
Araras, Serra das *mts* Brazil 138 B3
Ararat Austr. 104 C3
Ararat, Mount Turkey 85 C2
Araruama, Lago de *lag.* Brazil 139 D2
Arauca Col. 134 B2
Araxá Brazil 138 C1
Arbīl Iraq 85 C2
Arbroath U.K. 44 C2
Arbu Lut, Dasht-e *des.* Afgh. 78 A2
Arcachon France 52 B3
Arcata U.S.A. 118 A1

Archangel Rus. Fed. 34 D2
Archer *r.* Austr. 103 D1
Arco U.S.A. 118 D2
Arcos de la Frontera Spain 54 B2
Arctic Bay Can. 111 G2
Arctic Ocean 146
Arctic Red *r.* Can. 112 B1
Ardabīl Iran 85 C2
Ardahan Turkey 85 C1
Ārdalstangen Norway 41 B3
Ardennes *plat.* Belgium 48 B3
Ardestān Iran 85 D2
Ardlethan Austr. 105 D2
Ardmore U.S.A. 127 E2
Ardnamurchan, Point of *pt* U.K. 44 A2
Ardrossan Austr. 104 B3
Ardrossan U.K. 44 B3
Arena, Point U.S.A. 119 B3
Arendal Norway 41 B4
Arequipa Peru 134 B4
Arévalo Spain 54 C1
Arezzo Italy 56 B2
Argentan France 52 B2
Argentina *country* S. America 137 B4
Argentino, Lago *l.* Arg. 137 A6
Argenton-sur-Creuse France 52 C2
Argeș *r.* Romania 38 C2
Arghandāb *r.* Afgh. 78 A1
Argolikos Kolpos *b.* Greece 59 B3
Argos Greece 59 B3
Argostoli Greece 59 B3
Arguís Spain 55 C1
Argun' *r.* China/Rus. Fed. 73 E1
Argyle, Lake Austr. 102 B1
Ar Horqin Qi China *see* Tianshan
Århus Denmark 41 C4
Ariamsvlei Namibia 98 A2
Ari Atoll Maldives 77 B4
Arica Chile 136 A2
Arinagour U.K. 44 A2
Arinos Brazil 139 C1
Aripuanã Brazil 134 D4
Aripuanã *r.* Brazil 134 C3
Ariquemes Brazil 134 C3
Arīrahhā *r.* Brazil 138 B1
Arizona *state* U.S.A. 119 D5
Arkadelphia U.S.A. 124 B2
Arkalyk Kazakh. 81 D1
Arkansas *r.* U.S.A. 124 B1
Arkansas *state* U.S.A. 124 B1
Arkansas City U.S.A. 121 D3
Arkhangel'sk Rus. Fed. *see* Archangel
Arklow Rep. of Ireland 45 C2
Arkona, Kap *c.* Ger. 50 C2
Arkticheskogo Instituta, Ostrova *is* Rus. Fed. 61 H1
Arles France 53 C3
Arlit Niger 91 C3
Arlon Belgium 48 B3

Armagh U.K. 45 C1
Armant Egypt 92 D2
Armavir Rus. Fed. 39 F3
Armenia country Asia 85 C1
Armenia Col. 134 C2
Armería Mex. 128 B3
Armidale Austr. 105 E2
Armstrong Can. 114 B1
Armyans'k Ukr. 84 B1
Arnaud r. Can. 115 D1
Arnhem Neth. 48 B2
Arnhem, Cape Austr. 105 C1
Arnhem Bay Austr. 103 C1
Arnhem Land reg. Austr. 103 C1
Arno r. Italy 56 B2
Arno Bay Austr. 104 B2
Arnsberg Ger. 48 D2
Arnstadt Ger. 49 E2
Aroab Namibia 98 A2
Arona Italy 56 A1
Aros r. Mex. 128 B2
Arran i. U.K. 44 B3
Ar Raqqah Syria 84 B2
Arrée, Monts d' hills France 52 B2
Arriaga Mex. 129 C3
Ar Rimāl reg. Saudi Arabia 83 C2
Ar Riyāḍ Saudi Arabia see Riyadh
Ar Rustāq Oman 83 C2
Ar Ruṭbah Iraq 84 C2
Arsenajān Iran 85 D3
Arsen'yev Rus. Fed. 70 B2
Arta Greece 59 B3
Arteaga Mex. 128 B3
Artem Rus. Fed. 70 B2
Artemivs'k Ukr. 39 E2
Artenay France 52 C2
Artesia U.S.A. 126 D2
Arthur Point Austr. 103 E2
Arthur's Pass N.Z. 106 B3
Arthur's Town Bahamas 125 E4
Artigas Uru. 136 C4
Artillery Lake Can. 113 E1
Artsyz Ukr. 38 C2
Artux China 81 E3
Artvin Turkey 85 C1
Aru, Kepulauan is Indon. 63 C3
Arua Uganda 95 D2
Aruba terr. West Indies 131 D3
Arusha Tanz. 95 D3
Arvayheer Mongolia 72 C1
Arviat Can. 113 F1
Arvidsjaur Sweden 40 C2
Arvika Sweden 41 C4
Arzamas Rus. Fed. 35 D3
Arzew Alg. 55 C2
Arzfeld Ger. 48 C2
Aš Czech Rep. 49 F2
Asahi-dake vol. Japan 70 D2
Asahikawa Japan 70 D2
Asansol India 79 C2
Ascea Italy 56 C2
Ascensión Bol. 136 B2
Ascension i. S. Atlantic Ocean 97

Ascensión, Bahía de la b. Mex. 129 D3
Aschaffenburg Ger. 49 D3
Aschersleben Ger. 49 E2
Ascoli Piceno Italy 56 B2
Åsele Sweden 40 D3
Asenovgrad Bulg. 58 B2
Ashburton watercourse Austr. 102 A2
Ashburton N.Z. 106 B3
Ashdown U.S.A. 124 B2
Asheville U.S.A. 125 D1
Ashford U.K. 47 D4
Ashgabat Turkm. 80 C3
Ashington U.K. 46 C2
Ashkhabad Turkm. see Ashgabat
Ashland KY U.S.A. 122 D3
Ashland OH U.S.A. 122 D2
Ashland OR U.S.A. 118 B5
Ashland WI U.S.A. 122 B1
Ashmyany Belarus 36 C3
Ash Sharawrah Saudi Arabia 82 B3
Ash Shāriqah U.A.E. see Sharjah
Ash Sharqāṭ Iraq 85 C2
Ash Shiḥr Yemen 83 B3
Ash Shināṣ Oman 83 C2
Ash Shu'bah Saudi Arabia 83 B2
Ashuanipi Lake Can. 115 D1
Asilah Morocco 54 B1
Asinara, Golfo dell' b. Italy 56 A2
Asino Rus. Fed. 86 H3
Asipovichy Belarus 36 C3
'Asīr reg. Saudi Arabia 82 B2
Askim Norway 41 C4
Asmara Eritrea 92 B3
Åsnen l. Sweden 41 C4
Aspang-Markt Austria 31 D3
Aspen U.S.A. 120 B3
Aspiring, Mount N.Z. 106 A3
Assab Eritrea 93 C3
Assal, Lake Djibouti 96
Aş Salamīyah Saudi Arabia 83 B2
As Samāwah Iraq 85 C2
Aş Şanām reg. Saudi Arabia 83 C2
As Sarīr reg. Libya 91 E2
Assen Neth. 48 C1
Assesse Belgium 48 B2
Assiniboia Can. 113 E3
Assis Brazil 138 B2
Assisi Italy 53 E3
Aş Şubayḥiyah Kuwait 83 B2
Aş Sulaymānīyah Iraq 85 C2
As Sulayyil Saudi Arabia 82 B2
As Sūq Saudi Arabia 82 B2
As Suwaydā' Syria 84 B2
As Suways Egypt see Suez
Astakos Greece 59 B3
Astana Kazakh. 81 E1
Āstārā Iran 85 C2
Asti Italy 56 A2
Astorga Spain 54 B1
Astoria U.S.A. 118 B1

Astrakhan' Rus. Fed. 35 D4
Astravyets Belarus 36 C3
Astypalaia i. Greece 59 C3
Asunción Para. 136 C3
Aswān Egypt 92 B2
Asyūṭ Egypt 92 B2
Atacama, Desierto de des. Chile see Atacama Desert
Atacama, Salar de salt flat Chile 136 B3
Atacama Desert Chile 136 B3
Atakpamé Togo 90 C4
Atamyrat Turkm. 81 D3
'Ataq Yemen 82 B3
Atār Maur. 90 A2
Atascadero U.S.A. 119 B3
Atasu Kazakh. 81 E2
Atbara Sudan 92 B3
Atbara r. Sudan 92 B3
Atbasar Kazakh. 81 C1
Atchison U.S.A. 121 D3
Ath Belgium 48 A2
Athabasca Can. 112 D2
Athabasca r. Can. 113 D2
Athabasca, Lake Can. 113 E2
Athens Greece 59 B3
Athens GA U.S.A. 125 D2
Athens OH U.S.A. 122 D3
Athens TN U.S.A. 125 D1
Athens TX U.S.A. 127 E2
Athína Greece see Athens
Athlone Rep. of Ireland 45 C2
Athos mt. Greece 59 B2
Ati Chad 91 D3
Atikokan Can. 114 A2
Atiu i. Cook Is 109
Atlanta U.S.A. 125 D2
Atlantic U.S.A. 121 D2
Atlantic City U.S.A. 123 F3
Atlantic Ocean 144
Atlantis S. Africa 98 A3
Atlas Mountains Africa 90 B1
Atlas Saharien mts Alg. 90 C1
Atlin Can. 112 B2
Atlin Lake Can. 112 B2
Atmore U.S.A. 124 C2
Atoka U.S.A. 127 E2
Atrai r. India 79 C2
Aṭ Ṭā'if Saudi Arabia 82 B2
Attapu Laos 67 B2
Attawapiskat Can. 114 B1
Attawapiskat r. Can. 114 B1
Attawapiskat Lake Can. 114 B1
Aṭ Ṭur Egypt 92 B2
At Turbah Yemen 82 B3
Atyrau Kazakh. 80 C2
Aubenas France 53 C3
Aubry Lake Can. 112 C1
Auburn CA U.S.A. 119 B3
Auburn NE U.S.A. 121 D2
Auburn NY U.S.A. 123 E2

Aubusson France 52 C2
Auch France 52 C3
Auckland N.Z. 106 B2
Auckland Islands N.Z. 110
Audo Range mts Eth. 95 C3
Aue Ger. 49 F2
Augsburg Germany Ger. 50 C3
Augusta Sicilia 56 C3
Augusta GA U.S.A. 125 D2
Augusta ME U.S.A. 123 G2
Augustus, Mount Austr. 102 A3
Aulnoye-Aymeries France 48 A2
Aunglan Myanmar 66 A2
Aurangabad India 78 B3
Aurich Ger. 48 C1
Aurillac France 52 C3
Aurora CO U.S.A. 120 C3
Aurora IL U.S.A. 122 C2
Aus Namibia 98 A2
Austin MN U.S.A. 121 E2
Austin NV U.S.A. 119 C3
Austin TX U.S.A. 127 C3
Australes, Îles is Fr. Polynesia see Tubuai Islands
Australia country Oceania 102
Australian Capital Territory admin. div. Austr. 105 D3
Austria country Europe 50 C3
Autlán Mex. 128 B3
Autun France 52 C2
Auxerre France 52 C2
Avallon France 52 C2
Avalon Peninsula Can. 115 E2
Avaré Brazil 138 C3
Avarua Cook Is 101
Avdiyivka Ukr. 39 E2
Aveiro Port. 54 B1
Avellino Italy 56 B2
Avesnes-sur-Helpe France 48 A2
Avesta Sweden 41 D3
Avezzano Italy 56 B2
Aviemore U.K. 44 C2
Avignon France 52 C3
Ávila Spain 54 C1
Avilés Spain 54 C1
Avola Italy 56 C3
Avon r. England U.K. 47 C4
Avon r. England U.K. 47 B3
Avranches France 52 B2
Awanui N.Z. 106 B2
Awash Eth. 93 C4
Awash r. Eth. 93 C3
Awbārī Libya 91 D2
Aweil Sudan 93 A4
Awka Nigeria 94 A2
Axel Heiberg Island Can. 110 F1
Ay France 48 B3
Ayacucho Peru 134 B4
Ayagoz Kazakh. 81 F2
Ayakkum Hu salt l. China 72 B2
Ayamonte Spain 54 B2
Ayan Rus. Fed. 87 L3
Ayaviri Peru 134 B4
Aybak Afgh. 78 A1

Aydar r. Ukr. 39 E2
Aydın Turkey 59 C3
Ayeat, Gora h. Kazakh. 81 D2
Ayers Rock h. Austr. see Uluṟu
Aylesbury U.K. 47 C4
Ayllón Spain 54 C1
Aylmer Lake Can. 113 E1
Ayod Sudan 93 B4
Ayon, Ostrov i. Rus. Fed. 87 N2
'Ayoûn el 'Atroûs Maur. 90 B3
Ayr Austr. 103 D1
Ayr U.K. 44 B3
Ayre, Point of pt Isle of Man 46 A2
Aytos Bulg. 58 C2
Ayutthaya Thai. 67 B2
Ayvacık Turkey 59 C3
Ayvalık Turkey 59 C3
Azaouagh, Vallée de watercourse Mali/Niger 90 C3
Azerbaijan country Asia 85 C1
Azores aut. reg. Port. 32
Azores terr. N. Atlantic Ocean 32
Azov Rus. Fed. 39 E2
Azov, Sea of Rus. Fed./Ukr. 39 E2
Azraq, Baḩr al r. Eth./Sudan see Blue Nile
Azuaga Spain 54 B2
Azuero, Península de pen. Panama 130 B4
Azul Arg. 137 C4
Az Zaqāzīq Egypt 84 B2
Az Zarqā' Jordan 84 B2
Az Zaydīyah Yemen 82 B3
Azzel Matti, Sebkha salt pan Alg. 90 C2
Az Zuqur i. Yemen 82 B3

B

Baardheere Somalia 93 C4
Bābā, Kūh-e mts Afgh. 78 A1
Babadag Romania 58 C2
Babaeski Turkey 59 C2
Bāb al Mandab str. Africa/Asia 82 B3
Babana Indon. 65 C2
Babar i. Indon. 63 C3
Babati Tanz. 95 D3
Babayevo Rus. Fed. 37 E2
Babine r. Can. 112 C2
Babine Lake Can. 112 C2
Babruysk Belarus 36 C3
Babuyan i. Phil. 68 B1
Bábol Iran 85 D2
Babuyan Islands Phil. 68 B2
Bacabal Brazil 135 E3
Bacău Romania 38 C2
Bacchus Marsh Austr. 104 C3

Bachu China 81 E3
Back r. Can. 113 F1
Bac Liêu Vietnam 67 B3
Bacolod Phil. 68 B2
Bacqueville, Lac l. Can. 114 C1
Badajoz Spain 54 B2
Badarpur India 66 A1
Bad Berleburg Ger. 49 D2
Bad Bevensen Ger. 49 E1
Bad Ems Ger. 48 C2
Baden Austria 51 D3
Baden-Baden Ger. 50 B3
Bad Freienwalde Ger. 49 F1
Bad Harzburg Ger. 49 E2
Bad Hersfeld Ger. 49 D2
Bad Hofgastein Austria 50 C3
Bad Homburg vor der Höhe Ger. 49 D2
Badin Pak. 78 A2
Bad Ischl Austria 53 E2
Bādiyat ash Shām des. Asia see Syrian Desert
Bad Kissingen Ger. 49 E2
Bad Kreuznach Ger. 48 C3
Bad Lauterberg im Harz Ger. 49 E2
Bad Liebenwerda Ger. 49 F2
Bad Mergentheim Ger. 49 D3
Bad Nauheim Ger. 49 D2
Bad Neuenahr-Ahrweiler Ger. 48 C2
Bad Neustadt an der Saale Ger. 49 E2
Bad Oldesloe Ger. 49 E1
Bad Pyrmont Ger. 49 D2
Bad Salzuflen Ger. 49 D1
Bad Salzungen Ger. 49 E2
Bad Schwartau Ger. 50 C2
Bad Segeberg Ger. 50 C2
Badulla Sri Lanka 77 C4
Bad Zwischenahn Ger. 48 D1
Bafatá Guinea-Bissau 90 A3
Baffin Bay sea Can./Greenland 111 H2
Baffin Island Can. 111 H2
Bafia Cameroon 94 B2
Bafing r. Guinea/Mali 90 A3
Bafoulabé Mali 90 A3
Bafoussam Cameroon 94 B2
Bāfq Iran 85 D2
Bafra Turkey 84 B1
Bāft Iran 83 D2
Bafwasende Dem. Rep. Congo 95 C2
Bagamoyo Tanz. 95 D3
Bagani Namibia 96 B1
Bagansiapiapi Indon. 64 B1
Bagé Brazil 136 C4
Baghdād Iraq 85 C2
Baghlān Afgh. 78 A1
Bagnères-de-Luchon France 52 C3
Bagrationovsk Rus. Fed. 36 B3

Bagrax China see Bohu
Baguio Phil. **68** B2
Bagzane, Monts mts Niger **91** C3
Baharampur India **79** C2
Bahawalpur Pak. **78** B2
Bahía, Islas de la is Hond. **130** D3
Bahía Blanca Arg. **137** B4
Bahía Kino Mex. **128** A2
Bahía Tortugas Mex. **128** A2
Bahir Dar Eth. **93** B3
Bahraich India **79** C2
Bahrain country Asia **83** C2
Bahrīyah, Wāḩāt al oasis Egypt **92** A2
Bāhū Kālāt Iran **83** D2
Baia Mare Romania **38** B2
Baicheng China **73** B1
Baie-Comeau Can. **115** D2
Baihe China **69** B1
Baikal, Lake Rus. Fed. **73** D1
Bailín Yougí China see Daban
Baile Átha Cliath Rep. of Ireland see Dublin
Băileşti Romania **38** B3
Bainang China **72** C2
Bainbridge U.S.A. **125** D2
Bairiki Kiribati **100**
Bairin Youqi China see Daban
Bairnsdale Austr. **105** D3
Baishan China **69** B1
Baiyin China **74** A2
Baiyuda Desert Sudan **92** B3
Baja Hungary **51** D3
Baja California pen. Mex. **128** A1
Bajawa Indon. **65** D2
Bakel Senegal **90** A3
Baker CA U.S.A. **119** C3
Baker MT U.S.A. **120** C1
Baker OR U.S.A. **118** C2
Baker, Mount vol. U.S.A. **118** B1
Baker Foreland hd Can. **113** F1
Baker Island terr. N. Pacific Ocean **101**
Baker Lake Can. **113** F1
Baker Lake l. Can. **113** F1
Bakersfield U.S.A. **119** C3
Bakhchysaray Ukr. **39** D3
Bakherden Turkm. **80** C3
Bakhmach Ukr. **39** D1
Baku Azer. see Baku
Barköy Turkey **59** C2
Bakkaflói b. Iceland **40** [inset]
Bala U.K. **47** B3
Balabac Phil. **68** A3
Balabac i. Phil. **68** A3
Balabac Strait Malaysia/Phil. **65** C1
Balaiberkuak Indon. **65** C2
Balaklava Austr. **104** B2
Balaklava Ukr. **39** D3
Balakliya Ukr. **39** E2
Balakovo Rus. Fed. **35** D3
Bālā Morghāb Afgh. **78** A1
Balan Daği h. Turkey **59** C3

Balashov Rus. Fed. **35** D3
Balaton, Lake Hungary **51** D3
Balbina, Represa de resr Brazil **134** D3
Balbriggan Rep. of Ireland **45** C2
Balcanoona Austr. **104** B2
Balchik Bulg. **58** C2
Balclutha N.Z. **106** A4
Baldock Lake Can. **113** F2
Baldy Mountain h. Can. **113** E2
Baldy Peak U.S.A. **126** C2
Baleares, Islas is Spain see Balearic Islands
Balearic Islands is Spain **55** D2
Baleia, Ponta da pt Brazil **139** E1
Baleine, Grande Rivière de la r. Can. **114** C1
Baleine, Rivière à la r. Can. **115** D1
Baleshwar India **79** C2
Bali i. Indon. **65** C2
Baliguda India **79** C2
Balige Indon. **64** A1
Balıkesir Turkey **59** C3
Balikpapan Indon. **65** C2
Balimo P.N.G. **63** D3
Bali Sea Indon. see Bali, Laut
Balkanabat Turkm. **80** C3
Balkan Mountains Bulg./S.M. **58** B2
Balkhash Kazakh. **81** E2
Balkhash, Lake Kazakh. **81** E2
Balladonia Austr. **102** B3
Ballangen Norway **40** D2
Ballarat Austr. **104** C3
Ballard, Lake salt flat Austr. **102** B2
Ballater U.K. **44** C2
Ballena, Punta pt Chile **147**
Ballina Austr. **105** E1
Ballina Rep. of Ireland **45** B1
Ballinasloe Rep. of Ireland **45** B2
Ballinger U.S.A. **127** E2
Ballycastle U.K. **45** C1
Ballyclare U.K. **45** D1
Ballymena U.K. **45** C1
Ballymoney U.K. **45** C1
Ballyshannon Rep. of Ireland **45** B1
Balonne r. Austr. **103** D2
Balotra India **78** B2
Balrampur India **79** C2
Balranald Austr. **104** C2
Balş Romania **38** B3
Balsas Mex. **129** C3
Balta Ukr. **38** C2
Bălţi Moldova **38** C2
Baltic Sea g. Europe **41** D4
Baltimore U.S.A. **123** E3
Baltiysk Rus. Fed. **36** E3
Balvi Latvia **36** C2
Balykchy Kyrg. **81** E2
Balykshi Kazakh. **80** C2

Bam Iran **83** C2
Bamaga Austr. **103** D1
Bamaji Lake Can. **114** A1
Bamako Mali **90** B3
Bambari C.A.R. **94** C2
Bamberg Ger. **49** E3
Bambouti C.A.R. **95** C2
Bambuí Brazil **139** C2
Bamenda Cameroon **94** B2
Bāmīān Afgh. **78** A1
Bam Posht, Kūh-e mts Iran **78** A2
Bañados del Izozog swamp Bol. **136** B2
Bananal, Ilha do i. Brazil **135** D4
Banas r. India **78** B2
Banaz Turkey **59** C3
Ban Ban Laos **66** B2
Banbridge U.K. **45** C1
Banbury U.K. **47** C3
Banda Dem. Rep. Congo **95** C2
Banda India **79** C2
Banda, Laut sea Indon. **63** C3
Banda Aceh Indon. **64** A1
Bandar-e 'Abbās Iran **83** C2
Bandar-e Anzalī Iran **85** C2
Bandar-e Emām Khomeynī Iran **85** C2
Bandar-e Lengeh Iran **83** C2
Bandar-e Maqām Iran **83** C2
Bandar Lampung Indon. **64** B2
Bandar Seri Begawan Brunei **65** C1
Banda Sea Indon. see Banda, Laut
Bandeiras, Pico de mt. Brazil **139** D2
Bandelierkop S. Africa **99** C1
Banderas, Bahía de b. Mex. **128** B2
Bandırma Turkey **59** C2
Bandundu Dem. Rep. Congo **94** B3
Bandung Indon. **64** B2
Banff Can. **112** D2
Banff U.K. **44** C2
Banfora Burkina **90** B3
Banga Phil. **68** B3
Bangalore India **77** B3
Bangassou C.A.R. **94** C2
Banggai Indon. **65** D2
Banggai, Kepulauan is Indon. **65** D2
Banggi i. Malaysia **65** C1
Bangka i. Indon. **64** B2
Bangkalan Indon. **65** C2
Bangko Indon. **64** B2
Bangkok Thai. **67** B2
Bangladesh country Asia **79** C2
Bangor Northern Ireland U.K. **45** D1
Bangor Wales U.K. **46** A3
Bangor U.S.A. **123** G2

155

Bang Saphan Yai Thai. **67** A2
Bangui C.A.R. **94** B2
Bangweulu, Lake Zambia **97** B1
Ban Huai Khon Thai. **66** B2
Bani Mazār Egypt **84** B3
Bani Walid Libya **91** D1
Bāniyās Syria **84** B2
Banja Luka Bos.-Herz. **57** C2
Banjarmasin Indon. **65** C2
Banjul Gambia **90** A3
Banks Island B.C. Can. **112** B2
Banks Island N.W.T. Can. **110** D2
Banks Islands Vanuatu **110** F3
Banks Lake Can. **113** F1
Banks Peninsula N.Z. **106** B3
Bankura India **79** C2
Banmauk Myanmar **66** A1
Bann r. U.K. **45** C1
Ban Napè Laos **66** B2
Ban Na San Thai. **67** A3
Bannerman Town Bahamas **125** E4
Bannu Pak. **78** B1
Banswara India **78** B2
Ban Tha Kham Thai. **67** A3
Bantry Rep. of Ireland **45** B3
Bantry Bay Rep. of Ireland **45** B3
Banyuwangi Indon. **65** C2
Baochang China **74** B1
Baoding China **74** B2
Baoji China **74** A2
Bao Lôc Vietnam **67** B2
Baoqing China **70** B1
Baoshan China **66** A1
Baotou China **74** B1
Baotou Shan mt. China/N. Korea **69** B1
Bapaume France **48** A2
Ba'qūbah Iraq **85** C2
Bar S.M. **58** A2
Baracoa Cuba **131** C2
Baradine Austr. **105** D2
Baram r. Malaysia **65** C1
Baranis Egypt **82** A2
Baranavichy Belarus **39** F3
Baranivka Ukr. **38** C1
Barankul Kazakh. **80** C2
Baranof Island U.S.A. **112** B2
Barat Daya, Kepulauan is Indon. **63** C3
Barbacena Brazil **139** D2
Barbados country West Indies **131** E3
Barbastro Spain **55** D1
Barbate Spain **54** C2
Barberton S. Africa **99** D2
Barbezieux-St-Hilaire France **52** B2
Barcaldine Austr. **103** D2
Barcelona Spain **55** D1
Barcelona Venez. **134** C1
Barcelos Brazil **134** C3
Barcs Hungary **51** D3
Barddhaman India **79** C2
Bardejov Slovakia **51** E3
Bardsīr Iran **83** C2
Bareilly India **79** B2
Barentin France **47** D5

Barents Sea Arctic Ocean **34** D1
Barentu Eritrea **82** A3
Barfleur, Pointe de pt France **47** C5
Bar Harbor U.S.A. **123** G2
Bari Italy **57** C2
Barika Alg. **55** E2
Barinas Venez. **134** B2
Baripada India **79** C2
Barisal Bangl. **79** D2
Barisan, Pegunungan mts Indon. **64** B2
Barito r. Indon. **65** C2
Barkā Oman **83** C2
Barkly Tableland reg. Austr. **103** C1
Barkol China **72** C2
Bârlad Romania **38** C2
Bar-le-Duc France **53** D2
Barlee, Lake salt flat Austr. **102** A2
Barletta Italy **57** C2
Barmedman Austr. **105** D2
Barmer India **78** B2
Barmouth U.K. **47** A3
Barnato Austr. **105** C2
Barnaul Rus. Fed. **81** F1
Barneveld Neth. **48** B1
Barnsley U.K. **46** C3
Barnstaple U.K. **47** A4
Barquisimeto Venez. **134** C1
Barra i. U.K. **44** A2
Barraba Austr. **105** D2
Barra do Corda Brazil **135** E3
Barra do Garças Brazil **138** B1
Barra de São Manuel Brazil **134** D3
Barranca Lima Peru **134** B4
Barranca Loreto Peru **134** B3
Barranquilla Col. **134** B1
Barreiras Brazil **135** E4
Barretos Brazil **138** C2
Barrie Can. **114** C2
Barrier Range hills Austr. **104** C2
Barrington, Mount Austr. **105** E2
Barringun Austr. **105** D1
Barrow r. Rep. of Ireland **45** C2
Barrow U.S.A. **110** B2
Barrow, Point U.S.A. **110** B2
Barrow Creek Austr. **102** C2
Barrow-in-Furness U.K. **46** B2
Barrow Island Austr. **102** A2
Barry U.K. **47** B4
Barrys Bay Can. **114** C2
Barsalpur India **78** B2
Barstow U.S.A. **118** C2
Bar-sur-Aube France **53** C2
Bartın Turkey **84** B1
Bartle Frere, Mount Austr. **103** D1
Bartlesville U.S.A. **127** E1
Bartoszyce Pol. **51** E2
Barung i. Indon. **65** C2

Baruun-Urt Mongolia **73** D1
Barvinkove Ukr. **39** E2
Barwon r. Austr. **105** D2
Barysaw Belarus **36** C1
Basarabi Romania **38** C3
Basel Switz. **53** D2
Bashtanka Ukr. **39** D2
Basilan i. Phil. **68** B3
Basildon U.K. **47** D4
Basingstoke U.K. **47** C4
Baskatong, Réservoir resr Can. **114** C2
Basle Switz. see Basel
Basoko Dem. Rep. Congo **94** C2
Basra Iraq **85** C2
Bassein Myanmar **66** A2
Basse-Terre Guadeloupe **131** D3
Basseterre St Kitts and Nevis **131** D3
Bass Strait Austr. **103** D3
Bastak Iran **83** C2
Basti India **79** C2
Bastia France **53** D3
Bastogne Belgium **48** B2
Bastrop U.S.A. **124** B2
Bata Equat. Guinea **94** A2
Batagay Rus. Fed. **87** K2
Bataguassu Brazil **138** B2
Batan i. Phil. **68** B1
Batangas Phil. **68** B2
Batanghari r. Indon. **64** B2
Batan Islands Phil. **68** B1
Batavia U.S.A. **123** E2
Bataysk Rus. Fed. **39** E2
Batchawana Mountain h. Can. **114** B2
Batchelor Austr. **102** C1
Bătdâmbâng Cambodia **67** B2
Batemans Bay Austr. **105** E3
Batesville U.S.A. **124** B1
Batetskiy Rus. Fed. **37** D2
Bath U.K. **47** B4
Bathinda India **78** B1
Bathurst Can. **111** H3
Bathurst U.S.A. ... see Bathurst Inlet

Bathurst Inlet Can. **110** E2
Bathurst Inlet inlet Can. **110** E2
Bathurst Island Austr. **102** C1
Bathurst Island Can. **110** F1
Bātin, Wādī al watercourse Asia **82** B1
Batman Turkey **85** C2
Batna Alg. **91** C1
Baton Rouge U.S.A. **124** B2
Batopilas Mex. **128** B2
Batouri Cameroon **94** B2
Båtsfjord Norway **40** F1
Batticaloa Sri Lanka **77** C4
Battipaglia Italy **56** B2
Battle r. Can. **113** E2
Battle Creek U.S.A. **122** C2
Batu mt. Eth. **93** B4
Batu, Pulau-pulau is Indon. **64** A2

Batudaka i. Indon. 65 D2
Batu Pahat Malaysia 64 B1
Baubau Indon. 65 D2
Bauchi Nigeria 91 C3
Baures Brazil 138 C2
Bauru Brazil 138 C2
Bauska Latvia 36 B2
Bautzen Ger. 50 C2
Bavispe r. Mex. 128 B2
Bavly Rus. Fed. 35 E3
Bawean i. Indon. 65 C2
Bayamo Cuba 131 C2
Bayan Hot China 74 A2
Bayan Obo Kuangqu China 74 A1
Bayan Ul Hot China 74 B1
Bayburt Turkey 84 C1
Bay City MI U.S.A. 122 C2
Bay City TX U.S.A. 127 E3
Baydhabo Somalia 93 C4
Bayeux France 47 C5
Baykal, Ozero l. Rus. Fed. see
Baikal, Lake
Baykal'skiy Khrebet mts
Rus. Fed. 87 J3
Baymak Rus. Fed. 35 E3
Bayonne France 52 B3
Bayramiç Turkey 59 C3
Bayreuth Ger. 49 E3
Baza Spain 54 C2
Bazardyuzyu, Gora mt.
Azer./Rus. Fed. 85 C1
Bazdar Pak. 81 C2
Bazmān Iran 83 D2
Bazmān, Kūh-e mt. Iran 80 D2
Beachy Head U.K. 47 D4
Beacon Bay S. Africa 99 C3
Beagle Gulf Austr. 102 C1
Bealanana Madag. 97 [inset] D1
Beardmore Can. 114 B2
Bear Paw Mountain U.S.A.
118 E1
Beatrice U.S.A. 121 D2
Beatty U.S.A. 119 C3
Beaudesert Austr. 105 E1
Beaufort Austr. 104 C3
Beaufort Malaysia 65 C1
Beaufort U.S.A. 125 D2
Beaufort Sea Can./U.S.A. 110 D2
Beaufort West S. Africa 98 B3
Beauly r. U.K. 44 B2
Beaumont Belgium 48 B2
Beaumont NZ 106 A4
Beaumont U.S.A. 127 F2
Beaune France 53 C2
Beaune France 53 C2
Beauraing Belgium 48 B2
Beauséjour Can. 113 F2
Beauvais France 52 C2
Beauval Can. 113 E2
Beaver r. Can. 113 E2
Beaver U.S.A. 119 D3

Beaver Creek Can. 112 A1
Beaver Dam U.S.A. 122 C2
Beaver Hill Lake Can. 113 F2
Beaver Island U.S.A. 122 C1
Beaverlodge Can. 112 D2
Beawar India 78 B2
Bebedouro Brazil 138 C2
Bebra Ger. 49 D2
Béchar Alg. 90 B1
Beckley U.S.A. 122 D3
Bedford U.K. 47 C3
Bedford U.S.A. 122 C3
Beecroft Peninsula Austr.
105 E2
Beenleigh Austr. 105 E1
Beersheba Israel 84 B2
Beeville U.S.A. 127 E3
Bega Austr. 105 D3
Degur, Cap de c. Spain 55 D1
Behshahr Iran 85 D2
Bei'an China 73 E1
Beihai China 75 A3
Beijing China 74 B2
Beilen Neth. 48 C1
Beinn Mhòr h. U.K. 44 A2
Beira Moz. 97 C1
Beirut Lebanon 84 B2
Beja Port. 54 B2
Bejaïa Alg. 91 C1
Béjar Spain 54 B1
Beji r. Pak. 78 A2
Bekdash Turkm. 80 C2
Békéscsaba Hungary 51 F3
Bekily Madag. 97 [inset] D2
Bela Pak. 78 A2
Bela Crkva S.M. 58 B2
Belaga Malaysia 65 C1
Belarus country Europe 36 C3
Bela Vista Brazil 138 A2
Bela Vista Moz. 99 D2
Belawan Indon. 64 A1
Belaya r. Rus. Fed. 87 N2
Belaya Glina Rus. Fed. 39 F2
Belaya Kalitva Rus. Fed. 39 F2
Belchatów Pol. 51 D2
Belcher Islands Can. 111 C3
Beledweyne Somalia 93 C4
Belém Brazil 135 D2
Belen U.S.A. 126 C2
Belev Rus. Fed. 37 E3
Belfast U.K. 45 D1
Belfast U.S.A. 123 G2
Belfort France 53 D2
Belgaum India 77 B3
Belgium country Europe 48 B2
Belgorod Rus. Fed. 39 E1
Belgrade S.M. 58 B2
Beli Nigeria 91 D4
Belinyu Indon. 64 B2
Belitung i. Indon. 64 B2
Belize Belize 130 B3
Belize country Central America
130 B3

Bella Bella Can. 112 C2
Bellac France 52 C2
Bellata Austr. 105 D1
Belle Fourche U.S.A. 120 C2
Belle Fourche r. U.S.A. 120 C2
Belle Glade U.S.A. 125 D3
Belle-Île i. France 52 B2
Belle Isle i. Can. 115 E1
Belle Isle, Strait of Can. 115 E1
Belleville KS U.S.A. 121 D3
Bellevue U.S.A. 118 B1
Bellingham U.S.A. 118 B1
Bellinzona Switz. 53 D2
Belluno Italy 56 B1
Bellville S. Africa 98 A3
Belmonte Brazil 139 E1
Belmopan Belize 130 B3
Belmullet Rep. of Ireland 45 A1
Belogorsk Rus. Fed. 73 E1
Belo Horizonte Brazil 139 D1
Beloit U.S.A. 122 C2
Belomorsk Rus. Fed. 34 C2
Belorechensk Rus. Fed. 39 E3
Beloretsk Rus. Fed. 35 E3
Beloyarskiy Rus. Fed. 34 F2
Beloye, Ozero l. Rus. Fed. 37 E1
Beloye More sea Rus. Fed. see
White Sea
Belozersk Rus. Fed. 37 E1
Belukha, Gora mt.
Kazakh./Rus. Fed. 81 F2
Belush'ye Rus. Fed. 34 D2
Belyy Rus. Fed. 37 D2
Belyy, Ostrov i. Rus. Fed. 34 G1
Bemidji U.S.A. 121 E1
Benalla Austr. 105 D3
Benavente Spain 54 B1
Benbecula i. U.K. 44 A2
Bend U.S.A. 118 B2
Bendearg mt. S. Africa 99 C3
Bendigo Austr. 104 C3
Bene Moz. 97 C1
Benešov Czech Rep. 50 C3
Benevento Italy 56 B2
Bengal, Bay of sea Indian Ocean
77 C3
Bengbu China 74 B2
Benghazi Libya 91 E1
Bengkayang Indon. 64 B1
Bengkulu Indon. 64 B2
Benguela Angola 96 A1
Ben Hope h. U.K. 44 B1
Beni r. Bol. 136 B2
Beni Dem. Rep. Congo 95 C2
Beni-Abbès Alg. 90 B1
Benidorm Spain 55 C2
Beni Mellal Morocco 90 B1
Benin country Africa 90 C4
Benin, Bight of g. Africa 90 C4
Benin City Nigeria 91 C4
Beni-Saf Alg. 55 C2
Benjamin Constant Brazil
134 C3
Benjamín Hill Mex. 128 A1

Ben Lawers *mt.* U.K. **44** B2
Ben Macdui *mt.* U.K. **44** C2
Ben More *h.* U.K. **44** A2
Benmore, Lake N.Z. **106** B3
Ben More Assynt *h.* U.K. **44** B1
Bennett Can. **112** B2
Ben Nevis *mt.* U.K. **44** B2
Bennington U.S.A. **123** F2
Benoni S. Africa **99** C2
Benson U.S.A. **126** B2
Benteng Indon. **65** D2
Benton Harbor U.S.A. **122** C2
Bentonville U.S.A. **124** E1
Benue *r.* Nigeria **91** C4
Benwee Head Rep. of Ireland **45** B1
Ben Wyvis *mt.* U.K. **44** B2
Benxi China **74** C1
Beograd S.M. *see* Belgrade
Beohari India **79** C2
Beppu Japan **71** B4
Berane S.M. **58** A2
Berat Albania **59** A2
Berbérati C.A.R. **94** B2
Berck France **52** C1
Berdyans'k Ukr. **39** E2
Berdychiv Ukr. **38** C2
Berehove Ukr. **38** B2
Berens River Can. **113** F2
Berezhany Ukr. **38** B2
Berezivka Ukr. **38** D2
Berezne Ukr. **38** C1
Bereznik Rus. Fed. **34** D2
Berezniki Rus. Fed. **34** E3
Berga Spain **55** D1
Bergama Turkey **59** C3
Bergamo Italy **56** A1
Bergen *Mecklenburg-Vorpommern* Ger. **50** C2
Bergen *Niedersachsen* Ger. **49** D1
Bergen Norway **41** B3
Bergen op Zoom Neth. **48** B2
Bergerac France **52** C3
Bergheim (Erft) Ger. **48** C2
Bergisch Gladbach Ger. **48** C2
Bergland Namibia **98** A1
Bergsviken Sweden **40** E2
Beringen Belgium **48** B2
Bering Sea N. Pacific Ocean **87** N3
Bering Strait Rus. Fed./U.S.A. **87** O2
Berkeley U.S.A. **119** B3
Berkner Island Antarctica **107** A2
Berkovitsa Bulg. **58** B2
Berlevåg Norway **40** F1
Berlin Ger. **49** F1
Bermagui Austr. **105** E3
Bermejo Bol. **136** B3
Bermen, Lac *l.* Can. **115** D1
Bermuda *terr.* N. Atlantic Ocean **144** B3

Bern Switz. **53** D2
Bernau Ger. **49** F1
Bernburg (Saale) Ger. **49** E2
Bernkastel-Kues Ger. **48** C3
Beroroha Madag. **97** [inset] D3
Berounka *r.* Czech Rep. **49** G3
Berri Austr. **104** C2
Berrouaghia Alg. **55** D2
Berry Islands Bahamas **131** C2
Bersenbrück Ger. **48** C1
Bershad' Ukr. **38** C2
Berté, Lac *l.* Can. **115** D1
Bertoua Cameroon **94** B2
Beru *atoll* Kiribati **110**
Beruri Brazil **134** C3
Berwick-upon-Tweed U.K. **46** B2
Beryslav Ukr. **39** D2
Besalampy Madag. **97** [inset] D2
Besançon France **53** D2
Bessemer U.S.A. **124** C2
Besshoky, Gora *h.* Kazakh. **80** C2
Betanzos Spain **54** B1
Bethanie Namibia **98** A2
Bethlehem S. Africa **99** C2
Bethlehem U.S.A. **123** E2
Bethune France **48** A2
Betioky Madag. **97** [inset] D3
Betpak-Dala *plain* Kazakh. **81** E2
Betroka Madag. **97** [inset] D3
Betsiboka *r.* Madag. **97** [inset] D1
Bettendorf U.S.A. **121** E2
Bettiah India **79** C2
Betul India **78** B2
Betwa *r.* India **79** B2
Betws-y-coed U.K. **46** B3
Beverley U.K. **46** C3
Beverungen Ger. **49** D2
Beverwijk Neth. **48** B1
Bexhill U.K. **47** D4
Beykoz Turkey **59** C2
Beyla Guinea **90** B4
Beyneu Kazakh. **80** B2
Beypazarı Turkey **84** B1
Beyrouth Lebanon *see* Beirut
Beyşehir Turkey **84** B2
Beyşehir Gölü *l.* Turkey **84** B2
Beysug *r.* Rus. Fed. **39** E2
Bezhetsk Rus. Fed. **37** E2
Béziers France **53** C3
Bhadrak India **77** B3
Bhadravati India **77** B3
Bhagalpur India **79** C2
Bhairi Hol *mt.* Pak. **78** A2
Bhamo Myanmar **66** A1
Bhanjanagar India **79** C3
Bharatpur India **78** B2
Bharuch India **78** B2
Bhavnagar India **78** B2
Bhekuzulu S. Africa **99** D2
Bhilwara India **78** B2
Bhima *r.* India **77** B3
Bhiwani India **78** B2
Bhopal India **78** B2

Bhubaneshwar India **79** C2
Bhuj India **78** A2
Bhumiphol Dam Thai. **66** A2
Bhusawal India **78** B2
Bhutan *country* Asia **79** D2
Bia, Phou *mt.* Laos **66** B2
Biak *i.* Indon. **63** D3
Biała Podlaska Pol. **51** E2
Białogard Pol. **51** D2
Białystok Pol. **51** E2
Bianco Italy **57** C3
Biarritz France **52** B3
Biddeford U.S.A. **123** F2
Bideford U.K. **47** A4
Bideford Bay U.K. **47** A4
Biedenkopf Ger. **49** D2
Biel Switz. **53** D2
Bielefeld Ger. **49** D1
Biella Italy **56** A1
Bielsko-Biała Pol. **51** D3
Biên Hoa Vietnam **67** B2
Bienville, Lac *l.* Can. **114** C1
Big Bend Swaziland **99** D2
Big Hole *r.* U.S.A. **118** D1
Bighorn *r.* U.S.A. **120** B1
Bighorn Mountains U.S.A. **120** B2
Big Lake U.S.A. **127** C2
Big Rapids U.S.A. **122** C2
Big Sand Lake Can. **113** F2
Big Sioux *r.* U.S.A. **121** D2
Big Spring U.S.A. **127** D2
Big Timber U.S.A. **118** E1
Big Trout Lake Can. **114** B1
Big Trout Lake *l.* Can. **114** A1
Bihać Bos.-Herz. **57** C2
Bihar Sharif India **79** C2
Bihor, Vârful *mt.* Romania **38** B2
Bijār Iran **85** C2
Bijeljina Bos.-Herz. **57** C2
Bijie Polje Serb. S.M. **58** A2
Bijie China **75** A3
Bikaner India **78** B2
Bikin Rus. Fed. **70** B1
Bikin *r.* Rus. Fed. **70** B1
Bikoro Dem. Rep. Congo **94** B3
Bilaspur India **79** C2
Bila Tserkva Ukr. **38** D2
Bilauktaung Range *mts* Myanmar/Thai. **67** A2
Bilbao Spain **54** C1
Bilecik Turkey **59** C2
Bilgoraj Pol. **51** E2
Bilhorod-Dnistrovs'kyy Ukr. **38** D2
Bili Dem. Rep. Congo **95** C2
Bilibino Rus. Fed. **87** N2
Billings U.S.A. **118** E1
Bill of Portland *hd* U.K. **47** B4
Bilma Niger **91** D3

loela Austr. **103** E2
lohirs'k Ukr. **39** D2
lohir"ya Ukr. **38** C1
lovods'k Ukr. **39** E2
loxi U.S.A. **124** C2
lpa Morea Claypan *salt flat*
  Austr. **103** C2
lshausen Ger. **49** E2
ltine Chad **91** E3
lyayivka Ukr. **38** D2
mini Islands Bahamas **125** E3
na-Etawa India **79** B2
naija, Gunung *mt.* Indon.
  63 C3
ndura C. Equat. Guinea **94** A2
ngara Austr. **105** E1
ngharnten U.S.A. **103** D2
ngö Turkey **85** C2
njai Indon. **64** B2
ntuhan Indon. **64** B2
ntulu Malaysia **65** C1
nzhou China **74** B2
rao C.A.R. **94** C1
ratnagar Nepal **79** C2
rch Mountains Can. **112** D2
rdsville Austr. **103** C2
recik Turkey **84** B2
reun Indon. **64** A1
rganj Nepal **79** C2
rhan *mt.* Eth. **93** B3
rigüi Brazil **138** B2
rjand Iran **80** D2
rroonhead U.K. **46** B3
rraïnghan U.K. **47** C3
rmingham U.S.A. **124** C2
rmingham China **73** E1
rmin-Kebbi Nigeria **90** A2
rnin Konni Niger **91** C3
robidzhan Rus. Fed. **73** E1
rrsay U.K. **44** C1
'r Shalatayn Egypt **82** A2
rřzai Lith. **36** B2
rscay, Bay of *sea* France/Spain
  52 A2
rschofshofen Austria **50** C3
rscotasi Lake Can. **114** B2
rshkek Kyrg. **81** E2
rsho S. Africa **99** C3
rshop U.S.A. **119** C3
rshui China **73** E1
rskra Alg. **91** C1
rsmarck U.S.A. **120** C1
rsmarck Archipelago *is* P.N.G.
  63 D3
rsmarck Sea P.N.G. **106** E2
rssa, Djebel *mt.* Alg. **55** D2
rssau Guinea-Bissau **90** A3
rstcho Lake Can. **112** D2
rstrita Romania **38** C2
rstriţa *r.* Romania **38** C2

Bitburg Ger. **48** C3
Bitkine Chad **91** D3
Bitola Macedonia **59** B2
Bitonto Italy **57** C2
Bitterfontein S. Africa **98** A3
Bitterroot *r.* U.S.A. **118** D1
Bitterroot Range *mts* U.S.A.
  118 C1
Bityug *r.* Rus. Fed. **37** E3
Biu Nigeria **91** D3
Biwa-ko *l.* Japan **71** C3
Biysk Rus. Fed. **81** F1
Bizerte Tunisia **91** C1
Bjargtangar *hd* Iceland **40** [inset]
Bjästa Sweden **40** D3
Bjerkvik Norway **40** D2
Bjørnøya *i.* Arctic Ocean **86** D2
Black *r.* U.S.A. **124** B1
Blackall Austr. **105** D2
Blackburn U.K. **46** B3
Blackfoot U.S.A. **118** D2
Black Forest *mts* Ger. **50** B3
Black Hills U.S.A. **120** C2
Black Isle *pen.* U.K. **44** B2
Black Lake Can. **113** E2
Black Lake *l.* Can. **113** E2
Black Mountains U.K. **47** B4
Blackpool U.K. **46** B3
Black River *r.* Vietnam **66** B1
Black River Falls U.S.A. **122** B2
Blacksburg U.S.A. **123** D3
Black Sea Asia/Europe **84** B1
Blacksod Bay Rep. of Ireland
  45 A1
Blackstairs Mountains
  Rep. of Ireland **45** C2
Blackwater *r.* Rep. of Ireland
  45 C2
Blackwater Lake Can. **112** C1
Blackwood *r.* Austr. **102** A3
Blagoevgrad Bulg. **58** B2
Blagoveshchensk Rus. Fed.
  73 E1
Blair U.K. **121** D2
Blairgowrie U.K. **44** C2
Blakely U.S.A. **125** C2
Blanca, Bahía *b.* Arg. **137** B4
Blanche, Lake *salt flat* Austr.
  104 B1
Blanco *r.* Bol. **136** B2
Blanco, Cape U.S.A. **120** A2
Blanda *r.* Iceland **40** [inset]
Blanding U.S.A. **119** E3
Blanes Spain **55** D1
Blangkejeren Indon. **64** A1
Blankenheim Ger. **48** C2
Blansko Czech Rep. **51** D3
Blantyre Malawi **97** C3
Blaydon U.K. **46** C2
Blayney Austr. **105** D2
Blenheim N.Z. **106** B3
Blida Alg. **90** C1
Bloemfontein S. Africa **99** C2
Bloemhof S. Africa **99** C2

Bloemhof Dam S. Africa **99** C2
Blönduós Iceland **40** [inset]
Bloody Foreland *pt*
  Rep. of Ireland **45** B1
Bloomfield U.S.A. **126** C1
Bloomington *IL* U.S.A. **122** C2
Bloomington *IN* U.S.A. **122** C3
Blosseville Kyst *coastal area*
  Greenland **111** K2
Bluefield U.S.A. **122** D3
Bluefields Nic. **130** B3
Blue Mountains Austr. **105** D2
Blue Mountains U.S.A. **118** C1
Blue Nile *r.* Eth./Sudan **93** B3
Blue Ridge *mts* U.S.A. **125** D1
Blue Stack Mountains
  Rep. of Ireland **45** B1
Bluff N.Z. **106** A4
Bluff U.S.A. **119** E3
Blumenau Brazil **138** C3
Blyth U.K. **46** C2
Blythe U.S.A. **119** D4
Blytheville U.S.A. **124** C1
Bo Sierra Leone **90** A4
Boac Phil. **68** B2
Boa Esperança, Açude *resr*
  Brazil **135** E3
Boa Vista Brazil **134** C2
Bobadah Austr. **105** D2
Bobai China **75** B3
Bobaomby, Tanjona *c.* Madag.
  97 [inset] D1
Bobrov Rus. Fed. **37** E3
Bobrovytsya Ukr. **39** D1
Bobrynets' Ukr. **39** D2
Boby *mt.* Madag. **97** [inset] D2
Boca do Acre Brazil **134** C3
Bocaiúva Brazil **139** D1
Bochnia Pol. **51** E3
Bocholt Ger. **48** C2
Bochum Ger. **48** C2
Bochum S. Africa **99** C1
Bockenem Ger. **49** E1
Boda C.A.R. **94** B2
Bodaybo Rus. Fed. **87** J3
Bodélé *reg.* Chad **91** D3
Boden Sweden **40** E2
Bodmin U.K. **47** A4
Bodmin Moor *moorland* U.K.
  47 A4
Bodø Norway **40** C2
Bodrum Turkey **59** C3
Boende Dem. Rep. Congo **94** C3
Bogalusa U.S.A. **124** C2
Bogda Shan *mts* China **81** F2
Boggabilla Austr. **105** E1
Boggeragh Mountains
  Rep. of Ireland **45** B2
Bog of Allen *reg.* Rep. of Ireland
  45 C2
Bogong, Mount Austr. **105** D3
Bogor Indon. **64** B2
Bogoroditsk Rus. Fed. **37** E3

Bogotá Col. **134** B2
Bogotol Rus. Fed. **86** H3
Boguchany Rus. Fed. **87** I3
Boguchar Rus. Fed. **39** C2
Bo Hai g. China **74** B2
Bohai Wan b. China **74** B2
Bohlokong S. Africa **99** C2
Böhmer Wald *mts* Ger. **49** E1
Bojnürd Iran **85** D2
Bohodukhiv Ukr. **39** E1
Bohol *i.* Phil. **68** B3
Bohol Sea Phil. **68** B3
Bohu China **81** F2
Boi, r. Brazil **138** B1
Boise U.S.A. **118** C2
Boise City U.S.A. **127** C1
Boitumelong S. Africa **99** C2
Boizenburg Ger. **49** E1
Bojnürd Iran **85** D2
Bokatola Dem. Rep. Congo **94** B3
Bokele Dem. Rep. Congo **94** C3
Boknafjorden *sea chan.* Norway **41** B4
Bokoro Chad **91** D3
Bokovskaya Rus. Fed. **39** F2
Boksitogorsk Rus. Fed. **37** D2
Bokspits S. Africa **98** B2
Bolama Guinea-Bissau **90** A3
Bolangir India **79** C2
Bolbec France **52** C2
Bole China **81** F2
Boleko Dem. Rep. Congo **94** B3
Bolgatanga Ghana **90** B3
Bolhrad Ukr. **38** C2
Boli China **70** B1
Bolintin-Vale Romania **38** C3
Bolivia *country* S. America **136** B2
Bolkhov Rus. Fed. **37** E3
Bollène France **53** C3
Bollnäs Sweden **41** D3
Bollon Austr. **105** D1
Bolmen *l.* Sweden **41** C4
Bolobo Dem. Rep. Congo **94** B3
Bologna Italy **56** B2
Bologoye Rus. Fed. **37** D2
Bologoye Rus. Fed. **37** D2
Bolomba Dem. Rep. Congo **94** B3
Bolovens, Phouphieng *plat.* Laos **67** B2
Bol'shaya Martinovka Rus. Fed. **39** F2
Bol'shevik, Ostrov *i.* Rus. Fed. **87** I1
Bol'shezemel'skaya Tundra *low-land* Rus. Fed. **34** E2
Bol'shoy Aluy r. Rus. Fed. **87** M2
Bol'shoy Kamen' Rus. Fed. **70** B2
Bol'shoy Kavkaz *mts* Asia/Europe *see* Caucasus
Bolsward Neth. **48** B1
Bolton U.K. **46** B3
Bolu Turkey **84** B1
Bolzano Italy **56** B1

Boma Dem. Rep. Congo **94** B3
Bomaderry Austr. **105** E2
Bombala Austr. **105** D3
Bombay India *see* Mumbai
Bom Despacho Brazil **139** C1
Bomdila India **79** D2
Bom Jesus da Lapa Brazil **135** E4
Bemlo *i.* Norway **42** E2
Bonaire *i.* Neth. Antilles **131** D3
Bonaparte Archipelago *is* Austr. **102** B1
Bonavista Can. **115** C2
Bonavista Bay Can. **115** C2
Bondo Dem. Rep. Congo **94** C2
Bondoukou Côte d'Ivoire **90** B4
Bone, Teluk *g.* Indon. **65** D2
Bonerate, Kepulauan *is* Indon. **65** D2
Bonete, Cerro *mt.* Bol. **147**
Bongaigaon India **79** D2
Bongandanga Dem. Rep. Congo **94** C2
Bongor Chad **91** D3
Bongouanou Côte d'Ivoire **90** B4
Bông Son Vietnam **67** B2
Bonham U.S.A. **127** E2
Boniface France **53** D3
Bonifacio, Strait of France/Italy **56** A2
Bonito Brazil **138** A2
Bonn Ger. **48** C2
Bonners Ferry U.S.A. **118** C1
Bonnie Rock Austr. **102** A3
Bonnyville Can. **113** D2
Bontoc Phil. **68** B2
Bontosunggu Indon. **65** C2
Bontrug S. Africa **99** C3
Booligal Austr. **104** C2
Boonah Austr. **105** D1
Boonah Austr. **105** E1
Boone *IA* U.S.A. **121** E2
Boone *NC* U.S.A. **122** D3
Booneville U.S.A. **124** C2
Boorowa Austr. **105** D2
Boothia, Gulf of Can. **111** G2
Boothia Peninsula Can. **110** F2
Boppard Ger. **48** C2
Boquilla, Presa de la *resr* Mex. **128** B2
Bor S.M. **58** B2
Bor Sudan **93** B4
Boraha, Nosy *i.* Madag. **97** [inset] B1
Borås Sweden **41** C4
Boräzjän Iran **85** D3
Bordeaux France **52** B3
Borðdertown Austr. **104** C3
Bordj Bou Arréridj Alg. **55** D2
Bordj Bounaama Alg. **55** D2
Bordj Messaouda Alg. **91** C1

Bordj Omer Driss Alg. **91** C2
Borðoy *i.* Faroe Is **42** B1
Borgarnes Iceland **40** [inset]
Borgloesk Rus. Fed. **39** F1
Borisoglebsk Rus. Fed. **39** F1
Borisovka Rus. Fed. **39** E1
Borken Ger. **48** C2
Borkum Ger. **48** C1
Borkum *i.* Ger. **48** C1
Borlänge Sweden **41** D3
Borna Ger. **49** F2
Borneo *i.* Asia **65** C1
Bornholm *i.* Denmark **41** C4
Bornova Turkey **59** C3
Borodyanka Ukr. **38** C1
Borovichi Rus. Fed. **37** D2
Borovsk Rus. Fed. **37** E2
Borroloola Austr. **103** C1
Borşa Romania **38** B2
Borshchiv Ukr. **38** C2
Borshchovochnyy Khrebet *mts* Rus. Fed. **73** D1
Borüjerd Iran **85** C2
Boryslav Ukr. **38** B2
Boryspil' Ukr. **38** D1
Borzna Ukr. **39** D1
Borzya Rus. Fed. **73** D1
Bosanska Dubica Bos.-Herz. **57** C1
Bosanska Gradiška Bos.-Herz. **57** C1
Bosanski Novi Bos.-Herz. **57** C1
Bose China **75** A3
Boshof S. Africa **99** C2
Bosnia-Herzegovina *country* Europe **57** C2
Bosobolo Dem. Rep. Congo **94** B2
Bosporus *str.* Turkey **59** C2
Bossangoa C.A.R. **94** B2
Bossembélé C.A.R. **94** B2
Bosten Hu *l.* China **81** F2
Boston U.K. **46** C3
Boston U.S.A. **123** F2
Boston Mountains U.S.A. **124** E1
Botany Bay Austr. **105** E2
Botev *mt.* Bulg. **58** B2
Botevgrad Bulg. **84** A1
Bothnia, Gulf of Fin./Sweden **41** D3
Botoşani Romania **38** C2
Botshabelo S. Africa **99** C2
Botswana *country* Africa **96** B2
Botte Donato, Monte *mt.* Italy **57** C3
Bottrop Ger. **48** C2
Botucatu Brazil **138** C2
Bouaké Côte d'Ivoire **90** B4
Bouar C.A.R. **94** B2
Bouârfa Morocco **90** B1
Bougaa Alg. **55** E2
Bougainville Island P.N.G. **100**
Bougaroûn, Cap *c.* Alg. **55** E2
Bougouni Mali **90** B3
Bouillon Belgium **48** B3

ouira Alg. 55 D2
oujdour Western Sahara 90 A2
oulder U.S.A. 120 B2
oulder City U.S.A. 119 D3
oulogne-sur-Mer France 47 D4
52 C2
oulogne-Billancourt France 52 C2
oumango Gabon 94 B3
oumba r. Cameroon 94 B2
oumerdes Alg. 55 D2
ouna Côte d'Ivoire 90 B4
oundiali Côte d'Ivoire 90 B4
ountiful U.S.A. 118 D2
ourem Mali 90 B3
ourg-en-Bresse France 53 D2
ourges France 52 C2
ourke Austr. 105 D2
ourke U.K. 47 C4
ou Saâda Alg. 91 C1
ousso Chad 91 D3
outilimit Maur. 90 A3
ow r. Can. 113 D3
owen Can. 103 D2
ow Island Can. 113 D3
owling Green r. N/ U.S.A. 122 C3
owling Green OH U.S.A. 122 D2
owman U.S.A. 120 C1
oxberg Ger. 49 D3
oxtel Neth. 48 B2
oyabat Turkey 84 B1
oyang China 75 B3
oyle Rep. of Ireland 45 C2
oyuibe Bol. 136 B3
ozdağ mt. Turkey 59 C3
oz Dağlari mts Turkey 59 C3
ozeman U.S.A. 118 D1
ozoum C.A.R. 94 B2
ozüyük Turkey 59 D3
rač i. Croatia 57 C2
rachet, Lac au l. Can. 115 D2
racknell U.K. 47 C4
radenton U.S.A. 125 D3
radford U.K. 46 C3
rady U.S.A. 127 E2
raga Port. 54 B1
ragança Brazil 135 E3
ragança Port. 54 B1
ragança Paulista Brazil 139 C2
rahin Bangl. 66 A1
rahmanbaria Bangl. 66 A1
rahmapur India 77 C3
rahmaputra r. China/India 66 A1
raila Romania 38 C2
raine? U.S.A. 121 E2
raintree U.K. 47 D4
rake (Unterweser) Ger. 49 D1
rakwater Namibia 98 A1
ramsche Ger. 48 D1
ranco r. Brazil 134 C3
randenburg Ger. 49 F1
randon Can. 113 F3

Brandon Mountain h. Rep. of Ireland 45 A2
Brandvlei S. Africa 98 B3
Braniewo Pol. 51 D2
Brantford Can. 114 B2
Bras d'Or Lake Can. 115 D2
Brasil, Planalto do plat. Brazil 139 D1
Brasilândia Brazil 138 C1
Brasília Brazil 138 C1
Brasília de Minas Brazil 139 D1
Brasov Romania 38 C2
Bratislava Slovakia 51 D3
Bratsk Rus. Fed. 87 I3
Braunau am Inn Austria 50 C3
Braunschweig Ger. 49 E1
Bravo del Norte, Rio r. Mex./U.S.A. see Rio Grande
Brawley U.S.A. 119 C4
Bray Rep. of Ireland 45 C2
Brazil country S. America 135 D3
Brazilian Highlands mts Brazil 146
Brazos r. U.S.A. 127 E3
Brazzaville Congo 94 B3
Brčko Bos.-Herz. 57 C2
Brechin U.K. 44 C2
Brecht Belgium 48 B2
Breckenridge U.S.A. 127 C2
Břeclav Czech Rep. 51 D3
Brecon U.K. 47 B4
Brecon Beacons reg. U.K. 47 B4
Breda Neth. 48 B2
Bredasdorp S. Africa 98 B3
Bregenz Austria 50 D0
Breivikbotn Norway 40 E1
Brekstad Norway 40 B3
Bremen Ger. 49 D1
Bremerhaven Ger. 49 D1
Bremerton U.S.A. 118 B1
Bremervörde Ger. 49 D1
Brenham U.S.A. 127 E2
Brennero Italy 50 C3
Brenner Pass Austria/Italy 50 D3
Brentwood U.K. 47 D4
Brescia Italy 56 B1
Bressanone Italy 56 B1
Bressay i. U.K. 44 [inset]
Bressuire France 52 B2
Brest Belarus 36 B3
Brest France 52 B2
Breton Sound b. U.S.A. 124 C3
Breves Brazil 135 D3
Brewarrina Austr. 105 D1
Brewster U.S.A. 118 C1
Breytovo Rus. Fed. 37 E2
Brezovo Polje plain Croatia 57 C1
Bria C.A.R. 94 C2
Briançon France 53 D3
Briceni Moldova 38 C2

Bridgend U.K. 47 B4
Bridgeport CT U.S.A. 123 F2
Bridgeport NE U.S.A. 120 C2
Bridgetown Barbados 131 E3
Bridgewater Can. 115 D2
Bridgwater U.K. 47 B4
Bridlington U.K. 46 C2
Bridlington Bay U.K. 46 C2
Brig Switz. 53 D2
Brigham City U.S.A. 118 D2
Brighton N.Z. 106 B4
Brighton U.K. 47 C4
Brignoles France 53 D3
Brilon Ger. 49 D2
Brindisi Italy 57 C2
Brisbane Austr. 105 E1
Bristol U.K. 47 B4
Bristol U.S.A. 125 D1
Bristol Bay U.S.A. 87 F3
Bristol Channel est. U.K. 47 A4
British Columbia prov. Can. 112 C2
British Indian Ocean Territory terr. Indian Ocean 91
Britstown S. Africa 98 B3
Brittany reg. France 52 B2
Brive-la-Gaillarde France 52 C2
Brno Czech Rep. 51 D3
Broad r. U.S.A. 125 D2
Broadback r. Can. 114 C1
Broad Law h. U.K. 44 C3
Broadus U.S.A. 120 B1
Brochet Can. 113 E2
Brochet, Lac l. Can. 113 E2
Brockville Can. 114 C2
Brodick U.K. 44 B3
Brodnica Pol. 51 D2
Brody Ukr. 38 C1
Broken Arrow U.S.A. 127 E1
Broken Hill Austr. 104 C2
Bromsgrove U.K. 47 B3
Brønderslev Denmark 41 B4
Brønnøysund Norway 40 C2
Brooke's Point Phil. 68 A3
Brookhaven U.S.A. 124 B2
Brookings OR U.S.A. 118 B2
Brookings SD U.S.A. 121 D2
Brooks Can. 113 D2
Brooks Range mts U.S.A. 110 C2
Brooksville U.S.A. 125 D3
Broom, Loch inlet U.K. 44 B2
Broome Austr. 102 B1
Brothers U.S.A. 118 B2
Brovary Ukr. 38 D1
Brownfield U.S.A. 127 D2
Browning U.S.A. 118 D1
Brownsville TN U.S.A. 124 C1
Brownsville TX U.S.A. 127 E3
Brownwood U.S.A. 127 E2
Brú Iceland 40 [inset]
Bruay-la-Bussière France 52 C1
Bruchsal Ger. 49 D3
Bruges Belgium see Brugge
Brugge Belgium 48 A2

Brühl Ger. **49** D3
Bruint India **66** A1
Brumado Brazil **135** E4
Brumunddal Norway **41** C4
Brunei *country* Asia **65** C1
Brunico Italy **50** C3
Brunswick *GA* U.S.A. **125** D2
Brunswick *ME* U.S.A. **123** G2
Brush U.S.A. **120** C2
Brussels Belgium **48** B2
Bruxelles Belgium *see* Brussels
Bryan U.S.A. **127** E2
Bryansk Rus. Fed. **37** D3
Bryne Norway **42** B7
Bryn'kovskaya Rus. Fed. **39** E2
Bryukhovetskaya Rus. Fed. **39** E2
Brzeg Pol. **51** D2
Bucaramanga Col. **134** B2
Buchanan Liberia **90** A4
Bucharest Romania **38** C3
Bucholz im der Nordheide Ger. **49** D1
Bucin, Pasul *pass* Romania **38** C2
Bückeburg Ger. **49** D1
Buckeye U.S.A. **126** D2
Buckhaven U.K. **44** C2
Buckie U.K. **44** C2
Bucureşti Romania *see* Bucharest
Buda-Kashalyova Belarus **37** D3
Budapest Hungary **51** D3
Budaun India **79** B2
Bude U.K. **47** A4
Budennovsk Rus. Fed. **35** D4
Budoni Italy **56** A2
Buea Cameroon **94** A2
Buenaventura Mex. **128** B2
Buenaventura Col. **134** B2
Buendia, Embalse de *resr* Spain **54** C1
Buenópolis Brazil **139** D1
Buenos Aires Arg. **137** C4
Buffalo *NY* U.S.A. **123** E2
Buffalo *SD* U.S.A. **120** C1
Buffalo *WY* U.S.A. **120** B2
Buffalo Narrows Can. **110** E3
Buffels *watercourse* S. Africa **98** A2
Buftea Romania **38** C3
Bug *r.* Pol. **51** E2
Bugel, Tanjung *pt* Indon. **65** C2
Bugojno Bos.-Herz. **57** C2
Buguruslan Rus. Fed. **35** E3
Buhuşi Romania **38** C2
Builth Wells U.K. **47** B3
Buir Nur *l.* Mongolia **73** D1
Buitepos Namibia **98** A1
Bujanovac S.M. **58** B2
Bujumbura Burundi **95** C3
Bukavu Dem. Rep. Congo **95** C3
Bukhara Uzbek. *see* Buxoro
Bukittinggi Indon. **64** B2

Bukoba Tanz. **95** D3
Bulahdelal Austr. **105** E2
Bulawayo Zimbabwe **97** B2
Buldan Turkey **59** C3
Bulembu Swaziland **99** D2
Bulgan Mongolia **72** C1
Bulgaria *country* Europe **58** B2
Buller *r.* N.Z. **106** B3
Bulloo Downs Austr. **104** C1
Büllsport Namibia **98** A1
Bulukumba Indon. **65** D2
Bulungu Dem. Rep. Congo **94** B3
Bumba Dem. Rep. Congo **94** C2
Bumhkang Myanmar **66** A1
Buna Dem. Rep. Congo **94** B3
Bunbury Austr. **102** A3
Bunda Tanz. **95** D3
Bundaberg Austr. **103** E2
Bundarra Austr. **105** E2
Bundi India **78** B2
Bungo-suidō *sea chan.* Japan **71** B4
Bunia Dem. Rep. Congo **95** D2
Bunianga Dem. Rep. Congo **94** C3
Buôn Mê Thuôt Vietnam **67** B2
Bura Kenya **95** D3
Buraydah Saudi Arabia **82** B2
Burbach Ger. **48** D2
Burco Somalia **93** C4
Burë Eth. **93** B3
Bure *r.* U.K. **47** D3
Burgas Bulg. **58** C2
Burg bei Magdeburg Ger. **49** E1
Burgdorf Ger. **49** E1
Burgeo Can. **115** E2
Burgersfort S. Africa **99** D1
Burglengenfeld Ger. **49** F3
Burgos Spain **54** C1
Burhaniye Turkey **59** C3
Burhanpur India **78** B2
Burhave (Butjadingen) Ger. **49** D1
Burin Can. **115** E2
Buritis Brazil **139** C1
Burketown Austr. **103** C1
Burkina *country* Africa **90** B3
Burley U.S.A. **118** D2
Burlington *CO* U.S.A. **120** C3
Burlington *IA* U.S.A. **121** E2
Burlington *NC* U.S.A. **125** E1
Burney U.S.A. **118** B2
Burnie Austr. **103** D4
Burnley U.K. **46** B3
Burns U.S.A. **118** C2
Burqin China **81** F2
Burra Austr. **104** B2
Burrel Albania **58** B2
Burren *reg.* Rep. of Ireland **45** B2
Burrendong Reservoir Austr. **105** D2

Burren Junction Austr. **105** D2
Burriana Spain **55** C2
Burrinjuck Reservoir Austr. **105** D2
Burro, Serranías del *mts* Mex. **128** B2
Bursa Turkey **59** C2
Bür Safājah Egypt **92** B2
Bür Saʿīd Egypt *see* Port Said
Burton, Lac *l.* Can. **114** C1
Burtonport Rep. of Ireland **45** B1
Burton upon Trent U.K. **46** C3
Buru *i.* Indon. **63** C3
Burullus, Lake *l.* Egypt **84** B1
Burundi Burundi **95** C3
Bururi Burundi **95** C3
Burwash Landing Can. **112** B1
Buryn' Ukr. **39** D1
Bury St Edmunds U.K. **47** D3
Busanga Dem. Rep. Cong **94** C3
Büshehr Iran **85** D3
Bushenyi Uganda **95** D3
Businga Dem. Rep. Congo **94** C2
Busselton Austr. **102** A3
Bustamante Mex. **127** D3
Busuanga Phil. **68** A2
Buta Dem. Rep. Congo **94** C2
Butha-Buthe Lesotho **99** C2
Butiaba Uganda **95** D2
Butler U.S.A. **122** E2
Buton *i.* Indon. **65** D2
Butte U.S.A. **118** D1
Butterworth Malaysia **64** B1
Butt of Lewis *hd* U.K. **44** A1
Button Bay Can. **113** F2
Butuan Phil. **68** B3
Buturlinovka Rus. Fed. **37** E3
Butwal Nepal **79** C2
Butzbach Ger. **49** D2
Buulobarde Somalia **93** C4
Buur Gaabo Somalia **93** C5
Buurhakaba Somalia **93** C4
Buxoro Uzbek. **80** D3
Buxtehude Ger. **49** D1
Buy Rus. Fed. **37** F2
Buynaksk Rus. Fed. **35** D4
Büyükmenderes *r.* Turkey **59** C3
Buzai Gumbad Afgh. **78** B1
Buzău Romania **38** C2
Buzuluk Rus. Fed. **35** E3
Byala Bulg. **58** C2
Byalynichy Belarus **36** C3
Byarezina *r.* Belarus **36** D3
Byaroza Belarus **36** B3
Bydgoszcz Pol. **51** D2
Byerazino Belarus **36** C3
Byeshankovichy Belarus **36** C2
Bykhaw Belarus **37** D3
Bylot Island Can. **111** G2
Byrkjelo Norway **42** E1
Byrock Austr. **105** D2
Byron Bay Austr. **105** E1
Bytom Pol. **51** D2

C

Caaguazú, Cordillera de hills
Para. 138 A3
Caarapó Brazil 138 A2
Caazapá Para. 138 A2
Cabanatuan Phil. 68 B2
Cabeceira Rio Manso Brazil
138 A1
Cabimas Venez. 134 B1
Cabinda Angola 94 B3
Cabinda prov. Angola 94 B3
Cabo Frio Brazil 139 D2
Cabo Frio, Ilha do i. Brazil
139 D2
Cabonga, Réservoir resr Can.
114 C2
Caboolture Austr. 105 E1
Cabo Pantoja Peru 134 B3
Cabora Bassa, Lake resr Moz.
97 C1
Caborca Mex. 128 A1
Cabot Strait Can. 115 D2
Cabrera i. Spain 55 D2
Cabrera, Sierra de la mts Spain
54 B1
Cabriel r. Spain 55 C2
Caçador Brazil 138 B3
Čačak S.M. 58 B2
Cáceres Brazil 136 D4
Cáceres Spain 54 B3
Cache Creek Can. 112 C2
Cacheu Guinea-Bissau 90 A3
Cachimbo, Serra do hills Brazil
138 D3
Cachoeira Alta Brazil 138 B1
Cachoeiro de Itapemirim
Brazil 139 D2
Cacine Guinea-Bissau 90 A3
Cacolo Angola 94 B4
Caçu Brazil 138 B1
Čadca Slovakia 51 D3
Cadenberge Ger. 49 D1
Cadereyta Mex. 129 D2
Cadillac U.S.A. 122 C2
Cádiz Spain 54 B4
Cádiz, Golfo de g. Spain 54 B2
Caen France 52 B2
Caernarfon U.K. 46 A3
Caernarfon Bay U.K. 46 A3
Cafayate Arg. 136 B3
Cagliari Italy 56 A3
Cagliari, Golfo di b. Italy 56 A3
Caha Mountains Rep. of Ireland
45 B3
Cahir Rep. of Ireland 45 C2
Cahore Point Rep. of Ireland
45 C2
Cahors France 52 C3
Cahul Moldova 38 C2
Caia Moz. 97 C1

Caiabis, Serra dos hills Brazil
135 D4
Caianda Angola 96 B1
Caiapó, Serra do mts Brazil
138 B1
Caiapônia Brazil 138 B1
Caicos Islands
Turks and Caicos Is 131 C2
Cairngorm Mountains U.K.
44 C2
Cairnryan U.K. 44 B3
Cairns Austr. 103 D1
Cairo Egypt 92 B1
Caiundo Angola 96 A1
Cajamarca Peru 134 B3
Čakovec Croatia 56 B1
Calabar Nigeria 94 B2
Calafat Romania 58 B3
Calahorra Spain 55 C1
Calais France 52 C1
Calais U.S.A. 123 G1
Calama Chile 136 B3
Calamian Group is Phil. 68 A2
Calamocha Spain 55 C1
Calandula Angola 94 B3
Calang Indon. 64 A1
Calanscio Sand Sea des. Libya
91 E1
Calapan Phil. 68 B2
Călărași Romania 58 C3
Calatayud Spain 55 C1
Calau Ger. 49 F2
Calavan i. Phil. 68 B2
Calbayog Phil. 68 B2
Calcanhar, Ponta do pt Brazil
135 F3
Calçoene Brazil 135 D2
Calcutta India see Kolkata
Caldas da Rainha Port. 54 B2
Caldas Novas Brazil 138 C1
Caldera Chile 136 A3
Caldwell U.S.A. 118 C2
Caledon r. Lesotho/S. Africa
99 C3
Caleta Olivia Arg. 137 B5
Calf of Man i. Isle of Man 46 A2
Calgary Can. 112 D2
Cali Col. 134 B2
Calicut India see Kozhikode
Caliente U.S.A. 119 D3
California state U.S.A. 118 B2
California, Gulf of Mex. 119 D4
California Aqueduct canal U.S.A.
119 B3
Callabonna, Lake salt flat Austr.
104 C1
Callander U.K. 44 B2
Callao Peru 134 B4
Caltagirone Italy 56 B3
Caltanissetta Italy 56 B3
Caluquembe Angola 96 A1
Caluula Somalia 93 D3
Calvi France 55 D3
Calvià Spain 55 D2

Calvillo Mex. 128 B2
Calvinia S. Africa 98 A3
Calvo, Monte mt. Italy 57 C2
Camacho Mex. 128 B2
Camacupa Angola 96 A1
Camagüey Cuba 130 C2
Camana Peru 134 B4
Camapuã Brazil 138 B1
Ca Mau Vietnam 67 B3
Ca Mau, Mui c. Vietnam 67 B3
Cambodia country Asia 67 B2
Camborne U.K. 47 A4
Cambrai France 52 C1
Cambrian Mountains U.K. 47 B3
Cambridge N.Z. 106 C2
Cambridge U.K. 47 D3
Cambridge MA U.S.A. 123 F2
Cambridge MD U.S.A. 123 F3
Cambridge MN U.S.A. 121 E1
Cambridge OH U.S.A. 122 D2
Camden AR U.S.A. 124 B2
Camden ME U.S.A. 123 G2
Cameroon mt. Africa 94 B2
Cameroon, Mont vol. Cameroon
96
Cametá Brazil 135 E3
Camiguin i. Phil. 68 B2
Camirí Bol. 136 B3
Camocim Brazil 135 E3
Camooweal Austr. 103 C1
Camorta i. India 67 A3
Campana, Isla i. Chile 107 A5
Campbell, Cape N.Z. 106 B3
Campbell Island N.Z. 110
Campbell River Can. 112 C2
Campbellsville U.S.A. 122 C3
Campbellton Can. 123 G1
Campbelltown U.K. 44 B3
Campeche Mex. 129 C3
Campeche, Bahía de g. Mex.
129 C3
Camperdown Austr. 104 C3
Câmpina Romania 58 C2
Campina Grande Brazil 135 F3
Campinas Brazil 138 C2
Campina Verde Brazil 138 C1
Campobasso Italy 56 B2
Campo Belo Brazil 139 C2
Campo Grande Brazil 138 B2
Campo Maior Brazil 135 E3
Campo Mourão Brazil 138 B2
Campos Brazil 139 D2
Campos Altos Brazil 139 C1
Câmpulung Romania 58 C2
Cam Ranh Vietnam 67 B2
Camrose Can. 113 D2
Camsell Portage Can. 113 E2
Çan Turkey 59 C2
Canada country N. America
110 D2
Canadian U.S.A. 127 D1
Canadian r. U.S.A. 127 E1

Canadian Shield reg. Can. 121
Çanakkale Turkey 59 C2
Cananea Mex. 128 C3
Canary Islands terr.
N. Atlantic Ocean 90 A2
Canastra, Serra da mts Brazil
139 C1
Canatlán Mex. 128 B2
Canaveral, Cape U.S.A. 125 D3
Canavieiras Brazil 139 E1
Canberra Austr. 105 D3
Cancún Mex. 129 D2
Candelaria Mex. 129 C3
Cangamba Angola 96 A1
Cangas del Narcea Spain 54 B1
Canguçu Brazil 136 C4
Cangzhou China 74 B2
Caniapiscau Can. 115 D1
Caniapiscau r. Can. 115 D1
Caniapiscau, Lac l. Can. 115 C1
Cañitas de Felipe Pescador
Mex. 128 B2
Çankırı Turkey 84 B1
Canna i. U.K. 44 A2
Cannanore India 77 B3
Cannes France 53 D3
Cann River Austr. 105 D3
Canoas Brazil 136 C3
Canoinhas Brazil 138 B3
Canon City U.S.A. 120 B3
Canowindra Austr. 105 D2
Cantábrico, Mar sea Spain 54 C1
Cantábrico, Mar sea Spain 54 D1
Canterbury U.K. 47 D4
Canterbury Bight b. N.Z. 106 B3
Canterbury Plains N.Z. 106 B3
Cần Thơ Vietnam 67 B2
Canton China see Guangzhou
Canton MS U.S.A. 124 C2
Canton OH U.S.A. 122 D2
Canyon U.S.A. 127 D1
Canyon Ferry Lake U.S.A.
118 D1
Cao Bằng Vietnam 66 B1
Capão Bonito Brazil 138 C2
Caparaó, Serra do mts Brazil
139 D2
Cape Barren Island Austr.
103 D4
Cape Borda Austr. 104 B3
Cape Breton Island Can. 115 D2
Cape Coast Ghana 90 B4
Cape Cod Bay U.S.A. 123 F2
Cape Dorset Can. 111 G2
Cape Fear r. U.S.A. 125 E2
Cape Girardeau U.S.A. 121 F3
Capelle aan den IJssel Neth.
48 B2
Capenda-Camulemba Angola
94 B3
Cape Town S. Africa 98 A3
Cape Verde country
N. Atlantic Ocean 88

Cape York Peninsula Austr.
103 D1
Capim r. Brazil 135 E3
Capitol Hill N. Mariana Is 63 D1
Čapljina Bos.-Herz. 57 C2
Capraia, Isola di i. Italy 56 A2
Caprara, Punta pt Italy 56 A2
Capri, Isola di i. Italy 56 B2
Caprivi Strip reg. Namibia 96 B1
Caquetá r. Col. 134 C3
Caracal Romania 38 B3
Caracas Venez. 134 C1
Caransebeş Romania 38 B2
Caratasca, Laguna de lag. Hond.
130 B3
Caratinga Brazil 139 D1
Carauari Brazil 134 C3
Caravaca de la Cruz Spain
55 C2
Caravelas Brazil 139 E1
Carberry Can. 113 F3
Carbó Mex. 128 A2
Carbondale CO U.S.A. 120 B3
Carbondale IL U.S.A. 122 C3
Carbonear Can. 115 E2
Carbonita Brazil 139 D1
Carcaixent Spain 55 C2
Carcross Can. 112 B1
Cárdenas Mex. 129 C3
Cardiff U.K. 47 B4
Cardigan U.K. 47 A3
Cardigan Bay U.K. 47 A3
Cardston Can. 118 D1
Carei Romania 38 B2
Carentan France 52 B2
Carey, Lake salt flat Austr.
102 B2
Cargados Carajos Islands
Mauritius 97
Cariacica Brazil 139 D2
Caribbean Sea N. Atlantic Ocean
130 B3
Caribou Can. 123 G1
Caribou Lake Can. 114 B1
Caribou Mountains Can. 112 D2
Carignan France 48 B3
Carinda Austr. 105 D2
Cariñena Spain 55 C1
Carleton Place Can. 114 C2
Carletonville S. Africa 99 C2
Carlingford Lough inlet
Rep. of Ireland/U.K. 45 C1
Carlisle U.K. 46 B2
Carlisle U.S.A. 123 E2
Carlos Chagas Brazil 139 D1
Carlow Rep. of Ireland 45 C2
Carlsbad CA U.S.A. 119 C4
Carlsbad NM U.S.A. 126 C2
Carlyle Can. 120 C1
Carmacks Can. 112 B1
Carman Can. 113 F3
Carmarthen U.K. 47 A4

Carmarthen Bay U.K. 47 A4
Carmaux France 52 C3
Carmelita Guat. 129 C3
Carmen, Isla i. Mex. 128 A2
Carnac France 52 B2
Carnarvon S. Africa 98 B3
Carnegie, Lake salt flat Austr.
102 B2
Carn Eighe mt. U.K. 44 B2
Car Nicobar i. India 67 A3
Carnot C.A.R. 94 B2
Carnot, Cape Austr. 104 B2
Carnsore Point Rep. of Ireland
45 C2
Caroline Island atoll Kiribati 111
Caroline Islands N. Pacific Ocean
63 D2
Carpathian Mountains Europe
38 A2
Carpentaria, Gulf of Austr.
103 C1
Carpentras France 53 D3
Carrantuohill mt. Rep. of Ireland
45 B3
Carrara Italy 56 B2
Carrickmacross Rep. of Ireland
45 C2
Carrick-on-Shannon
Rep. of Ireland 45 B2
Carrick-on-Suir Rep. of Ireland
45 C2
Carrington U.S.A. 121 D1
Carrizo Springs U.S.A.
127 E3
Carrizozo U.S.A. 126 C2
Carroll U.S.A. 121 E2
Carrollton U.S.A. 125 C2
Carrot River Can. 113 E2
Carson City U.S.A. 119 C3
Cartagena Col. 134 B1
Cartagena Spain 55 C2
Cartago Costa Rica 130 B4
Carúaru Brazil 135 F3
Casablanca Morocco 90 B1
Casa de Janos Mex. 128 B1
Casa Grande U.S.A. 126 B2
Casale Monferrato Italy
56 A1
Casarano Italy 57 C2
Cascade U.S.A. 118 C2
Cascade Range mts Can./U.S.A.
118 B2
Cascavel Brazil 138 B2
Caserta Italy 56 B2
Cashel Rep. of Ireland 45 C2
Casino Austr. 105 E1
Caspe Spain 55 C1
Casper U.S.A. 120 B2
Caspian Lowland
Kazakh./Rus. Fed. 80 B2
Caspian Sea l. Asia/Europe
80 B2
Cássia Brazil 138 C2

ssiar Can. **112** C2
ssiar Mountains Can. **112** B2
ssilândia Brazil **138** B1
ssino Italy **56** B2
stanhal Brazil **135** E3
staño r. Arg. **136** B4
staños Mex. **128** B2
steljaloux France **52** C3
stelló de la Plana Spain
  5 C2
stelo Branco Port. **54** B2
sterton Austr. **104** C3
stlebar Rep. of Ireland **45** B2
stlebay U.K. **44** A2
stleblayney Rep. of Ireland
  5 C1
stlederg U.K. **45** C1
ntle Douglas U.K **44** C3
stlegar Can. **112** D3
stleisland Italy **56** B2
  5 B2
stlemaine Austr. **104** C3
stle Mountain Can. **112** B1
stlereagh r. Austr. **105** D2
stle Rock U.S.A. **120** C3
stres France **52** C3
atries St Lucia **131** D3
stro Brazil **138** C2
stro Chile **137** A5
strovillari Italy **57** C3
stacaos Peru **134** A3
staguases Brazil **139** D2
stalao Brazil **138** C1
staluña aut. comm. Spain **55** D1
stamarca Arg. **136** B3
standuanes i. Phil. **68** B2
standua Brazil **100** D2
stania Italy **56** C3
stanzaró Italy **57** C3
starman Phil. **68** B2
stbalogan Phil. **68** B2
stherine, East Mount Egypt see
  Kâtrina, Jabal
st Island Bahamas **131** C2
stoche, Cabo c. Mex. **129** D2
stskill Mountains U.S.A.
  23 F2
stuayan Phil. **68** B3
stubvick, Mount Can. **115** D1
stuca r. Col. **134** B2
stucaia Brazil **135** F3
stucasus mts Asia/Europe **85** C1
studry France **48** A2
stulonia Italy **56** B3
stusapacal Can. **115** D2
stuvaillon France **53** D3
stvan Rep. of Ireland **45** C2
stvernoso, Serra do mts Brazil
  38 B3
sxias Brazil **135** E3
sxias do Sul Brazil **136** C3
sxito Angola **100** B2
syenne Fr. Guiana **135** D2

Cayman Islands terr. West Indies
  130 B3
Cazombo Angola **96** B1
Ceballos Mex. **128** B2
Cebu Phil. **68** B2
Cebu i. Phil. **68** B2
Cecil Plains Austr. **105** E1
Cecina Italy **56** B2
Cedar r. U.S.A. **122** D2
Cedar Falls U.S.A. **121** E2
Cedar Lake Can. **113** E2
Cedar Rapids U.S.A. **121** E2
Cedros, Isla i. Mex. **128** A2
Ceduna Austr. **102** C3
Ceeldheere Somalia **93** C4
Ceerigaabo Somalia **93** C3
Cefalù Italy **56** B3
Celaya Mex. **129** C2
Celebes i. Indon. **65** D2
Celebes Sea Indon./Phil. **62** C2
Celestún Mex. **129** C2
Celle Ger. **49** E1
Celtic Sea Rep. of Ireland/U.K.
  43 B3
Central, Cordillera mts Col.
  134 B2
Central, Cordillera mts Peru
  134 B4
Central, Cordillera mts Phil.
  68 B2
Central African Republic country
  Africa **94** C2
Central Brahui Range mts Pak.
  78 A2
Central City U.S.A. **121** D2
Central Russian Upland hills
  Rus. Fed. **37** E3
Central Siberian Plateau
  Rus. Fed. **87** J2
Cephalonia i. Greece **59** B3
Ceram Sea Indon. see
  Seram, Laut
Ceres S. Africa **98** A3
Céret France **52** C3
Cerezo de Abajo Spain **54** C1
Cerignola Italy **56** C2
Cernavodă Romania **38** C2
Cerritos Mex. **129** C1
Cerro Azul Brazil **138** C2
Cerro Azul Mex. **129** C2
Cerro de Pasco Peru **134** B4
Cervione France **53** D3
Cervo Spain **54** B1
Cesena Italy **56** D2
Cēsis Latvia **35** N2
České Budějovice Czech Rep.
  50 C3

Český Les mts Czech Rep./Ger.
  49 F3
Çeşme Turkey **59** C3
Cessnock Austr. **105** E2
Cetinje S.M. **58** A2
Cetraro Italy **57** C3
Ceuta N. Africa **54** B2
Cévennes mts France **53** C3
Chābahār Iran **83** D2
Chabyêr Caka salt l. China **79** C1
Chachapoyas Peru **134** B3
Chachersk Belarus **37** D3
Chachoengsao Thai. **67** B2
Chad country Africa **91** D3
Chad, Lake Africa **91** D3
Chadaasan Mongolia **72** C1
Chadan Rus. Fed. **81** G1
Chadron U.S.A. **120** C2
Chaghcharān Afgh. **78** A3
Chagny France **50** A3
Chagoda Rus. Fed. **37** E2
Chagos Archipelago is B.I.O.T.
  66
Chaibaaa India **79** C2
Chainat Thai. **67** B2
Chaiyaphum Thai. **67** B2
Chakonipau, Lac l. Can. **115** D1
Chala Peru **134** B4
Chalap Dalan mts Afgh. **78** A1
Chaleur Bay inlet Can. **115** D2
Chalisgaon India **78** B2
Chalki i. Greece **59** C3
Chalkida Greece **59** B3
Challans France **52** B2
Challenger Deep sea feature
  N. Pacific Ocean **142** C4
Challis U.S.A. **118** D2
Châlons-en-Champagne France
  53 C2
Chalon-sur-Saône France **53** C2
Cham Ger. **49** F3
Chama U.S.A. **126** C1
Chama Zambia **97** C1
Chaman Pak. **78** A1
Chambal r. India **78** B2
Chamberlain U.S.A. **121** D2
Chambéry France **53** D2
Chambeshi Zambia **97** C1
Champaign U.S.A. **122** C2
Champlain, Lake Can./U.S.A.
  114 C2
Champotón Mex. **129** C3
Chañaral Chile **136** A3
Chandeleur Islands U.S.A.
  123 D3
Chandigarh India **78** B1
Chandler U.S.A. **126** B2
Chandrapur India **79** B3
Chang, Ko i. Thai. **67** B2
Changane r. Moz. **97** C2
Changara Moz. **97** C1
Changbai China **69** B1
Changbai Shan mts
  China/N. Korea **69** B1

Changchun China **69** B1
Changde China **75** B3
Ch'angdo N. Korea **69** B3
Changhua Taiwan **75** C3
Changhŭng S. Korea **69** B3
Chang Jiang r. China see Yangtze
Changjin-gang r. N. Korea **69** B1
Changsha China **75** B3
Changsŏng S. Korea **69** B3
Changting China **75** B3
Ch'angwŏn S. Korea **69** B3
Changzhi China **74** B2
Changzhou China **74** B2
Chania Greece **59** F3
Channel Islands English Chan.
  47 B5
Channel Islands U.S.A. **119** C4
Channel-Port-aux-Basques Can.
  115 E2
Chanthaburi Thai. **67** B2
Chany, Ozero salt l. Rus. Fed.
  81 E1
Chaouèn Morocco **54** B2
Chaoyang Guangdong China
  75 B3
Chaoyang Liaoning China **74** C1
Chaozhou China **75** B3
Chapayev Kazakh. **80** C1
Chapecó Brazil **138** B3
Chapleau Can. **114** B2
Chaplygin Rus. Fed. **37** E3
Chaplynka Ukr. **39** D2
Charcas Mex. **129** B2
Chardzhev Turkm. see
  Turkmenabat
Charente r. France **52** B2
Chārīkār Afgh. **78** A1
Charleroi Belgium **48** B2
Charles, Cape U.S.A. **123** E3
Charleston IL U.S.A. **122** C3
Charleston SC U.S.A. **125** E2
Charleston WV U.S.A. **122** D3
Charleston Peak U.S.A. **119** C3
Charleville Austr. **103** D2
Charleville-Mézières France
  53 C2
Charlotte U.S.A. **125** D1
Charlotte Harbor b. U.S.A.
  125 D3
Charlottesville U.S.A. **123** E3
Charlottetown Can. **115** D2
Charlton Austr. **104** C3
Charlton Island Can. **114** C1
Charters Towers Austr. **103** D2
Chartres France **52** C2
Chashniki Belarus **35** C3
Chasŏng N. Korea **69** B1
Chassiron, Pointe de pt France
  52 B2
Châteaubriant France **52** B2
Château-du-Loir France **52** C2
Châteaudun France **52** C2
Châteaulin France **52** B2
Château-Thierry France **53** C2

Chateh Can. **112** D2
Châtelet Belgium **48** B2
Châtellerault France **52** C2
Chatham Can. **122** D2
Chatham Islands N.Z. **111**
Chattahoochee r. U.S.A. **125** D2
Chattanooga U.S.A. **125** C1
Châu Đôc Vietnam **67** B2
Chauk Myanmar **66** A1
Chaumont France **53** D2
Chauny France **53** C2
Chaves Brazil **135** E3
Chaves Port. **54** B1
Chavigny, Lac l. Can. **114** C1
Chavusy Belarus **37** D3
Chayevo Rus. Fed. **37** E2
Chaykovskiy Rus. Fed. **34** E3
Cheb Czech Rep. **50** C2
Cheboksary Rus. Fed. **35** D3
Chech'ŏn S. Korea **69** B2
Chegga Maur. **90** B2
Chehalis U.S.A. **118** B1
Cheju S. Korea **69** B3
Cheju-do i. S. Korea **69** B3
Cheju-haehyŏp sea chan.
  S. Korea **69** B3
Chekhov Rus. Fed. **37** E2
Chelan, Lake U.S.A. **118** B1
Cheleken Turkm. **85** D2
Chelghoum el Aïd Alg. **55** E2
Chélif, Oued r. Alg. **55** D2
Chełm Pol. **51** D2
Chełmno Pol. **51** D2
Chelmsford U.K. **47** D4
Cheltenham U.K. **47** B4
Chelyabinsk Rus. Fed. **35** F3
Chemnitz Ger. **49** F2
Chenachane Alg. **90** B2
Chengde China **74** B1
Chengdu China **74** A2
Chennai India **77** C3
Chenzhou China **75** B3
Cherbourg France **52** B2
Cheremkhovo Rus. Fed. **72** C1
Cherepovets Rus. Fed. **37** E2
Cherkasy Ukr. **39** D2
Cherkessk Rus. Fed. **35** D4
Chernihiv Ukr. **39** D1
Chernivka Ukr. **39** D2
Chernivtsi Ukr. **38** C2
Chernyakhiv Ukr. **38** C1
Chernyakhovsk Rus. Fed. **36** B3
Chernyanka Rus. Fed. **37** E3
Chernyshevskiy Rus. Fed. **87** J2
Chernyshkovskiy Rus. Fed. **39** F2
Cherskogo, Khrebet mts
  Rus. Fed. **87** L2
Chertkovo Rus. Fed. **39** F2
Chervonohrad Ukr. **38** B1
Chervyen' Belarus **36** C3
Cherykaw Belarus **37** D3
Chesapeake Bay U.S.A. **123** E3
Cheshskaya Guba b. Rus. Fed.
  34 D2

Chester U.K. **46** B3
Chester SC U.S.A. **125** D2
Chesterfield U.K. **46** C3
Chesterfield, Îles is
  New Caledonia **103** E1
Chesterfield Inlet Can. **113** F1
Chesterfield Inlet inlet Can.
  113 F1
Chesuncook Lake U.S.A. **123**
Chetumal Mex. **129** D3
Chetwynd Can. **112** C2
Cheviot Hills U.K. **46** B2
Cheyenne U.S.A. **120** C2
Cheyenne r. U.S.A. **120** C2
Cheyenne Wells U.S.A. **120** C3
Chhapra India **79** C2
Chhatarpur India **79** B2
Chiai Taiwan **75** C3
Chiang Dao Thai. **66** A2
Chiang Mai Thai. **66** A2
Chiang Rai Thai. **66** A2
Chibi China **75** B3
Chiboma Moz. **97** C2
Chibougamau Can. **114** C2
Chicago U.S.A. **122** C2
Chichagof Island U.S.A. **112** B2
Chichester U.K. **47** C4
Chichester Range mts Austr.
  102 A2
Chickasha U.S.A. **127** E1
Chiclayo Peru **134** B3
Chico r. Arg. **137** B5
Chico U.S.A. **119** B3
Chicoutimi Can. **115** C2
Chidley, Cape Can. **121**
Chieti Italy **56** B2
Chifeng China **74** B1
Chifre, Serra do mts Brazil
  139 D1
Chiganak Kazakh. **81** E2
Chigubo Moz. **97** C2
Chigu Co l. China **66** A1
Chihuahua Mex. **128** B2
Chikhachevo Rus. Fed. **36** C2
Chilanko r. Can. **112** C2
Chilas Jammu and Kashmir **78**
Childress U.S.A. **127** D2
Chile country S. America **136** A
Chilika Lake India **79** C3
Chililabombwe Zambia **96** B1
Chilko r. Can. **112** C2
Chilko Lake Can. **112** C2
Chillán Chile **137** A4
Chillicothe MO U.S.A. **121** E3
Chillicothe OH U.S.A. **122** D3
Chilliwack Can. **112** C3
Chiloé, Isla de i. Chile **137** A5
Chilpancingo Mex. **129** C3
Chiltern Austr. **105** D3
Chilung Taiwan **75** C3
Chimala Tanz. **95** D3
Chimbas Arg. **136** B4
Chimbote Peru **134** B3

Chimboy Uzbek. **80** C2
Chimoio Moz. **97** C1
Chimtargha, Qullai *mt.* Tajik. **81** D3
China *country* Asia **72** B2
Chincha Alta Peru **134** B4
Chinchaga *r.* Can. **112** D2
Chinchorro, Banco *sea feature* Mex. **129** D3
Chinde Moz. **97** C1
Chindo S. Korea **69** B3
Chin-do *i.* S. Korea **69** B3
Chindu China **72** C2
Chindwin *r.* Myanmar **66** A1
Chinghwa N. Korea **69** B2
Chingola Zambia **96** B1
Chinguar Angola **96** A1
Chinhae S. Korea **69** B2
Chinhoyi Zimbabwe **97** C1
Chiniot Pak. **78** B1
Chinju S. Korea **69** B2
Chinko *r.* C.A.R. **94** C2
Chinle U.S.A. **126** C1
Chinmen Taiwan **75** B3
Chino Japan **71** C3
Chino Valley U.S.A. **126** B2
Chinsali Zambia **95** D4
Chioggia Italy **56** B1
Chios Greece **59** C3
Chios *i.* Greece **59** C3
Chipata Zambia **97** C1
Chipindo Angola **96** A1
Chipipe China **99** A2
Chiplun India **77** B3
Chippenham U.K. **47** B4
Chir *r.* Rus. Fed. **39** F2
Chirchiq Uzbek. **81** D2
Chiredzi Zimbabwe **97** C2
Chiricahua Peak U.S.A. **126** C2
Chiriquí, Golfo de *b.* Panama **130** B4
Chiri-san *mt.* S. Korea **69** B2
Chirripo *mt.* Costa Rica **130** B4
Chirundu Zimbabwe **97** C1
Chisasibi Can. **114** C1
Chisholm U.S.A. **121** E1
Chişinău Moldova **38** C2
Chita Rus. Fed. **73** D1
Chitado Angola **96** A1
Chitato Angola **96** C3
Chitipa Malawi **95** D3
Chitradurga India **77** B3
Chitral Pak. **78** B1
Chitré Panama **130** B4
Chittagong Bangl. **79** D2
Chittaurgarh India **78** B2
Chitungwiza Zimbabwe **97** C1
Chiume Angola **96** B1
Chivhu Zimbabwe **97** C1
Chixoy China **75** B2
Chkalovsk Rus. Fed. **37** F2
Choiseul *i.* Solomon Is **110**
Choix Mex. **128** B2
Chojnice Pol. **51** D2

Ch'ok'ē Mountains Eth. **93** B3
Chokurdakh Rus. Fed. **87** L2
Chókwé Moz. **97** C2
Cholet France **52** B2
Chomutov Czech Rep. **50** C2
Chona *r.* Rus. Fed. **87** J2
Ch'ŏnan S. Korea **69** B2
Ch'ŏngjin N. Korea **69** B1
Chŏngju N. Korea **69** B2
Ch'ŏngp'yŏng N. Korea **69** B2
Chongqing China **75** A3
Chongqing *mun.* China **74** A2
Chŏngup S. Korea **69** B2
Chŏnju S. Korea **69** B2
Chonos, Archipiélago de los *is* Chile **137** A5
Chopimzinho Brazil **138** B3
Chornomors'ke Ukr. **39** D2
Chortkiv Ukr. **38** C2
Ch'ŏrwŏn S. Korea **69** B2
Ch'osan N. Korea **69** B1
Chōshi Japan **71** D3
Choszczno Pol. **51** D2
Choûm Maur. **90** A2
Choybalsan Mongolia **73** D1
Choyr Mongolia **73** D2
Christchurch N.Z. **106** B3
Christchurch U.K. **47** C4
Christian, Cape Can. **111** H2
Christina S. Africa **99** C2
Christina, Mount N.Z. **106** A3
Christmas Island *terr.* Indian Ocean **62** B3
Chrysi *i.* Greece **59** C4
Chubut *r.* Arg. **137** B5
Chudniv Ukr. **38** C1
Chudovo Rus. Fed. **37** D2
Chügaku Mountains U.S.A. **110** C2
Chūgoku-sanchi *mts* Japan **71** B4
Chuguyevka Rus. Fed. **70** B2
Chuhuyiv Ukr. **39** E2
Chukchi Sea Rus. Fed./U.S.A. **87** O2
Chukotskiy Poluostrov *pen.* Rus. Fed. **87** O2
Chula Vista U.S.A. **119** C4
Chulym Rus. Fed. **86** H3
Chumbicha Arg. **136** B3
Chumikan Rus. Fed. **87** L3
Chumphon Thai. **67** A2
Ch'unch'ŏn S. Korea **69** B2
Chuncheon Chile *see* Chongqing
Chuquicamata Chile **136** B3
Chur Switz. **53** D2
Churchill Can. **113** F2
Churchill *r.* Man. Can. **113** F2
Churchill *r.* Nfld. and Lab. Can. **115** D1
Churchill, Cape Can. **113** F2
Churchill Falls Can. **115** D1
Churchill Lake Can. **113** E2
Churu India **78** B2

Chute-des-Passes Can. **115** C2
Chuuk *is* Micronesia **110**
Chuxiong China **66** B1
Ciadîr-Lunga Moldova **38** C2
Ciamis Indon. **64** B2
Cianjur Indon. **64** B2
Cianorte Brazil **138** B2
Ciechanów Pol. **51** E2
Ciego de Ávila Cuba **130** C2
Cienfuegos Cuba **130** B2
Cieza Spain **55** C2
Cigüela *r.* Spain **54** C2
Cihanbeyli Turkey **84** B2
Cihuatlán Mex. **128** B3
Cíjara, Embalse de *resr* Spain **54** C2
Cilacap Indon. **64** B2
Cimarron *r.* U.S.A. **127** E1
Cimişlia Moldova **38** C2
Cimone, Monte *mt.* Italy **56** B2
Cincinnati U.S.A. **122** D3
Çine Turkey **59** C3
Ciney Belgium **48** B2
Cintalapa Mex. **120** O0
Circle AK U.S.A. **110** C2
Circle MT U.S.A. **120** B1
Cirebon Indon. **64** B2
Cirencester U.K. **47** C4
Cirò Marina Italy **57** C3
Citrusdal S. Africa **98** A3
Città di Castello Italy **53** E3
Ciudad Altamirano Mex. **129** B3
Ciudad Bolívar Venez. **134** C2
Ciudad Camargo Mex. **128** B2
Ciudad Constitución Mex. **128** A2
Ciudad del Carmen Mex. **129** C3
Ciudad Delicias Mex. *see* **128** B2
Ciudad de Valles Mex. **129** C2
Ciudad Guayana Venez. **134** C2
Ciudad Guerrero Mex. **126** C3
Ciudad Guzmán Mex. **128** B3
Ciudad Ixtepec Mex. **129** C3
Ciudad Juárez Mex. **128** B1
Ciudad Mante Mex. **129** C2
Ciudad Mier Mex. **129** C2
Ciudad Obregón Mex. **128** B2
Ciudad Real Spain **54** C2
Ciudad Rio Bravo Mex. **129** C2
Ciudad Rodrigo Spain **54** B1
Ciudad Victoria Mex. **129** C2
Ciutadella de Menorca Spain **55** D1
Cıvan Dağı *mt.* Turkey **59** C3
Civitanova Marche Italy **56** B2
Civitavecchia Italy **56** B2
Civray France **52** C2
Çivril Turkey **59** C3
Clacton-on-Sea U.K. **47** D4
Claire, Lake Can. **113** D2
Clanwilliam S. Africa **98** A3
Clare Australia **104** B2
Clare Island Rep. of Ireland **45** A2

Claremont U.S.A. **123** F2
Claremorris Rep. of Ireland **45** B2
Clarence N.Z. **106** B3
Clarenville Can. **115** E2
Claresholm Can. **112** D2
Clarinda U.S.A. **121** D2
Clarión, Isla *i.* Mex. **128** A3
Clarkebury S. Africa **99** C3
Clark Fork *r.* U.S.A. **118** C1
Clark Hill Reservoir U.S.A. **125** D2
Clarksburg U.S.A. **123** D3
Clarksdale U.S.A. **124** B2
Clarksville *AR* U.S.A. **124** B1
Clarksville *TN* U.S.A. **124** C1
Claro *r.* Brazil **138** B1
Clayton U.S.A. **127** D1
Clear, Cape Rep. of Ireland **45** B3
Cleare, Cape U.S.A. **110** C3
Clear Lake U.S.A. **121** D2
Clear Lake *l.* U.S.A. **119** B3
Clearwater Can. **112** D2
Clearwater *r.* Can. **113** D2
Clearwater U.S.A. **125** D3
Clearwater *r.* U.S.A. **118** C1
Cleburne U.S.A. **127** D2
Clermont Austr. **127** D1
Clermont *r.* Can. **113** D2
Clermont U.S.A. **125** D3
Clermont-en-Argonne France **48** B3
Clermont-Ferrand France **52** C2
Clervaux Lux. **48** B3
Cleveland *MS* U.S.A. **124** B2
Cleveland *OH* U.S.A. **122** D2
Cleveland *TN* U.S.A. **125** C1
Cleveland, Mount U.S.A. **118** D1
Clewiston U.S.A. **125** D3
Clifden Rep. of Ireland **45** A2
Clifton Austr. **105** E1
Clifton U.S.A. **126** C2
Clinton Can. **112** C2
Clinton *IA* U.S.A. **121** E2
Clinton *OK* U.S.A. **127** E1
Clisham *h.* U.K. **44** A2
Clitheroe U.K. **46** B3
Clonakilty Rep. of Ireland **45** B3
Cloncurry Austr. **103** D2
Clonmel Rep. of Ireland **45** C2
Cloppenburg Ger. **48** B3
Cloud Peak U.S.A. **120** B2
Clovis U.S.A. **127** D2
Cluff Lake Mine Can. **113** E2
Cluj-Napoca Romania **38** B2
Cluny Austr. **103** C2
Cluses France **53** D2
Clutha *r.* N.Z. **106** A4
Clyde *r.* U.K. **44** B3
Clyde, Firth of *est.* U.K. **44** B3
Clydebank U.K. **44** B3
Clyde River Can. **111** H2
Coaldale U.S.A. **118** C2
Coal River Can. **112** C2
Coari Brazil **134** C3
Coari *r.* Brazil **134** C3
Coastal Plain U.S.A. **124** B2
Coast Mountains Can. **112** C2

Coast Ranges *mts* U.S.A. **118** B2
Coatbridge U.K. **44** B3
Coats Island Can. **113** G1
Coats Land *reg.* Antarctica **107** A2
Coatzacoalcos Mex. **129** C3
Cobán Guat. **130** A3
Cobar Austr. **105** D2
Cóbh Rep. of Ireland **45** B3
Cobija Bol. **136** B2
Cobourg Can. **123** E2
Cobourg Peninsula Austr. **102** C1
Cobram Austr. **105** D3
Coburg Ger. **49** E2
Cochabamba Bol. **136** B2
Cochem Ger. **48** C2
Cochin India **77** B4
Cochrane Can. **114** B2
Cockburn Austr. **104** C2
Cockburn Town
   Turks and Caicos Is *see*
   Grand Turk
Cockscomb *mt.* S. Africa **98** B3
Coco *r.* Hond./Nic. **130** B3
Cocos Islands *terr.* Indian Ocean **62** A3
Cod, Cape U.S.A. **123** F2
Codigoro Italy **56** B2
Cod Island Can. **115** D1
Codó Brazil **135** E3
Cody U.S.A. **120** B2
Coesfeld Ger. **48** C2
Coeur d'Alene U.S.A. **118** C1
Coffee Bay S. Africa **99** C3
Coffeyville U.S.A. **121** D3
Coffs Harbour Austr. **105** E2
Cognac France **52** B2
Cohuna Austr. **104** C3
Coiba, Isla de *i.* Panama **130** B4
Coihaique Chile **137** A5
Coimbatore India **77** B3
Coimbra Port. **54** B1
Colac Austr. **104** C3
Colatina Brazil **139** D1
Colby U.S.A. **120** C3
Colchester U.K. **47** D4
Cold Lake Can. **113** D2
Coldstream U.K. **44** C3
Coleman U.S.A. **127** D2
Coleraine U.K. **45** C1
Coles, Punta de *pt* Peru **146**
Colesberg S. Africa **99** C3
Colima Mex. **128** B3
Colima, Nevado *de vol.* Mex. **128** B3
Coll *i.* U.K. **44** A2
Collarenebri Austr. **105** D1
Collier Bay Austr. **102** B1
Collingwood N.Z. **106** B3
Collo Alg. **55** E2
Collooney Rep. of Ireland **45** B1
Colmar France **53** D2
Cologne Ger. **48** C2

Colômbia Brazil **138** C2
Colombia *country* S. America **134** B2
Colombo Sri Lanka **77** B4
Colomiers France **52** C3
Colón Panama **130** C4
Colonna, Capo *c.* Italy **57** C3
Colonsay *i.* U.K. **44** A2
Colorado *r.* Arg. **137** B4
Colorado *r.* Mex./U.S.A. **126** A2
Colorado *r.* U.S.A. **127** E3
Colorado *state* U.S.A. **120** B3
Colorado Plateau U.S.A. **120** B3
Colorado Springs U.S.A. **120** C3
Cölpin Ger. **49** F1
Columbia *MO* U.S.A. **121** E3
Columbia *SC* U.S.A. **125** D2
Columbia *TN* U.S.A. **124** C1
Columbia *r.* U.S.A. **118** B1
Columbia, Mount U.S.A. **112** D2
Columbia Falls U.S.A. **118** D1
Columbia Mountains Can. **112** C2
Columbia Plateau U.S.A. **118** C1
Columbus *GA* U.S.A. **125** D2
Columbus *IN* U.S.A. **122** C3
Columbus *MS* U.S.A. **124** C2
Columbus *NE* U.S.A. **121** D2
Columbus *NM* U.S.A. **126** C2
Columbus *OH* U.S.A. **122** D3
Colville U.S.A. **118** C1
Colville *r.* U.S.A. **110** C2
Colville Lake Can. **110** D2
Colwyn Bay U.K. **46** B3
Comacchio Italy **56** B2
Comalcalco Mex. **129** C3
Comăneşti Romania **38** C2
Comencho, Lac *l.* Can. **114** C1
Comeragh Mountains
   Rep. of Ireland **45** C2
Comilla Bangl. **79** D2
Comines Belgium **48** A2
Comino, Capo *c.* Italy **56** A2
Comitán de Domínguez Mex. **129** C3
Como Italy **56** A1
Como, Lake Italy **56** A1
Comodoro Rivadavia Arg. **137** B5
Comorin, Cape India **67**
Comoros *country* Africa **97** D1
Compiègne France **52** C2
Compostela Mex. **128** B2
Comrat Moldova **38** C2
Conceição da Barra Brazil **139** E1
Conceição do Araguaia Brazil **135** E3
Concepción Arg. **136** B3
Concepción Chile **137** A4
Concepción Mex. **128** C2
Conception, Point U.S.A. **119** B4

Conchas Lake U.S.A. **126** D1
Conchos *r. Nuevo León/Tamaulipas* Mex. **129** D2
Conchos *r.* Mex. **128** B2
Concord U.S.A. **119** B3
Concord *NH* U.S.A. **123** F2
Concordia Argentina **136** C4
Concordia U.S.A. **121** D3
Condobolin Austr. **105** D2
Condom France **52** C3
Condon U.S.A. **118** B1
Conegliano Italy **56** E1
Conflict Group *is* P.N.G. **103** E1
Congdü China **79** C2
Congo *r.* Congo/Dem. Rep. Congo **94** C3
Congo *r.* Congo/Dem. Rep. Congo **94** C3
Congo, Democratic Republic of *country* Africa **94** C3
Congo Basin Dem. Rep. Congo **97**
Conklin Can. **113** D2
Conn, Lough *l.* Rep. of Ireland **45** B1
Connaught *reg.* Rep. of Ireland **45** B1
Connecticut *r.* U.S.A. **123** F2
Connecticut *state* U.S.A. **123** F2
Connemara *reg.* Rep. of Ireland **45** B2
Conrad U.S.A. **118** D1
Conroe U.S.A. **127** E2
Conselheiro Lafaiete Brazil **139** D2
Conselheiro Pena Brazil **139** D1
Consett U.K. **46** D2
Côn Son *i.* Vietnam **67** B3
Constance, Lake U.S.A. **104** A1
Constanța Romania **38** C3
Constantine Alg. **91** C1
Contact U.S.A. **118** D2
Contreras, Isla *i.* Chile **137** A6
Conway *AR* U.S.A. **124** B1
Coober Pedy Austr. **104** A1
Cook, Mount N.Z. **106** B3
Cook U.S.A. **125** C1
Cook Inlet *sea chan.* U.S.A. **110** B2
Cook Islands S. Pacific Ocean **101**
Cook Islands *terr.* S. Pacific Ocean **101**
Cook's Harbour Can. **115** E1
Cook Strait N.Z. **106** B3
Cooktown Austr. **103** D3
Coolabah Austr. **105** D2
Coolangatta Austr. **105** E1
Coolgardie Austr. **102** B3
Cooma Austr. **105** D3
Coombah Austr. **104** C2
Coonabarabran Austr. **105** D2

Coonalpyn Austr. **104** B3
Coonamble Austr. **105** D2
Cooper Creek *watercourse* Austr. **104** B1
Coos Bay U.S.A. **118** B2
Cootamundra Austr. **105** D2
Copala Mex. **128** B3
Copenhagen Denmark **41** C4
Copertino Italy **57** C2
Copiapó Chile **136** B3
Copper Harbor U.S.A. **122** C1
Coppermine Can. *see* Kugluktuk
Coquimbo Chile **136** B3
Corabia Romania **38** B3
Coração de Jesus Brazil **139** D1
Coral Bay Austr. **102** A2
Coral Harbour Can. **111** G2
Coral Sea S. Pacific Ocean **103** E1
Coral Sea Islands Territory *terr.* Austr. **100**
Corangamite, Lake Austr. **104** C3
Corby U.K. **47** C3
Corcovado, Golfo de *sea chan.* Chile **137** A5
Cordele U.S.A. **125** D2
Cordillera Range *mts* Phil. **68** B3
Córdoba Arg. **136** B4
Córdoba Mex. **129** C3
Córdoba Spain **54** C2
Córdoba, Sierras de *mts* Arg. **136** B4
Cordova U.S.A. **112** A1
Corfu *i.* Greece **59** A3
Coria Spain **54** B2
Corinth U.S.A. **124** C2
Corinth, Gulf of *sea chan.* Greece **59** B3
Corinto Brazil **139** D1
Cork Rep. of Ireland **45** B3
Çorlu Turkey **59** C2
Cornélio Procópio Brazil **138** B2
Corner Brook Can. **115** E2
Corner Inlet *b.* Austr. **105** D3
Corning *CA* U.S.A. **118** B3
Corning *NY* U.S.A. **123** E2
Corno, Monte *mt.* Italy **56** B2
Cornwall Can. **114** C2
Cornwallis Island Can. **110** F1
Coro Venez. **134** C1
Coromandel Can. **113** D2
Coromandel Peninsula N.Z. **106** C2
Coronation Can. **113** D2
Coronation Gulf Can. **110** E2
Coronel Oviedo Para. **136** C3
Corovodë Albania **59** B2
Corozal Belize **129** G3
Corpus Christi U.S.A. **127** E3
Correntina Brazil **135** E4

Corrib, Lough *l.* Rep. of Ireland **45** B2
Corrientes Arg. **136** C3
Corrientes, Cabo *c.* Arg. **146**
Corrientes, Cabo *c.* Mex. **128** B2
Corryong Austr. **105** D3
Corse *i.* France *see* Corsica
Corse, Cap *c.* France **53** D3
Corsica *i.* France **53** D3
Corsicana U.S.A. **127** E2
Cortés U.S.A. **120** C3
Cortland U.S.A. **123** E2
Cortona Italy **56** B2
Coruche Port. **54** B2
Çoruh Turkey *see* Artvin
Çorum Turkey **84** B1
Corumbá Brazil **136** C2
Corumbá *r.* Brazil **138** C1
Corvallis U.S.A. **118** B2
Corwen U.K. **46** B3
Cosamaloapan Mex. **129** C3
Cosenza Italy **57** C3
Cosne-Cours-sur-Loire France **52** C2
Costa Blanca *coastal area* Spain **55** C2
Costa Brava *coastal area* Spain **55** D1
Costa del Sol *coastal area* Spain **54** B2
Costa de Mosquitos *coastal area* Nic. **130** B3
Costa Rica Brazil **138** B1
Costa Rica *country* Central America **130** B3
Costa Rica Mex. **128** B2
Costești Romania **38** B3
Cotabato Phil. **68** B3
Côte d'Ivoire *country* Africa **90** B4
Cotopaxi, Volcán *vol.* Ecuador **134** B3
Cotswold Hills U.K. **47** B4
Cottage Grove U.S.A. **118** B2
Cottbus Ger. **50** C2
Coubre, Pointe de la *pt* France **52** B2
Couëdic, Cape du Austr. **104** B3
Council Bluffs U.S.A. **121** D2
Courland Lagoon *b.* Lith./Rus. Fed. **36** B2
Courtenay Can. **112** C3
Coutances France **52** B2
Coutras France **52** B2
Couvin Belgium **48** B2
Coventry U.K. **47** C3
Covington U.S.A. **122** D3
Cowan, Lake *salt flat* Austr. **102** B3
Cowdenbeath U.K. **44** C2
Cowlitz *r.* U.S.A. **118** B1
Cowra Austr. **105** D2

Coxim Brazil **138** B1
Cox's Bazar Bangl. **79** D2
Cozumel Mex. **129** D2
Cozumel, Isla de *i.* Mex. **129** D2
Cradock S. Africa **99** C3
Craig U.S.A. **120** B2
Crailsheim Ger. **49** E3
Craiova Romania **38** B3
Cranberry Portage Can. **113** F2
Cranbourne Austr. **105** D3
Cranbrook Can. **112** D3
Crateús Brazil **135** E2
Crato Brazil **135** F3
Crawford U.S.A. **120** B3
Crawfordsville U.S.A. **122** C2
Crawley U.K. **47** C4
Crazy Mountains U.S.A. **118** D1
Cree *r.* Can. **113** E2
Creel Mex. **128** B2
Cree Lake Can. **113** E2
Cremona Italy **56** B1
Crépy-en-Valois France **48** A3
Cres *i.* Croatia **56** B2
Crescent City U.S.A. **118** B2
Creston U.S.A. **121** E2
Crestview U.S.A. **124** C2
Crete *i.* Greece **59** B3
Creus, Cap de *c.* Spain **55** D1
Creutzwald France **48** C3
Crewe U.K. **46** B3
Crianlarich U.K. **44** B2
Criciúma Brazil **136** D3
Crieff U.K. **44** C2
Crimea *pen.* Ukr. **39** D2
Crimmitschau Ger. **49** F2
Crnomelj Slovenia **56** C1
Croagh Patrick *h.* Rep. of Ireland **45** B2
Croatia *country* Europe **57** C1
Crocker, Banjaran *mts* Malaysia **65** C1
Croker Island Austr. **63** C3
Cromer U.K. **46** D3
Cromwell N.Z. **106** A4
Crookston U.S.A. **121** D1
Crookwell Austr. **105** D2
Cross City U.S.A. **125** D3
Crossett U.S.A. **124** B2
Cross Fell *h.* U.K. **46** B2
Cross Lake Can. **113** F2
Crotone Italy **57** C3
Crowley U.S.A. **124** B2
Crowsnest Pass Can. **112** D3
Cruz Alta Brazil **136** C3
Cruz del Eje Arg. **136** B4
Cruzeiro Brazil **139** D2
Cruzeiro do Sul Brazil **134** B3
Crystal Brook Austr. **104** B2
Crystal Falls U.S.A. **122** C1
Csongrád Hungary **51** E2
Cuando *r.* Angola/Zambia **96** B1
Cuangar Angola **96** A1

Cuango *r.* Angola/
Dem. Rep. Congo **94** B3
Cuanza *r.* Angola **94** B3
Cuatro Ciénegas Mex. **127** D3
Cuauhtémoc Mex. **128** B2
Cuautla Mex. **129** C3
Cuba *country* West Indies **130** B2
Cubal Angola **96** A1
Cubango *r.* Angola/Namibia **96** B1
Cúcuta Col. **134** B2
Cuddalore India **77** B3
Cuddapah India **77** B3
Cuemba Angola **96** A1
Cuenca Ecuador **134** B3
Cuenca Spain **55** C1
Cuenca, Serranía de *mts* Spain **55** C1
Cuernavaca Mex. **129** C3
Cuiabá Brazil **138** A1
Cuillin Sound *sea chan.* U.K. **44** A2
Cuilo Angola **94** B3
Cuito *r.* Angola **96** B1
Cuito Cuanavale Angola **96** A1
Cukai Malaysia **64** B1
Culcairn Austr. **105** D3
Culgoa *r.* Austr. **105** D1
Culiacán Mex. **128** B2
Culion *i.* Phil. **68** A2
Cullera Spain **55** C2
Cullman U.S.A. **124** C2
Culuene *r.* Brazil **135** D4
Cumaná Venez. **134** C1
Cumberland *r.* U.S.A. **122** C3
Cumberland Lake Can. **113** E2
Cumberland Peninsula Can. **111** H2
Cumberland Plateau U.S.A. **125** C1
Cumberland Sound *sea chan.* Can. **111** H2
Cumbernauld U.K. **44** C3
Cummings U.S.A. **118** B3
Cunene *r.* Angola **96** A1
Cuneo Italy **56** A2
Cunnamulla Austr. **105** D1
Cupar U.K. **44** C2
Curaçao *i.* Neth. Antilles **131** D3
Curicó Chile **137** A4
Curitiba Brazil **138** C3
Curitibanos Brazil **138** B3
Curnamona Austr. **104** B2
Currie Austr. **103** D3
Curtis Island Austr. **103** E2
Curuá *r.* Brazil **135** D3
Cururupu Brazil **135** E3
Curvelo Brazil **139** D1
Cusco Peru **134** B4
Cut Bank U.S.A. **118** D1
Cuttack India **79** C2
Cuxhaven Ger. **49** D1
Cuyo Islands Phil. **68** B2
Cuzco Peru *see* Cusco
Cyangugu Rwanda **95** C3

Cyclades *is* Greece **59** B3
Cypress Hills Can. **113** D3
Cyprus *country* Asia **92** B1
Czech Republic *country* Europe **50** C3
Częstochowa Pol. **51** D2

D

Daban China **74** B1
Dacca Bangl. *see* Dhaka
Dachau Ger. **50** C3
Dadu Pak. **78** A2
Daegu S. Korea *see* Taegu
Daet Phil. **68** B2
Dagana Senegal **90** A3
Dagupan Phil. **68** B2
Da Hinggan Ling *mts* China **74** B1
Dahlak Archipelago *is* Eritrea **92** C3
Dahlem Ger. **48** C2
Dahm, Ramlat *des.* Saudi Arabia/Yemen **82** B3
Dahme Ger. **49** F2
Daik Indon. **64** B2
Dakar Senegal **90** A3
Daketa Shet' *watercourse* Eth. **95** E2
Dākhilah, Wāḥāt al *oasis* Egypt **92** A2
Dakhla Oasis Egypt *see* Dākhilah, Wāḥāt al
Dakoank India **67** A3
Đakovica S.M. **58** B2
Đakovo Croatia **57** C1
Dala Angola **96** B1
Dalain Hob China **72** C2
Dalälven *r.* Sweden **41** D3
Dalaman Turkey **59** C3
Dalaman *r.* Turkey **59** C3
Dalandzadgad Mongolia **72** C2
Đà Lat Vietnam **67** B2
Dalbandin Pak. **78** A2
Dalby Austr. **105** E1
Dale *Hordaland* Norway **42** E1
Dale *Sogn og Fjordane* Norway **42** E1
Dale Hollow Lake U.S.A. **125** C1
Dalgety Austr. **105** D3
Dalhart U.S.A. **127** D1
Dalhousie Can. **123** G1
Dali China **66** B1
Dalian China **74** C2
Dalkeith U.K. **44** C3
Dallas U.S.A. **127** E2
Dall Island U.S.A. **112** B2
Dalmatia *reg.* Bos.-Herz./Croatia **57** C2
Dal'negorsk Rus. Fed. **70** C2
Dal'nerechensk Rus. Fed. **70** B1

aloa Côte d'Ivoire **90** B4
alrymple, Mount Austr. **103** D2
alsmynni Iceland **40** [inset]
altenganj India **79** C2
alton U.S.A. **125** D2
aly r. Austr. **102** C1
aly Waters Austr. **102** C1
aman India **78** B2
amanhür Egypt **84** B2
amascus Syria **84** B2
amaturu Nigeria **91** D3
amghan Iran **85** D2
ammam Saudi Arabia **83** C2
amoh India **79** B2
amongo Ghana **90** B4
ampir, Selat sea chan. Indon.
53 C3
amroh India **66** A1
amxung China **79** D1
anané Côte d'Ivoire **90** B4
a Näng Vietnam **67** B2
anbury U.S.A. **123** F2
andong China **74** C1
angriga Belize **130** B3
angshan China **74** B2
antu China **74** B2
anube r. Austria/Ger. **50** D3
anube r. Bulg./Croatia/S.M.
58 C3
anube r. Hungary **51** D3
anube r. Romania **50** C2
anube Delta Romania/Ukr.
58 C2
anville IL U.S.A. **122** C2
anville KY U.S.A. **122** D3
anville VA U.S.A. **123** E3
anzhou China **75** A4
aoxian China **75** B3
apaong Togo **90** C3
a Qaidam Zhen China **72** C2
aqing China **73** E1
ar es Salaam Tanz. **95** D3
argai Pak. **85** I3
argaville U.S.A. **106** B2
arhan Mongolia **72** D1
arién, Golfo del g. Col. **134** D2
arjiling India **79** C2
arlag China **72** C2
arling r. Austr. **104** C2
arling Downs hills Austr.
105 D1

Darling Range hills Austr. **102** A3
Darlington U.K. **46** C2
Darlington Point Austr. **105** D2
Darlowo Pol. **51** D2
Darmstadt Ger. **49** D3
Darnah Libya **91** E1
Darnick Austr. **104** C2
Daroca Spain **55** C1
Dartford U.K. **47** D4
Dartmoor hills U.K. **47** A4
Dartmouth Can. **115** D2
Dartmouth U.K. **47** B4
Daru P.N.G. **63** D3
Darvaza Turkm. **80** C2
Darwin Austr. **102** C1
Dashoguz Turkm. **80** C2
Dasht r. Pak. **78** A2
Datadian Indon. **65** C1
Datça Turkey **59** C3
Datong China **74** B1
Datu Piang Phil. **68** B3
Daud Khel Pak. **78** B1
Daugava r. Latvia **36** B2
Daugavpils Latvia **36** C2
Daun Ger. **48** C2
Dauphin Can. **113** E2
Dauphin Lake Can. **113** F2
Davangere India **77** B3
Davao Phil. **68** B3
Davao Gulf Phil. **68** B3
Davenport U.S.A. **121** E2
Daveyton S. Africa **99** C2
David Panama **130** B4
Davidson Can. **113** E2
Davis U.S.A. **119** B3
Davis Inlet Can. **115** D1
Davis Sea Antarctica **107** F3
Davis Strait Can./Greenland
111 I2
Davos Switz. **53** D2
Dawgah Oman **83** C3
Dawson Can. **112** B1
Dawson U.S.A. **125** D2
Dawson Creek Can. **112** C2
Dawsons Landing Can. **112** C2
Dawu China **72** C2
Dax France **52** B3
Da Xueshan mts China **72** C2
Dayr az Zawr Syria **84** C2
Dayton U.S.A. **122** D3
Daytona Beach U.S.A. **125** D3
Da Yunhe canal China **74** B2
Dazhou China **74** A2
De Aar S. Africa **98** B3
Dead Sea salt l. Asia **84** B2
De'an China **75** B3
Deán Funes Arg. **136** B4
Dease Lake Can. **112** C2
Death Valley depr. U.S.A. **119** C3
Deauville France **52** C2
Debar Macedonia **59** B2
Debrecen Hungary **51** E3
Debre Markos Eth. **93** B3
Debre Zeyit Eth. **93** B4

Decatur AL U.S.A. **124** C2
Decatur IL U.S.A. **122** C3
Deccan plat. India **77** B3
Děčín Czech Rep. **50** C2
Dedović Rus. Fed. **36** C2
Dedza Malawi **97** C1
Dee r. England/Wales U.K. **46** B3
Dee r. Scotland U.K. **44** C2
Deepwater Austr. **105** E1
Deer Lodge U.S.A. **118** D1
Defiance U.S.A. **122** D2
Dêgê China **72** C2
Deggendorf Ger. **50** C3
Degtevo Rus. Fed. **39** F2
Dehra Dun India **79** B1
Dehri India **79** C2
Dehui China **73** E2
Deinze Belgium **48** A2
Dej Romania **30** B2
De Kalb U.S.A. **122** C2
Dekese Dem. Rep. Congo **94** C3
Delano U.S.A. **119** C3
Delano Peak U.S.A. **119** D3
Delap-Uliga-Djarrit Marshall Is
100
Delārām Afgh. **78** A1
Delaronde Lake Can. **113** E2
Delaware U.S.A. **122** D2
Delaware r. U.S.A. **123** E3
Delaware state U.S.A. **123** E3
Delaware Bay U.S.A. **123** E3
Delegate Austr. **105** D3
Delémont Switz. **53** D2
Delft Neth. **48** A1
Delfzijl Neth. **48** C1
Delgado, Cabo c. Moz. **95** E4
Delhi India **78** B2
Deli i. Indon. **64** B2
Déline Can. **112** C1
Delitzsch Ger. **49** F2
Dellys Alg. **55** D2
Delmenhorst Ger. **49** D1
Delnice Croatia **56** B1
De-Longa, Ostrova is Rus. Fed.
87 M1
Deloraine Can. **113** E3
Delphi tourist site Greece **59** B3
Del Rio U.S.A. **127** D3
Delta CO U.S.A. **120** B3
Delta UT U.S.A. **119** D3
Delta Junction U.S.A. **110** C2
Delvinë Albania **59** B3
Demanda, Sierra de la mts Spain
54 C1
Demba Dem. Rep. Congo **94** C3
Dembī Dolo Eth. **93** B4
Demidov Rus. Fed. **37** D2
Deming U.S.A. **126** C2
Demirci Turkey **59** C3
Demmin Ger. **50** C2
Demopolis U.S.A. **124** C2
Dempo, Gunung vol. Indon.
64 B2
Demyansk Rus. Fed. **37** D2

De Naawte S. Africa **98** B3
Denakil *reg.* Eritrea/Eth. **93** C3
Den Burg Neth. **48** B1
Dendermonde Belgium **48** B2
Dengkou China **74** A1
Dengzhou China **74** B2
Den Haag Neth. *see* **The Hague**
Denham Austr. **102** A2
Den Helder Neth. **48** B1
Deniliquin Austr. **104** C3
Denio U.S.A. **118** C2
Denison *IA* U.S.A. **121** D2
Denison *TX* U.S.A. **127** D2
Denizli Turkey **59** C3
Denman Austr. **105** E2
Denmark Austr. **102** A3
Denmark *country* Europe **41** C4
Denmark Strait
 Greenland/Iceland **111** K2
Denpasar Indon. **65** C2
D'Entrecasteaux, Point Austr.
 102 A3
Denver U.S.A. **120** B3
Deogarh *Orissa* India **79** C2
Deogarh *Rajasthan* India **78** B2
Deoghar India **79** C2
Deolali Mah. Rep. **87** L2
Dégên China **66** A1
De Queen U.S.A. **124** E2
Dera Ghazi Khan Pak. **78** B1
Dera Ismail Khan Pak. **78** B1
Derbent Rus. Fed. **35** D4
Derby Austr. **102** B1
Derby U.K. **46** C3
Dereham U.K. **47** D3
Derg, Lough *l.* Rep. of Ireland
 45 B2
Derhachi Ukr. **39** E1
De Ridder U.S.A. **124** E2
Derkul *r.* Rus. Fed./Ukr. **39** E2
Dêrub China **79** B1
Derudeb Sudan **92** B3
De Rust S. Africa **98** B3
Derventa Bos.-Herz. **57** C2
Derwent *r.* U.K. **46** C3
Derzhavinsk Kazakh. **81** D1
Desaguadero *r.* Bol. **136** B2
Désappointement, Îles du *is*
 Fr. Polynesia **111**
Deschambault Lake Can. **113** E2
Deschutes *r.* U.S.A. **118** B1
Desê Eth. **93** B3
Deseado Arg. **137** B5
Deseado *r.* Arg. **137** B5
Des Moines U.S.A. **121** D2
Des Moines *r.* U.S.A. **121** E2
Desna *r.* Rus. Fed./Ukr. **39** D1
Desnogorsk Rus. Fed. **37** D3
Dessau Ger. **49** F2
Destruction Bay Can. **112** B1
Desventuradas, Islas de los *is*
 S. Pacific Ocean **133**
Detmold Ger. **49** D2

Detroit U.S.A. **122** D2
Detroit Lakes U.S.A. **121** D1
Deurne Neth. **48** B2
Deva Romania **38** B1
Deventer Neth. **48** C1
Deveron *r.* U.K. **44** C2
Devêt Skal *h.* Czech Rep. **51** D3
Devil's Lake U.S.A. **121** D1
Devil's Paw *mt.* U.S.A. **112** B2
Devli India **78** B2
Devnya Bulg. **58** C2
Devon Can. **112** D2
Devon Island Can. **111** F1
Devonport Austr. **103** D4
Dewas India **78** B2
Deyong, Tanjung *pt* Indon. **63** D3
Dezfūl Iran **85** C2
Dezhou China **74** B2
Dhahran Saudi Arabia **83** C2
Dhaka Bangl. **79** C2
Dhamār Yemen **82** B3
Dhamtari India **79** C2
Dhanbad India **79** C2
Dhankuta Nepal **79** C2
Dharmanagar India **66** A1
Dharmjaygarh India **79** C2
Dharwad India **77** B3
Dhule India **78** B2
Diablo, Picacho del *mt.* Mex.
 128 A1
Diamantina *watercourse* Austr.
 103 C2
Diamantina, Chapada *plat.* Brazil
 135 E4
Diamantino Brazil **135** D4
Diapaga Burkina **90** C3
Dibā al Hiṣn U.A.E. **83** C2
Dibrugarh India **76** D2
Dickinson U.S.A. **120** C1
Dickson U.S.A. **124** C1
Dicle *r.* Turkey *see* **Tigris**
Die France **53** D3
Diefenbaker, Lake Can. **113** D2
Diéma Mali **90** B3
Diên Châu Vietnam **66** B2
Diepholz Ger. **49** D1
Dieppe France **52** C2
Diffa Niger **91** D3
Digby Can. **115** D2
Digne-les-Bains France **53** D3
Digoin France **53** C2
Digos Phil. **68** B3
Digul *r.* Indon. **63** D3
Dijlah, Nahr *r.* Iraq/Syria **66**
Dijon France **53** D2
Dikhil Djibouti **93** C3
Dikili Turkey **59** C3
Dila Eth. **93** B4
Dili East Timor **63** C3
Dillenburg Ger. **49** D2
Dillon U.S.A. **118** D1
Dilolo Dem. Rep. Congo **94** C4
Dimapur India **66** A1

Dimashq Syria *see* **Damascus**
Dimboola Austr. **104** C3
Dimitrovgrad Bulg. **58** C2
Dimitrovgrad Rus. Fed. **35** D3
Dinagat *i.* Phil. **68** B2
Dinan France **52** B2
Dinant Belgium **48** B2
Dinar Turkey **84** B2
Dinār, Kūh-e *mt.* Iran **85** D2
Dinaric Alps *mts*
 Bos.-Herz./Croatia **36**
Dindigul India **77** B3
Dingelstädt Ger. **49** E2
Dingle Rep. of Ireland **45** A2
Dingle Bay Rep. of Ireland **45** A2
Dingwall U.K. **44** B2
Dinkelsbühl Ger. **49** E3
Dionísio Cerqueira Brazil **138** I
Diourbel Senegal **90** A3
Dipolog Phil. **68** B3
Dir Pak. **78** B1
Direction, Cape Austr. **103** D1
Dirê Dawa Eth. **93** C4
Dirico Angola **96** B1
Dirk Hartog Island Austr. **102** A
Dirranbandi Austr. **105** D1
Dirs Saudi Arabia **82** B3
Disappointment, Cape
 S. Georgia **137** E6
Disappointment, Lake *salt flat*
 Austr. **102** B2
Discovery Bay Austr. **104** C3
Dismal Swamp U.S.A. **123** E3
Diss U.K. **47** D3
Dittaino *r.* Italy **56** C3
Diu India **78** B2
Divinópolis Brazil **139** D2
Divo Côte d'Ivoire **90** B4
Dixon U.S.A. **122** C2
Dixon Entrance *sea chan.*
 Can./U.S.A. **112** B2
Diyarbakır Turkey **84** C2
Djado Niger **91** D2
Djado, Plateau du Niger **91** D2
Djambala Congo **94** B3
Djanet Alg. **91** C2
Djelfa Alg. **90** C1
Djéma C.A.R. **95** C2
Djenné Mali **90** B3
Djibo Burkina **90** B3
Djibouti *country* Africa **93** C3
Djibouti Djibouti **93** C3
Dmitriyevka Rus. Fed. **37** E3
Dmitriyev-L'govskiy Rus. Fed.
 37 E3
Dmitrov Rus. Fed. **37** E2
Dnepr *r.* Rus. Fed. *see* **Dnieper**
Dnieper *r.* Rus. Fed. **37** D3
Dnieper *r.* Ukr. **39** D2
Dniester *r.* Ukr. **39** D2
Dnipro *r.* Ukr. *see* **Dnieper**
Dniprodzerzhyns'k Ukr. **39** E2
Dnipropetrovs'k Ukr. **39** E2
Dniprorudne Ukr. **39** D2

Dnister r. Ukr. see Dniester
Dno Rus. Fed. **36** C2
Doba Chad **91** D4
Döbeln Ger. **49** F2
Doberai, Jazirah pen. Indon. **63** C3
Dobo Indon. **63** C3
Doboj Bos.-Herz. **57** C2
Dobrich Bulg. **58** C2
Dobrinka Rus. Fed. **37** F3
Dobrush Belarus **37** D3
Dodecanese is Greece **59** C3
Dodekanisos is Greece see Dodecanese
Dodge City U.S.A. **120** C3
Dodoma Tanz. **95** D3
Dodinchem Neth. **48** C2
Dogai Coring salt l. China **70** C1
Dokkum Neth. **48** B1
Dokshytsy Belarus **36** C3
Dokuchayevs'k Ukr. **39** E2
Dolak, Pulau i. Indon. **63** D3
Dole France **53** D2
Dolgellau U.K. **47** B3
Dolinsk Rus. Fed. **73** F1
Dolisie Congo see Loubomo
Dolyna Ukr. **38** D2
Domažlice Czech Rep. **50** C3
Dombås Norway **41** B3
Dombóvár Hungary **51** D3
Dome Creek Can. **112** C4
Dominica country West Indies **131** D3
Dominican Republic country West Indies **131** C3
Domodedovo Rus. Fed. **37** D2
Domokos Greece **59** B3
Dompu Indon. **65** C2
Don r. Rus. Fed. **37** E3
Don r. U.K. **44** C2
Donald Austr. **104** C3
Donau r. Austria/Ger. see Danube
Donauwörth Ger. **50** C3
Don Benito Spain **54** B2
Doncaster U.K. **46** C3
Dondo Angola **94** B3
Dondo Moz. **97** C3
Dondra Head Sri Lanka **77** C4
Donegal Rep. of Ireland **45** B1
Donegal Bay Rep. of Ireland **45** B1
Donets'k Ukr. **39** E2
Donets'kyy Kryazh hills Rus. Fed./Ukr. **39** E2
Dongara Austr. **102** A3
Dongchuan China **75** A3
Dongfang China **75** A4
Dongfanghong China **70** B1

Donggala Indon. **65** C2
Donggang China **69** A2
Dongguan China **75** B3
Đông Hới Vietnam **66** B2
Dongou Congo **94** B2
Dongsheng China see Ordos
Dongtai China **74** C2
Dongting Hu l. China **75** B3
Dongying China **74** B2
Donnellys Crossing N.Z. **106** B2
Donostia - San Sebastián Spain **55** C1
Dooxo Nugaaleed val. Somalia **93** C4
Dorchester U.K. **47** B4
Dordabis Namibia **98** A1
Dordogne r. France **52** B2
Dordrecht Neth. **48** B2
Deré Lake Can. **113** E2
Dori Burkina **90** B3
Doring r. S. Africa **98** A3
Dornoch U.K. **44** B2
Dornoch Firth est. U.K. **44** B2
Dorogobuzh Rus. Fed. **37** D3
Dorohoi Romania **38** C1
Döröö Nuur salt l. Mongolia **72** C1
Dorotea Sweden **40** D3
Dorre Island Austr. **102** A2
Dorrigo Austr. **105** E2
Dorsale Camerounaise slope Cameroon/Nigeria **94** B2
Dortmund Ger. **48** C2
Dos Bahías, Cabo c. Arg. **137** B5
Dosse r. Ger. **49** F1
Dosso Niger **90** C3
Dothan U.S.A. **125** C2
Douai France **52** C1
Douala Cameroon **94** A2
Douarnenez France **52** B2
Doubtful Sound N.Z. **106** A4
Douentza Mali **90** B3
Douglas Isle of Man **46** A2
Douglas S. Africa **98** B2
Douglas AK U.S.A. **112** B2
Douglas AZ U.S.A. **126** C2
Douglas GA U.S.A. **125** D2
Douglas WY U.S.A. **120** B2
Dourada, Serra hills Brazil **138** B1
Dourados Brazil **138** B2
Dourados, Serra dos hills Brazil **138** B2
Douro r. Port. **54** B1
Dover U.K. **47** D4
Dover U.S.A. **123** E3
Dover, Strait of France/U.K. **47** D3
Downpatrick U.K. **45** D1
Dowshī Afgh. **78** A1
Dōzen is Japan **71** B3
Dozois, Réservoir resr Can. **114** C2
Dracena Brazil **138** B2

Drachten Neth. **48** C1
Drăgăneşti-Olt Romania **38** B3
Drăgăşani Romania **38** B3
Drahichyn Belarus **36** C3
Drakensberg mts Lesotho/S. Africa **99** C2
Drakensberg mts S. Africa **99** C2
Drake Passage S. Atlantic Ocean **107** L4
Drama Greece **59** B2
Drammen Norway **41** C4
Drau r. Austria **56** B1
Drava r. Europe **57** C1
Drepano, Akra pt Greece **59** B3
Dresden Ger. **49** F2
Dreux France **52** C2
Drina r. Bos.-Herz./S.M. **57** C2
Drniš Croatia **57** C2
Drobeta - Turnu Severin Romania **38** B3
Drochtersen Ger. **49** D1
Drogheda Rep. of Ireland **45** C2
Drohobych Ukr. **38** B2
Drosh Pak. **78** B1
Drouin Austr. **105** D3
Drummond Island U.S.A. **122** D1
Drummondville Can. **115** C2
Druskininkai Lith. **36** B3
Druzhkivka Ukr. **39** E2
Dryden Can. **114** A2
Drysdale r. Austr. **102** B1
Dubā Saudi Arabia **82** A2
Dubai U.A.E. **83** C2
Dubawnt Lake Can. **113** E1
Dubayy U.A.E. see Dubai
Dubbagh, Jabal ad mt. Saudi Arabia **82** A2
Dubbo Austr. **105** D2
Dublin Rep. of Ireland **45** C2
Dublin U.S.A. **125** D2
Dubno Ukr. **38** C1
Du Bois U.S.A. **123** E2
Dubrovnik Croatia **57** C2
Dubrovytsya Ukr. **38** C1
Dubrowna Belarus **37** D3
Dubuque U.S.A. **121** E2
Ducie Island atoll Pitcairn Is **111**
Duck Bay Can. **113** E2
Đức Trong Vietnam **67** B2
Duderstadt Ger. **49** E2
Dudinka Rus. Fed. **86** H2
Dudley U.K. **47** B3
Duero r. Spain **54** B1
Duffreboy, Lac l. Can. **115** C1
Dufftown U.K. **44** C2
Dugi Rat Croatia **57** C2
Duisburg Ger. **48** C2
Dukathole S. Africa **99** C3
Dukhān Qatar **83** C2
Dulan China **72** C2
Dulce r. Arg. **136** B4
Dülmen Ger. **48** C2
Dulovo Bulg. **58** C2
Duluth U.S.A. **121** E1

Dumaguete Phil. **68** B3
Dumai Indon. **64** B1
Dumaran *i.* Phil. **68** B2
Dumas *AR* U.S.A. **124** B2
Dumas *TX* U.S.A. **127** D1
Dumbarton U.K. **44** B3
Dumfries U.K. **44** C3
Duna *r.* Hungary *see* Danube
Dunakeszi Hungary **51** D3
Dunărea *r.* Romania *see* Danube
Dunaújváros Hungary **51** D3
Dunayivtsi Ukr. **38** C2
Dunbar U.K. **44** C3
Dunbeath U.K. **44** C1
Duncan U.S.A. **112** C3
Duncan U.S.A. **127** C2
Duncansby Head U.K. **44** C1
Dundalk Rep. of Ireland **45** C1
Dundalk Bay Rep. of Ireland **45** C2
Dundas Greenland **111** H1
Dundee S. Africa **99** D2
Dundee U.K. **44** C2
Dunedin N.Z. **106** B4
Dunfermline U.K. **44** C2
Dungannon U.K. **45** C1
Dungarvan Rep. of Ireland **45** C2
Dungeness *hd* U.K. **47** D4
Dungiven U.K. **45** C1
Dungog Austr. **105** E2
Dungu Dem. Rep. Congo **95** C2
Dungun Malaysia **64** B1
Dunhua China **69** B1
Dunhuang China **72** C2
Dunkerque France *see* Dunkirk
Dunkirk France **52** C1
Dunkirk U.S.A. **123** E2
Dún Laoghaire Rep. of Ireland
45 C2
Dunmurry U.K. **45** D1
Dunnet Head U.K. **44** C1
Duns U.K. **44** C3
Dupnitsa Bulg. **59** B2
Dupree U.S.A. **120** C1
Durack *r.* Austr. **102** B1
Durango Mex. **128** B2
Durango Spain **54** C1
Durango U.S.A. **120** B3
Durant U.S.A. **127** E2
Durazno Uru. **137** C4
Durban S. Africa **99** D2
Durban-Corbières France **52** C3
Durbanville S. Africa **98** A3
Düren Ger. **48** C2
Durg India **79** C2
Durham U.K. **44** C2
Durham U.S.A. **125** E1
Durmā Indon. **64** B1
Durmitor *mt.* S.M. **58** A2
Durness U.K. **44** B1
Durrës Albania **59** A2
Dursey Island Rep. of Ireland
45 A3
Dursunbey Turkey **59** C3

D'Urville, Tanjung *pt* Indon.
63 D3
D'Urville Island N.Z. **106** B3
Dushan China **75** A3
Dushanbe Tajik. **81** D3
Düsseldorf Ger. **48** C2
Duyun China **75** A3
Dvorichna Ukr. **39** E2
Dwarka India **78** A2
Dworshak Reservoir U.S.A.
118 C1
Dyat'kovo Rus. Fed. **37** D3
Dyce U.K. **44** C2
Dyer, Cape Can. **111** H2
Dyersburg U.S.A. **124** C1
Dyfrdwy *r. England/Wales* U.K. *see*
Dee
Dyje *r.* Austria/Czech Rep. **51** D3
Dylewska Góra *h.* Pol. **51** D2
Dymytrov Ukr. **39** E2
Dzamin Öböö Mongolia **73** D2
Dzaoudzi Mayotte **97** D1
Dzhankoy Ukr. **39** D2
Dzhizak Uzbek. *see* Jizzax
Dzhubga Rus. Fed. **39** E3
Dzhugdzhur, Khrebet *mts*
Rus. Fed. **87** L3
Dzhungarskiy Alatau, Khrebet
mts China/Kazakh. **81** E2
Dzhusaly Kazakh. **80** C2
Działdowo Pol. **51** E2
Dzuunmod Mongolia **72** D1
Dzyarzhynsk Belarus **36** C3

E

Eagle *r.* Can. **115** E1
Eagle Cap *mt.* U.S.A. **118** C1
Eagle Lake Can. **114** A2
Eagle Lake U.S.A. **118** B2
Eagle Pass U.S.A. **127** D3
Eagle Plain Can. **110** C2
Ear Falls Can. **114** A1
East Antarctica *reg.* Antarctica
107 F2
Eastbourne U.K. **47** D4
East China Sea N. Pacific Ocean
73 E2
East Coast Bays N.Z. **106** B2
Eastend Can. **118** C1
Eastern Cape *prov.* S. Africa
99 C3
Eastern Desert Egypt **90** B2
Eastern Ghats *mts* India **77** B3
East Falkland *i.* Falkland Is.
137 C6
East Frisian Islands Ger. **48** C1
East Kilbride U.K. **44** B3
Eastleigh U.K. **47** C4
East Liverpool U.S.A. **123** D2

East London S. Africa **99** C3
Eastmain Can. **114** C1
Eastmain *r.* Can. **114** C1
Eastman U.S.A. **125** D2
East Sea N. Pacific Ocean *see*
Japan, Sea of
East Siberian Sea Rus. Fed.
87 L2
East St Louis U.S.A. **122** B3
East Timor *country* Asia **61**
Eau Claire U.S.A. **122** B2
Eau Claire, Lac à *l. l.* Can.
114 C1
Eauripik *atoll* Micronesia **63** D2
Ebano Mex. **129** C2
Ebbw Vale U.K. **47** B4
Eberswalde-Finow Ger. **49** F1
Eboli Italy **56** C2
Ebolowa Cameroon **94** B2
Ebro *r.* Spain **55** D1
Ech Chélif Alg. **90** C1
Echeverria, Pico *mt.* Mex.
128 A2
Echoing *r.* Can. **113** F2
Echternach Lux. **48** C3
Echuca Austr. **104** C3
Écija Spain **54** B2
Eckernförde Ger. **50** B2
Ecuador *country* S. America
134 B3
Ed Eritrea **92** C3
Ed Damazin Sudan **93** B3
Ed Damer Sudan **92** B3
Ed Debba Sudan **92** B3
Ed Dueim Sudan **92** B3
Eddystone Point Austr. **103** D4
Ede Neth. **48** B1
Edéa Cameroon **94** B2
Edéia Brazil **138** C1
Eden Austr. **105** D3
Eden *r.* U.K. **46** B2
Edenburg S. Africa **99** C2
Edenderry Rep. of Ireland **45** C2
Edenhope Austr. **104** C3
Edessa Greece **59** B2
Edgeøya *i.* Svalbard **86** D1
Edinburg U.S.A. **127** E3
Edinburgh U.K. **44** C3
Edirne Turkey **59** C2
Edmonton Can. **112** D2
Edmundston Can. **123** G1
Edremit Turkey **59** C3
Edremit Körfezi *b.* Turkey **59** C3
Edson Can. **112** D2
Edward's Creek Austr. **104** A1
Edwards Plateau U.S.A. **127** D2
Éfaté *i.* Vanuatu **110**
Egan Range *mts* U.S.A. **119** D3
Eger Hungary **51** E3
Egersund Norway **41** B4
Egilsstaðir Iceland **40** [inset]
Eğirdir Turkey **84** B2
Eğirdir Gölü *l.* Turkey **84** B2

gletons France 52 C2
gkveinot Rus. Fed. 87 O2
gypt country Africa 92 A2
hen Haddang China 74 A2
ibergen Neth. 48 C1
lfel hills Ger. 48 C2
igg i. U.K. 44 A2
ight Degree Channel India/Maldives 77 B4
ighty Mile Beach Austr. 102 B1
ilat Israel 84 B3
ilenburg Ger. 49 F2
linbeck Ger. 49 D2
lindhoven Neth. 48 B2
lirunepé Brazil 134 C3
iseb watercourse Namibia 96 B1
isenach Ger. 49 D2
lisenhüttenstadt Ger. 50 C2
isenstadt Austria 51 D3
lisleben Lutherstadt Ger. 49 E2
ivissa Spain 55 D2
lvissa i. Spain see Ibiza
ijeda Madag. 97 [inset] D2
kenäs Fin. 41 E4
kibastuz Kazakh. 81 E1
kostrovskaya Imandra, Ozero l. Rus. Fed. 40 G2
ksjö Sweden 41 C4
kwan r. Can. 114 B1
la Myanmar 66 A2
lassona Greece 59 B3
Iba, Isola d' i. Italy 56 B2
Ibasan Albania 59 B2
I Bayadh Alg. 90 C1
Ibert, Mount U.S.A. 120 B3
Ibeuf France 52 C2
Ibistan Turkey 84 B2
lblag Pol. 51 D2
I'brus mt. Rus. Fed. 35 G4
Iburz Mountains Iran 85 C2
I Callao Venez. 134 C2
I Campo U.S.A. 127 C3
I Centro U.S.A. 119 C4
I Cerro Bol. 136 B2
Iche-Elc Spain 55 C2
Ilda Spain 55 C2
Idorado Arg. 138 B3
I Dorado Mex. 128 B3
I Dorado AR U.S.A. 124 B2
I Dorado KS U.S.A. 121 D3
I Ejido plat. Alg. 90 B2
I Ejido Spain 54 C2
I Eulma Alg. 55 F2
Ieuthera i. Bahamas 131 C2
Elgin U.K. 44 C2
Elgin U.S.A. 122 C2
I Fasher Sudan 93 A3
I Fuerte Mex. 128 B2
I Geneina Sudan 93 A3

El Golfo de Santa Clara Mex. 128 A1
Elgon, Mount Uganda 95 D2
El Hammâmi reg. Maur. 90 A2
El Higo Mex. 128 C2
El Homr Alg. 90 C2
Elim U.S.A. 110 B2
Elista Rus. Fed. 35 D4
Elizabeth U.S.A. 123 F2
Elizabeth City U.S.A. 125 E1
Elizabethtown U.S.A. 122 C3
El Jadida Morocco 90 B1
Elk Pol. 51 E2
Elk City U.S.A. 127 E1
Elkhovo Bulg. 58 C2
Elko Can. 112 D3
Elko U.S.A. 118 C2
Elk Point Can. 113 D2
Elief Ringnes Island Can. 110 F1
Ellendale U.S.A. 121 D1
Ellensburg U.S.A. 118 B1
Ellesmere, Lake N.Z. 106 B3
Ellesmere Island Can. 111 G1
Ellesmere Port U.K. 46 B3
Ellice r. Can. 110 F2
Ellon U.K. 44 C2
Ellsworth U.S.A. 123 G2
Ellsworth Mountains Antarctica 107 K2
Elmalı Turkey 59 C3
El Milia Alg. 55 E2
Elmira U.S.A. 123 F2
Elmshorn Ger. 49 D1
El Muglad Sudan 93 A3
El Obeid Sudan 93 B3
El Oro Mex. 128 B2
El Oued Alg. 91 C1
El Paso U.S.A. 126 C2
El Porvenir Mex. 128 B1
El Prat de Llobregat Spain 55 D1
El Progreso Hond. 129 D3
El Reno U.S.A. 127 E1
Elsa Can. 112 B1
El Salado Mex. 129 B2
El Salto Mex. 128 B2
El Salvador country Central America 130 B3
El Sauz Mex. 126 C3
El Socorro Mex. 128 A1
Elsterwerda Ger. 49 F2
Elva Estonia 36 C2
Elvas Port. 54 B2
Elverum Norway 41 C3
El Wak Kenya 95 E2
Ely U.K. 47 D3
Ely MN U.S.A. 121 E1
Ely NV U.S.A. 119 D3
Emämrüd Iran 85 D2
Emån r. Sweden 41 D4
Emba Kazakh. 80 C2
Emba r. Kazakh. 80 C2
Embalenhle S. Africa 99 C2

Emborcação, Represa de resr Brazil 138 C1
Embu Kenya 95 D3
Emden Ger. 48 C1
Emerald Austr. 103 D2
Emet Turkey 59 C3
eMijindini S. Africa 99 D2
Emi Koussi mt. Chad 91 D3
Emine, Nos pt Bulg. 58 C2
Emirdağ Turkey 84 B2
Emmaste Estonia 36 B2
Emmeloord Neth. 48 B1
Emmen Neth. 48 C1
Emory Peak U.S.A. 127 D3
Empalme Mex. 128 A2
Empangeni S. Africa 99 D2
Empoli Italy 56 B2
Emporia KS U.S.A. 121 D3
Emporia VA U.S.A. 123 E3
Emzinoni S. Africa 99 C2
Encarnación Mex. 128 B2
Encarnación Para. 136 C3
Encrucilhada Brazil 139 D1
Ende Indon. 65 D2
Endicott Mountains U.S.A. 110 B2
Enerhodar Ukr. 39 D2
Engel's Rus. Fed. 35 D3
Enggano i. Indon. 64 B2
England admin. div. U.K. 46 C3
English Channel France/U.K. 47 C5
Enid U.S.A. 127 E1
Enkhuizen Neth. 48 B1
Enköping Sweden 41 D4
Enna Italy 56 B3
Ennadai Lake Can. 113 E1
En Nahud Sudan 93 A3
Ennedi, Massif mts Chad 91 E3
Enngonia Austr. 105 D1
Ennis Rep. of Ireland 45 B2
Ennis U.S.A. 127 D2
Enniscorthy Rep. of Ireland 45 C2
Enniskillen U.K. 45 C1
Enns r. Austria 50 C3
Enontekiö Fin. 40 E2
Ensay Austr. 105 D3
Enschede Neth. 48 C1
Ensenada Mex. 128 A1
Enshi China 75 A2
Enterprise Can. 112 D1
Enterprise AL U.S.A. 125 C2
Enterprise OR U.S.A. 118 C1
Entroncamento Port. 54 B2
Enugu Nigeria 91 C4
Épernay France 48 A3
Épinal France 53 D2
Epsom U.K. 47 C4
Equatorial Guinea country Africa 94 A2
Erbendorf Ger. 49 F3
Erbeskopf h. Ger. 48 C3
Erciş Turkey 85 C2

Erdao Jiang *r.* China **69** B1
Erdek Turkey **59** C2
Erdemli Turkey **84** B2
Erechim Brazil **136** C3
Ereğli *Konya* Turkey **84** B2
Ereğli *Zonguldak* Turkey **84** B1
Erenhot China **74** B1
Erevan Armenia *see* Yerevan
Erfurt Ger. **49** E2
Ergani Turkey **84** B2
'Erg Chech *des.* Alg./Mali **90** B2
Ergene *r.* Turkey **59** C2
Erie U.S.A. **123** D2
Erie, Lake Can./U.S.A. **122** D2
Erimo-misaki *c.* Japan **70** D2
Eritrea *country* Africa **92** B3
Erkner Ger. **49** F1
Erlangen Ger. **49** E2
Erldunda Austr. **102** C2
Ermelo S. Africa **99** C2
Ermoupoli Greece **59** B3
Ernakulam India **77** B4
Er Rachidia Morocco **90** B1
Er Rahad Sudan **93** B3
Errigal *h.* Rep. of Ireland **45** B1
Erris Head Rep. of Ireland **45** A1
Erromango *i.* Vanuatu **110**
Erseka Albania **59** B2
Ertil' Rus. Fed. **37** F3
Erwitte Ger. **49** D2
Erzgebirge *mts* Czech Rep./Ger. **50** C2
Erzincan Turkey **84** B2
Erzurum Turkey **84** B2
Esbjerg Denmark **35** H4
Escalante U.S.A. **119** D3
Escanaba U.S.A. **122** C1
Escárcega Mex. **129** C3
Escatrón Spain **55** C1
Esch-sur-Alzette Lux. **48** B3
Eschede Ger. **49** E1
Eschwege Ger. **49** E2
Eschweiler Ger. **48** C2
Escondido Mex. **128** B2
Escuinapa Mex. **128** B2
Eşen Turkey **59** C3
Eşfahān Iran **85** D2
Esikhawini S. Africa **99** D2
Esk *r.* U.K. **46** B2
Esker Can. **115** D1
Eskifjörður Iceland **40** [inset]
Eskilstuna Sweden **41** D4
Eskişehir Turkey **84** B2
Eslāmābād-e Gharb Iran **85** C2
Esler Dağı *mt.* Turkey **59** C3
Eşme Turkey **59** C3
Esmeraldas Ecuador **134** B2
Espakeh Iran **83** D2
Espalion France **52** C3
Espanola Can. **114** B2
Espanola U.S.A. **126** C1
Esperance Austr. **102** B3

Esperanza Mex. **128** B2
Espichel, Cabo *c.* Port. **54** B2
Espinhaço, Serra do *mts* Brazil **139** D1
Espiritu Santo *i.* Vanuatu **142** D6
Espíritu Santo, Isla *i.* Mex. **128** A2
Espoo Fin. **41** E3
Esquel Arg. **137** A5
Essaouira Morocco **90** B1
Es Semara Western Sahara **90** A2
Essen Ger. **48** C2
Essequibo *r.* Guyana **134** D2
Esso Rus. Fed. **87** M3
Estados, Isla de los *i.* Arg. **137** B6
Estância Brazil **135** F4
Estcourt S. Africa **99** C2
Estella Spain **55** C1
Estepona Spain **54** B2
Esterhazy Can. **113** E2
Esteros Para. **136** B2
Estevan Can. **120** C1
Estherville U.S.A. **121** E2
Eston Can. **113** D2
Estonia *country* Europe **36** C2
Estrela, Serra da *mts* Port. **54** B1
Estremoz Port. **54** B2
Etadunna Austr. **104** B1
Étain France **48** B3
Étampes France **52** C2
Étaples France **52** C1
Etawah India **79** B2
eThandukukhanya S. Africa **99** D2
Ethiopia *country* Africa **93** B4
Ethiopian Highlands *plat.* Eth. **93** B4
Etna, Monte *vol.* Italy **56** C3
Etne Norway **42** E2
Etolin Island U.S.A. **112** B2
Etosha Pan *salt pan* Namibia **96** A1
Ettelbruck Lux. **48** C3
Etten-Leur Neth. **48** B2
Euabalong Austr. **105** D2
Euboea *i.* Greece *see* Evvoia
Eucla Austr. **102** B3
Eufaula U.S.A. **125** C2
Eufaula Lake *resr* U.S.A. **127** E1
Eugene U.S.A. **118** B2
Eugenia, Punta *pt* Mex. **128** A2
Eulo Austr. **105** D1
Eunice U.S.A. **127** D2
Euphrates *r.* Asia **84** C2
Eureka *MT* U.S.A. **118** C1
Eureka *NV* U.S.A. **119** C3
Euriowie Austr. **104** C2
Euroa Austr. **105** D3
Europa Point Gibraltar **54** B2
Eutsuk Lake Can. **112** C2

Evans, Lac *l.* Can. **114** C1
Evans Head Austr. **105** E1
Evans Strait Can. **113** G1
Evanston *IL* U.S.A. **120** A2
Evanston *WY* U.S.A. **118** D2
Evansville U.S.A. **122** C3
Evaton S. Africa **99** C2
Everard, Lake *salt flat* Austr. **104** B2
Everest, Mount China/Nepal **79** C2
Everett U.S.A. **118** B1
Evergem Belgium **48** A2
Everglades *swamp* U.S.A. **125** D3
Evinayong Equat. Guinea **94** B3
Evje Norway **41** B4
Évora Port. **54** B2
Évreux France **52** C2
Evros *r.* Greece/Turkey **59** C2
Evrotas *r.* Greece **59** B3
Evrychou Cyprus **84** B2
Evvoia *i.* Greece **59** B3
Exaltación Bol. **136** B2
Exe *r.* U.K. **47** B4
Exeter U.K. **47** B4
Exmoor *hills* U.K. **47** B4
Exmouth U.K. **47** B4
Exmouth Gulf Austr. **102** A2
Exuma Cays *is* Bahamas **131** C2
Eyasi, Lake *salt flat* S.A. Austr. **104** B1
Eyasi, Lake *salt flat* S.A. Austr. **104** B1
Eyjafjörður Austr. **104** B2
Eysturoy *i.* Faroe Is **42** B1
Ezakheni S. Africa **99** D2
Ezhou China **75** B2
Ezhva Rus. Fed. **34** E2
Ezine Turkey **59** C3

Fabens U.S.A. **126** C2
Faborg Denmark **50** C1
Fabriano Italy **56** B2
Fachi Niger **91** D3
Fada-N'Gourma Burkina **90** C3
Faenza Italy **56** B2
Fafanlap Indon. **63** C3
Fāgāraş Romania **38** B2
Fagatogo American Samoa **101**
Fagernes Norway **41** B3
Fagersta Sweden **41** D4
Faguibine, Lac *l.* Mali **90** B3
Fagurhólsmýri Iceland **40** [inset]
Fairbanks U.S.A. **110** C2
Fairfield U.S.A. **119** B3
Fair Isle *i.* U.K. **44** [inset]
Fairmont *MN* U.S.A. **121** E2
Fairmont *WV* U.S.A. **123** D3

Fairweather, Mount Can./U.S.A. **112** B2
Fais *i.* Micronesia **63** D2
Faisalabad Pak. **78** B1
Faith U.S.A. **120** C1
Faizabad India **79** C2
Fakarava *atoll* Fr. Polynesia **111**
Faku China **69** A1
Falcon Lake Mex./U.S.A. **127** E3
Falfurrias U.S.A. **127** C3
Falher Can. **112** D2
Falkenberg Ger. **49** F2
Falkenberg Sweden **41** C4
Falkensee Ger. **49** F1
Falkirk U.K. **44** C3
Falkland Islands *terr.*
  S. Atlantic Ocean **137** C6
Falköping Sweden **41** C4
Fallon U.S.A. **119** C3
Fall River U.S.A. **123** F2
Falls City U.S.A. **121** D2
Falmouth U.K. **47** A4
False Bay S. Africa **98** A3
Falso, Cabo *c.* Mex. **120**
Falster *i.* Denmark **41** C5
Fălticeni Romania **38** C2
Falun Sweden **41** C3
Fameck France **48** C3
Fangzheng China **73** E1
Fano Italy **56** E2
Fan Si Pan *mt.* Vietnam **66** B1
Faradje Dem. Rep. Congo **95** C2
Farafangana Madag. **97** [inset] D2
Farāfirah, Wāḥāt al *oasis* Egypt
  92 A2
Farah Afgh. **78** A1
Farah Rūd *watercourse* Afgh.
  78 A1
Faranah Guinea **90** A3
Farasān, Jazā'ir *is* Saudi Arabia
  82 B3
Farewell, Cape Greenland
  111 J2
Farewell, Cape N.Z. **106** B3
Fargo U.S.A. **121** D1
Farg'ona Uzbek. **81** E2
Faribault U.S.A. **121** E2
Faribault, Lac *l.* Can. **115** C1
Farmington NM U.S.A. **126** C1
Faro Port. **54** B2
Fårö *i.* Sweden **36** A2
Faroe Islands *terr.*
  N. Atlantic Ocean **42** B1
Farrashband Iran **79** B2
Fāryāb Iran **83** C2
Fasā Iran **85** D3
Fasano Italy **57** C2
Fastiv Ukr. **38** C1
Fatehgarh India **79** B2
Fatehpur India **79** C2
Fauske Norway **40** D2
Faxaflói *b.* Iceland **40** [inset]
Faya Chad **91** D3
Fayetteville *AR* U.S.A. **124** B1

Fayetteville *NC* U.S.A. **125** E1
Fazilka India **78** B1
Fdérik Maur. **90** A2
Fear, Cape U.S.A. **125** E2
Featherston N.Z. **106** C3
Fécamp France **52** C2
Fehmarn *i.* Ger. **50** C2
Feia, Lagoa *lag.* Brazil **139** D2
Feijó Brazil **134** B3
Feilding N.Z. **106** C3
Feira de Santana Brazil **135** F4
Felanitx Spain **55** D2
Feldberg Ger. **49** F1
Felipe C. Puerto Mex. **129** D3
Felixlândia Brazil **139** D1
Felixstowe U.K. **47** D4
Felsberg Ger. **49** D2
Femunden *l.* Norway **41** C3
Fengcheng *Liaoning* China **69** A1
Fengqing China **66** A1
Fengyüan Taiwan **75** C3
Fengzhen China **73** B1
Feodosiya Ukr. **39** E2
Fer, Cap de *c.* Alg. **56** A2
Fergus Falls U.S.A. **121** D1
Ferkessédougou Côte d'Ivoire
  90 B4
Fermo Italy **56** B2
Fermont Can. **115** D1
Fermoy Rep. of Ireland **45** B2
Fernandina Beach U.S.A.
  128 D2
Fernandópolis Brazil **138** B2
Fernie Can. **112** D3
Ferrara Italy **56** B2
Ferro, Capo *c.* Italy **56** A2
Ferrol Spain **54** B1
Ferwert Neth. **48** B1
Feshi Dem. Rep. Congo **94** B3
Festus U.S.A. **121** E3
Fethiye Turkey **59** C3
Fetlar *i.* U.K. **44** [inset]
Feucht Ger. **49** E3
Feuilles, Rivière aux *r.* Can.
  114 C1
Feyzābād Afgh. **79** B1
Fez Morocco *see* Fès
Fianarantsoa Madag. **97** [inset]
  D2
Fier Albania **59** A2
Fife Ness *pt* U.K. **44** C2
Figeac France **52** C3
Figueira da Foz Port. **54** B1
Figueres Spain **55** D1
Figuig Morocco **90** B1
Fiji *country* S. Pacific Ocean **100**
Fik' Eth. **95** E2
Filadelfia Para. **136** B3
Filchner Ice Shelf Antarctica
  107 A2
Filey U.K. **46** C2
Findhorn *r.* U.K. **44** C2
Findlay U.S.A. **122** D2

Fingal Austr. **103** D4
Finger Lakes U.S.A. **123** E2
Finisterre, Cape Spain **54** B1
Finland *country* Europe **40** F3
Finland, Gulf of Europe **41** E4
Finlay *r.* Can. **112** C2
Finley U.S.A. **105** D3
Finne *ridge* Ger. **49** E2
Finnmarksvidda *reg.* Norway
  40 E2
Finspång Sweden **41** D4
Finsterwalde Ger. **49** F2
Fionnphort U.K. **44** A2
Firenze Italy *see* Florence
Firminy France **53** C2
Firozabad India **79** B2
Firozpur India **78** B1
Firūzābād Iran **85** D3
Fish *watercourse* Namibia **98** A2
Fish *r.* S. Africa **98** B3
Fisher Strait Can. **113** G1
Fishguard U.K. **47** A4
Fisterra, Cabo *c.* Spain *see*
  Finisterre, Cape
Fitchburg U.S.A. **123** F2
Fitzgerald Can. **113** D2
Fitzroy Crossing Austr. **102** B1
Fizi Dem. Rep. Congo **95** C3
Fjällsjöälven *r.* Sweden **40** D3
Flagstaff S. Africa **99** C3
Flagstaff U.S.A. **126** R1
Flaherty Island Can. **114** C1
Flamborough Head U.K. **46** C2
Fläming *hills* Ger. **49** F1
Flaming Gorge Reservoir U.S.A.
  120 B2
Flathead *r.* U.S.A. **118** D1
Flathead Lake U.S.A. **118** D1
Flattery, Cape Austr. **103** D1
Flattery, Cape U.S.A. **118** B1
Fleetwood U.K. **46** B3
Flekkefjord Norway **41** B4
Flensburg Ger. **50** B2
Flers France **52** B2
Flinders *r.* Austr. **103** D1
Flinders Bay Austr. **102** A3
Flinders Island Austr. **103** D3
Flinders Ranges *mts* Austr.
  104 B2
Flin Flon Can. **113** E2
Flint U.S.A. **122** D2
Florac France **55** D1
Florence Italy **56** B2
Florence *AL* U.S.A. **124** C2
Florence *AZ* U.S.A. **126** B2
Florence *OR* U.S.A. **118** B2
Florence *SC* U.S.A. **125** E2
Florencia Col. **134** B2
Flores Guat. **130** B3
Flores *i.* Indon. **65** D2
Flores, Laut *sea* Indon. *see* Flores, Laut
Flores Sea Indon. *see* Flores, Laut
Floresta Brazil **135** F3
Floriano Brazil **135** E3

Florianópolis Brazil **138** C3
Florida Uru. **137** C4
Florida state U.S.A. **125** C2
Florida, Straits of
Bahamas/U.S.A. **130** B2
Florida Keys is U.S.A. **125** D4
Florina Greece **59** B2
Florø Norway **41** B3
Foča Bos.-Herz. **57** C2
Foggia Italy **56** C2
Fogo Island Can. **115** E2
Foix France **52** C3
Fokino Rus. Fed. **37** D3
Foleyet Can. **114** B2
Foligno Italy **56** C2
Folkestone U.K. **47** D4
Folkston U.S.A. **125** D2
Follonica Italy **56** C2
Fond-du-Lac Can. **110** E3
Fond du Lac r. Can. **113** E2
Fond du Lac U.S.A. **122** C2
Fondevila Spain **54** B1
Fondi Italy **56** B2
Fonseca, Golfo de b.
Central America **130** B3
Fonte Boa Brazil **134** C4
Fontenay-le-Comte France
52 B2
Fontur pt Iceland **40** [inset]
Forbes Austr. **105** D2
Forchheim Ger. **49** E3
Førde Norway **41** B3
Fords Bridge Austr. **105** D1
Fordyce U.S.A. **124** B2
Forel, Mt Can. **124** C2
Forest Hill Austr. **105** D3
Forestville Can. **115** D2
Forfar U.K. **44** C2
Forks U.S.A. **118** B1
Forlì Italy **56** C2
Formby U.K. **46** D2
Formentera i. Spain **55** D2
Formentor, Cap de c. Spain
55 D2
Formiga Brazil **139** C2
Formosa Arg. **136** E3
Formosa Brazil **138** C1
Forrest Austr. **102** B3
Forrest City U.S.A. **124** B1
Forssa Fin. **41** E3
Forster Austr. **105** E2
Forsyth U.S.A. **118** E1
Fort Abbas Pak. **78** B2
Fort Albany Can. **114** B1
Fortaleza Brazil **135** F3
Fort Augustus U.K. **44** B2
Fort Benton U.S.A. **118** D1
Fort Bragg U.S.A. **119** B3
Fort Chimo Can. see **Kuujjuaq**
Fort Chipewyan Can. **113** D2
Fort Collins U.S.A. **120** B2
Fort-de-France Martinique
131 D3
Fort Dodge U.S.A. **121** E2

Fort Frances Can. **114** A2
Fort George Can. see **Chisasibi**
Fort Good Hope Can. **110** D2
Forth r. U.K. **44** C2
Forth, Firth of est. U.K. **44** C2
Fort Lauderdale U.S.A. **125** D3
Fort Liard Can. **112** C1
Fort Mackay Can. **113** D2
Fort McMurray Can. **113** D2
Fort Morgan U.S.A. **120** C2
Fort Myers U.S.A. **125** D3
Fort Nelson Can. **112** C2
Fort Nelson r. Can. **112** C2
Fort Payne U.S.A. **125** C2
Fort Peck U.S.A. **120** B1
Fort Peck Reservoir U.S.A.
120 B1
Fort Pierce U.S.A. **125** D3
Fort Providence Can. **112** D1
Fort Qu'Appelle Can. **113** E2
Fort Resolution Can. **112** D1
Fort Rupert Can. see
Waskaganish
Fort Saskatchewan Can. **112** D2
Fort Scott U.S.A. **121** E3
Fort Severn Can. **114** B1
Fort-Shevchenko Kazakh. **80** C2
Fort Simpson Can. **112** C1
Fort Smith Can. **113** D1
Fort Smith U.S.A. **124** B1
Fort St James Can. **112** C2
Fort St John Can. **112** C2
Fort Stockton U.S.A. **127** D2
Fort Sumner U.S.A. **126** C2
Fort Vermilion Can. **112** D2
Fort Walton Beach U.S.A. **124** C2
Fort Wayne U.S.A. **122** C2
Fort William U.K. **44** B2
Fort Worth U.S.A. **127** E2
Fort Yukon U.S.A. **110** C2
Foshan China **75** B3
Fosna pen. Norway **40** C3
Foss Iceland **40** [inset]
Fossá Iceland **40** [inset]
Fossano Italy **56** A2
Foster Austr. **105** D3
Fougères France **52** B2
Foula i. U.K. **44** [inset]
Foumi r. Greece **59** C3
Foveaux Strait N.Z. **106** A4
Fowler U.S.A. **120** C3
Fowlers Bay Austr. **102** C3
Fox Creek Can. **112** D2
Fox Basin g. Can. **111** G2
Foxe Channel Can. **111** G2
Foxe Peninsula Can. **111** G2
Fox Glacier N.Z. **106** B3
Foxton N.Z. **106** C3
Foyle, Lough b.
Rep. of Ireland/U.K. **45** C1
Foz de Areia, Represa de resr
Brazil **138** B3

Foz do Cunene Angola **96** A1
Foz do Iguaçu Brazil **138** B3
Fraga Spain **55** D1
Franca Brazil **138** C2
France country Europe **52** C2
Franceville Gabon **94** B3
Francis Case, Lake U.S.A.
121 D2
Francisco Sá Brazil **139** D1
Francistown Botswana **96** B1
François Lake Can. **112** C2
Frankenberg (Eder) Ger. **49** D2
Frankenhöhe hills Ger. **49** E3
Frankenwald mts Ger. **49** E2
Frankfort U.S.A. **122** D3
Frankfurt am Main Ger. **49** D2
Frankfurt an der Oder Ger.
50 C2
Fränkische Alb hills Ger. **50** C3
Fränkische Schweiz reg. Ger.
49 E3
Franklin D. Roosevelt Lake resr
U.S.A. **118** C1
Franklin Mountains Can. **112** C1
Frantsa-Iosifa, Zemlya is
Rus. Fed. **86** F1
Franz Josef Glacier N.Z. **106** B3
Frasca, Capo della c. Italy
56 A3
Frascati Italy **56** B2
Fraser r. B.C. Can. **112** C3
Fraser r. Nfld. and Lab. Can.
115 D1
Fraserburg S. Africa **98** B3
Fraserburgh U.K. **44** C2
Fraserdale Can. **114** B2
Fraser Island Austr. **103** E2
Fraser Lake Can. **112** C2
Fray Bentos Uru. **137** C4
Fredericia Denmark **41** B4
Frederick U.S.A. **127** E2
Fredericksburg VA U.S.A. **123** E3
Frederick Sound sea chan. U.S.A.
112 B2
Fredericton Can. **111** H3
Frederikshavn Denmark **41** C4
Fredrikstad Norway **41** C4
Freeport IL U.S.A. **122** C2
Freeport TX U.S.A. **127** E3
Freeport City Bahamas **130** C2
Free State prov. S. Africa **99** C2
Freetown Sierra Leone **90** A4
Freiberg Ger. **49** F2
Freiburg im Breisgau Ger. **50** B3
Freising Ger. **50** C3
Freistadt Austria **50** C3
Freital Ger. **49** F2
Fréjus France **53** D3
Fremantle Austr. **102** A3
Fremont NE U.S.A. **121** D2
Fremont OH U.S.A. **122** D2
French Guiana terr. S. America
135 D2
Frenchman r. U.S.A. **118** E1

French Polynesia *terr.*
S. Pacific Ocean **101** D2
Frenda Alg. **55** D2
Fresnillo Mex. **128** B2
Fresno U.S.A. **119** C3
Freu, Cap des *c.* Spain **55** D2
Freyming-Merlebach France
53 D2
Frías Arg. **136** B3
Friedland Ger. **49** F1
Friedrichshafen Ger. **50** B3
Friesack Ger. **49** F1
Friesoythe Ger. **48** C1
Frobisher Bay Can. *see* Iqaluit
Frolovo Rus. Fed. **35** D4
Frome, Lake *salt flat* Austr. **104** B2
Frome Downs Austr. **104** B2
Frontera Mex. **129** C3
Fronteras Mex. **128** B1
Frosinone Italy **56** B2
Frøya *i.* Norway **40** B3
Frýdek-Místek Czech Rep. **51** D3
Fu'an China **75** B3
Fuenlabrada Spain **54** C1
Fuerte Olimpo Para. **136** D3
Fuerteventura *i.* Canary Is **90** A2
Fuga *i.* Phil. **68** B2
Fujairah U.A.E. **83** C2
Fuji Japan **71** C3
Fujian *prov.* China **75** B3
Fuji-san *vol.* Japan **71** C3
Fukui Japan **71** B4
Fukuoka Japan **71** A4
Fukushima Japan **71** D3
Fukuda Ger. **49** D2
Fulda *r.* Ger. **49** D2
Fuling China **75** A3
Fulton U.S.A. **121** E3
Fumay France **53** C2
Funafuti *atoll* Tuvalu **110**
Funchal Madeira **90** A1
Fundy, Bay of *g.* Can. **115** D2
Funhalouro Moz. **99** D1
Funing Yunnan China **75** A3
Funtua Nigeria **91** C3
Fürgun, Küh-e *mt.* Iran **83** C2
Furmanovo Rus. Fed. **37** F2
Furnas, Represa *resr* Brazil
139 C2
Furneaux Group *is* Austr. **103** D4
Fürstenwalde Ger. **49** G1
Fürth Ger. **49** E3
Furth im Wald Ger. **49** F3
Furukawa Japan **70** C3
Fushun China **74** C1
Fusong China **69** B1
Fuwayriṭ Qatar **83** C2
Fuxin China **74** C1
Fuyang China **74** B2
Fuyu China **73** E1
Fuyun China **76** C2
Fuzhou *Fujian* China **75** B3
Fuzhou *Jiangxi* China **75** B3
Fyn *i.* Denmark **41** C4

G

Gaalkacyo Somalia **93** C4
Gabela Angola **96** A1
Gabès Tunisia **91** D1
Gabès, Golfe de *g.* Tunisia **91** D1
Gabgaba, Wadi *watercourse*
Sudan **82** A2
Gabon *country* Africa **94** B3
Gaborone Botswana **99** C1
Gabrovo Bulg. **58** C2
Gadag India **77** B3
Gadebusch Ger. **49** E1
Gadsden U.S.A. **124** C2
Gáeşti Romania **38** C3
Gaeta Italy **56** B2
Gafsa Tunisia **91** C1
Gagarin Rus. Fed. **37** E2
Gagnoa Côte d'Ivoire **90** B4
Gagnon Can. **115** D1
Gagra Georgia **83** C1
Gaiab *watercourse* Namibia **98** A2
Gaillac France **52** C3
Gainesville *FL* U.S.A. **125** D3
Gainesville *GA* U.S.A. **125** D2
Gainesville *TX* U.S.A. **127** E2
Gainsborough U.K. **46** C2
Gairdner, Lake *salt flat* Austr.
104 B2
Gairloch U.K. **44** B2
Galana *r.* Kenya **95** D3
Galapagos Islands Ecuador **132**
Galashiels U.K. **44** C3
Galaţi Romania **38** C2
Galdhøpiggen *mt.* Norway **41** B3
Galena Bay Can. **112** D2
Galera, Punta *pt* Chile **147**
Galesburg U.S.A. **122** B2
Galeshewe S. Africa **98** B2
Galich Rus. Fed. **37** F2
Galichskaya Vozvyshennost' *hills*
Rus. Fed. **37** F2
Galicia *aut. comm.* Spain **54** B1
Galilee, Sea of *l.* Israel **84** B2
Gallatin U.S.A. **125** C1
Galle Sri Lanka **77** C4
Gallinas, Punta *pt* Col. **134** B1
Gallipoli Italy **57** C2
Gallipoli Turkey **59** C2
Gällivare Sweden **40** E2
Gallup U.S.A. **126** C1
Galtat Zemmour Western Sahara
90 A2
Galtymore *h.* Rep. of Ireland
45 B2
Galveston U.S.A. **127** E3
Galveston Bay U.S.A. **127** E3
Galway Rep. of Ireland **45** B2
Galway Bay Rep. of Ireland **45** B2
Gamá Brazil **138** C1

Gamalakhe S. Africa **99** D3
Gambia, The *country* Africa
90 A3
Gambier, Îles *is* Fr. Polynesia
111
Gambier Islands Austr. **104** B3
Gamboma Congo **94** B3
Ganado U.S.A. **126** C1
Ganāveh Iran **85** C3
Gäncä Azer. **85** C1
Gandadiwata, Bukit *mt.* Indon.
65 C2
Gandajika Dem. Rep. Congo
94 C3
Gander Can. **115** E2
Gander *r.* Can. **115** E2
Gandesa Spain **55** D1
Gandhidham India **78** B2
Gandhinagar India **78** B2
Gandhi Sagar *resr* India **78** B2
Gandía Spain **55** C2
Ganga *r.* Bangl./India *see* Ganges
Ganganagar India **78** B2
Gangca China **79** C2
Gangdisê Shan *mts* China
79 C1
Ganges, Mouths of the
Bangl./India **79** C2
Ganges *r.* India **79** C2
Gangtok India **79** C2
Gannett Peak U.S.A. **120** B2
Gansbaai S. Africa **98** A3
Gansu *prov.* China **74** A2
Ganzhou China **75** B3
Gao Mali **90** B3
Gap France **53** D3
Gap Carbon *hd* Alg. **55** C2
Gar China **79** C1
Garah Austr. **105** D1
Garanhuns Brazil **135** F3
Garbahaarrey Somalia **95** E2
Garberville U.S.A. **118** B2
Garbsen Ger. **49** D1
Garça Brazil **138** C2
Garça, Lake Italy **56** B1
Gardelegen Ger. **49** E1
Garden City U.S.A. **120** C3
Gardez Afgh. **78** A1
Gargždai Lith. **36** B2
Gariep Dam *resr* S. Africa
99 C3
Garies S. Africa **98** A3
Garissa Kenya **95** D3
Garmisch-Partenkirchen Ger.
50 C3
Garnpung Lake *imp. l.* Austr.
104 C2
Garonne *r.* France **52** B3
Garoowe Somalia **93** C4
Garoua Cameroon **94** B2
Garry Lake Can. **113** E1
Garsen Kenya **95** E3
Garut Indon. **64** B2
Garut U.S.A. **122** C2
Garza García Mex. **129** B2

Garzê China **72** C2

Gascony, Gulf of France **52** B3

Gascoyne r. Austr. **102** A2

Gashua Nigeria **91** D3

Gaspé Can. **115** D2

Gaspé, Péninsule de pen. Can. **115** D2

Gaston, Lake U.S.A. **125** E1

Gastonia U.S.A. **125** D2

Gata, Cabo de c. Spain **55** C2

Gatchina Rus. Fed. **36** D2

Gateshead U.K. **46** C2

Gatesville U.S.A. **127** E2

Gatineau r. Can. **114** C2

Gatton Austr. **105** E1

Gauer Lake Can. **113** F2

Gausta mt. Norway **41** B4

Gauteng prov. S. Africa **99** C2

Gavdos i. Greece **59** C4

Gävle Sweden **41** D3

Gavrilov-Yam Rus. Fed. **37** E2

Gawai Myanmar **66** A1

Gawler Austr. **104** B2

Gawler Ranges hills Austr. **104** B2

Gaya India **79** C2

Gaya Niger **90** C3

Gaylord U.S.A. **122** D1

Gaza Gaza **84** B2

Gaza terr. Asia **84** B2

Gaz-Achak Turkm. **80** C3

Gazandzhyk Turkm. **80** C3

Gaziantep Turkey **92** B1

Gbarnga Liberia **90** B4

Gdańsk Pol. **51** D2

Gdańsk, Gulf of Pol./Rus. Fed. **51** D2

Gdov Rus. Fed. **36** C2

Gdynia Pol. **51** D2

Gedaref Sudan **92** B3

Gediz r. Turkey **59** C3

Gedser Denmark **50** C2

Geel Belgium **48** B2

Geelong Austr. **104** C3

Geesthacht Ger. **49** E1

Gê'gyai China **79** C1

Geikie r. Can. **110** F3

Geita Tanz. **95** D3

Gejiu China **75** A3

Gela Italy **56** B3

Gelendzhik Rus. Fed. **39** E3

Gelibolu Turkey see Gallipoli

Gelsenkirchen Ger. **48** C2

Gemena Dem. Rep. Congo **94** B2

Gemlik Turkey **59** C2

Gemona del Friuli Italy **53** E2

Genalē Wenz r. Eth. **93** C4

General Acha Arg. **137** B4

General Alvear Arg. **137** B4

General Roca Arg. **137** B4

General Santos Phil. **68** B3

Genesee r. U.S.A. **123** E2

Geneva Switz. **53** D2

Geneva, Lake France/Switz. **53** D2

Genève Switz. see Geneva

Genil r. Spain **54** B2

Genk Belgium **48** B2

Genoa Italy **56** A2

Génova Italy see Genoa

Gent Belgium see Ghent

Genthin Ger. **49** F1

George r. Can. **115** D1

George S. Africa **98** B3

George, Lake FL U.S.A. **125** D3

George, Lake NY U.S.A. **123** F2

Georgetown Guyana **135** D2

George Town Malaysia **64** B1

Georgetown SC U.S.A. **125** E2

Georgetown TX U.S.A. **127** E2

George V Land reg. Antarctica **107** H3

Georgia country Asia **85** C1

Georgia state U.S.A. **125** D2

Georgian Bay Can. **123** D2

Georgina watercourse Austr. **103** C2

Georgiyevka Kazakh. **81** F2

Georgiyevsk Rus. Fed. **35** D4

Gera Ger. **49** F2

Geral, Serra mts Brazil **138** C3

Geraldine N.Z. **106** B3

Geraldton Austr. **102** A2

Gerede Turkey **84** B1

Gereshk Afgh. **78** A1

Gerlachovský štít mt. Slovakia **51** E3

Germany country Europe **50** B2

Gersfeld (Rhön) Ger. **49** D2

Gettysburg SD U.S.A. **120** D1

Gevgelija Macedonia **59** B2

Ghaap Plateau S. Africa **98** B2

Ghadāmis Libya **91** C1

Ghaghara r. India **79** C2

Ghana country Africa **90** B4

Ghanzi Botswana **96** B2

Ghardaïa Alg. **90** C1

Gharyān Libya **91** D1

Ghatal India **79** C2

Ghazaouet Alg. **55** C2

Ghaziabad India **79** B2

Ghazipur India **79** C2

Ghazni Afgh. **78** A1

Ghent Belgium **48** A2

Gherla Romania **38** B2

Ghisonaccia France **53** D3

Giaginskaya Rus. Fed. **39** F3

Giant's Causeway lava field U.K. **45** C1

Giarre Italy **56** C3

Giaveno Italy **56** A1

Gibeon Namibia **98** A2

Gibraltar Gibraltar **54** B2

Gibraltar, Strait of Morocco/Spain **54** B2

Gibson Desert Austr. **102** B2

Gichgeniyn Nuruu mts Mongolia **72** C1

Gidolē Eth. **93** B4

Gien France **52** C2

Gießen Ger. **49** D2

Gifhorn Ger. **49** E1

Gifu Japan **71** C3

Gigha i. U.K. **44** B3

Gijón-Xixón Spain **54** B1

Gila r. U.S.A. **126** B2

Gila Bend U.S.A. **126** B2

Gilbert r. Austr. **103** D1

Gilbert Islands Kiribati **110**

Gildford U.S.A. **118** D1

Gilgandra Austr. **105** D2

Gilgit Jammu and Kashmir **78** B1

Gilgit r. Jammu and Kashmir **78** B1

Gillam Can. **113** F2

Gillette U.S.A. **120** B2

Gillingham U.K. **47** D4

Gilmour Island Can. **114** C1

Gimli Can. **113** F2

Ginir Eth. **93** C4

Ginosa Italy **57** C2

Gippsland reg. Austr. **105** D3

Girdar Dhor r. Pak. **78** A2

Girdi Iran **83** D1

Giresun Turkey **84** B1

Girona Spain **55** D1

Girvan U.K. **44** B3

Gisborne N.Z. **106** C2

Gitarama Rwanda **95** C3

Giulianova Italy **56** B2

Giurgiu Romania **38** C3

Giuvala, Pasul pass Romania **38** C2

Givors France **53** C2

Giyani S. Africa **99** D1

Giza Egypt **92** B2

Gjirokastër Albania **59** B2

Gjoa Haven Can. **110** F2

Gjøvik Norway **41** C3

Glace Bay Can. **115** E2

Glacier Peak vol. U.S.A. **118** B1

Gladstone Austr. **103** E2

Gláma mts Iceland **40** [inset]

Glan r. Ger. **48** C3

Glanaruddery Mountains Rep. of Ireland **45** B2

Glasgow U.K. **44** B3

Glasgow KY U.S.A. **122** C3

Glasgow MT U.S.A. **118** E1

Glauchau Ger. **49** F2

Glazov Rus. Fed. **34** E3

Glazunovka Rus. Fed. **37** E3

Glen Coe val. U.K. **44** B2

Glendale U.S.A. **126** B2

Glendive U.S.A. **120** C1

Glenelg r. Austr. **104** C3

Glen Innes Austr. **105** E1

Glenmorgan Austr. **105** D1

Glennallen U.S.A. **110** C2

Glenrothes U.K. **44** C2

Glens Falls U.S.A. **123** F2

Glen Shee val. U.K. **44** C2

Glenwood U.S.A. **126** C2
Glenwood Springs U.S.A. **120** B3
Gliwice Pol. **51** D2
Globe U.S.A. **126** B2
Głogów Pol. **51** D2
Glomfjord Norway **40** C3
Glomma r. Norway **41** C4
Gloucester Austr. **105** D2
Gloucester U.K. **47** B4
Glubokoye Kazakh. **31** F1
Glückstadt Ger. **49** D1
Gmünd Austria **50** C3
Gmunden Austria **50** C3
Gnarrenburg Ger. **49** D1
Gniezno Pol. **51** D2
Gnjilane S.M. **58** B2
Goalpara India **79** G4
Goba Eth. **93** C4
Gobabis Namibia **98** A1
Gobi *des.* China/Mongolia **74** I1
Goch Ger. **48** C2
Gochas Namibia **98** A1
Godavari r. India **77** C3
Goderich Can. **114** B2
Godhra India **78** B2
Gods r. Can. **113** F2
Gods Lake Can. **113** F2
Godthåb Greenland *see* Nuuk
Godwin Austen *mt.*
  China/Jammu and Kashmir *see*
  K2
Goéland, Lac au *l.* Can. **114** C2
Goélands, Lac aux *l.* Can.
  115 D1
Goes Neth. **48** B3
Goiânia Brazil **138** C1
Goiás Brazil **138** B1
Goio-Erê Brazil **138** B2
Gökçeada *i.* Turkey **59** C2
Gokwe Zimbabwe **97** B1
Gol Norway **41** B3
Golaghat India **66** A4
Gol'chikha Rus. Fed. **34** H1
Gölcük Turkey **59** C2
Gołdap Pol. **51** E2
Goldberg Ger. **49** F1
Gold Coast Austr. **105** E1
Gold Coast *coastal area* Ghana
  90 B4
Golden Can. **112** C2
Golden Bay N.Z. **106** B3
Goldenberg Ger. **50** C2
Golden Hinde *mt.* Can. **112** C3
Goldfield U.S.A. **118** C3
Gold River Can. **112** C3
Goldsboro U.S.A. **125** E1
Goleta U.S.A. **119** C4
Golmud China **72** C1
Golpāyegān Iran **85** D2
Golspie U.K. **44** C2
Goma Dem. Rep. Congo **95** C3
Gomati r. India **79** C2
Gombe Nigeria **91** D3
Gómez Palacio Mex. **128** B2
Gonaïves Haiti **131** C3

Gonbad-e Kavus Iran **85** D2
Gonder Eth. **93** B3
Gondia India **79** C2
Gondomar Port. **54** B1
Gongola r. Nigeria **91** D4
Gongpolgon Austr. **105** D2
Gongzhuling China **69** A1
Gonzáles Mex. **129** C2
Gonzales U.S.A. **127** E3
Good Hope, Cape of S. Africa
  98 A3
Gooding U.S.A. **118** D2
Goodland U.S.A. **120** C3
Goodooga Austr. **105** D1
Goole U.K. **46** C3
Goondiwindi Austr. **105** E1
Goose Lake U.S.A. **118** B2
Gorakhpur India **79** C2
Goražde Bos.-Herz. **57** C2
Goré Chad **91** D4
Gorē Eth. **93** B4
Gore N.Z. **106** A4
Gorey Rep. of Ireland **45** C2
Gorgān Iran **85** D2
Gori Georgia **85** C1
Gorlice Pol. **51** E3
Görlitz Ger. **50** C2
Gornji Vakuf Bos.-Herz. **57** C2
Gorno-Altaysk Rus. Fed. **81** F1
Gornotrakiyska Nizina *lowland*
  Bulg. **56** C2
Gornyak Rus. Fed. **81** F1
Goroka P.N.G. **63** D3
Gorokhovets Rus. Fed. **37** F2
Gorom Gorom Burkina **90** B3
Gorontalo Indon. **65** C1
Gorshechnoye Rus. Fed. **37** E3
Gorumna Island Rep. of Ireland
  45 B2
Goryachiy Klyuch Rus. Fed.
  39 E3
Gorzów Wielkopolski Pol. **50** D2
Gosford Austr. **105** D2
Goshogawara Japan **70** D2
Goslar Ger. **49** E2
Gospić Croatia **56** C2
Gosport U.K. **47** C4
Gostivar Macedonia **58** B2
Göta älv r. Sweden **41** C4
Gotha Ger. **49** E2
Gothenburg Sweden **41** C4
Gothenburg U.S.A. **120** C2
Gotland *i.* Sweden **41** D4
Gotse Delchev Bulg. **59** B2
Gotska Sandön *i.* Sweden **41** D4
Gōtsu Japan **71** B4
Göttingen Ger. **49** D2
Gott Peak Can. **112** C2
Gouda Neth. **48** B2
Gouin, Réservoir *resr* Can.
  114 C2

Goulburn Austr. **105** D2
Goulburn r. N.S.W. Austr.
  105 C3
Goundam Mali **90** B3
Gouraya Alg. **55** D2
Gourdon France **52** C3
Gouré Niger **91** D3
Gourits r. S. Africa **98** B3
Gourma-Rharous Mali **90** B3
Gourock Range *mts* Austr.
  105 D3
Governador Valadares Brazil
  139 D1
Governor's Harbour Bahamas
  125 E3
Govĭ Altayn Nuruu *mts* Mongolia
  72 C2
Gower *pen.* U.K. **47** A4
Goya Arg. **136** C3
Göyçay Azer. **85** C1
Gozha Co *salt l.* China **79** C1
Graaf-Reinet S. Africa **98** B3
Grabow Ger. **49** F1
Grachevka Rus. Fed. **35** C3
Gräfenhainichen Ger. **49** F2
Grafton Austr. **105** E1
Grafton U.S.A. **120** D1
Graham U.S.A. **127** E2
Graham Island Can. **112** B2
Graham Land *reg.* Antarctica
  107 K3
Grahamstown S. Africa **99** C3
Grajaú Brazil **135** E3
Grammos *mt.* Greece **59** B2
Grampian Mountains U.K.
  44 B2
Granada Nic. **130** B3
Granada Spain **54** C2
Granby Can. **123** F1
Gran Canaria *i.* Canary Is **90** A2
Gran Chaco *reg.* Arg./Para.
  136 B3
Grand r. U.S.A. **120** C2
Grand Bahama *i.* Bahamas
  130 C2
Grand Bank Can. **115** E2
Grand Canal China *see* Da Yunhe
Grand Canyon U.S.A. **126** B1
Grand Canyon *gorge* U.S.A.
  126 B1
Grand Cayman *i.* Cayman Is
  130 B3
Grand Coulee U.S.A. **118** C1
Grande r. Bol. **136** B2
Grande r. Brazil **139** B2
Grande, Bahía *b.* Arg. **137** B6
Grande, Ilha *i.* Brazil **139** D2
Grande Cache Can. **112** D2
Grande Comore *i.* Comoros *see*
  Njazidja
Grande Prairie Can. **112** D2
Grand Erg de Bilma *des.* Niger
  91 D3

Grand Erg Occidental *des.* Alg.
90 B1
Grand Erg Oriental *des.* Alg.
91 D2
Grande-Rivière Can. **115** D2
Grand Falls *N.B.* Can. **123** D4
Grand Falls *Nfld. and Lab.* Can.
115 D2
Grand Forks Can. **112** D3
Grand Forks U.S.A. **121** D1
Grandin, Lac *l.* Can. **112** D1
Grand Island U.S.A. **121** C3
Grand Isle U.S.A. **124** B3
Grand Junction U.S.A. **120** B3
Grand-Lahou Côte d'Ivoire **90** B4
Grand Lake *N.B.* Can. **115** D2
Grand Lake *Nfld. and Lab.* Can.
115 D2
Grand Marais U.S.A. **121** E1
Grândola Port. **54** B2
Grand Rapids Can. **113** F2
Grand Rapids *MI* U.S.A. **122** C2
Grand Rapids *MN* U.S.A. **121** E1
Grand Teton *mt.* U.S.A. **120** A2
Grand Turk Turks and Caicos Is
131 D2
Grangeville U.S.A. **118** C1
Granite Peak U.S.A. **118** E1
Granitola, Capo *c.* Italy **56** B3
Gränna Sweden **41** C4
Gransee Ger. **49** F1
Grantham U.K. **46** C3
Grantown-on-Spey U.K. **44** C2
Grants U.S.A. **126** C1
Grants Pass U.S.A. **118** B2
Granville France **52** B2
Granville Lake Can. **113** C2
Grão Mogol Brazil **139** D1
Grarem Alg. **55** E2
Graskop S. Africa **99** D1
Grasse France **52** D3
Grave, Pointe de *pt* France
52 B2
Gravesend Austr. **105** E1
Gravesend U.K. **44** B3
Graz Austria **51** D3
Great Abaco *i.* Bahamas **131** C2
Great Australian Bight *g.* Austr.
102 B3
Great Barrier Island N.Z. **106** C2
Great Barrier Reef Austr. **103** D1
Great Basin U.S.A. **119** C3
Great Bear Lake Can. **112** D1
Great Belt *sea chan.* Denmark
41 C4
Great Bend U.S.A. **121** D3
Great Coco Island Cocos Is
67 A2
Great Dividing Range *mts* Austr.
105 C3
Greater Antilles *is* Caribbean Sea
130 B2
Great Falls U.S.A. **118** D1
Great Fish *r.* S. Africa **99** C3

Great Fish Point S. Africa **99** C3
Great Inagua *i.* Bahamas **131** C2
Great Karoo *plat.* S. Africa **98** B3
Great Kei *r.* S. Africa **99** C3
Great Malvern U.K. **47** B3
Great Namaqualand *reg.* Namibia
98 A2
Great Nicobar *i.* India **67** A3
Great Ouse *r.* U.K. **47** D3
Great Plains *reg.* U.S.A. **121**
Great Rift Valley Africa **95** D3
Great Ruaha *r.* Tanz. **95** D4
Great Salt Lake U.S.A. **118** D2
Great Salt Lake Desert U.S.A.
118 D2
Great Sand Sea *des.* Egypt/Libya
92 A2
Great Sandy Desert Austr.
102 B2
Great Slave Lake Can. **112** D1
Great Smoky Mountains U.S.A.
125 D1
Great Victoria Desert Austr.
102 B2
Great Yarmouth U.K. **47** D3
Gredos, Sierra de *mts* Spain
54 C3
Greece *country* Europe **59** B3
Greeley U.S.A. **120** C2
Greem-Bell, Ostrov *i.* Rus. Fed.
86 G1
Green *r.* Can. **122** G1
Green *r.* *KY* U.S.A. **125** C1
Green *r.* *WY* U.S.A. **120** B3
Green Bay U.S.A. **122** C2
Green Bay *b.* U.S.A. **122** C1
Greenbrier *r.* U.S.A. **123** D3
Greeneville U.S.A. **125** D1
Greenfield U.S.A. **123** F2
Green Lake Can. **113** E2
Greenland *terr.* N. America
111 J2
Greenland Sea
Greenland/Svalbard **86** B1
Greenock U.K. **44** B3
Green River *UT* U.S.A. **119** D3
Green River U.S.A. **120** B3
Greensburg *PA* U.S.A. **123** E2
Green Swamp U.S.A. **125** E2
Green Valley U.S.A. **126** B2
Greenville Liberia **90** B4
Greenville *AL* U.S.A. **124** C2
Greenville *MS* U.S.A. **124** B2
Greenville *NC* U.S.A. **125** E1
Greenville *SC* U.S.A. **125** D2
Greenville *TX* U.S.A. **127** C2
Greenwell Point Austr. **105** E2
Greenwood U.S.A. **125** D2
Gregory, Lake *salt flat* Austr.
102 B2
Gregory Range *hills* Austr.
103 D1
Greifswald Ger. **50** C2
Greiz Ger. **49** F2

Grená Denmark **41** C4
Grenada U.S.A. **124** C2
Grenada *country* West Indies
131 D3
Grenfell Austr. **105** D2
Grenfell Can. **113** E2
Grenoble France **52** D3
Grenville, Cape U.S.A. **103** D1
Gresham U.S.A. **118** B1
Greven Ger. **48** C1
Grevena Greece **59** B2
Grevenbroich Ger. **48** C2
Greybull U.S.A. **120** B2
Grey Hunter Peak Can. **112** B1
Grey Islands Can. **115** E1
Greymouth N.Z. **106** B3
Grey Range *hills* Austr. **104** C1
Greystones Rep. of Ireland **45** C1
Gribanovskiy Rus. Fed. **39** F1
Griffin U.S.A. **125** D2
Griffith Austr. **105** D2
Grimma Ger. **49** F2
Grimmen Ger. **50** C2
Grimsby U.K. **46** C3
Grimshaw Can. **112** D2
Grímsstaðir Iceland **40** [inset]
Griqualand East *reg.* S. Africa
99 C3
Griqualand West *reg.* S. Africa
98 B3
Grise Fiord Can. **111** G1
Groblersdal S. Africa **99** C2
Groblershoop S. Africa **98** B2
Groix, Île de *i.* France **52** B2
Gronau (Westfalen) Ger. **48** C1
Grong Norway **40** C3
Groningen Neth. **48** C1
Grootdrink Austr. **103** C1
Grootfontein Namibia **96** A1
Groot Karas Berg *plat.* Namibia
98 A2
Groot Swartberge S. Africa
98 B3
Groot Winterberg *mt.* S. Africa
99 C3
Großer Rachel *mt.* Ger. **49** F3
Grosser Speikkogel *mt.* Austria
50 C3
Grosseto Italy **56** D3
Groß-Gerau Ger. **49** D3
Großglockner *mt.* Austria **50** C3
Groß-Hesepe Ger. **48** C1
Gross Ums Namibia **98** A1
Groswater Bay Can. **115** E1
Groundhog *r.* Can. **114** B2
Grover Beach U.S.A. **119** B3
Groznyy Rus. Fed. **35** D4
Grudziądz Pol. **51** D2
Grünau Namibia **98** A2
Grundarfjörður Iceland **40** [inset]
Gryazi Rus. Fed. **37** E3
Gryazovets Rus. Fed. **37** F3
Gryfice Pol. **50** C2
Gryfino Pol. **50** C2

Grytviken S. Georgia **137** E6
Guacanayabo, Golfo de b. Cuba **130** C2
Guadalajara Mex. **128** B2
Guadalcanal i. Solomon Is **110**
Guadalquivir r. Spain **54** D5
Guadalupe i. Mex. **116** B4
Guadalupe, Sierra de mts Spain **54** B2
Guadalupe Peak U.S.A. **126** D2
Guadalupe Victoria Mex. **128** B2
Guadarrama, Sierra de mts Spain **54** C1
Guadeloupe terr. West Indies **131** D3
Guadiana r. Port./Spain **54** B4
Guadix Spain **54** C2
Guaira Brazil **138** E2
Guajira, Península de la pen. Col. **131** C3
Guam terr. N. Pacific Ocean **63** D2
Guamuchil Mex. **128** B2
Guanambi Brazil **135** E4
Guanare Venez. **134** C2
Guane Cuba **130** B2
Guang'an China **75** B3
Guangchang China **75** B3
Guangdong prov. China **75** B3
Guangxi Zhuangzu Zizhiqu aut. reg. China **75** A3
Guangyuan China **74** A2
Guangzhou China **75** B3
Guanling China **75** A3
Guantánamo Cuba **131** C2
Guaporé r. Bol./Brazil **136** B2
Guarapuava Brazil **138** B3
Guaraqueçaba Brazil **138** C3
Guaratingueta Brazil **139** C2
Guarda Port. **54** B1
Guarujá Brazil **139** C2
Guasave Mex. **128** B2
Guatemala country Central America **130** A3
Guatemala City Guat. **130** A3
Guaviare r. Col. **134** C2
Guayaquil Ecuador **134** B3
Guayaquil, Golfo de g. Ecuador **146**
Guayaramerín Bol. **136** B2
Guaymas Mex. **128** A2
Guba Eth. **93** B3
Guba Dolgaya Rus. Fed. **34** E1
Gubbio Italy **53** E1
Gubkin Rus. Fed. **37** E3
Guelmine Morocco **90** A2
Guelph Can. **114** B2
Guémez Mex. **129** C2
Guéret France **52** E3
Guernsey i. Channel Is **47** B5
Guerrero Negro Mex. **128** A2
Guers, Lac l. Can. **115** D1
Guiana Highlands mts Guyana/Venez. **134** C2

Guider Cameroon **94** B3
Guidonia-Montecelio Italy **56** B2
Guigang China **75** A3
Guignicourt France **48** A3
Guija Moz. **99** D1
Guildford U.K. **47** D3
Guilin China **75** B3
Guillaume-Delisle, Lac l. Can. **114** C1
Guimarães Port. **54** B1
Guinea country Africa **90** A3
Guinea, Gulf of **90** C4
Guinea-Bissau country Africa **90** A3
Guingamp France **52** B2
Guiratinga Brazil **138** B1
Güiria Venez. **134** C1
Guiyang China **75** A3
Guizhou prov. China **75** A3
Gujranwala Pak. **78** B1
Gujrat Pak. **78** B1
Gukovo Rus. Fed. **39** E2
Gulang China **74** A2
Gulargambone Austr. **105** D2
Gulbarga India **77** B3
Gulbene Latvia **36** C2
Gulfport U.S.A. **124** C2
Gulian China **73** E1
Guliston Uzbek. **81** D2
Gul'kevichi Rus. Fed. **39** F2
Gull Lake Can. **113** E2
Gulu Uganda **95** D2
Gumare Botswana **98** B1
Gumdag Turkm. **80** C2
Gummersbach Ger. **48** C2
Guna India **78** B2
Gundagai Austr. **105** D3
Gungu Dem. Rep. Congo **94** B3
Gunisao r. Can. **113** F2
Gunnedah Austr. **105** E2
Gunnison CO U.S.A. **120** B3
Gunnison UT U.S.A. **119** D3
Gunnison r. U.S.A. **120** B3
Guntakal India **77** B3
Gunungsitoli Indon. **64** A1
Gunungtua Indon. **64** A1
Günzburg Ger. **50** C3
Gunzenhausen Ger. **49** E3
Guojiaba China **74** B2
Gurgaon India **78** B2
Gurguéia r. Brazil **135** E3
Guri, Embalse de resr Venez. **134** C2
Gurinhatã Brazil **138** C1
Gurupi r. Brazil **135** E3
Gusau Nigeria **91** C3
Gushan China **69** A2
Gushgy Turkm. **78** A1
Gus'-Khrustal'nyy Rus. Fed. **37** F2
Guspini Italy **56** A3
Gustavus U.S.A. **112** B2

Güstrow Ger. **49** F1
Gütersloh Ger. **49** D2
Guwahati India **79** D2
Guyana country S. America **134** D2
Guymon U.S.A. **127** D1
Guyra Austr. **105** E2
Guyuan China **74** A2
Guzmán Mex. **128** B1
Guzmán, Lago de l. Mex. **128** B1
Gwadar Pak. **78** A2
Gwalior India **79** B2
Gwanda Zimbabwe **97** C2
Gwardafuy, Gees c. Somalia **93** D3
Gweebarra Bay Rep. of Ireland **45** B1
Gweedore Rep. of Ireland **45** B1
Gweru Zimbabwe **97** B1
Gwydir r. Austr. **105** E2
Gyangzê China **79** C2
Gyaring Co l. China **79** C1
Gyaring Hu l. China **72** C1
Gydan Peninsula Rus. Fed. **34** G1
Gydanskiy Poluostrov pen. Rus. Fed. see Gydan Peninsula
Gyigang China **66** A1
Gympie Austr. **105** E1
Gyöngyös Hungary **51** D3
Győr Hungary **51** D3
Gypsumville Can. **113** F2
Gyrfalcon Islands Can. **115** D1
Gyula Hungary **51** E3
Gyumri Armenia **85** C1
Gyzylarbat Turkm. **80** C2

H

Haapsalu Estonia **36** B2
Haarlem Neth. **48** B1
Haarstrang ridge Ger. **49** C2
Haast N.Z. **106** A3
Habbān Yemen **82** B3
Ḩabbānīyah, Hawr al l. Iraq **85** C2
Hachijō-jima i. Japan **71** C4
Hachinohe Japan **70** D2
Hacufera Moz. **97** C2
Hadd, Ra's al pt Oman **83** C2
Hadejia Nigeria **91** D3
Haderslev Denmark **41** B4
Hadyach Ukr. **39** D1
Haeju N. Korea **69** B2
Haeju-man b. N. Korea **69** B2
Haenam S. Korea **69** B3
Ḩafar al Bāţin Saudi Arabia **82** B2
Haflong India **66** A1
Hagar Nish Plateau Eritrea **82** A3
Hagåtña Guam **63** D2
Hagen Ger. **48** C2

Hagenow Ger. **49** E1
Hagensberg Can. **112** C2
Hagerstown U.S.A. **123** E3
Hagfors Sweden **41** C3
Hagi Japan **71** B4
Ha Giang Vietnam **66** B1
Hag's Head Rep. of Ireland **45** B2
Hague, Cap de la France **52** B2
Haicheng China **69** A1
Hai Duong Vietnam **66** B1
Haifa Israel **84** B2
Haikou China **75** B3
Hāʼil Saudi Arabia **82** B2
Hailar China see Hulun Buir
Hailuoto i. Fin. **40** E2
Hainan i. China **73** D3
Hainan prov. China **75** A4
Hainich ridge Ger. **49** E2
Hainleite ridge Ger. **49** E2
Hai Phong Vietnam **66** B1
Haiti country West Indies **131** C3
Haiya Sudan **92** B3
Hajdúböszörmény Hungary
51 E3
Hajhir mt. Yemen **83** C3
Hajjah Yemen **82** B3
Ḩājjīābād Iran **85** D3
Hajmā' Oman **83** C3
Haka Myanmar **66** A1
Hakkâri Turkey **85** C2
Hakodate Japan **70** D2
Halab Syria see Aleppo
Halabān Saudi Arabia **82** B2
Halaib Sudan **92** B3
Ḩalāniyāt, Juzur al is Oman
83 C3
Halban Mongolia **72** C1
Halberstadt Ger. **49** E2
Halcon, Mount Phil. **68** B3
Halden Norway **41** C4
Haldensleben Ger. **49** E1
Haldwani India **79** B2
Hāleh Iran **83** C2
Halfmoon Bay N.Z. **106** A4
Halifax Can. **115** D2
Halifax U.K. **46** C3
Halla-san mt. S. Korea **69** B3
Hall Beach Can. **111** G2
Halle Belgium **48** B2
Hallein Austria **50** C3
Halle (Saale) Ger. **49** E2
Hallock U.S.A. **121** D1
Halls Creek Austr. **102** C3
Halmahera i. Indon. **63** C2
Halmstad Sweden **41** C4
Ham France **48** A3
Hamada Japan **71** B4
Hamadān Iran **85** C2
Ḩamāh Syria **84** B2
Hamamatsu Japan **71** C4
Hamar Norway **41** C3

Ḩamāţah, Jabal mt. Egypt **92** B2
Hambantota Sri Lanka **77** C4
Hamburg Ger. **49** D1
Ḩamḑ, Wādī al watercourse
Saudi Arabia **82** A2
Ḩamḑah Saudi Arabia **82** B2
Hämeenlinna Fin. **41** E3
Hameln Ger. **49** D1
Hamersley Range mts Austr.
102 A2
Hamhŭng N. Korea **69** B2
Hami China **72** C2
Hamid Sudan **92** B2
Hamilton Austr. **104** C3
Hamilton Can. **114** C2
Hamilton N.Z. **106** C2
Hamilton U.K. **44** B3
Hamilton AL U.S.A. **124** C2
Hamilton MT U.S.A. **118** D1
Hamilton OH U.S.A. **122** D3
Hamina Fin. **41** F3
Hamm Ger. **49** C2
Hammada du Drâa plat. Alg.
90 B2
Ḩammār, Hawr al imp. l. Iraq
85 C2
Hammelburg Ger. **49** D2
Hammerdal Sweden **40** D3
Hammerfest Norway **40** E1
Hammond U.S.A. **124** C2
Hammonton U.S.A. **123** F3
Hāmūn-e Jaz Mūriān salt marsh
Iran **83** C2
Hāmūn-i-Lora dry lake Afgh./Pak.
78 A2
Hāmūn-i-Mashkel salt flat Iran
83 C2
Hamun-i-Mashkel salt flat Pak.
78 A2
Hanak Saudi Arabia **82** A2
Hanamaki Japan **70** D3
Hanau Ger. **49** D2
Hancheng China **74** B2
Handan China **74** B2
Hanford U.S.A. **119** C3
Hangayn Nuruu mts Mongolia
72 C1
Hangzhou China **75** C2
Hangzhou Wan b. China **74** C2
Hanko Fin. **41** E4
Hanksville U.S.A. **119** D3
Hanmer Springs N.Z. **106** B3
Hanna Can. **112** C2
Hannibal U.S.A. **121** E3
Hannover Ger. **49** D1
Hannoversch Münden Ger.
49 D2
Hanöbukten b. Sweden **41** C4
Ha Nôi Vietnam **66** B1
Hanoi Vietnam see Ha Nôi
Hanover S. Africa **98** B3
Hantsavichy Belarus **36** C4
Hanumana India **79** C2
Hanumangarh India **78** B2

Hanzhong China **74** A2
Hao atoll Fr. Polynesia **111**
Haparanda Sweden **40** E2
Happy Valley - Goose Bay Can.
115 D1
Haql Saudi Arabia **82** A2
Ḩaraḑh Saudi Arabia **83** B3
Haradok Belarus **36** C2
Harare Zimbabwe **97** C1
Ḩarāsīs, Jiddat al des. Oman
83 C3
Har-Ayrag Mongolia **73** D1
Harbin China **73** E1
Harbour Breton Can. **115** E2
Harda India **78** B2
Hardangerfjorden sea chan.
Norway **41** B4
Harderwijk Neth. **48** B1
Hardeveld mts S. Africa **98** A3
Hardin U.S.A. **118** E1
Hardisty Lake Can. **112** D1
Hardwar (Emes) Ger. **48** C1
Härer Eth. **93** C4
Hargeysa Somalia **93** C4
Harghita-Mădăraş, Vârful mt.
Romania **38** C2
Hari Rūd r. Afgh./Iran **78** A1
Harlingen Neth. **48** B1
Harlingen U.S.A. **127** E3
Harlow U.K. **47** D4
Harlowton U.S.A. **118** E1
Harnes France **48** A3
Harney Basin U.S.A. **118** C2
Harney Lake U.S.A. **118** C2
Härnösand Sweden **41** D3
Har Nuur l. Mongolia **72** C1
Harper Liberia **90** B4
Harricanaw r. Can. **114** C1
Harrington Austr. **105** E2
Harrington Harbour Can. **115** E1
Harris pen. U.K. **44** A2
Harris, Lake salt flat Austr.
104 B2
Harris, Sound of sea chan. U.K.
44 A2
Harrisburg IL U.S.A. **122** C3
Harrisburg PA U.S.A. **123** E2
Harrismith S. Africa **99** C2
Harrison U.S.A. **124** B1
Harrison, Cape U.S.A. **115** E1
Harrison Bay U.S.A. **110** B2
Harrisonburg U.S.A. **123** E3
Harrisonville U.S.A. **121** E3
Harrogate U.K. **46** C3
Hârşova Romania **38** C3
Harstad Norway **40** D2
Hartbees watercourse S. Africa
98 B2
Hartford U.S.A. **123** F2
Hartland Point U.K. **47** A4
Hartlepool U.K. **46** C3
Hartley Bay Can. **112** C2
Harts r. S. Africa **99** C2
Hartwell Reservoir U.S.A. **125** D2

ar Us Nuur l. Mongolia **72** C1
Harvey U.S.A. **120** C1
Harwich U.K. **47** D4
Harz hills Ger. **49** C2
Hasselt Belgium **48** B2
Hassleholm Sweden **41** C4
Hastings Austr. **105** D3
Hastings N.Z. **106** C2
Hastings U.K. **47** D4
Hastings MN U.S.A. **121** E2
Hastings NE U.S.A. **121** D2
Hatay Turkey see Antakya
Hatchet Lake Can. **113** E2
Hatfield Austr. **104** C2
Hatgal Mongolia **72** C1
Ha Tinh Vietnam **66** B2
Hatteras, Cape U.S.A. **125** E1
Hattiesburg U.S.A. **124** C2
Hat Yai Thai. **67** B3
Haud reg. Eth. **93** C4
Haugesund Norway **41** B4
Haukeligrend Norway **41** B4
Haukraki Gulf N.Z. **106** C2
Hauterive Can. **115** D2
Havana Cuba **130** B2
Havant U.K. **47** C4
Havel r. Ger. **49** F1
Havelberg Ger. **49** F1
Havelock N.Z. **106** B3
Havelock North N.Z. **106** C2
Haverfordwest U.K. **47** A4
Havlíčkův Brod Czech Rep. **51** D3
Havøysund Norway **40** E1
Havre U.S.A. **118** E1
Havre Aubert Can. **115** D2
Havre-St-Pierre Can. **115** D1
Hawaii i. U.S.A. **120**
Hawaiian Islands
  N. Pacific Ocean **142** E3
Hawea, Lake N.Z. **106** A3
Hawera N.Z. **106** B2
Hawick U.K. **44** C3
Hawke Bay N.Z. **106** C2
Hawker Austr. **104** B2
Hawkers Gate Austr. **104** C1
Hawthorne U.S.A. **119** C3
Hay Austr. **104** C2
Hay r. Can. **112** D1
Haydon U.S.A. **118** C1
Hayes r. Man. Can. **113** F2
Hayes r. Nunavut Can. **111** F2
Haytboshi tog'i mt. Uzbek.
  81 D2
Hayrabolu Turkey **59** C2
Hay River Can. **112** D1
Hays U.S.A. **121** D3
Hays Yemen **82** B3
Haysyn Ukr. **38** C2
Haywards Heath U.K. **47** C4
Hazarajat reg. Afgh. **78** A1
Hazard U.S.A. **122** D3
Hazaribagh India **79** C2
Hazaribagh Range mts India
  79 C2

Hazebrouck France **48** A2
Hazelton Can. **112** C2
Healesville Austr. **105** D3
Hearst Can. **114** B2
Hebei prov. China **74** B2
Hebel Austr. **105** D1
Heber Springs U.S.A. **124** B1
Hebi China **74** B2
Hebron Can. **115** D1
Hecate Strait Can. **112** B2
Hechi China **75** A3
Hede Sweden **41** C3
Heerenveen Neth. **48** B1
Heerhugowaard Neth. **48** B1
Heerlen Neth. **48** B2
Hefa Israel see Haifa
Hefei China **74** B2
Hefeng China **75** B3
Hegang China **73** E1
Heide Ger. **50** B2
Heidelberg Ger. **49** D3
Heilbronn Ger. **49** D3
Heilongjiang prov. China **70** B1
Heilong Jiang r. China **73** E1
Heinola Fin. **41** F3
Helagsfjället mt. Sweden **40** C3
Helena AR U.S.A. **124** B2
Helena MT U.S.A. **118** D1
Helensburgh U.K. **44** B2
Helgoland i. Ger. **50** B2
Helgoländer Bucht g. Ger. **50** B2
Hella Iceland **40** [inset]
Hellevoetsluis Neth. **48** B2
Hellín Spain **55** C2
Helmand r. Afgh. **78** A1
Helmbrechts Ger. **49** E2
Helmeringhausen Namibia **98** A2
Helmond Neth. **48** B2
Helmsdale U.K. **44** C1
Helmsdale r. U.K. **44** C1
Helmstedt Ger. **49** E1
Helong China **69** B1
Helsingborg Sweden **41** C4
Helsingfors Fin. see Helsinki
Helsingør Denmark **41** C4
Helsinki Fin. **41** F3
Helvick Head Rep. of Ireland
  45 C2
Hemel Hempstead U.K. **47** C4
Hemnesberget Norway **40** C2
Henan prov. China **74** B2
Henderson KY U.S.A. **122** C3
Henderson NC U.S.A. **125** E1
Henderson NV U.S.A. **119** D3
Henderson TX U.S.A. **127** F2
Hendon U.K. **47** C4
Hengduan Shan mts China **66** A1
Hengelo Neth. **48** C1
Hengshui China **74** B2
Hengxian China **75** A3
Hengyang China **75** B3
Heniches'k Ukr. **39** D2
Henrietta Maria, Cape Can.
  114 B1

Henry Kater, Cape Can.
  111 H2
Henstedt-Ulzburg Ger. **49** D1
Hentiesbaai Namibia **96** A2
Hepu China **75** A3
Herāt Afgh. **78** A1
Herbert Can. **113** E2
Hereford U.K. **47** B3
Hereford U.S.A. **127** D2
Herford Ger. **49** D1
Herma Ness hd U.K. **44** [inset]
Hermanus S. Africa **98** A3
Hermidale Austr. **105** D2
Hermiston U.S.A. **118** C1
Hermit Islands P.N.G. **63** D3
Hermosillo Mex. **128** A2
Hernandarias Para. **138** B3
Herne Ger. **48** C2
Herning Denmark **41** B4
Herrieden Ger. **49** E3
Hertford U.K. **47** C4
Hervey Bay Austr. **103** E2
Herzberg Ger. **49** F2
Herzesprung Ger. **49** E3
Heshan China **75** A3
Hess r. Can. **112** B1
Hesselberg h. Ger. **49** E3
Hessisch Lichtenau Ger. **49** D2
Hettinger U.S.A. **120** C1
Hettstedt Ger. **49** E2
Hexham U.K. **46** B2
Heyuan China **75** B3
Heywood Austr. **104** C3
Heze China **74** B2
Hezhou China **75** B3
Hiawatha U.S.A. **121** D3
Hibbing U.S.A. **121** E1
Hicks Bay N.Z. **106** C2
Hidaka-sanmyaku mts Japan
  70 D2
Hidalgo del Parral Mex.
  128 B2
Hidrolândia Brazil **138** C1
High Desert U.S.A. **118** B2
High Level Can. **112** D2
High Point U.S.A. **125** E1
High Prairie Can. **112** D2
High River Can. **112** D2
Highrock Lake Can. **113** E2
High Wycombe U.K. **47** C4
Hiiumaa i. Estonia **36** B2
Híjar reg. Saudi Arabia **82** A2
Hikurangi mt. N.Z. **106** C2
Hildburghausen Ger. **49** E2
Hildesheim Ger. **49** D1
Hillah Iraq **85** C2
Hillsboro TX U.S.A. **127** E2
Hillston Austr. **105** D2
Hilton Head Island U.S.A.
  125 D2
Hilversum Neth. **48** B1
Himalaya mts Asia **79** B1
Himeji Japan **71** B4
Himeville S. Africa **99** C3

Hinchinbrook Island Austr. **103** D1
Hindu Kush *mts* Afgh./Pak. **78** A1
Hinesville U.S.A. **125** D2
Hinganghat India **79** C2
Hinis Turkey **85** C2
Hinnøya i. Norway **40** D2
Hinthada Myanmar **66** A2
Hinton Can. **112** D2
Hirakud Reservoir India **79** C2
Hirosaki Japan **70** D2
Hiroshima Japan **71** B4
Hirschberg Ger. **49** E2
Hirson France **53** C2
Hisar India **78** B2
Hispaniola i. Caribbean Sea **131** C2
Hit Iraq **85** C2
Hitachi Japan **71** D3
Hitachinaka Japan **71** D3
Hitra i. Norway **40** B3
Hiva Oa i. Fr. Polynesia **111**
Hjälmaren l. Sweden **41** D4
Hjalmar Lake Can. **113** E1
Hjørring Denmark **41** C4
Hlabisa S. Africa **99** D2
Hliŏ Iceland **40** [inset]
Hlobyne Ukr. **39** D2
Hlukhiv Ukr. **39** D1
Hlotse Lesotho **99** C2
Hlybokaye Belarus **36** C2
Ho Ghana **90** C4
Hoachanas Namibia **98** A1
Hobart Austr. **103** D4
Hobart U.S.A. **127** E1
Hobbs U.S.A. **127** D2
Hobro Denmark **41** B4
Hobyo Somalia **93** C4
Hoceima, Baie d'Al b. Morocco **54** C2
Hồ Chí Minh City Vietnam **67** B2
Hồd reg. Maur. **90** B3
Hodeidah Yemen **82** B3
Hódmezóvásárhely Hungary **51** E3
Hodna, Chott el salt l. Alg. **55** D2
Hoek van Holland Neth. see
  Hook of Holland
Hoeyang N. Korea **69** B2
Hof Ger. **49** F2
Höfn Austurland Iceland **40** [inset]
Höfn Vestfirðir Iceland **40** [inset]
Hofsjökull ice cap Iceland
  40 [inset]
Hófu Japan **71** B4
Hoggar plat. Alg. **91** C2
Högsby Sweden **41** D4
Hegste Breakulen mt. Norway
  41 B3
Hohe Rhön reg. Ger. **49** D2
Hohe Venn moorland Belgium
  48 C2
Hohhot China **74** B1
Hoh Xil Shan mts China **79** C1

Hội An Vietnam **67** B2
Hojai India **66** A1
Hokitika N.Z. **106** B3
Hokkaidō i. Japan **70** D2
Holbæk Denmark **41** C4
Holbrook U.S.A. **126** B2
Holdrege U.S.A. **121** D2
Holguín Cuba **131** C2
Hóll Iceland **40** [inset]
Holland U.S.A. **122** C2
Hollum Neth. **48** B1
Holly Springs U.S.A. **124** C2
Hollywood CA U.S.A. **119** C4
Hollywood FL U.S.A. **125** D3
Holm Norway **40** C2
Holman Can. **110** E2
Holmsund Sweden **40** E3
Holoog Namibia **98** A2
Holstebro Denmark **41** B4
Holston r. U.S.A. **125** D1
Holyhead U.K. **46** A3
Holy Island England U.K. **46** C2
Holy Island Wales U.K. **46** A3
Holyoke U.S.A. **120** C2
Holzminden Ger. **49** D2
Homberg (Efze) Ger. **49** D2
Hombori Mali **90** B3
Homburg Ger. **48** C3
Home Bay Can. **111** H2
Homestead U.S.A. **125** D3
Homs Syria **84** B2
Homyel' Belarus **37** D2
Hondeklipbaai S. Africa **98** A3
Hondo r. Belize/Mex. **129** D3
Hondo U.S.A. **127** E3
Honduras country
  Central America **130** B3
Hønefoss Norway **41** C3
Honey Lake salt l. U.S.A. **118** B2
Hồng Gai Vietnam **66** B1
Honghu China **75** B3
Hongjiang China **75** A3
Hong Kong China **75** B3
Hong Kong aut. reg. China **75** B3
Hongwón N. Korea **69** B1
Hongze Hu l. China **74** B2
Honiara Solomon Is **100**
Honjō Japan **71** D3
Honningsvåg Norway **40** F1
Honshū i. Japan **71** B3
Hood, Mount U.S.A. **118** B1
Hood Point Austr. **102** A3
Hood River U.S.A. **118** B1
Hoogeveen Neth. **48** C1
Hoogezand-Sappemeer Neth.
  48 C1
Hook of Holland Neth. **48** B2
Hoonah U.S.A. **112** B2
Hoorn Neth. **48** B1
Hoorn, Îles de is
  Wallis and Futuna Is **111**
Hope Can. **112** C3
Hope U.S.A. **124** B2
Hopedale Can. **115** D1
Hope Mountains Can. **115** D1
Hopetoun Austr. **104** C3

Hopetown S. Africa **98** B2
Hopewell U.S.A. **123** E3
Hopewell Islands Can. **114** C1
Hopkins, Lake salt flat Austr.
  102 B2
Hopkinsville U.S.A. **122** C3
Horasan Turkey **85** C1
Horažďovice Czech Rep. **49** F3
Horki Belarus **37** D3
Horlivka Ukr. **39** E2
Hormak Iran **83** D2
Hormuz, Strait of Iran/Oman
  83 C2
Horn c. Iceland **40** [inset]
Horn, Cape Chile **137** B6
Hornell U.S.A. **123** E2
Hornsea U.K. **46** C3
Horodenka Ukr. **38** C2
Horodnya Ukr. **39** D1
Horodok Khmel'nyts'ka Oblast' Ukr.
  38 C2
Horodok L'viv's'ka Oblast' Ukr.
  38 B2
Horokhiv Ukr. **38** B1
Horse Islands Can. **115** E1
Horsham Austr. **104** C3
Horton r. Can. **110** D2
Hosa'ina Eth. **93** B4
Hoshab Pak. **78** A2
Hoshiarpur India **78** B1
Hotan China **79** C1
Hotazel S. Africa **98** B2
Hot Springs AR U.S.A. **124** B2
Hot Springs SD U.S.A. **120** C2
Hottah Lake Can. **112** D1
Houma China **74** B2
Houma U.S.A. **124** B3
Houston Can. **112** C2
Houston U.S.A. **127** E3
Houwater S. Africa **98** B3
Hove U.K. **47** C4
Hövsgöl Nuur l. Mongolia **72** C1
Hövüün Mongolia **72** C2
Howar, Wadi watercourse Sudan
  92 A3
Howe, Cape Austr. **105** D3
Howland Island terr.
  N. Pacific Ocean **101**
Höxter Ger. **49** D2
Hoy i. U.K. **44** C2
Høyanger Norway **41** B3
Hoyerswerda Ger. **50** C2
Hpapun Myanmar **66** A2
Hradec Králové Czech Rep.
  51 D2
Hrasnica Bos.-Herc. **57** C2
Hrebinka Ukr. **39** D1
Hrodna Belarus **36** B3
Hsi-hseng Myanmar **66** A1
Hsinchu Taiwan **75** C3
Hsinying Taiwan **75** C3
Huacho Peru **134** B4
Huade China **74** B1

Huadian China **69** B1
Huai'an China **74** B2
Huaibei China **74** B2
Huaihua China **75** A3
H:ainan China **74** B2
Huaiyang China **74** B2
Huaiyin China see Huai'an
Huajuápan de León Mex. **129** C3
Huaki Indon. **63** C3
Hualien Taiwan **75** B1
Huallaga r. Peru **134** B3
Huambo Angola **96** A1
Huancavelica Peru **134** B4
Huancayo Peru **134** B3
Huangchuan China **74** B2
Huang Hai sea N. Pacific Ocean **146**
see Yellow Sea
Huangnihe China **69** B1
Huangshan China **75** B3
Huangshi China **75** R?
Huangtu Gaoyuan plat. China **74** A2
Huangyan China **75** B3
Huanren China **69** B1
Huánuco Peru **134** B3
Huanuni Bol. see H∠
Huaráz Peru **134** B3
Huarmey Peru **134** B4
Huascarán, Nevado de mt. Peru **146**
Huasco Chile **136** A3
Huasco r. Chile **136** A3
Huatabampo Mex. **128** B2
Huatusco Mex. **129** C3
Huayuan China **75** A3
Huayxay Laos **66** B1
Hubei prov. China **74** B2
Hubli India **77** B3
Huddersfield U.K. **46** C1
Hudiksvall Sweden **41** D3
Hudson r. U.S.A. **123** F2
Hudson Bay Can. **113** E2
Hudson Bay sea Can. **111** G3
Hudson's Hope Can. **112** C2
Hudson Strait Can. **111** H2
Huế Vietnam **66** B2
Huehuetenango Guat. **130** A3
Huehueto, Cerro mt. Mex. **128** B2
Huejutle Mex. **129** C2
Huelva Spain **54** B5
Huércal-Overa Spain **55** C2
Huesca Spain **55** C1
Huéscar Spain **54** C2
Hughes Austr. **102** B3
Hugo U.S.A. **127** E2
Huhudi S. Africa **98** B2
Huib-Hoch Plateau Namibia **98** A2
Huichang China **75** B3
Huich'on N. Korea **69** B1
Huila Plateau Angola **96** A1
Huili China **66** B1
Huinan China **69** B1

Huixtla Mex. **129** C3
Huize China **75** A3
Huizhou China **75** B3
Hukuntsi Botswana **98** B1
Hulayfah Saudi Arabia **82** B2
Hulin China **70** D1
Hull Can. **114** C2
Hulun Buir China **73** D1
Hulun Nur l. China **73** D1
Hulyaypole Ukr. **39** E2
Humaitá Brazil **134** B3
Humber est. U.K. **46** C3
Humboldt U.S.A. **124** C1
Humboldt r. U.S.A. **118** C2
Humenné Slovakia **51** E3
Humphreys Peak U.S.A. **126** B1
Húnaflói b. Iceland **40** [inset]
Hunan prov. China **75** B3
Hunchun China **69** C1
Hunedoara Romania **38** B2
Hünfeld Ger. **49** D2
Hungary country Europe **51** D3
Hungerford Austr. **104** C1
Hüngnam N. Korea **69** B2
Hun He r. China **69** A1
Hunstanton U.K. **46** D3
Hunter r. Austr. **105** E2
Hunter Islands Austr. **103** D4
Huntingdon U.K. **47** C3
Huntington IN U.S.A. **122** C2
Huntington WV U.S.A. **122** D3
Huntly N.Z. **106** C2
Huntly U.K. **44** C2
Huntsville Can. **114** C2
Huntsville AL U.S.A. **124** C2
Huntsville TX U.S.A. **127** E2
Huron r. U.S.A. **121** D2
Huron, Lake Can./U.S.A. **122** D2
Hurricane U.S.A. **119** D3
Húsavík Iceland **40** [inset]
Huşi Romania **38** C2
Husn Al 'Abr Yemen **82** B3
Husnes Norway **42** E2
Husum Ger. **50** B1
Hutanopan Indon. **64** A1
Hutchinson U.S.A. **121** D3
Huzhou China **74** C2
Hvalnes Iceland **40** [inset]
Hvannadalshnúkur vol. Iceland **40** [inset]
Hvar i. Croatia **57** C2
Hwange Zimbabwe **96** B1
Hyannis U.S.A. **120** C2
Hyargas Nuur salt l. Mongolia **72** C1
Hyden Austr. **102** A3
Hyderabad India **77** B3
Hyderabad Pak. **78** A2
Hyères France **53** D3
Hyères, Îles d' is France **53** D3
Hyesan N. Korea **69** B1
Hyllestad Norway **42** E1
Hyōno-sen mt. Japan **71** B3

Hyvinkää Fin. **41** E3

Ialomiţa r. Romania **38** C3
Ianca Romania **38** C2
Iaşi Romania **38** C2
Ibadan Nigeria **90** C4
Ibagué Col. **134** B2
Ibarra Ecuador **134** B2
Ibb Yemen **82** B3
Ibbenbüren Ger. **48** C1
Ibiraçu Brazil **139** D1
Ibiza i. Spain **55** D2
Ibotirama Brazil **135** E4
Ibrā' Oman **83** C2
Ibrī Oman **83** C2
Ica Peru **134** B4
İçel Turkey see Mersin
Iceland country Europe **40** [inset]
Ichinoseki Japan **70** D3
Ichnya Ukr. **39** D1
Ich'ŏn N. Korea **69** B2
Idabel U.S.A. **127** F2
Idaho state U.S.A. **118** D2
Idaho Falls U.S.A. **118** D2
Idar-Oberstein Ger. **48** C3
Idfū Egypt **92** B2
Idhān Awbārī des. Libya **91** D2
Idhān Murzūq des. Libya **91** D2
Idiofa Dem. Rep. Congo **94** B3
Idlib Syria **84** B2
Iepê Brazil **138** B2
Ieper Belgium **48** A2
Ifakara Tanz. **95** D3
Ifanadiana Madag. **97** [inset] D2
Ife Nigeria **90** C4
Ifôghas, Adrar des hills Mali **90** C3
Igan Malaysia **65** C1
Igarapuri India **78** B3
Iğdır Turkey **85** C2
Iglesias Italy **56** A3
Igloolik Can. **111** G2
Ignace Can. **114** A2
Ignalina Lith. **36** C2
Igneada Turkey **58** C2
Igrim Rus. Fed. **34** F2
Iguaçu r. Brazil **138** B3
Iguaçu Falls arg./Brazil **138** B3
Iguala Mex. **129** C3
Igualada Spain **55** D1
Iguape Brazil **138** C2
Iguatemi Brazil **138** B2
Iguatemi r. Brazil **138** B2
Iguatu Brazil **135** F3
Iguéla Gabon **94** A3
Ihbulag Mongolia **73** D2
Ihosy Madag. **97** [inset] D2
Iisalmi Fin. **40** F3
Ijebu-Ode Nigeria **90** C4
IJmuiden Neth. **48** B1

IJssel r. Neth. 48 B1
IJsselmeer l. Neth. 48 B1
Ikageng S. Africa 99 C2
Ikaria i. Greece 59 C3
Ikela Dem. Rep. Congo 94 C3
Ikhtiman Bulg. 58 B2
Iki i. Japan 71 A4
Iksan S. Korea 69 B2
Ilagan Phil. 68 B2
Ilam Iran 85 C2
Ilawa Pol. 51 D2
Ilazárán, Küh-e mt. Iran 83 C2
Île-à-la-Crosse, Lac l. Can. 113 E2
Ilebo Dem. Rep. Congo 94 C3
Ileret Kenya 99 C2
Ilford U.K. 47 D4
Ilfracombe U.K. 47 A4
Ilha Grande, Baía de b. Brazil 139 D2
Ilha Grande, Represa resr Brazil 138 B2
Ilha Solteira, Represa resr Brazil 138 B2
Ilhavo Port. 54 B1
Ilhéus Brazil 135 F4
Iligan Phil. 68 B3
Ilicapel Chile 136 A4
Illichivs'k Ukr. 38 D2
Illinois r. U.S.A. 122 B3
Illinois state U.S.A. 122 C3
Illintsi Ukr. 38 C2
Illizi Alg. 91 C2
Il'men', Ozero l. Rus. Fed. 37 D2
Ilmenau Ger. 49 E2
Ilo Peru 134 B4
Iloilo Phil. 68 B3
Ilorin Nigeria 90 C4
Iluka Austr. 105 E1
Ilulissat Greenland 111 I2
Imi Eth. 93 C4
Imola Italy 56 D2
Imperatriz Brazil 135 E3
Imperial U.S.A. 120 C2
Impfondo Congo 94 B2
Imphal India 66 M1
Imroz Turkey 59 C2
In Aménas Alg. 91 C2
Inari Fin. 40 F2
Inarijärvi l. Fin. 40 F2
Inawashiro-ko l. Japan 71 D3
Ince Burun pt Turkey 84 B1
Inch'ŏn S. Korea 69 B2
Incomati r. Moz. 99 D2
Indalsta Norway 42 I7
Inda Silasē Eth. 82 A3
Independence CA U.S.A. 119 C3
Independence IA U.S.A. 121 E2
Independence KS U.S.A. 121 D3
Independence MO U.S.A. 121 E3
Independence Mountains U.S.A. 118 C2
Inderborskiy Kazakh. 80 C2
India country Asia 76 B2

Indiana U.S.A. 123 E2
Indiana state U.S.A. 122 C2
Indianapolis U.S.A. 122 C3
Indian Ocean 50
Indianola IA U.S.A. 121 E2
Indianola MS U.S.A. 124 B2
Indian Springs U.S.A. 119 C3
Indiga Rus. Fed. 34 D2
Indigirka r. Rus. Fed. 87 L2
Indija S.M. 58 B1
Indio U.S.A. 119 C4
Indonesia country Asia 62 B3
Indore India 78 B2
Indramayu, Tanjung pt Indon. 64 B2
Indre r. France 52 C2
Indus r. China/Pakistan 78 B1
Indus r. China/Pakistan 76 A2
Indus, Mouths of the Pak. 78 A2
Inebolu Turkey 84 B1
Inegöl Turkey 59 C2
Infiernillo, Presa resr Mex. 128 B3
Inglewood Austr. 105 E1
Ingolstadt Ger. 50 C3
Ingomar Austr. 104 B1
Ingraj Bazar India 79 C2
Inhambane Moz. 97 C2
Inishbofin i. Rep. of Ireland 45 A2
Inishmore i. Rep. of Ireland 45 B2
Inishowen pen. Rep. of Ireland 45 C1
Inland Kaikoura Range mts N.Z. 106 B3
Inn r. Europe 50 C3
Inner Mongolia aut. reg. China see Nei Mongol Zizhiqu
Inner Sound sea chan. U.K. 44 B2
Innisfail Austr. 103 D1
Innsbruck Austria 50 C3
Inongo Dem. Rep. Congo 94 B3
Inowrocław Pol. 51 D2
In Salah Alg. 90 C2
Insein Myanmar 66 A2
Inta Rus. Fed. 34 F2
International Falls U.S.A. 121 E1
Inukjuak Can. 114 C1
Inuvik Can. 110 D2
Inveraray U.K. 44 B2
Invercargill N.Z. 106 A4
Inverell Austr. 105 E1
Invergordon U.K. 44 B2
Invermere Can. 112 D2
Inverness U.K. 44 B2
Inverurie U.K. 44 C2
Investigator Strait Austr. 104 B3
Inya Rus. Fed. 81 F1
Inyonga Tanz. 95 D3
Inzhavino Rus. Fed. 39 F1
Ioannina Greece 59 B3
Iola U.S.A. 121 D3
Iona i. U.K. 44 A2
Ionian Islands admin. reg. Greece 59 A3

Ionian Sea Greece/Italy 59 A3
Ionioi Nisoi admin. reg. Greece see Ionian Islands
Ios i. Greece 59 C3
Iowa state U.S.A. 121 E2
Iowa City U.S.A. 121 E2
Ipameri Brazil 138 C1
Ipatinga Brazil 139 D1
Ipatovo Rus. Fed. 85 C1
Ipelegeng S. Africa 99 C2
Ipiales Col. 134 B2
Ipoh Malaysia 64 B1
Ipora Brazil 138 B1
Ippy C.A.R. 94 C2
Ipswich Austr. 105 E1
Ipswich U.K. 47 D3
Iqaluit Can. 111 H2
Iquique Chile 136 A3
Iquitos Peru 134 B3
Irai Brazil 138 B3
Irakleio Greece see Iraklion
Iraklion Greece 59 C3
Iran country Asia 85 D2
Iran, Pegunungan mts Indon. 65 C1
Īrānshahr Iran 83 D2
Irapuato Mex. 128 B2
Iraq country Asia 85 C2
Irati Brazil 138 B3
Irbid Jordan 84 B2
Irbit Rus. Fed. 34 F3
Irecê Brazil 135 E4
Ireland i. Rep. of Ireland/U.K. 36
Ireland, Republic of country Europe 45 B2
Irema Dem. Rep. Congo 94 C3
Irgiz Kazakh. 80 D2
Irigui reg. Mali/Maur. 90 B3
Iringa Tanz. 95 D3
Iriri r. Brazil 135 D3
Irish Sea Rep. of Ireland/U.K. 43 B3
Irkutsk Rus. Fed. 72 C1
Iron Knob Austr. 104 B2
Iron Mountain U.S.A. 122 C1
Ironwood U.S.A. 122 B1
Irosin Phil. 68 B2
Irō-zaki pt Japan 71 C4
Irpin' Ukr. 38 D1
Irrawaddy r. Myanmar 66 A2
Irrawaddy, Mouths of the Myanmar 67 A2
Irtysh r. Kazakh./Rus. Fed. 81 E1
Irún Spain 55 C1
Irvine U.K. 44 B3
Isabela Phil. 68 B3
Isabela, Cordillera mts Nic. 130 B3
Ísafjörður Iceland 40 [inset]
Isahaya Japan 71 B4
Isar r. Ger. 53 E2
Isbister U.K. 44 [inset]
Ischia, Isola d' i. Italy 56 B2
Ise Japan 71 C4

...ere, Pointe *pt* Fr. Guiana 146
...ernhagen Ger. 49 D1
...e-wan *b.* Japan 71 C4
...eyin Nigeria 90 C4
...nikari-wan *b.* Japan 70 D2
...nim *r.* Kazakh./Rus. Fed. 81 E1
...ninomaki Japan 70 D3
...npeming U.S.A. 122 C1
...klar Dağı *mts* Turkey 59 C2
...kli Turkey 59 C3
...l'kul' Rus. Fed. 81 E1
...pingo S. Africa 99 D2
...ro Dem. Rep. Congo 95 C2
...kenderun Turkey 84 B2
...kitim Rus. Fed. 86 H3
...kut *r.* Can. 112 B2
...amabad Pak. 78 B1
...and Lagoon *salt flat* Austr. 104 B2
...and Lake Can. 113 F2
...lands, Bay of N.Z. 106 B2
...ay *i.* U.K. 44 A3
...e of Man *i.* Irish Sea 46 A2
...moili Somoni, Qullai *mt.* Tajik. 81 E3
...a Egypt 82 A2
...ola di Capo Rizzuto Italy 57 C3
...merlüh Bulg. 58 C2
...abirito Brazil 139 D1
...abuna Brazil 135 C4
...acoatiara Brazil 134 D3
...af Brazil 138 C2
...aipu, Represa de *resr* Brazil 138 B3
...aituba Brazil 135 D3
...ajai Brazil 138 C3
...ajubá Brazil 139 C2
...aly *country* Europe 56 B2
...amarandiba Brazil 139 D1
...ambacuri Brazil 139 D1
...ambé, Pico de *mt.* Brazil 139 D1
...anagar India 66 A1
...anhaém Brazil 138 C2
...anhém Brazil 139 D1
...aobim Brazil 139 D1
...apajpe Brazil 138 C1
...apebi Brazil 139 E1
...apemirim Brazil 139 D2
...aperuna Brazil 139 D2
...apetinga Brazil 135 E4
...apetininga Brazil 138 C2
...apeva Brazil 138 C2
...apicuru Mirim Brazil 135 E3

Itapuranga Brazil 138 C1
Itararé Brazil 135 D3
Itarsi India 78 B2
Itaúna Brazil 139 D2
Itbayat *r.* Phil. 68 B1
Ithaca U.S.A. 123 E2
Ith Hils *ridge* Ger. 49 D1
Itimbiri *r.* Dem. Rep. Congo 94 C2
Itinga Brazil 139 D1
Itiquira Brazil 138 B1
Itiquira *r.* Brazil 138 A1
Ittoqqortoormiit Greenland 111 K2
Itu Brazil 138 C2
Itui *r.* Brazil 134 B3
Ituiutaba Brazil 138 C1
Itumbiara Brazil 138 C1
Iturama Brazil 138 B1
Itzehoe Ger. 50 B2
Iui'tin Rus. Fed. 87 O2
Ivai *r.* Brazil 138 B2
Ivalo Fin. 40 F2
Ivanava Belarus 36 C3
Ivanhoe Austr. 104 C2
Ivankiv Ukr. 38 C1
Ivano-Frankivs'k Ukr. 38 B2
Ivanovo Rus. Fed. 37 F2
Ivatsevichy Belarus 36 C3
Ivdel' Rus. Fed. 34 F2
Ivinheima Brazil 138 B2
Ivinheima *r.* Brazil 138 B2
Ivittuut Greenland 111 J3
Ivrea Italy 56 A1
Ivrindi Turkey 59 C3
Ivujivik Can. 111 G2
Iwaki Japan 71 F3
Iwakuni Japan 71 B4
Iwamizawa Japan 70 D2
Iwye Belarus 36 C3
Ixopo S. Africa 99 D3
Ixtlán Mex. 128 D2
Izabal, Lago de *l.* Guat. 129 D3
Izamal Mex. 129 D2
Izberbash Rus. Fed. 85 C1
Izhevsk Rus. Fed. 34 E3
Izmayil Ukr. 38 C2
Izmir Turkey 59 C3
Iznik Gölü *l.* Turkey 59 C2
Izumo Japan 71 B3
Izyaslav Ukr. 38 C1
Izyum Ukr. 39 E2

J

Jabalón *r.* Spain 54 C2
Jabalpur India 79 B2
Jabiru Austr. 102 C1
Jablanica Bos.-Herz. 57 C2
Jaboatão Brazil 135 F4
Jaboticabal Brazil 138 C2

Jaca Spain 55 C1
Jacareacanga Brazil 135 D3
Jacareí Brazil 139 C2
Jacinto Brazil 139 D1
Jackman U.S.A. 123 F1
Jackson *AL* U.S.A. 124 C2
Jackson *MI* U.S.A. 122 D2
Jackson *MS* U.S.A. 124 B2
Jackson *TN* U.S.A. 124 C1
Jackson *WY* U.S.A. 120 A2
Jackson Head N.Z. 106 A3
Jacksonville *AR* U.S.A. 124 B2
Jacksonville *FL* U.S.A. 125 D2
Jacksonville *IL* U.S.A. 122 B3
Jacksonville *NC* U.S.A. 125 E2
Jacksonville *TX* U.S.A. 127 E2
Jacmel Haiti 131 C3
Jacobabad Pak. 78 A2
Jacobina Brazil 135 E4
Jacques Cartier, Mont *mt.* Can. 115 D2
Jacunda Brazil 135 D3
Jacupiranga Brazil 138 C2
Jaùovnik, *mt.* Bos.-Herz. 57 C2
Jaén Spain 54 C2
Jaffa, Cape Austr. 104 B3
Jaffna Sri Lanka 77 B4
Jagdalpur India 77 C3
Jaguariaíva Brazil 138 C2
Jahrom Iran 85 D3
Jaipur India 78 B2
Jaisalmer India 78 B2
Jakarta Indon. 68 B2
Jäkkvik Sweden 40 D2
Jakobstad Fin. 40 E3
Jalālābād Afgh. 78 B1
Jalandhar India 78 B1
Jalapa Mex. 129 C3
Jales Brazil 138 B2
Jalgaon India 78 B2
Jalingo Nigeria 91 D4
Jalna India 78 B3
Jalpa Mex. 128 B2
Jālū Libya 91 E2
Jamaica *country* West Indies 130 C3
Jamalpur Bangl. 79 C2
Jambi Indon. 64 B2
James *r.* N. Dakota/S. Dakota U.S.A. 121 D2
James *r.* VA U.S.A. 123 E3
James Bay Can. 114 B1
Jameson Land *reg.* Greenland 111 K2
Jamestown Austr. 104 B2
Jamestown *ND* U.S.A. 121 D1
Jamestown *NY* U.S.A. 123 E2
Jammu India 78 B1
Jammu and Kashmir *terr.* Asia 78 B1
Jamnagar India 78 B2
Jämsä Fin. 41 F3
Jamshedpur India 79 C2
Jamuna *r.* Bangl. 79 C2

Janakpur Nepal **79** C2
Janaúba Brazil **139** D1
Jandaq Iran **85** D2
Janesville U.S.A. **122** C2
Jan Mayen *terr.* Arctic Ocean **86** B2
Jansenville S. Africa **98** B3
Januária Brazil **135** E4
Japan *country* Asia **71** C3
Japan, Sea of N. Pacific Ocean **73** E2
Japurá *r.* Brazil **134** C3
Jaraguá Brazil **138** C1
Jaraguari Brazil **138** B2
Jardim Brazil **138** A2
Jargalant Mongolia **73** D1
Jarocin Pol. **51** D2
Jarosław Pol. **51** E2
Järpen Sweden **40** C3
Jartai China **74** A2
Jarū Brazil **134** C4
Jarud China *see* Lubei
Jask Iran **83** D2
Jasło Pol. **51** E3
Jasper Can. **112** D2
Jasper *IN* U.S.A. **122** C3
Jasper *TX* U.S.A. **127** F2
Jastrzębie-Zdrój Pol. **51** D3
Jászberény Hungary **51** D3
Jataí Brazil **138** B1
Jaú Brazil **138** C2
Jaú *r.* Brazil **134** C3
Jaunpur India **79** C2
Java *i.* Indon. **64** B2
Java Sea Indon. *see* Jawa, Laut
Java Trench *sea feature*
Indian Ocean **145** H6
Jawa *i.* Indon. *see* Java
Jawa, Laut *sea* Indon. **64** C2
Jaya, Puncak *mt.* Indon. **63** D3
Jayapura Indon. **63** D3
Jeannin, Lac *l.* Can. **115** D1
Jebel, Bahr el *r.* Sudan/Uganda *see* White Nile
Jebel Abyad Plateau Sudan **92** A3
Jedburgh U.K. **44** C3
Jeddah Saudi Arabia **82** A2
Jefferson, Mount U.S.A. **119** C3
Jefferson City U.S.A. **121** E3
Jejuí Guazú *r.* Para. **138** A2
Jēkabpils Latvia **36** C2
Jelenia Góra Pol. **51** D2
Jelgava Latvia **36** B2
Jember Indon. **65** C2
Jena Ger. **49** E2
Jengish Chokusu *mt.* China/Kyrg. *see* Pobeda Peak
Jenin West Bank **84** B2
Jennings U.S.A. **124** B2
Jequié Brazil **135** E4

Jequitaí Brazil **139** D1
Jequitinhonha Brazil **139** D1
Jequitinhonha *r.* Brazil **139** E1
Jérémie Haiti **131** C3
Jerez Mex. **128** B2
Jerez de la Frontera Spain **54** B2
Jerome U.S.A. **118** D2
Jersey *i.* Channel Is. **47** B5
Jerumenha Brazil **135** E3
Jerusalem Israel/West Bank **84** B2
Jervis Bay Territory *admin. div.* Austr. **105** E3
Jesenice Slovenia **56** B1
Jesi Italy **56** B2
Jessore Bangl. **79** C2
Jesup U.S.A. **125** D2
Jesús Carranza Mex. **129** C3
Jhalawar India **78** B2
Jhang Pak. **78** B1
Jhansi India **79** B2
Jharsuguda India **79** C2
Jhelum Pak. **78** B1
Jiamusi China **70** B1
Ji'an *Jiangxi* China **75** B3
Ji'an *Jilin* China **69** B1
Jiangsu *prov.* China **75** B3
Jiangxi *prov.* China **75** B3
Jiangyou China **74** A2
Jianli China **75** B3
Jianqiao China **74** B2
Jianyang *Fujian* China **75** B3
Jianyang *Sichuan* China **74** A2
Jiaohe China **69** B1
Jiaozhou China **74** C2
Jiaozuo China **74** B2
Jiaxing China **74** C2
Jiayuguan China **72** C2
Jiddah Saudi Arabia *see* Jeddah
Jiehkkevárri *mt.* Norway **40** D2
Jiexiu China **74** B2
Jihlava Czech Rep. **51** D3
Jijel Alg. **58** C1
Jijiga Eth. **93** C4
Jilin China **69** B1
Jilin *prov.* China **74** C1
Jilin Hada Ling *mts* China **69** A1
Jima Eth. **93** B4
Jiménez *Chihuahua* Mex. **128** B2
Jiménez *Tamaulipas* Mex. **129** C2
Jinan China **74** B2
Jinchang China **74** A2
Jincheng China **74** B2
Jindabyne Austr. **105** D3
Jindřichův Hradec Czech Rep. **50** D3
Jingdezhen China **75** B3
Jinggangshan China **75** B3
Jinghong China **66** B1
Jingmen China **74** B2
Jingning China **74** A2
Jingtai China **74** A2

Jingxi China **75** A3
Jingyu China **69** B1
Jingyuan China **74** A2
Jingzhou *Hubei* China **75** B2
Jingzhou *Hubei* China **75** B2
Jinhua China **75** B3
Jining *Nei Mongol* China **74** B1
Jining *Shandong* China **74** B2
Jinja Uganda **95** D2
Jinka Eth. **93** B4
Jinotepe Nic. **130** B3
Jinsha China **75** B3
Jinsha Jiang *r.* China *see* Yangtze
Jinshi China **75** B3
Jinzhong China **74** B2
Jinzhou China **74** C1
Jiparaná *r.* Brazil **134** C3
Jirang China **79** C1
Jirkov Czech Rep. **49** F2
Jiroft Iran **83** C2
Jishou China **75** B3
Jiu *r.* Romania **38** B3
Jiuding Shan *mt.* China **74** A2
Jiujiang China **75** B3
Jiwani Pak. **83** D2
Jixi China **69** B1
Jīzān Saudi Arabia **82** B3
Jizzax Uzbek. **81** D2
Joaçaba Brazil **138** B3
João Pessoa Brazil **135** F3
João Pinheiro Brazil **139** C1
Jodhpur India **78** B2
Joensuu Fin. **40** F3
Jõetsu Japan **71** C3
Jofane Moz. **97** C2
Jõgeva Estonia **36** C2
Johannesburg S. Africa **99** C2
John Day U.S.A. **118** C2
John Day *r.* U.S.A. **118** B1
John H. Kerr Reservoir U.S.A. **123** E3
John o'Groats U.K. **44** C1
Johnson City U.S.A. **125** D1
Johnson's Crossing Can. **112** B1
Johnstone U.K. **44** B3
Johor Bahru Malaysia **64** B1
Jõhvi Estonia **36** C2
Joinville Brazil **138** C3
Joinville France **52** C2
Jokkmokk Sweden **40** D2
Jökulsá á Fjöllum *r.* Iceland **40** [inset]
Joliet U.S.A. **122** C2
Joliette Can. **114** C2
Jolo Phil. **68** B3
Jolo *i.* Phil. **68** B3
Jombang Indon. **65** C2
Jomsom Nepal **79** C2
Jonava Lith. **36** B2
Jonesboro *AR* U.S.A. **124** B1
Jonesboro *LA* U.S.A. **124** B2
Jones Sound *sea chan.* Can. **111** G1
Jönköping Sweden **41** C4
Jonquière Can. **115** C2
Joplin U.S.A. **121** E3

ordan country Asia 84 B2
ordan r. Asia 84 B2
ordan Valley U.S.A. 118 C2
orhat India 66 A1
erpeland Norway 41 B4
os Nigeria 91 C4
osé Cardel Mex. 129 C3
oseph, Lac l. Can. 115 D1
oseph Bonaparte Gulf Austr.
102 B1
os Plateau Nigeria 91 C4
otunheimen mts Norway 41 B3
ouberton S. Africa 99 C2
uan de Fuca Strait Can./U.S.A.
118 B1
uan Fernández, Archipiélago is
S. Pacific Ocean 133
uaréz Mex. 129 B2
uàzeiro Brazil 135 E3
uàzeiro do Norte Brazil 135 F3
uba Sudan 93 B4
ubba r. Somalia 93 C5
ubba l. India 66 B2
úcar r. Spain 55 C2
uchitán Mex. 129 C3
udenburg Austria 50 C3
uigalpa Nic. 130 B3
uist l. Ger. 48 C1
uiz de Fora Brazil 139 D2
uliaca Peru 134 B4
umla Nepal 79 C2
unagadh India 78 B2
unction U.S.A. 127 F2
unction City U.S.A. 121 D3
undiaí Brazil 100 C2
uneau U.S.A. 112 B3
unee Austr. 105 D2
ungfrau mt. Switz. 53 D2
uniata r. U.S.A. 123 E2
unsele Sweden 40 D3
untura U.S.A. 118 C2
uquiá Brazil 138 C2
ur r. Sudan 93 A4
ura mts France/Switz. 53 D2
ura l. U.K. 44 B2
urbarkas lth. 36 B2
ürmala Latvia 36 B2
urua r. Brazil 134 C3
uruena r. Brazil 134 D3
utaí r. Brazil 134 C3
üterbog Ger. 49 F2
utland pen. Denmark 36
uventud, Isla de la l. Cuba
130 B2
uxian China 74 B2
waneng Botswana 98 B3
yväskylä Fin. 41 F3

K

K2 mt. China/Jammu and Kashmir
78 B1

Kabaena l. Indon. 65 D2
Kabalo Dem. Rep. Congo 95 C3
Kabinakagami Lake Can. 114 B2
Kabinda Dem. Rep. Congo 94 C3
Kabompo Zambia 96 B1
Kabongo Dem. Rep. Congo
95 C3
Kābul Afgh. 78 A1
Kaburuang l. Indon. 68 B3
Kabwe Zambia 97 C3
Kachchh, Gulf of India 78 A2
Kachchh, Rann of marsh India
78 B2
Kachug Rus. Fed. 87 J3
Kaçkar Daği mt. Turkey 85 C1
Kadavu l. Fiji 110
Kadiköy Turkey 59 C2
Kadmat atoll India 77 B3
Kadom Rus. Fed. 37 F3
Kadoma Zimbabwe 97 C3
Kadonkani Myanmar 67 A2
Kadugli Sudan 93 A3
Kaduna Nigeria 91 C3
Kaduy Rus. Fed. 37 E2
Kadzharom Rus. Fed. 34 E2
Kaédi Maur. 90 A3
Kaesŏng N. Korea 69 B2
Kafue r. Zambia 96 B1
Kafue r. Zambia 96 B1
Kaga Bandoro C.A.R. 94 B2
Kagal'nitskaya Rus. Fed. 39 F2
Kagoshima Japan 71 B4
Kaharlyk Ukr. 38 D2
Kahayan r. Indon. 65 C2
Kahemba Dem. Rep. Congo
94 B3
Kahnūj Iran 83 C2
Kahperusvaarat mts Fin. 40 D2
Kahramanmaraş Turkey 84 B2
Kahürak Iran 83 C2
Kai, Kepulauan is Indon. 63 C3
Kaiama Nigeria 91 C4
Kaiapoi N.Z. 106 B3
Kaifeng China 74 B2
Kaiingveld reg. S. Africa 98 B2
Kaikoura N.Z. 106 B3
Kaili China 75 A3
Kaimana Indon. 63 C3
Kaimanawa Mountains N.Z.
106 C2
Kainan Japan 71 C4
Kainji Reservoir Nigeria 90 C3
Kaipara Harbour N.Z. 106 B2
Kairana India 78 B2
Kairouan Tunisia 91 D1
Kaitaia N.Z. 106 B2
Kaitawa N.Z. 106 C2
Kaiwatu Indon. 63 C3
Kaiyuan Liaoning China 69 A1
Kaiyuan Yunnan China 75 A3
Kajaani Fin. 40 F3
Kakamas S. Africa 98 B2
Kakamega Kenya 95 D2
Kakhovka Ukr. 39 D2

Kakhovs'ke Vodoskhovyshche
resr Ukr. 39 D2
Kakinada India 77 C3
Kaktovik U.S.A. 110 C2
Kalabo Zambia 96 B1
Kalach Rus. Fed. 39 F1
Kalacha Dida Kenya 95 D2
Kalajoki Fin. 40 E3
Kalamare Botswana 99 C1
Kalamaria Greece 59 B2
Kalamata Greece 59 B3
Kalamazoo U.S.A. 122 C2
Kalanchak Ukr. 39 D2
Kalao l. Indon. 65 D2
Kalaotoa l. Indon. 65 D2
Kalasin Thai. 66 B2
Kalāt Afgh. 78 A1
Kalāt Iran 83 C2
Kalat Pak. 78 A2
Kalbarri Austr. 102 A2
Kalecik Turkey 84 B1
Kalema Dem. Rep. Congo
94 C3
Kalemie Dem. Rep. Congo
95 C3
Kalemyo Myanmar 66 A1
Kalevala Rus. Fed. 40 G2
Kalgoorlie Austr. 102 B3
Kaliakra, Nos pt Bulg. 58 C2
Kalima Dem. Rep. Congo
95 C3
Kalimantan reg. Indon. 65 C2
Kaliningrad Rus. Fed. 36 B3
Kalininskaya Rus. Fed. 39 E2
Kalinkavichy Belarus 36 C3
Kalispell U.S.A. 118 D1
Kalisz Pol. 51 D2
Kalitva r. Rus. Fed. 39 F2
Kalix Sweden 40 E2
Kalixälven r. Sweden 40 E2
Kalkan Turkey 59 C3
Kallavesi l. Fin. 40 F3
Kallsjön l. Sweden 40 C3
Kalmar Sweden 41 D4
Kalmarsund sea chan. Sweden
41 D4
Kalomo Zambia 96 B1
Kalone Peak Can. 112 C2
Kalpa India 79 B1
Kalpeni atoll India 77 B3
Kalpi India 79 B2
Kaltag U.S.A. 110 B2
Kaltenkirchen Ger. 49 D1
Kaluga Rus. Fed. 37 E3
Kalundborg Denmark 41 C4
Kalush Ukr. 38 B2
Kalyazin Rus. Fed. 37 E2
Kalymnos l. Greece 59 C3
Kama Dem. Rep. Congo 95 C3
Kama r. Rus. Fed. 34 E3
Kamaishi Japan 70 D3
Kamanjab Namibia 96 A1
Kamarān l. Yemen 82 B3

Kamarod Pak. **78** A2
Kambalda Austr. **102** B3
Kamchatka Peninsula Rus. Fed. **87**
Kamchiya r. Bulg. **58** D2
Kamenitsa mt. Bulg. **58** D2
Kamenjak, Rt pt Croatia **56** B2
Kamenka, Rus. Fed. **39** E1
Kamen'-na-Obi Rus. Fed. **81** F1
Kamenmomostskiy Rus. Fed. **39** F3
Kamenolomni Rus. Fed. **39** F2
Kamenskoye Rus. Fed. **87** N2
Kamensk-Shakhtinskiy Rus. Fed. **39** F2
Kamensk-Ural'skiy Rus. Fed. **34** F3
Kamiesberge mts S. Africa **98** A3
Kamieskroon S. Africa **98** A3
Kamilukuak Lake Can. **113** I1
Kamina Dem. Rep. Congo **95** C5
Kaminak Lake Can. **113** I1
Kamloops Can. **112** C2
Kamonia Dem. Rep. Congo **94** C3
Kampala Uganda **95** D2
Kampar r. Indon. **64** B1
Kampen Neth. **48** B1
Kampene Dem. Rep. Congo **95** C3
Kamphaeng Phet Thai. **66** A2
Kâmpóng Spœ Cambodia **67** B2
Kâmpôt Cambodia **67** B2
Kamsack Can. **113** I2
Kamsuuma Somalia **93** C4
Kam"yanets'-Podil's'kyy Ukr. **38** C2
Kam"yanka-Buz'ka Ukr. **38** B1
Kamyshevatskaya Rus. Fed. **39** E2
Kamyshin Rus. Fed. **35** I3
Kanab U.S.A. **119** D3
Kananga Dem. Rep. Congo **95** C4
Kanash Rus. Fed. **35** I3
Kanawha r. U.S.A. **130** C4
Kanazawa Japan **71** C3
Kanbalu Myanmar **66** A1
Kanchanaburi Thai. **67** A2
Kanchipuram India **77** B3
Kandahār Afgh. **78** A1
Kandalaksha Rus. Fed. **40** G2
Kandangan Indon. **65** C2
Kandhkot Pak. **78** A2
Kandi Benin **90** C3
Kandla India **78** B2
Kandos Austr. **105** C2
Kandyagash Kazakh. **80** C2
Kanevskaya Rus. Fed. **39** E2
Kang Botswana **96** B2
Kangaatsiaq Greenland **111** I1
Kangal Turkey **84** B2

Kangän Iran **83** C2
Kangar Malaysia **64** B1
Kangaroo Island Austr. **104** B3
Kangchenjunga mt. India/Nepal **79** F2
Kangean, Kepulauan is Indon. **65** C2
Kangeq c. Greenland **111** J2
Kangersuatsiaq Greenland **111** I2
Kanggye N. Korea **69** B1
Kangiqsualujjuaq Can. **115** D1
Kangiqsujuaq Can. **111** H2
Kangirsuk Can. **111** H2
Kangmar China **79** C2
Kangnŭng S. Korea **69** B2
Kangping China **69** A1
Kanin, Poluostrov pen. Rus. Fed. **34** D2
Kanin Nos Rus. Fed. **34** D2
Kaniv Ukr. **39** D2
Kankaanpää Fin. **41** E3
Kankakee U.S.A. **122** C2
Kankan Guinea **90** B3
Kanker India **79** C2
Kano Nigeria **91** C3
Kanonpunt pt S. Africa **98** B3
Kanoya Japan **71** B4
Kanpur India **79** C2
Kansas r. U.S.A. **120** E3
Kansas state U.S.A. **121** D3
Kansas City U.S.A. **121** E3
Kansk Rus. Fed. **87** I3
Kantemirovka Rus. Fed. **39** E2
Kanton atoll Kiribati **111**
KaNyamazane S. Africa **99** D2
Kanye Botswana **99** C1
Kaohsiung Taiwan **75** C3
Kaokoveld plat. Namibia **96** A1
Kaolack Senegal **90** A3
Kaoma Zambia **96** B1
Kapanga Dem. Rep. Congo **94** C3
Kapchagay Kazakh. **81** E2
Kapchagayskoye
Vodokhranilishche resr Kazakh.
81 E2
Kapellen Belgium **48** B2
Kapiri Mposhi Zambia **97** B1
Kapisillit Greenland **111** I2
Kapiskau r. Can. **114** B1
Kapit Malaysia **65** C1
Kapoe Thai. **67** A3
Kapoeta Sudan **93** B4
Kaposvár Hungary **51** D3
Kapuas r. Indon. **65** B2
Kapunda Austr. **104** B2
Kapuskasing Can. **114** B2
Kapyl' Belarus **36** C3
Kara Togo **90** C4
Kara r. Turkey **59** C3
Karabalyk Kazakh. **80** D1
Karabaur, Uval hills
Kazakh./Uzbek. **85** D1

Kara-Bogaz-Gol, Zaliv b. Turkm.
80 C2
Karabük Turkey **84** B1
Karabutak Kazakh. **80** D2
Karachev Rus. Fed. **37** D3
Karachi Pak. **78** A2
Karaganda Kazakh. **81** E2
Karagayly Kazakh. **81** E2
Karaginskiy Zaliv b. Rus. Fed.
87 M3
Karaj Iran **85** D2
Karakelong i. Indon. **68** B3
Karakol Kyrg. **81** E2
Karakoram Range mts Asia **81** E3
Karakum, Peski des. Kazakh. see
Karakum Desert
Karakum Desert Kazakh. **80** C2
Karakum Desert Turkm. see
Karakumy, Peski
Karakumy, Peski des. Turkm.
80 D3
Karaman Turkey **92** B1
Karamay China **81** F2
Karamea N.Z. **106** B3
Karamea Bight b. N.Z. **106** B3
Karapınar Turkey **84** B2
Karasburg Namibia **98** A2
Kara Sea Rus. Fed. **34** G1
Kárášjohka Norway see Karasjok
Karasjok Norway **40** F2
Karasuk Rus. Fed. **81** E1
Karatau Kazakh. **81** E2
Karatau, Khrebet mts Kazakh.
81 D2
Karatayka Rus. Fed. **34** F2
Karatsu Japan **71** A4
Karawang Indon. **64** B2
Karbalā' Iraq **85** C2
Karcag Hungary **51** E3
Kardítsa Greece **59** C3
Kärdla Estonia **41** E4
Kareeberge mts S. Africa **98** B3
Kareli India **79** B2
Kargil India **78** B1
Kariba Zimbabwe **97** B1
Kariba, Lake resr
Zambia/Zimbabwe **97** B1
Karimata, Pulau-pulau is Indon.
64 B2
Karimata, Selat str. Indon. **64** B2
Karimnagar India **77** B3
Karimunjawa, Pulau-pulau is
Indon. **65** C2
Karkinits'ka Zatoka g. Ukr.
39 D2
Karkinits'ka Zatoka b. Ukr. **37**
Karlivka Ukr. **39** E2
Karl Marks, Qullai mt. Tajik.
78 B1
Karlovac Croatia **56** C1
Karlovy Vary Czech Rep. **50** C2
Karlshamn Sweden **41** C4
Karlskrona Sweden **41** C4

arlsruhe Ger. **49** D3
arlstad Sweden **41** C4
arlstadt Ger. **49** D3
arma Belarus **37** D3
armey i. Norway **41** B4
aroi Zimbabwe **97** B1
aronga Malawi **97** C1
arora Eritrea **92** B3
arpathos i. Greece **59** C3
arpenisi Greece **59** B3
arratha Austr. **102** A2
ars Turkey **85** C1
arodi Pak. **78** A2

arshi Turkm. **35** E4
arshi Uzbek. see Qarshi
arskiye Vorota, Proliv str.
Rus. Fed. **34** E2
arskoye More sea Rus. Fed. see
Kara Sea
arstädt Ger. **49** D3
artal Turkey **59** C2
artaly Rus. Fed. **38** F3
arwar India **77** B3
arystos Greece **59** C3
asabonika Lake Can. **114** B1
asaji Dem. Rep. Congo **94** C4
asama Zambia **95** D4
asane Botswana **96** B1
asanguli Dem. Rep. Congo
94 B3
asba Lake Can. **113** C1
asenga Dem. Rep. Congo **95** C4
asese Uganda **95** D2
asfah Iran **85** D2
asnary Rus. Fed. **39** F2
ashi China **81** E3
ashima-nada b. Japan **71** D3
asin Rus. Fed. **37** E2
ashira Rus. Fed. **37** E3
ashirskoye Rus. Fed. **37** E3
ashiwazaki Japan **71** C3
ashmir Iran **80** C3
ashmir terr. Asia see
Jammu and Kashmir
ashmor Pak. **78** A2
ashyukulu Dem. Rep. Congo
95 C3
asimov Rus. Fed. **37** F3
asinken Fin. **41** E3
asongo Dem. Rep. Congo **95** C3
asongo-Lunda
Dem. Rep. Congo **94** B3
asos i. Greece **59** C3
assala Sudan **92** B3
assel Ger. **49** D2
asserine Turkey **84** B1
astelli Greece **59** B3
asterlee Belgium **48** C4
astsyukovichy Belarus **37** D3
asulu Tanz. **95** D3

Kasungu Malawi **97** C1
Katahdin, Mount U.S.A. **123** G1
Katako-Kombe Dem. Rep. Congo
94 C3
Katanning Austr. **102** A3
Katchall i. India **67** A3
Katerini Greece **59** B2
Kate's Needle mt. Can./U.S.A.
112 B2
Katete Zambia **97** C1
Katha Myanmar **66** A1
Katherine r. Austr. **102** C1
Kathiawar pen. India **78** B2
Kathlehong S. Africa **99** C2
Kathmandu Nepal **79** C2
Katihar India **79** C2
Katikati N.Z. **106** C3
Katima Mulilo Namibia **96** B1
Katoomba Austr. **105** C2
Katowice Pol. **51** D2
Kātrīnā, Jabal mt. Egypt **84** B3
Katrineholm Sweden **41** D4
Katsina Nigeria **90** C3
Katsuura str. Denmark/Sweden
41 C4
Katwijk aan Zee Neth. **48** B1
Kauai i. U.S.A. **120**
Kauhajoki Fin. **41** E3
Kaukauna U.S.A. **122** C2
Kautokeino Norway **40** E2
Kavala Greece **59** B2
Kavalerovo Rus. Fed. **70** C2
Kavaratti atoll India **77** B3
Kavarna Bulg. **58** C2
Kavir, Dasht-e des. Iran **85** D2
Kawakawa N.Z. **106** B2
Kawanishi Japan **71** C3
Kawartha Lakes Can. **114** O2
Kawasaki Japan **71** C3
Kawerau N.Z. **106** C2
Kawlin Myanmar **66** A1
Kawm Umbū Egypt **82** A2
Kaxgar He r. China **81** E3
Kaya Burkina **90** B3
Kayan r. Indon. **65** C1
Kaycee U.S.A. **120** B2
Kayenta U.S.A. **121** D4
Kayes Mali **90** A3
Kaynar Kazakh. **81** E2
Kayseri Turkey **84** B2
Kazakhstan country Asia **80** D2
Kazakhskiy Zaliv b. Kazakh.
80 D1
Kazakhstan country Asia **80** D2
Kazan' Rus. Fed. **35** D3
Kazanlŭk Bulg. **84** A1
Kazanskaya Rus. Fed. **39** F2
Kazbek mt. Georgia/Rus. Fed.
35 D4
Kāzerūn Iran **85** D3
Kazincbarcika Hungary **51** E3
Kea i. Greece **59** B3
Keady U.K. **45** C1

Kearney U.S.A. **121** D2
Kearny U.S.A. **126** B2
Kebkabiya Sudan **92** A3
Kebnekaise mt. Sweden **40** D2
K'ebrī Dehar Eth. **93** C4
Kebumen Indon. **65** B2
Kechika r. Can. **112** C2
Kecskemét Hungary **51** D3
Kėdainiai Lith. **36** B2
Kédougou Senegal **90** A3
Kędzierzyn-Koźle Pol. **51** D2
Keele r. Can. **112** C1
Keele Peak Can. **112** B1
Keeling Taiwan see Chilung
Keene U.S.A. **123** F2
Keetmanshoop Namibia **98** A2
Keewatin Can. **113** F3
Kefallonia i. Greece see
Cephalonia
Keflavík Iceland **40** [inset]
Kegen Kazakh. **81** E2
Keg River Can. **112** D2
Kehsi Mansam Myanmar **66** A1
Keighley U.K. **46** D0
Keila Estonia **36** B2
Keimoes S. Africa **98** B2
Keitele l. Fin. **40** F3
Keith Austr. **104** C3
Keith Arm b. Can. **112** C1
Kékes mt. Hungary **51** E3
Kekes-Uayu, Gora h. Rus. Fed.
40 G2
Kelheim Ger. **50** C3
Kelkit r. Turkey **84** B1
Keller Lake Can. **112** C1
Kellogg U.S.A. **118** C1
Kelloselkä Fin. **40** F2
Kells Rep. of Ireland **45** C2
Kelmė Lith. **36** B2
Kelowna Can. **112** D3
Kelso U.K. **44** C3
Kelso U.S.A. **118** B1
Keluang Malaysia **64** B1
Kem' Rus. Fed. **34** C2
Kemerovo Rus. Fed. **86** H3
Kemi Fin. **40** E2
Kemijärvi Fin. **40** F2
Kemijoki r. Fin. **40** E2
Kemmerer U.S.A. **120** A2
Kempele Fin. **40** F3
Kempsey Austr. **105** C2
Kempt, Lac l. Can. **114** C2
Kempten (Allgäu) Ger. **50** C3
Kempton Park S. Africa **99** C2
Kenai U.S.A. **110** B2
Kendal U.K. **46** B2
Kendari Indon. **65** C2
Kendawangan Indon. **65** C2
Kendégué Chad **91** D3
Kenema Sierra Leone **90** A4
Kenge Dem. Rep. Congo **94** B3
Kengtung Myanmar **66** A1
Kenhardt S. Africa **98** B2
Kénitra Morocco **90** B1

Kenmare Rep. of Ireland **45** B3
Kenmare U.S.A. **120** C1
Kenn Ger. **48** C3
Kennett U.S.A. **113** F3
Kennewick U.S.A. **118** C1
Kenora Can. **113** F3
Kenosha U.S.A. **122** C2
Kent U.S.A. **126** C3
Kentau Kazakh. **81** D2
Kentucky r. U.S.A. **122** C3
Kentucky *state* U.S.A. **122** D3
Kentucky Lake U.S.A. **122** C3
Kenya *country* Africa **95** D2
Kenya, Mount Kenya **95** D3
Keokuk U.S.A. **121** E2
Keonjhar India **79** C2
Kerang Austr. **104** C3
Kerava Fin. **36** C1
Kerch Ukr. **39** E2
Kerema P.N.G. **63** D3
Keren Eritrea **92** B3
Kericho Kenya **95** D3
Kerikeri N.Z. **106** B2
Kerinci, Gunung *vol.* Indon.
  64 B2
Kerkyra Greece **59** A3
Kerkyra *i.* Greece *see* Corfu
Kerma Sudan **92** B3
Kermadec Islands
  S. Pacific Ocean **111**
Kermān Iran **83** C1
Kermānshāh Iran **85** C2
Kermit U.S.A. **127** C2
Kern r. U.S.A. **119** C3
Kerpen Ger. **48** C2
Kerville U.S.A. **127** C2
Kesagami Lake Can. **114** B1
Keşan Turkey **59** C2
Kesennuma Japan **70** D3
Keshod India **78** B2
Keswick U.K. **46** B2
Keszthely Hungary **51** D3
Ket' r. Rus. Fed. **86** H3
Ketapang Indon. **65** C2
Ketchikan U.S.A. **112** B2
Ketchum U.S.A. **118** D2
Kettering U.K. **47** C3
Keurau Fin. **41** E3
Kevelaer Ger. **48** C2
Kewanee U.S.A. **122** C2
Keweenaw Bay U.S.A. **122** C1
Keweenaw Peninsula U.S.A.
  122 C1
Key Largo U.S.A. **125** D3
Key West U.S.A. **125** D4
Kgotsong S. Africa **99** C2
Khabarovsk Rus. Fed. **73** F1
Khadyzhensk Rus. Fed. **84** B1
Khagrachari Bangl. **66** A1
Khairpur Pak. **78** A2
Khakhea Botswana **98** B1
Khamar-Daban, Khrebet *mts*
  Rus. Fed. **72** C1

Khambhat India **78** B2
Khambhat, Gulf of India **78** B3
Khamgaon India **78** B2
Khamir Yemen **82** B3
Khamis Mushayṭ Saudi Arabia
  82 B3
Khammam India **77** C3
Khānābād Afgh. **78** A1
Khandwa India **78** B2
Khandyga Rus. Fed. **87** L2
Khanewal Pak. **78** B1
Khanka, Lake China/Rus. Fed.
  70 B2
Khanpur Pak. **78** B2
Khantau Kazakh. **81** E2
Khantayskoye, Ozero *l.* Rus. Fed.
  87 I2
Khanty-Mansiysk Rus. Fed.
  34 F2
Khao Chum Thong Thai. **67** A3
Khao Laem Reservoir Thai.
  67 A2
Kharabali Rus. Fed. **35** D4
Kharagpur India **79** C2
Khārān r. Iran **83** C2
Khārijah, Wāḥāt al *oasis* Egypt
  92 B2
Kharkiv Ukr. **39** E2
Khar'kov Ukr. *see* Kharkiv
Kharovsk Rus. Fed. **37** F2
Khartoum Sudan **92** B3
Khāsh Iran **83** D2
Khashm el Girba Dam Sudan
  82 A3
Khasi Hills India **79** D2
Khaskovo Bulg. **58** C2
Khayamnandi S. Africa **99** C3
Khaybar Saudi Arabia **82** A2
Khayelitsha S. Africa **98** A3
Khemis Miliana Alg. **55** D2
Khenâmèh Iran **85** D3
Kherson Ukr. **39** D2
Kheta r. Rus. Fed. **87** I2
Khilok Rus. Fed. **73** D1
Khimki Rus. Fed. **37** E2
Khmel'nyts'kyy Ukr. **38** C2
Khokhol'skiy Rus. Fed. **37** E3
Kholm Afgh. **78** A1
Kholm Rus. Fed. **37** D2
Kholmsk Rus. Fed. **70** C1
Kholm-Zhirkovskiy Rus. Fed.
  37 D2
Khomas Highland *hills* Namibia
  98 A1
Khonj Iran **83** C2
Khon Kaen Thai. **66** B2
Khoper r. Rus. Fed. **39** F2
Khorol Ukr. **39** D2
Khorramābād Iran **85** C2
Khorramshahr Iran **85** C2
Khorugh Tajik. **81** E3
Khowst Afgh. **78** A1
Khromtau Kazakh. **80** C1

Khrystynivka Ukr. **38** C2
Khŭjand Tajik. **81** D2
Khulays Saudi Arabia **82** A2
Khulna Bangl. **79** C2
Khushab Pak. **78** B1
Khust Ukr. **38** B2
Khuzdar Pak. **78** A2
Khvormūj Iran **85** C2
Khvoy Iran **85** C2
Khvoynaya Rus. Fed. **37** D2
Khyber Pass Afgh./Pak. **78** B1
Kiama Austr. **105** E2
Kiambi Dem. Rep. Congo **95** C3
Kibiti Tanz. **95** D3
Kičevo Macedonia **59** B2
Kidal Mali **90** C3
Kidderminster U.K. **47** B3
Kidira Senegal **90** A3
Kidnappers, Cape N.Z. **106** C2
Kiel Ger. **50** C2
Kielce Pol. **51** E2
Kielder Water resr U.K. **46** B2
Kieler Bucht *b.* Ger. **41** C5
Kiev Ukr. **38** D1
Kiffa Maur. **90** A3
Kigali Rwanda **95** D3
Kigoma Tanz. **95** C3
Kihnu *i.* Estonia **36** B2
Kiiminki Fin. **40** F2
Kii-suidō *sea chan.* Japan **71** B4
Kikinda S.M. **58** B1
Kikondja Dem. Rep. Congo **95** C3
Kikwit Dem. Rep. Congo **94** B3
Kilchu N. Korea **69** B1
Kilembe Dem. Rep. Congo **94** B3
Kilgore U.S.A. **127** F2
Kilimanjaro *vol.* Tanz. **95** D3
Kilis Turkey **84** B2
Kiliya Ukr. **38** C2
Kilkeel U.K. **45** D1
Kilkenny Rep. of Ireland **45** C2
Kilkis Greece **59** B2
Killarney Rep. of Ireland **45** B2
Killeen U.S.A. **127** E2
Killybegs Rep. of Ireland **45** B1
Kilmarnock U.K. **44** B3
Kilmore Austr. **105** C3
Kilosa Tanz. **95** D3
Kilrush Rep. of Ireland **45** B2
Kilwa Dem. Rep. Congo **95** C3
Kilwa Masoko Tanz. **95** D3
Kimba Austr. **104** B2
Kimball U.S.A. **120** C2
Kimberley S. Africa **98** B2
Kimberley Plateau Austr. **102** B1
Kimch'aek N. Korea **69** B1
Kimch'ŏn S. Korea **69** B2
Kimmirut Can. **111** H2
Kimovsk Rus. Fed. **37** E3
Kimpese Dem. Rep. Congo **94** B3
Kimry Rus. Fed. **37** E2
Kinabalu, Gunung *mt.* Malaysia
  65 C1
Kinbasket Lake Can. **112** D2

194

Lincardine Can. **114** B2
Linda Dem. Rep. Congo **95** C3
Lindia Guinea **90** A3
Lindu Dem. Rep. Congo **95** C3
Ling Rus. Fed. **37** F2
Ling City U.S.A. **119** B3
Ling George Islands Can. **114** C1
Lingisepp Rus. Fed. **36** C2
Lings Island Austr. **103** D3
Ling Leopold Ranges hills Austr. **102** B1
Lingman U.S.A. **126** B1
Lings r. U.S.A. **119** B3
Lingscote Austr. **104** B3
Ling's Lynn U.K. **47** D3
Lingsmill Group is Kiribati **110**
Ling Sound b. Austr. **102** B1
Lings Peak U.S.A. **118** D2
Lingsport U.S.A. **125** D1
Lingston Can. **114** C2
Lingston Jamaica **131** C3
Lingston U.S.A. **123** F2
Lingston South East Austr. **104** B3
Lingston upon Hull U.K. **46** C3
Lingstown St Vincent **131** D3
Lingsville U.S.A. **127** E3
Lingswood U.K. **47** B4
Lingussie U.K. **44** B2
Ling William Island Can. **110** F2
Ling William's Town S. Africa **99** C3
Linna Sweden **41** C4
Linsale Rep. of Ireland **45** B3
Linshasa Dem. Rep. Congo **94** B3
Linston U.S.A. **125** E1
Lintyre pen. U.K. **44** B3
Lipawa, Lac l. Can. **114** C2
Lireyevsk Rus. Fed. **37** E3
Liribati country Pacific Ocean **101**
Linkkale Turkey **84** B2
Lirillov Rus. Fed. **37** E2
Liringa, Mount
   Kenya, Mount
Lirishi Rus. Fed. **37** D2
Liritimati atoll Kiribati **111**
Lirkağaç Turkey **59** C3
Lirkcaldy U.K. **44** C2
Lirkcudbright U.K. **44** B3
Lirkenes Norway **40** G2
Lirkcbnummi Fin. **36** B1
Lirkland Lake Can. **114** B2
Lirksville U.S.A. **121** E2
Lirkūk Iraq **85** C2
Lirkwall U.K. **44** C1
Lirov Kaluzhskaya Oblast' Rus. Fed. **37** D3
Lirov Kirovskaya Oblast' Rus. Fed. **34** D3
Lirovo-Chepetsk Rus. Fed. **34** E3

Kirovohrad Ukr. **39** D2
Kirovsk Rus. Fed. **40** G2
Kirovs'ke Ukr. **39** E2
Kirriemuir U.K. **44** C2
Kirsanov Rus. Fed. **39** F1
Kirthar Range mts Pak. **78** A2
Kiruna Sweden **40** E2
Kiryū Japan **71** C3
Kirzhach Rus. Fed. **37** E2
Kisangani Dem. Rep. Congo **95** C2
Kisantu Dem. Rep. Congo **94** B3
Kisaran Indon. **64** A1
Kiselevsk Rus. Fed. **86** H3
Kishanganj India **79** C2
Kishinev Moldova see Chişinău
Kishkenekol' Kazakh. **81** E1
Kishorganj Bangl. **66** H2
Kishtwar Jammu and Kashmir **78** B1
Kisii Kenya **95** D3
Kiskunfélegyháza Hungary **51** D3
Kiskunhalas Hungary **51** D3
Kislovodsk Rus. Fed. **35** D4
Kismaayo Somalia **93** C5
Kisoro Uganda **95** C3
Kissidougou Guinea **90** A4
Kissimmee U.S.A. **125** D3
Kissimmee, Lake U.S.A. **125** D3
Kississing Lake Can. **113** F2
Kisumu Kenya **95** D3
Kita Mali **90** B3
Kitakami-gawa r. Japan **70** D3
Kita-Kyūshū Japan **71** B4
Kitami Japan **70** D2
Kitchener Can. **114** B2
Kitee Fin. **41** Q3
Kitgum Uganda **95** D2
Kitimat Can. **112** C2
Kitunda Tanz. **95** D3
Kitwanga Can. **112** C2
Kitwe Zambia **97** B1
Kitzingen Ger. **49** E3
Kiuruvesi Fin. **40** F3
Kızılca Dağ mt. Turkey **59** C3
Kızılırr Rus. Fed. **35** D4
Kjellefjord Norway **40** F1
Kjøpsvik Norway **40** D2
Kladno Czech Rep. **50** C2
Klagenfurt Austria **50** C3
Klaipėda Lith. **36** B2
Klaksvík Faroe Is **42** B1
Klamath r. U.S.A. **118** B2
Klamath Falls U.S.A. **118** B2
Klamath Mountains U.S.A. **118** B2
Klang Malaysia **64** B1
Klaukol U.S.A. **112** B2
Klawock U.S.A. **112** B2
Kleena Kleene Can. **112** C2
Kleinbegin S. Africa **98** B2
Kleinsee S. Africa **98** A2
Klerksdorp S. Africa **99** C2

Kletnya Rus. Fed. **37** D3
Klimavichy Belarus **37** D3
Klimovo Rus. Fed. **37** D3
Klimovsk Rus. Fed. **37** E2
Klin Rus. Fed. **37** E2
Klinovec mt. Czech Rep. **49** F2
Klintehamn Sweden **41** D4
Klintsy Rus. Fed. **37** D3
Ključ Bos.-Herz. **57** C2
Kłodzko Pol. **51** D2
Klosterneuburg Austria **51** D3
Klötze (Altmark) Ger. **49** E1
Kluane Lake Can. **112** B1
Kluczbork Pol. **51** D2
Klukwan U.S.A. **112** B2
Klupro Pak. **78** A2
Klyaz'ma r. Rus. Fed. **37** F2
Klyetsk Belarus **36** C3
Knästen h. Sweden **41** C3
Knee Lake Can. **113** F2
Knetzgau Ger. **49** E2
Knin Croatia **57** C2
Knittelfeld Austria **50** C3
Književa E.M. **60** D2
Knokke-Heist Belgium **48** A2
Knoxville U.S.A. **125** D1
Knysna S. Africa **98** B3
Kōbe Japan **71** C4
København Denmark see Copenhagen
Koblenz Ger. **48** C2
Kobroör i. Indon. **63** C3
Kobryn Belarus **36** B3
Kočani Macedonia **58** B2
Kocasu r. Turkey **59** C2
Koch Bihar India **79** C2
Kōchi Japan **71** B4
Kōchübey Rus. Fed. **35** D4
Kodarma India **79** C2
Kodiak Island U.S.A. **110** B3
Kodok Sudan **93** B4
Kodyma Ukr. **38** C2
Kodzhaele mt. Bulg./Greece **59** C2
Koës Namibia **98** A2
Koffiefontein S. Africa **98** C2
Koforidua Ghana **90** B4
Kōfu Japan **71** C3
Kogaluk r. Can. **115** D1
Kohat Pak. **78** B1
Kohima India **66** H4
Kohtla-Järve Estonia **36** C2
Kokand Uzbek. see Qo'qon
Kokkola Fin. **40** E3
Kokomo U.S.A. **122** C2
Kokpekti Kazakh. **81** F2
Koksharau Kazakh. **81** C1
Koksoak r. Can. **115** D1
Kokstad S. Africa **99** C3
Koktokay China see Fuyun
Kolaka Indon. **65** D2
Kola Peninsula Rus. Fed. **34** C2
Kolari Fin. **40** E2
Kolda Senegal **90** A3

Kolding Denmark 41 B4
Koléa Alg. 55 D2
Kolguyev, Ostrov i. Rus. Fed. 34 D2
Kolhapur India 71 C3
Kolkasrags pt Latvia 36 B2
Kolkata India 71 C2
Kolmanskop Namibia 98 A2
Köln Ger. see Cologne
Kolokani Mali 90 B3
Kolomna Rus. Fed. 37 E2
Kolomyya Ukr. 38 C2
Kolonedale Indon. 65 C2
Kolonkwaneng Botswana 98 B2
Kolpashevo Rus. Fed. 86 H3
Kolpny Rus. Fed. 37 E3
Kol'skiy Poluostrov pen. Rus. Fed. see Kola Peninsula
Koluli Eritrea 82 B3
Kolwezi Dem. Rep. Congo 95 C4
Kolymskaya Nizmennost' lowland Rus. Fed. 87 M2
Kolymskiy, Khrebet mts Rus. Fed. 87 N2
Komaki Japan 71 C3
Komandorskiye Ostrova is Rus. Fed. 87 N3
Komárno Slovakia 51 D3
Komati r. Swaziland 98 D2
Komatsu Japan 71 C3
Kominternivs'ke Ukr. 38 D2
Komiža Croatia 57 C2
Komotini Greece 59 C2
Komsberg mts S. Africa 98 B3
Komsomolets, Ostrov i. Rus. Fed. 87 I1
Komsomol'sk Rus. Fed. 37 F2
Komsomol'sk Ukr. 39 D2
Komsomol'sk-na-Amure Rus. Fed. 73 F1
Konakovo Rus. Fed. 37 E2
Kondagaon India 79 C3
Kondoa Tanz. 95 D3
Kondopoga Rus. Fed. 34 C2
Kondrovo Rus. Fed. 37 E3
Kong Christian IX Land reg. Greenland 111 J2
Kong Frederik VI Kyst coastal area Greenland 111 J2
Kongju S. Korea 69 B2
Kongolo Dem. Rep. Congo 95 C3
Kongsberg Norway 41 B4
Kongsvinger Norway 41 C3
Kongur Shan mt. China 81 E3
Königswinter Ger. 48 C2
Königs Wusterhausen Ger. 49 F1
Konin Pol. 51 D2
Konjic Bos.-Herz. 57 C2
Konklep watercourse Namibia 98 A2
Konotop Ukr. 39 D1
Konstantinovsk Rus. Fed. 39 F2

Konstanz Ger. 50 B3
Kontagora Nigeria 91 C3
Kon Tum Vietnam 67 B2
Kon Tum, Cao Nguyên plat. Vietnam 67 B2
Konya Turkey 84 B2
Konz Ger. 48 C3
Kooskia U.S.A. 118 C1
Kootenay Lake Can. 112 D3
Kópasker Iceland 40 [inset]
Koper Slovenia 56 B1
Koprivnica Croatia 57 C1
Korablino Rus. Fed. 37 E3
Koraput India 77 C3
Korbach Ger. 49 D2
Korçë Albania 59 B2
Korčula Croatia 57 C2
Korčula i. Croatia 57 C2
Korea, North country Asia 69 B1
Korea, South country Asia 69 B2
Korea Bay g. China/N. Korea 69 A2
Korea Strait Japan/S. Korea 69 B3
Korenovsk Rus. Fed. 39 E2
Korets' Ukr. 38 C1
Körfez Turkey 59 C2
Korhogo Côte d'Ivoire 90 B4
Korinthos Greece see Corinth
Köris-hegy h. Hungary 51 D3
Kōriyama Japan 71 D3
Korkuteli Turkey 84 B2
Korla China 81 F2
Körmend Hungary 51 D3
Koroc r. Can. 115 D1
Korocha Rus. Fed. 39 E1
Korogwe Tanz. 95 D3
Koror Palau 63 C2
Korosten' Ukr. 38 C1
Korostyshiv Ukr. 38 C1
Koro Toro Chad 91 D3
Korsakov Rus. Fed. 70 D1
Korsør Denmark 50 C1
Korsun'-Shevchenkivs'kyy Ukr. 39 D2
Kortrijk Belgium 48 A2
Koryakskiy Khrebet mts Rus. Fed. 87 N2
Koryazhma Rus. Fed. 34 D2
Koryŏng S. Korea 69 B2
Koryukivka Ukr. 39 D1
Kos Greece 59 C3
Kos i. Greece 59 C3
Koscian Pol. 51 D2
Kosciuszko, Mount Austr. 105 D3
Kosh-Agach Rus. Fed. 81 F2
Košice Slovakia 51 E3
Kosŏng N. Korea 69 B2
Kosovo prov. S.M. 58 B2
Kosovska Mitrovica S.M. 58 B2
Kosrae atoll Micronesia 110
Kossou, Lac de l. Côte d'Ivoire 90 B4
Kostanay Kazakh. 80 D1

Koster S. Africa 99 C2
Kosti Sudan 93 B3
Kostomuksha Rus. Fed. 40 G3
Kostroma Rus. Fed. 37 F2
Kostroma r. Rus. Fed. 37 F2
Kostrzyn Pol. 50 C2
Koszalin Pol. 51 D2
Kőszeg Hungary 51 D3
Kota India 78 B2
Kotaagung Indon. 64 B2
Kotabaru Indon. 65 C2
Kota Belud Malaysia 65 C1
Kota Bharu Malaysia 64 B1
Kotabumi Indon. 64 B2
Kota Kinabalu Malaysia 65 C1
Kota Samarahan Malaysia 65 C1
Kotel'nich Rus. Fed. 34 D3
Kotel'nyy, Ostrov i. Rus. Fed. 87 L1
Köthen (Anhalt) Ger. 49 E2
Kotka Fin. 41 F3
Kotlas Rus. Fed. 34 D2
Kotlik U.S.A. 110 B2
Kotor Varoš Bos.-Herz. 57 C2
Kotovsk Rus. Fed. 37 F3
Kotovs'k Ukr. 38 C2
Kotzebue U.S.A. 110 B2
Kotzebue Sound sea chan. U.S.A. 110 B2
Kötzting Ger. 49 F3
Koudougou Burkina 90 B3
Kougaberge mts S. Africa 98 B3
Koulamoutou Gabon 94 B3
Koulikoro Mali 90 B3
Koundâra Guinea 90 A3
Kourou Fr. Guiana 135 D2
Koutiala Mali 90 B3
Kouvola Fin. 41 F3
Kovdor Rus. Fed. 40 G2
Kovel' Ukr. 38 B1
Kovrov Rus. Fed. 37 F2
Kowhitirangi N.Z. 106 B3
Koyda Rus. Fed. 34 D2
Koyukuk r. U.S.A. 110 B2
Kozani Greece 59 B2
Kozelets' Ukr. 38 D1
Kozel'sk Rus. Fed. 37 E3
Kozyatyn Ukr. 38 C2
Krabi Thai. 67 A3
Kra Buri Thai. 67 A2
Krâchéh Cambodia 67 B2
Kragerø Norway 41 B4
Kragujevac S.M. 58 B2
Krakatau i. Indon. 64 B2
Kraków Pol. 51 D2
Kramators'k Ukr. 39 E2
Kramfors Sweden 40 D3
Krasino Rus. Fed. 34 E1
Krāslava Latvia 36 C2
Krasnaya Gora Rus. Fed. 37 D3
Krasnaya Gorbatka Rus. Fed. 37 F2

rasnoarmeysk Rus. Fed. **35** D3
rasnoarmiys'k Ukr. **39** E2
rasnodar Rus. Fed. **39** E2
rasnodon Ukr. **39** E2
rasnogvardeyskoye
Belgorodskaya Oblast' Rus. Fed.
39 E1
rasnogvardeyskoye
Stavropol'skiy Kray Rus. Fed.
39 F2
rasnohrad Ukr. **39** E2
rasnoarmiys'ke Ukr. **39** D2
rasnokamsk Rus. Fed. **34** E3
rasnoperekops'k Ukr. **39** D2
rasnoufimsk Rus. Fed. **34** E3
rasnoyarsk Rus. Fed. **87** I3
rasnoye-na-Volge Rus. Fed.
37 F2
rasnyy Rus. Fed. **37** D3
rasnyy Kholm Rus. Fed. **37** E2
rasnyy Luch Ukr. **35** C4
rasnyy Sulin Rus. Fed. **39** F2
rasyliv Ukr. **38** D2
refeld Ger. **48** C2
remenchuk Ukr. **39** D2
remenchuts'ka
Vodoskhovyshche *resr* Ukr.
39 D2
reminna Ukr. **39** E2
rems an der Donau Austria
51 D3
resttsy Rus. Fed. **37** D2
retinga Lith. **36** B2
reuztal Ger. **48** C2
ribl Cameroon **94** A2
rikellos Greece **59** B3
ril'on, Mys *c.* Rus. Fed. **70** D1
rishna *r.* India **77** C3
rishnanagar India **79** C2
ristiansand Norway **41** B4
ristianstad Sweden **41** C4
ristiansund Norway **40** B3
ristinehamn Sweden **41** C4
riti *i.* Greece *see* Crete
riževci Croatia **57** C1
rk *i.* Croatia **56** B1
rokom Sweden **40** C3
rolevets' Ukr. **39** D1
ronach Ger. **49** E2
röng Kaôh Rŏng Cambodia
67 B2
ronprins Frederik Bjerge
nunataks Greenland **111** J2
roonstad S. Africa **99** C2
ropotkin Rus. Fed. **39** F2
rosno Pol. **51** E3
rui Indon. **64** B2
rujë Albania **58** A2
rumovgrad Bulg. **59** C2
rung Thep Thai. *see* Bangkok
rupël Belarus **36** C3
ruševac S.M. **58** B2
rušné Hory *mts* Czech Rep.
49 F2

Kruzof Island U.S.A. **112** B2
Krychaw Belarus **37** D3
Krymsk Rus. Fed. **39** E3
Krytiko Pelagos *sea* Greece
59 C3
Kryvyy Rih Ukr. **39** D2
Ksabi Alg. **90** B2
Ksar Chellala Alg. **55** D2
Ksar el Boukhari Alg. **55** D2
Kshenskiy Rus. Fed. **37** E3
Kü', Jabal al *h.* Saudi Arabia
78 B4
Kuala Belait Brunei **65** C1
Kuala Kerai Malaysia **64** B1
Kuala Lipis Malaysia **64** B1
Kuala Lumpur Malaysia **64** B1
Kualapembuang Indon.
65 C2
Kuala Terengganu Malaysia
64 B1
Kualatungal Indon. **64** B2
Kuandian China **69** A1
Kuantan Malaysia **64** B1
Kubanʼ *r.* Rus. Fed. **39** F2
Kubenskoye, Ozero *l.* Rus. Fed.
37 E2
Kubrat Bulg. **58** C2
Kubuang Indon. **65** C1
Kuching Malaysia **65** C1
Kuçovë Albania **59** A2
Kudat Malaysia **65** C1
Kufstein Austria **60** C3
Kugaaruk Can. **111** G2
Kugluktuk Can. **110** E2
Kuhmo Fin. **40** F3
Kûhrân, Kûh-e *mt.* Iran **83** C2
Kuiseb *watercourse* Namibia
98 A1
Kuito Angola **96** A1
Kuivaniemi Fin. **40** F2
Kujang N. Korea **69** B2
Kukës Albania **58** B2
Kula Turkey **59** C3
Kula Kangri *mt.* Bhutan/China
79 D2
Kulandy Kazakh. **80** C2
Kuldiga Latvia **36** B2
Kulebaki Rus. Fed. **37** F2
Kulmbach Ger. **49** E2
Kŭlob Tajik. **81** D3
Kulʼsary Kazakh. **80** C2
Kulunda Rus. Fed. **81** E1
Kulundinskoye, Ozero *salt l.*
Rus. Fed. **81** E1
Kulusuk Greenland **111** J2
Kumagaya Japan **71** C3
Kumamoto Japan **71** B4
Kumanovo Macedonia **58** B2
Kumasi Ghana **90** B4
Kumba Cameroon **94** A2
Kumertau Rus. Fed. **35** E3
Kumi S. Korea **69** B2
Kumla Sweden **41** D4
Kumo Nigeria **91** D3

Kumon Range *mts* Myanmar
66 A1
Kumylzhenskiy Rus. Fed. **39** F2
Kunashir, Ostrov *i.* Rus. Fed.
70 E2
Kunene *r.* Angola/Namibia **96** A1
Kungei Alatau *mts* Kazakh./Kyrg.
81 E2
Kungsbacka Sweden **41** C4
Kungu Dem. Rep. Congo **94** B2
Kungur Rus. Fed. **34** E3
Kunhing Myanmar **66** A1
Kunlun Shan *mts* China **79** B1
Kunming China **75** A3
Kunsan S. Korea **69** B2
Kununurra Austr. **102** B1
Künzelsau Ger. **49** D3
Kuopio Fin. **40** F3
Kupa *r.* Croatia/Slovenia **56** C1
Kupang Indon. **63** C3
Kupiškis Lith. **36** B2
Kupreanof Island U.S.A. **112** B2
Kupʼʼyans'k Ukr. **39** E2
Kŭrp China *i.* **91** B4
Kurashiki Japan **71** B4
Kurayoshi Japan **71** B3
Kurchatov Rus. Fed. **37** E3
Kürdzhali Bulg. **58** C2
Kure Japan **71** B4
Kuressaare Estonia **36** B2
Kurgan Rus. Fed. **35** F3
Kurganinsk Rus. Fed. **39** F3
Kurikka Fin. **41** E3
Kuril Islands Rus. Fed. **87** L3
Kurilʼsk Rus. Fed. **87** L3
Kurmuk Sudan **93** B3
Kurnool India **77** B3
Kuroiso Japan **71** C3
Kurri Kurri Austr. **105** E2
Kursk Rus. Fed. **37** E3
Kuruman S. Africa **98** B2
Kuruman *watercourse* S. Africa
98 B2
Kurume Japan **71** B4
Kurumkan Rus. Fed. **87** J3
Kurunegala Sri Lanka **77** C4
Kuşadası Turkey **59** C3
Kuşadası Körfezi *b.* Turkey
59 C3
Kuş Gölü *l.* Turkey **59** C2
Kushchevskaya Rus. Fed. **39** E2
Kushiro Japan **70** D2
Kushmurun Kazakh. **80** D1
Kushtia Bangl. **79** C2
Kuskokwim *r.* U.S.A. **87** P2
Kuskokwim Mountains U.S.A.
110 B2
Kussharo-ko *l.* Japan **70** D2
Kütahya Turkey **59** C3
Kʼutʼaisi Georgia **85** C1
Kutno Pol. **51** D2
Kutu Dem. Rep. Congo **94** B3
Kuujjua *r.* Can. **110** E2
Kuujjuaq Can. **115** D1

197

Kuujjuarapik Can. **114** C1
Kuusamo Fin. **40** F2
Kuvango Angola **96** A1
Kuvshinovo Rus. Fed. **37** D2
Kuwait *country* Asia **83** B2
Kuwait Kuwait **83** B2
Kuybyshevskoye
  Vodokhranilishche *resr*
  Rus. Fed. **35** D3
Kuybysheve Ukr. **39** E2
Kuytun China **81** F2
Kuznetsk Rus. Fed. **35** D3
Kuznetsovs'k Ukr. **38** C1
Kvalsund Norway **40** F1
Kwajalein *atoll* Marshall Is **110**
KwaMashu S. Africa **99** D2
Kwandang Indon. **65** D1
Kwangju S. Korea **69** B2
Kwanmo-bong *mt.* N. Korea
  69 B1
Kwanobuhle S. Africa **99** C3
Kwanonzame S. Africa **98** B3
Kwatinidubu S. Africa **99** C3
Kwazulu-Natal *prov.* S. Africa
  99 D2
Kwekwe Zimbabwe **97** B1
Kwenge *r.* Dem. Rep. Congo **94** B3
Kwidzyn Pol. **51** D2
Kwilu *r.* Angola/Dem. Rep. Congo
  94 B3
Kwoka *mt.* Indon. **65** D2
Kyabram Austr. **105** D3
Kyaikto Myanmar **66** A2
Kyakhta Rus. Fed. **72** D1
Kyancutta Austr. **104** B2
Kyaukpadaung Myanmar **66** A1
Kyaukpyu Myanmar **66** A2
Kybartai Lith. **36** B3
Kyeintali Myanmar **66** A2
Kyeburg India **78** B1
Kyiv Ukr. *see* Kiev
Kyklades *is* Greece *see* Cyclades
Kyle Can. **113** E2
Kyle of Lochalsh U.K. **44** B2
Kyll *r.* Ger. **48** C3
Kyllini *mt.* Greece **59** B3
Kymi Greece **59** B3
Kyneton Austr. **104** C3
Kyoga, Lake Uganda **95** D2
Kyogle Austr. **105** E1
Kyŏnggi-man b. S. Korea **69** B2
Kyŏngju S. Korea **69** B2
Kyōto Japan **71** C4
Kypshak, Ozero *salt l.* Kazakh.
  81 D1
Kyrgyzstan *country* Asia **81** E2
Kyritz Ger. **49** F1
Kyrönjoki *r.* Fin. **40** E3
Kythira *i.* Greece **59** B3
Kythnos *i.* Greece **59** B3
Kyūshū *i.* Japan **71** B4
Kyustendil Bulg. **58** B2
Kyyivs'ke Vodoskhovyshche *resr*
  Ukr. **38** D1

Kyzyl Rus. Fed. **72** C2
Kyzylkum Desert Kazakh./Uzbek.
  80 D2
Kyzyl-Mazhalyk Rus. Fed. **81** G1
Kyzylorda Kazakh. **81** D2

La Angostura, Presa de *resr*
  Mex. **129** C3
Laascaanood Somalia **93** C4
La Asunción Venez. **134** C1
Laâyoune Western Sahara **90** A2
Laba *r.* Rus. Fed. **39** F2
La Babia Mex. **128** B2
La Banda Arg. **136** B3
La Baule-Escoublac France
  52 B2
Labé Guinea **90** A3
Laberge, Lake Can. **112** B1
La Biche, Lac *l.* Can. **113** D2
Labinsk Rus. Fed. **39** F3
Labouheyre France **52** B3
Labrador *reg.* Can. **115** D1
Labrador City Can. **115** D1
Labrador Sea Can./Greenland
  111 I2
Lábrea Brazil **134** C3
Labuan Malaysia **65** C1
Labuhanbajo Indon. **65** C2
Labuhanbilik Indon. **64** B1
Labuna Indon. **63** C3
Laburta Myanmar **66** A2
Labytnangi Rus. Fed. **34** F2
Laç Albania **58** A2
La Capelle France **53** C2
Laccadive Islands India **77** B3
Lac du Bonnet Can. **113** F2
La Ceiba Hond. **130** B3
Lachlan *r.* Austr. **105** C2
Lachute Can. **123** F1
La Ciotat France **53** D3
Lac la Biche Can. **113** D2
Lac-Mégantic Can. **115** C2
Lacombe Can. **112** D2
La Concepción Panama **130** B4
Laconia U.S.A. **123** F2
La Crosse U.S.A. **122** B2
La Cruz Mex. **128** B2
La Cuesta Mex. **128** B2
Ladakh Range *mts* India **79** B1
Ladismith S. Africa **98** B3
Ladozhskoye Ozero *l.* Rus. Fed.
  see Ladoga, Lake
Ladysmith S. Africa **99** C2
Lae P.N.G. **63** D3
Læsø *i.* Denmark **41** C4
La Fayette U.S.A. **125** C2
Lafayette *IN* U.S.A. **122** C2
Lafayette *LA* U.S.A. **124** B2
Lafia Nigeria **91** C4
La Flèche France **52** B2

Laforge Can. **115** C1
Läft Iran **83** C2
La Galite *i.* Tunisia **56** A3
Lagan' Rus. Fed. **35** D4
Laghouat Alg. **90** C1
Lagoa Santa Brazil **139** D1
Lagoda, Laba Rus. Fed. **37** D1
Lagos Nigeria **90** C4
Lagos Port. **54** B2
La Grande U.S.A. **118** C1
La Grande 2, Réservoir *resr* Can.
  114 C1
La Grande 3, Réservoir *resr* Can.
  114 C1
La Grande 4, Réservoir *resr* Can.
  115 C1
Lagrange Austr. **102** B1
La Grange U.S.A. **125** C2
La Gran Sabana *plat.* Venez.
  134 C2
Laguna Brazil **136** D3
Laguna, Picacho de la *mt.* Mex.
  128 A2
La Habana Cuba *see* Havana
Lahad Datu Malaysia **65** C1
Lahat Indon. **64** B2
Laḩij Yemen **82** B3
Lāhījān Iran **85** C2
Lahore Pak. **78** B1
Lahri Pak. **78** A2
Lahti Fin. **41** F3
Laï Chad **91** D4
Laidley Austr. **105** E1
Lainsburg S. Africa **98** B3
Lainioälven *r.* Sweden **40** E2
Lairg U.K. **44** B1
Laives Italy **56** B1
Laiwu China **74** B2
Laiyang China **74** C2
Laizhou China **74** B2
Laizhou Wan b. China **74** B2
Lajamanu Austr. **102** C1
Lajes Brazil **136** C3
La Junta Mex. **128** B2
La Junta U.S.A. **120** C3
Lake Cargelligo Austr. **105** D2
Lake Cathie Austr. **105** E2
Lake Charles U.S.A. **124** B2
Lake City *FL* U.S.A. **125** D2
Lake City *SC* U.S.A. **125** E2
Lake Havasu City U.S.A.
  126 B2
Lakeland U.S.A. **125** D3
Lake Louise Can. **112** D2
Lake Oswego U.S.A. **118** B1
Lake Paringa N.Z. **106** A3
Lake Providence U.S.A. **124** B2
Lakes Entrance Austr. **105** D3
Lakewood *CO* U.S.A. **120** B3
Lakewood *NJ* U.S.A. **123** F2
Lakhdaria Alg. *see* Lakhdaria
Lakh Worth U.S.A. **125** D3
Lakhpat India **78** A2
Lakki Pak. **78** B1

Lakonikos Kolpos b. Greece 59 B3
Lakselv Norway 40 E1
Laksha U.S.A. 120 C3
Lalín Spain 54 B1
Lalitpur India 79 B2
La Louvière Belgium 48 B2
La Maddalena Italy 56 A2
Lamag Malaysia 65 C1
La Manche str. France/U.K. see English Channel
Lamar U.S.A. 120 C3
Lamard Iran 83 C2
La Marmora, Punta mt. Italy 56 A3
La Martre, Lac l. Can. 112 D1
Lambaréné Gabon 94 B3
Lambert's Bay S. Africa 98 A3
La Merced Peru 134 B4
Lameroo Austr. 104 C3
Lamesa U.S.A. 127 D2
Lamia Greece 59 B3
Lamoni U.S.A. 121 E2
Lampang Thai. 66 A2
Lampasas U.S.A. 127 E2
Lampazos Mex. 129 B2
Lamphun Thai. 66 A2
Lamu Kenya 95 E3
Lanbi Kyun i. Myanmar 67 A2
Lancang Jiang r. China see Mekong
Lancaster U.K. 46 B2
Lancaster OH U.S.A. 122 D3
Lancaster PA U.S.A. 123 E2
Lancaster SC U.S.A. 125 D2
Lancaster Sound str. Can. 111 G2
Landau in der Pfalz Ger. 48 D3
Landeck Austria 50 C3
Land's End U.K. 47 A4
Landshut Ger. 50 C3
Landskrona Sweden 41 C4
Lanett U.S.A. 125 C2
Langberg mts S. Africa 98 B3
Langdon U.S.A. 121 D1
Langeland i. Denmark 41 C4
Langen Ger. 49 D1
Langeoog Ger. 48 C1
Langeoog i. Ger. 48 C1
Langgöns Ger. 49 D2
Langjökull ice cap Iceland 40 [inset]
Langogne France 53 C3
Langon France 52 B3
Langres France 53 D2
Langsa Indon. 64 A1
Länkäran Azer. 85 C2
Lannion France 52 B2
Lansing U.S.A. 122 D2
Lanxi China 75 B3
Lanzarote i. Canary Is 90 A2

Lanzhou China 74 A2
Laoag Phil. 68 B2
Lao Cai Vietnam 66 B1
Laohekou China 74 B2
Lao Ling mts China 69 B1
Laon France 53 C2
Laos country Asia 66 B2
Laotougou China 69 B1
Lapa Brazil 138 C3
La Palma i. Canary Is 90 A2
La Palma Panama 130 C4
La Paz Bol. 136 B2
La Paz Hond. 130 B3
La Paz Mex. 128 A2
La Pedrera Col. 134 C3
La Pérouse Strait Japan/Rus. Fed. 70 D1
La Pesca Mex. 129 C2
La Piedad Mex. 128 B2
La Plata Arg. 137 C4
La Plata, Río de sea chan. Arg./Uru. 137 C4
La Quiaca Arg. 136 B3
Lār Iran 83 C2
Larache Morocco 90 B1
Laramie U.S.A. 120 B2
Laramie Mountains U.S.A. 120 B2
Laranda Turkey see Karaman
Laranjeiras do Sul Brazil 138 B3
Larantuka Indon. 65 D2
Larba i. Indon. 65 C2
Laredo Spain 54 C1
Laredo U.S.A. 127 E3
Largs U.K. 44 B3
La Rioja Arg. 136 B3
Larisa Greece 59 B3
Larkana Pak. 78 A2
Larnaca Cyprus 84 B2
Larne U.K. 45 D1
La Rochelle France 52 B2
La Roche-sur-Yon France 52 B2
La Roda Spain 55 C2
La Romana Dom. Rep. 131 D3
La Ronge Can. 110 E3
La Ronge, Lac l. Can. 110 E3
Larrimah Austr. 102 C1
Larsen Ice Shelf Antarctica 107 A3
Larvik Norway 41 C4
Las Cruces U.S.A. 126 C2
La Serena Chile 136 A3
Las Heras Arg. 137 B4
Lashio Myanmar 66 A1

Lashkar Gāh Afgh. 78 A1
La Sila reg. Italy 57 C3
Las Lomitas Arg. 136 B3
Las Nieves Mex. 128 B2
Las Palmas de Gran Canaria Canary Is 90 A2
La Spezia Italy 56 A2
Las Plumas Arg. 137 B5
Last Mountain Lake Can. 113 C2
Lastovo i. Croatia 57 C2
Las Tres Vírgenes, Volcán vol. Mex. 128 A2
Las Tunas Cuba 131 C2
Las Varas Chihuahua Mex. 128 B2
Las Varas Nayarit Mex. 128 B2
Las Vegas NM U.S.A. 126 C1
Las Vegas NV U.S.A. 119 C3
Latakia Syria 84 B2
La Teste-de-Buch France 52 B3
Latina Italy 56 B2
La Tuque Can. 115 C2
Latvia country Europe 36 B2
Lauchhammer Ger. 49 F2
Lauf an der Pegnitz Ger. 49 E3
Launceston Austr. 103 D4
Launceston U.K. 47 A4
Laura Austr. 103 D1
Laurel MS U.S.A. 124 C2
Laurel MT U.S.A. 118 E1
Lauria Italy 57 C2
Laurinburg U.S.A. 125 E2
Lausanne Switz. 53 D2
Laut i. Indon. 65 C2
Lautersbach (Hessen) Ger. 49 D2
Laut Kecil, Kepulauan is Indon. 65 C2
Lauwersmeer l. Neth. 48 C1
Laval France 52 B2
Lavapié, Punta c. Chile 147
Lavras Brazil 139 D2
Lawrence U.S.A. 121 D3
Lawrenceburg U.S.A. 124 C1
Lawton U.S.A. 127 E2
Lawz, Jabal al mt. Saudi Arabia 82 A2
Laxå Sweden 41 C4
Lazarevac S.M. 58 B2
Lázaro Cárdenas Baja California Mex. 128 A1
Lázaro Cárdenas Michoacán Mex. 128 B3
Leader Can. 113 E2
Leadville U.S.A. 120 B3
Leaf Rapids Can. 113 E2
Leavenworth U.S.A. 121 E3
Lebach Ger. 48 C3
Lebanon country Asia 84 B2
Lebanon MO U.S.A. 121 E3
Lebanon NH U.S.A. 123 F2
Lebanon OR U.S.A. 118 B2
Lebanon PA U.S.A. 123 E2
Lebedyan' Rus. Fed. 37 E3

Lebedyn Ukr. **39** D1
Lębork Pol. **51** D2
Lebowakgomo S. Africa **99** C1
Lebrija Spain **54** B2
Lebu Chile **137** A4
Le Bugue France **52** C3
Le Catelet France **48** A2
Lecce Italy **57** C2
Lecco Italy **56** A1
Lech r. Austria/Ger. **50** C3
Lechaina Greece **59** B3
Lechang China **75** B3
Ledesma Spain **54** B1
Leduc Can. **112** D2
Leech Lake U.S.A. **121** E1
Leeds U.K. **46** C3
Leer (Ostfriesland) Ger. **48** C1
Leesburg U.S.A. **125** D3
Leesville U.S.A. **124** B2
Leeton Austr. **105** D2
Leeu-Gamka S. Africa **98** B3
Leeuwarden Neth. **48** B1
Leeuwin, Cape Austr. **102** A3
Leeward Islands Caribbean Sea **131** D3
Lefkada Greece **59** B3
Lefkada i. Greece **59** B3
Lefkosia Cyprus see Nicosia
Legaspi Phil. **68** B2
Legnago Italy **56** B1
Legnica Pol. **51** D2
Leh India **79** B1
Le Havre France **52** C2
Lehututu Botswana **98** B1
Leiah Pak. **78** B1
Leibnitz Austria **51** D3
Leicester U.K. **47** C3
Leichhardt r. Austr. **103** C1
Leiden Neth. **48** B1
Leie r. Belgium **48** A2
Leigh Creek Austr. **104** B2
Leikanger Norway **41** B3
Leimen Ger. **49** D2
Leine r. Ger. **49** D1
Leinster reg. Rep. of Ireland **45** C2
Leipzig Ger. **49** F2
Leiranger Norway **40** C2
Leiria Port. **54** B2
Leirvik Norway **41** B4
Leixlip Rep. of Ireland **45** C2
Leiyang China **75** B3
Leizhou China **75** B3
Leizhou Bandao pen. China **75** A3
Lelystad Neth. **48** B1
Le Maire, Estrecho de sea chan. Arg. **137** B6
Léman, Lac l. France/Switz. see Geneva, Lake
Le Mans France **52** C2
Le Mars U.S.A. **121** D2
Leme Brazil **138** C3
Lemesos Cyprus see Limassol

Lemieux Islands Can. **111** H2
Lemmon U.S.A. **120** C1
Lemoore U.S.A. **119** C3
Le Moyne, Lac l. Can. **115** D1
Le Murge hills Italy **57** C2
Lena r. Rus. Fed. **87** K2
Lendery Rus. Fed. **40** G3
Lengerich Ger. **48** C1
Lengshuijiang China **75** B3
Lengshuitan China **75** B3
Leninne Ukr. **39** E2
Leningradskaya Rus. Fed. **39** E2
Leninskiy Rus. Fed. **37** E3
Lensk Rus. Fed. **87** J2
Lentini Italy **56** C3
Léo Burkina **90** B3
Leoben Austria **50** D3
León Mex. **128** B2
León Nic. **130** B3
León Spain **54** B1
Leonardville Namibia **98** A1
Leonora Austr. **102** B2
Lephalale S. Africa **99** C1
Lephepe Botswana **99** C1
Leping China **75** B3
Le Puy-en-Velay France **53** C2
Lerala Botswana **99** C1
Lérida Col. **134** B3
Leros i. Greece **59** C3
Le Roy, Lac l. Can. **114** C1
Lerum Sweden **41** C4
Lerwick U.K. **44** [inset]
Lesbos i. Greece **59** C3
Les Cayes Haiti **131** C3
Leshan China **72** C3
Leshukonskoye Rus. Fed. **34** D2
Leskovac S.M. **58** B2
Lesosibirsk Rus. Fed. **87** I3
Lesotho country Africa **99** C2
Lesozavodsk Rus. Fed. **70** B1
Les Sables-d'Olonne France **52** B2
Lesser Antilles is Caribbean Sea **131** D3
Lesser Caucasus mts Asia **85** C1
Lesser Slave Lake Can. **112** D2
Lesvos i. Greece see Lesbos
Leszno Pol. **51** D2
Letchworth U.K. **47** C4
Lethbridge Can. **113** D3
Lethem Guyana **134** D2
Leticia Col. **134** C3
Letlhakeng Botswana **99** C1
Letsok-aw Kyun i. Myanmar **67** A2
Letsopa S. Africa **99** C2
Leucate, Étang de l. France **52** C3
Leuser, Gunung mt. Indon. **64** A1
Leuven Belgium **48** B2
Levadeia Greece **59** B3
Levelland U.S.A. **127** C2
Lévêque, Cape Austr. **102** B1

Leverkusen Ger. **48** C2
Levice Slovakia **51** D3
Levin N.Z. **106** C3
Lewis, Isle of i. U.K. **44** A1
Lewisburg U.S.A. **123** D3
Lewis Range mts U.S.A. **118** D1
Lewiston ID U.S.A. **118** C1
Lewiston ME U.S.A. **123** F2
Lewistown U.S.A. **118** E1
Lexington KY U.S.A. **122** D3
Lexington NC U.S.A. **125** D3
Lexington VA U.S.A. **123** E3
Leyte i. Phil. **68** B2
Lezhë Albania **58** A2
Lezhnevo Rus. Fed. **37** F2
L'gov Rus. Fed. **37** E3
Lhagoi Kangri mt. China **79** C2
Lhasa China **79** D2
Lhazê China **79** C2
Lhokseumawe Indon. **64** A1
Liancourt Rocks i.
    N. Pacific Ocean **69** C2
Lianjiang China **75** B3
Lianshan China **74** C1
Lianyungang China **74** C1
Lianzhou China **75** B3
Liaocheng China **74** B2
Liaodong Bandao pen. China **74** C1
Liaodong Wan b. China **74** C1
Liao He r. China **69** A1
Liaoning prov. China **74** C1
Liaoyang China **74** C1
Liaoyuan China **69** B1
Libby U.S.A. **118** C1
Libenge Dem. Rep. Congo **94** B2
Liberal U.S.A. **120** C3
Liberec Czech Rep. **50** D2
Liberia country Africa **90** B4
Liberia Costa Rica **130** B3
Libourne France **52** B3
Libreville Gabon **94** A2
Libya country Africa **91** D2
Libyan Desert Egypt/Libya **91** E2
Libyan Plateau Egypt **92** A1
Licata Italy **56** B3
Lichinga Moz. **97** C1
Lichtenburg S. Africa **99** C2
Lichtenfels Ger. **49** E2
Lida Belarus **36** C3
Liděping Sweden **41** C4
Liebenwalde Ger. **49** F1
Liebig, Mount Austr. **102** C2
Liechtenstein country Europe **53** D2
Liège Belgium **48** B2
Lieksa Fin. **40** G3
Lienz Austria **50** C3
Liepāja Latvia **36** B2
Liévin France **48** A2
Liezen Austria **50** C3
Liffey r. Rep. of Ireland **45** C2
Lifford Rep. of Ireland **45** C1
Lightning Ridge Austr. **105** D1

Ligonha r. Moz. **97** C1

Ligurian Sea France/Italy **56** A2

Likasi Dem. Rep. Congo **95** C4

Likhoslavl' Rus. Fed. **37** E2

Liku Indon. **64** B1

Lilla Edet Sweden **41** C4

Lille France **52** C1

Lillehammer Norway **41** C3

Lillestrøm Norway **41** C4

Lilongwe Malawi **97** C1

Lima Peru **134** B4

Lima U.S.A. **122** D2

Limassol Cyprus **84** B2

Limavady U.K. **45** C1

Limay r. Arg. **137** B4

Limbach-Oberfrohna Ger. **49** F2

Limbaži Latvia **36** B2

Limbe Cameroon **94** A2

Limburg an der Lahn Ger. **48** D2

Lime Acres S. Africa **98** B2

Limerick Rep. of Ireland **45** B2

Limfjorden sea chan. Denmark **41** B4

Limnos i. Greece **59** C3

Limoges France **52** C2

Limón Hond. C.A. **120** C3

Limoux France **52** C3

Limpopo prov. S. Africa **99** C1

Limpopo r. S. Africa/Zimbabwe **99** D2

Linares Chile **137** A4

Linares Mex. **129** C2

Linares Spain **54** C2

Lincang China **66** B3

Lincoln U.K. **46** C3

Lincoln IL U.S.A. **122** C2

Lincoln NE U.S.A. **121** D2

Linden Guyana **135** D2

Lindi r. Dem. Rep. Congo **95** C3

Lindi Tanz. **95** D3

Lindisfarne i. U.K. see Holy Island

Lindsay Can. **123** E2

Line Islands Kiribati **143** E4

Linfen China **74** B2

Lingayen Phil. **68** B2

Lingelihle S. Africa **99** C3

Lingen (Ems) Ger. **48** C1

Lingga, Kepulauan is Indon. **64** B2

Lingshui China **75** A4

Linguère Senegal **90** A3

Linhares Brazil **139** D1

Linhe China **74** A1

Linköping Sweden **41** D4

Linkou China **70** B1

Linnhe, Loch inlet U.K. **44** B2

Linqing China **74** B2

Lins Brazil **138** C2

Linton U.S.A. **120** C1

Linxi China **74** B1

Linxia China **74** A2

Linyi Shandong China **74** B2

Linyi Shandong China **74** B2

Linying China **74** B2

Linz Austria **50** D3

Lion, Golfe du g. France **53** C3

Lipari Italy **56** B3

Lipari, Isole is Italy **56** B3

Lipetsk Rus. Fed. **37** E3

Lipin Bor Rus. Fed. **37** E1

Lipova Romania **38** D2

Lippstadt Ger. **49** D2

Liqing China **75** B3

Lisala Dem. Rep. Congo **94** C2

Lisboa Port. see Lisbon

Lisbon Port. **54** B2

Lisburn U.K. **45** C1

Liscannor Bay Rep. of Ireland **45** B2

Lisieux France **52** C2

Liskeard U.K. **47** A4

Liski Rus. Fed. **37** E3

Lismore Austr. **105** E1

Lismore Rep. of Ireland **45** B2

Litang Guangxi China **75** A3

Litang Sichuan China **72** C2

Litchfield IL U.S.A. **122** C3

Litchfield MN U.S.A. **121** E1

Lithgow Austr. **105** E2

Lithino, Akra c. Greece **59** B4

Lithuania country Europe **36** B2

Litoměřice Czech Rep. **50** C2

Little Abaco i. Bahamas **131** C2

Little Andaman i. India **67** A2

Little Belt sea chan. Denmark see
Lille Bælt

Little Falls U.S.A. **121** E1

Littlefield U.S.A. **127** D2

Littlehampton U.K. **47** C4

Little Karoo plat. S. Africa **98** B3

Little Minch sea chan. U.K. **44** A2

Little Missouri r. U.S.A. **120** C1

Little Nicobar i. India **67** A3

Little Rock U.S.A. **124** B2

Liujiachang China **75** B3

Liuzhou China **75** A3

Līvāni Latvia **36** C2

Livermore, Mount U.S.A. **126** D2

Liverpool Can. **115** D2

Liverpool U.K. **46** B3

Liverpool Range mts Austr. **105** D2

Livingston MT U.S.A. **118** D1

Livingston TX U.S.A. **127** F2

Livingstone Zambia **96** B1

Livno Bos.-Herz. **57** C2

Livny Rus. Fed. **37** E3

Livonia U.S.A. **122** D2

Livorno Italy **56** B2

Liwale Tanz. **95** D3

Lizard Point U.K. **47** A5

Ljubljana Slovenia **56** B1

Ljungan r. Sweden **41** D3

Ljungby Sweden **41** C4

Ljusdal Sweden **41** D3

Ljusnan r. Sweden **41** D3

Llandeilo U.K. **47** B4

Llandovery U.K. **47** B4

Llandrindod Wells U.K. **47** B3

Llandudno U.K. **46** B3

Llanelli U.K. **47** A4

Llangefni U.K. **46** A3

Llano Estacado plain U.S.A. **127** D2

Llanos reg. Col./Venez. **134** C2

Lleida Spain **55** D1

Lliria Spain **55** C2

Llodio Spain **54** C1

Lloyd George, Mount Can. **112** C2

Lloyd Lake Can. **113** E2

Lloydminster Can. **113** D2

Llullaillaco, Volcán vol. Chile **136** B3

Lobatse Botswana **99** C2

Lobito Angola **96** A1

Lochboisdale U.K. **44** A2

Lochgilphead U.K. **44** B2

Lochinver U.K. **44** B1

Lochmaddy U.K. **44** A2

Lochnagar mt. U.K. **44** C2

Lock Austr. **104** B2

Lockerbie U.K. **44** C3

Lockport U.S.A. **123** E2

Lodeynoye Pole Rus. Fed. **37** C2

Lodi U.S.A. **122** C2

Løding Norway **40** C2

Lodwar Kenya **95** D2

Łódź Pol. **51** D2

Loei Thai. **66** B2

Loeriesfontein S. Africa **98** A3

Lofoten is Norway **40** C2

Logan U.S.A. **118** D2

Logan, Mount Can. **112** A1

Logansport U.S.A. **122** C2

Logatec Slovenia **56** B1

Logroño Spain **54** C1

Löhne Ger. **49** D1

Lohne (Oldenburg) Ger. **49** D1

Loikaw Myanmar **66** A2

Loi Lan mt. Myanmar/Thai. **66** A2

Loire r. France **52** B2

Loja Ecuador **134** B3

Loja Spain **54** C2

Lokan tekojärvi l. Fin. **40** F2

Lokeren Belgium **48** B2

Lokichar Kenya **95** D2

Loknya Rus. Fed. **37** D2

Lokoja Nigeria **91** C4

Lokot' Rus. Fed. **37** D3

Loks Land i. Can. **111** H2

Lolland i. Denmark **41** C5

Lolwane S. Africa **98** B2

Lom Bulg. **58** B2

Lomami r. Dem. Rep. Congo **95** C2

Lomas de Zamora Arg. **137** C4

Lombok i. Indon. **65** C2

Lombok, Selat sea chan. Indon. **65** C2

Lomé Togo **90** C4
Lomela r. Dem. Rep. Congo
94 C3
Lomme France **48** A2
Lommel Belgium **48** B2
Lomond, Loch l. U.K. **44** B2
Lomonosov Rus. Fed. **36** C1
Lompobattang, Gunung mt.
Indon. **65** C2
Lompoc U.S.A. **119** B4
Lom Sak Thai. **66** B2
Łomża Pol. **51** C2
London Can. **114** B2
London U.K. **47** C4
London U.S.A. **122** B3
Londonderry U.K. **45** C1
Londonderry, Cape Austr.
102 B1
Londrina Brazil **138** B2
Longa r. Dem. Rep. Congo
94 C3
Longa, Proliv sea chan. Rus. Fed.
87 N2
Long Akah Malaysia **65** C1
Long Bay U.S.A. **125** E2
Long Beach U.S.A. **119** C4
Longford Rep. of Ireland **45** C2
Longiram Indon. **65** C2
Long Island Bahamas **131** C2
Long Island Can. **114** C1
Long Island P.N.G. **63** D3
Long Island U.S.A. **123** F2
Longlac Can. **114** B2
Longmont U.S.A. **120** B2
Long Point Can. **123** D2
Long Range Mountains Can.
115 E2
Longreach Austr. **103** D2
Longtown U.K. **46** B2
Longuyon France **53** D2
Longview TX U.S.A. **127** E2
Longview WA U.S.A. **118** B1
Longxi China **74** A2
Longxi Shan mt. China **75** B3
Long Xuyên Vietnam **67** B2
Longyan China **75** B3
Longyearbyen Svalbard **86** D1
Lons-le-Saunier France **50** B3
Lookout, Cape U.S.A. **125** E2
Loop Head Rep. of Ireland **45** B2
Lop Buri Thai. **67** B2
Lopez Phil. **68** B2
Lop Nur salt flat China **72** C2
Lopori r. Dem. Rep. Congo
94 B2
Lora del Rio Spain **54** B2
Lorain U.S.A. **122** D2
Loralai Pak. **78** A1
Lorca Spain **55** C2
Lord Howe Island Austr. **103** E3
Lordsburg U.S.A. **126** C2
Lorena Brazil **139** C2
Loreto Bol. **136** B2
Loreto Mex. **128** A2
Lorient France **52** B2
Lorn, Firth of est. U.K. **44** B2

Lorne Austr. **104** C3
Los Alamos U.S.A. **126** C1
Los Aldamas Mex. **127** E3
Los Ángeles Chile **137** A4
Los Angeles U.S.A. **119** C4
Los Banos U.S.A. **119** B3
Los Blancos Arg. **136** B3
Losevo Rus. Fed. **39** F1
Lošinj i. Croatia **56** B2
Los Mochis Mex. **128** B2
Losombo Dem. Rep. Congo
94 B2
Los Roques, Islas is Venez.
131 D3
Lossiemouth U.K. **44** C2
Los Teques Venez. **134** C1
Los Vilos Chile **136** A4
Lot r. France **52** C3
Loth U.K. **44** C1
Lotikipi Plain Kenya **95** D2
Loto Dem. Rep. Congo **94** C3
Louangnamtha Laos **66** B1
Louangphabang Laos **66** B2
Loubomo Congo **94** B3
Loudéac France **52** B2
Loudi China **75** B3
Louga Senegal **90** A3
Loughborough U.K. **47** C3
Loughrea Rep. of Ireland **45** B2
Louhans France **52** B3
Louisburgh Rep. of Ireland **45** B2
Louisiade Archipelago is P.N.G.
103 E1
Louisiana state U.S.A. **124** B2
Louisville KY U.S.A. **122** C3
Louisville MS U.S.A. **124** C2
Louny Czech Rep. **49** F2
Lourdes France **52** B3
Lousã Port. **54** B1
Louth Austr. **105** D2
Louth U.K. **46** C3
Lovat' r. Rus. Fed. **37** D2
Lovech Bulg. **58** B2
Loveland U.S.A. **120** B2
Lovelock U.S.A. **118** C2
Lovington U.S.A. **127** D2
Lowa Dem. Rep. Congo **95** C3
Lowell U.S.A. **123** F2
Lower Arrow Lake Can. **112** D3
Lower Hutt N.Z. **106** B3
Lower Lough Erne l. U.K. **45** C1
Lowestoft U.K. **47** D3
Łowicz Pol. **51** D2
Lowville U.S.A. **123** E2
Loxton Austr. **104** C2
Loyauté, Îles is New Caledonia
110
Loyew Belarus **37** D3
Løypskardtinden mt. Norway
42 F2
Loznica S.M. **58** A2
Lozova Ukr. **39** E2
Luacano Angola **96** B1
Lu'an China **74** B2

Luanda Angola **94** B3
Luangwa r. Zambia **97** C1
Luanshya Zambia **97** B1
Luarca Spain **54** B1
Luau Angola **96** B1
Lubaczów Pol. **51** E2
Lubango Angola **96** A1
Lubao Dem. Rep. Congo **95** C3
Lubartów Pol. **51** E2
Lübbecke Ger. **49** D1
Lübben Ger. **49** F2
Lübbenau Ger. **49** F2
Lubbock U.S.A. **127** D2
Lübeck Ger. **49** E1
Lubei China **74** C1
Lubin Pol. **51** D2
Lublin Pol. **51** E2
Lubny Ukr. **39** D1
Lubudi Dem. Rep. Congo **95** C3
Lubuklinggau Indon. **64** B2
Lubumbashi Dem. Rep. Congo
95 C4
Lubungu Zambia **96** B1
Lubutu Dem. Rep. Congo **95** C3
Lucala Angola **94** B3
Lucan Rep. of Ireland **45** C2
Lucapa Angola **94** C3
Luce Bay U.K. **44** B3
Lucélia Brazil **138** B2
Lucena Phil. **68** B2
Lucena Spain **54** C2
Lučenec Slovakia **51** D3
Lucera Italy **56** C2
Lucerne Switz. **53** D2
Lüchow Ger. **49** E1
Lucira Angola **96** A1
Luckau Ger. **49** F2
Luckenwalde Ger. **49** F1
Luckhoff S. Africa **98** B2
Lucknow India **79** C2
Lucusse Angola **96** B1
Lüderitz Namibia **98** A2
Ludhiana India **78** B1
Ludlow U.K. **47** B3
Ludlow U.S.A. **119** C4
Ludogorie reg. Bulg. **58** C2
Ludvika Sweden **41** D3
Ludwigsburg Ger. **50** B3
Ludwigsfelde Ger. **49** F1
Ludwigshafen am Rhein Ger.
49 D3
Ludwigslust Ger. **49** E1
Ludza Latvia **36** C2
Luebo Dem. Rep. Congo **94** C3
Luena Angola **96** B1
Lüeyang China **74** A2
Lufeng China **75** B3
Lufkin U.S.A. **127** F2
Luga Rus. Fed. **36** C2
Luga r. Rus. Fed. **36** C2
Lugano Switz. **53** D2
Lugenda r. Moz. **97** C1
Lugo Italy **56** B2
Lugo Spain **54** B1
Lugoj Romania **58** B1
Luhans'k Ukr. **39** E2

Luhombero Tanz. **95** D3
Luhyny Ukr. **38** C1
Luiana Angola **96** B1
Luilaka r. Dem. Rep. Congo
94 C3
Luiro r. Fin. **40** F2
Lukavac Bos.-Herz. **57** C2
Lukenie r. Dem. Rep. Congo **94** B3
Lukeville U.S.A. **126** C2
Lukh r. Rus. Fed. **37** F3
Lukhovitsy Rus. Fed. **37** E3
Luków Pol. **51** E2
Lukulu Zambia **96** B1
Luleå Sweden **40** E2
Luleburgaz Turkey **58** C2
Liliang Shan mts China **74** B2
Lumajang Indon. **65** C2
Lumajangdong Co salt l. China
79 C1
Lumbala Kāquengue Angola
96 B1
Lumbala N'guimbo Angola **96** B1
Lumberton U.S.A. **125** E2
Lumbis Indon. **65** C1
Lumphăt Cambodia **67** B2
Lumsden N.Z. **113** C2
Lumsden Can. **123** D2
Lumsden N.Z. **106** A4
Lünd Sweden **41** C4
Lundazi Zambia **97** C1
Lundy i. U.K. **47** A4
Lüneburg Ger. **49** E1
Lüneburger Helde reg. Ger.
49 E1
Lunéville France **53** D2
Lünga r. Zambia **96** B1
Lungnaquilla Mountain h.
Rep. of Ireland **45** C2
Lungwebungu r. Zambia **96** B1
Lunl r. India **78** B2
Luninyets Belarus **36** C3
Lunsar Sierra Leone **90** A4
Luntai China **81** F2
Luoding China **75** B3
Luohe China **74** B2
Luoyang China **75** A3
Lupanshui China **75** A3
Lupeni Romania **58** B2
Lupilichi Moz. **97** C1
Lúrio Moz. **97** D1
Lurio r. Moz. **97** D1
Lusaka Zambia **97** B1
Lusambo Dem. Rep. Congo
94 C3
Lushnjë Albania **59** A2
Lusk U.S.A. **120** C2
Lut, Dasht-e des. Iran **80** C3
Lutherstadt Wittenberg Ger.
49 F2
Luton U.K. **47** C4
Luts'k Ukr. **36** C1
Lutselk'e Can. **113** D1
Luts'k Ukr. **36** C1
Lutzputs S. Africa **98** B2
Lutzville S. Africa **98** A3

Luuq Somalia **93** C4
Luverne U.S.A. **121** D2
Luvua r. Dem. Rep. Congo
95 C3
Luwero Uganda **95** D2
Luwuk Indon. **65** D2
Luxembourg country Europe
48 C1
Luxembourg Lux. **48** C1
Luxolweni S. Africa **99** C3
Luxor Egypt **92** B2
Luzern Switz. see Lucerne
Luzhou China **75** A3
Luziânia Brazil **138** C1
Luzon i. Phil. **68** B2
Luzon Strait Phil. **68** B1
L'viv Ukr. **38** B2
L'vov Ukr. see L'viv
Lyakhavichy Belarus **36** C3
Lyakhawichy Sweden **40** D0
Lydenburg S. Africa **99** D2
Lyel'chytsy Belarus **36** C3
Lyepyel' Belarus **36** C3
Lyme Bay U.K. **47** B4
Lynchburg U.S.A. **123** E3
Lynn Lake Can. **113** E2
Lynx Lake Can. **113** E1
Lyon France **53** C2
Lyozna Belarus **37** D2
Lys'va Rus. Fed. **35** E3
Lysychans'k Ukr. **39** E2
Lytham St Anne's U.K. **46** B3
Lyuban' Belarus **36** C3
Lyubertsy Rus. Fed. **37** E2
Lyubeshiv Ukr. **38** C1
Lyubim Rus. Fed. **37** F2
Lyubotyn Ukr. **39** E2
Lyubytino Rus. Fed. **37** D2
Lyudinovo Rus. Fed. **37** D3

M

Ma'ān Jordan **84** B2
Maardu Estonia **36** C2
Maarianhamina Fin. see
Mariehamn
Ma'arrat an Nu'mān Syria see
Maaseik Belgium **48** B2
Maasin Phil. **68** B2
Maastricht Neth. **48** B2
Mabalane Moz. **97** C2
Mabaruma Guyana **134** D2
Mabote Moz. **97** C2
Mabule Botswana **98** B1
Mabutsane Botswana **98** B1
Macaé Brazil **139** D2
Macaloge Moz. **97** C1
Macapá Brazil **135** D2
Macará Brazil **139** D1
Macassar Strait Indon. see
Makassar, Selat
Macau China **75** B3
Macau aut. reg. China **75** B3
Macclesfield U.K. **46** B3

Macdonald, Lake salt flat Austr.
102 B2
Macdonnell Ranges mts Austr.
102 C2
MacDowell Lake Can. **114** A1
Macedo de Cavaleiros Port.
54 B1
Macedon mt. Austr. **104** C3
Macedonia country Europe **58** B2
Maceió Brazil **135** F3
Macerata Italy **56** B2
Macfarlane, Lake salt flat Austr.
104 B2
Macgillycuddy's Reeks mts
Rep. of Ireland **45** B3
Mach Pak. **78** A2
Machaila Moz. **97** C2
Machakos Kenya **95** D3
Machala Ecuador **134** B3
Machanga Moz. **97** C2
Macheng China **74** B2
Machias U.S.A. **123** G2
Machiques Venez. **134** B1
Machu Picchu Peru **134** B4
Macia Moz. **99** D2
Măcin Romania **58** C2
Macintyre r. Austr. **105** E1
Mackay Austr. **103** D2
Mackay, Lake salt flat Austr.
102 B2
McKay Lake Can. **113** D1
Mackenzie Can. **112** C2
Mackenzie r. Can. **112** B1
Mackenzie Bay Can. **110** C2
Mackenzie King Island Can.
110 C1
Mackenzie Mountains Can.
112 B1
Macksville Austr. **105** E2
Maclean Austr. **105** E1
MacLeod, Lake imp. l. Austr.
102 A2
Macomb U.S.A. **122** B2
Macomer Italy **56** A2
Mâcon France **53** C2
Macon GA U.S.A. **125** D2
Macon MO U.S.A. **121** E3
Macquarie r. Austr. **105** D2
Macquarie Island
S. Pacific Ocean **110**
Macquarie Marshes Austr. **105** D2
Macroom Rep. of Ireland **45** B3
Macumba watercourse Austr.
104 B1
Macuspana Mex. **129** C3
Macuzari, Presa resr Mex.
128 B2
Madadeni S. Africa **99** D2
Madagascar country Africa
97 [inset] D2
Madama Niger **91** D2
Madan Bulg. **59** B2
Madang P.N.G. **63** D3

Madeira *r.* Brazil **134** D3
Madeira *terr.* N. Atlantic Ocean **90** A1
Madeleine, Îles de la *is* Can. **115** D2
Madera Mex. **128** B2
Madgaon India **77** B3
Madingou Congo **94** B3
Madison *IN* U.S.A. **122** C4
Madison *WI* U.S.A. **122** C3
Madison *r.* U.S.A. **118** D1
Madisonville U.S.A. **122** C3
Madiun Indon. **65** C2
Mado Gashi Kenya **95** D3
Madoi China **72** C2
Madona Latvia **36** C2
Madrakah Saudi Arabia **82** A2
Madras India *see* Chennai
Madras U.S.A. **118** B2
Madre, Laguna *lag.* Mex. **129** C2
Madre de Dios *r.* Peru **134** C4
Madre del Sur, Sierra *mts* Mex. **129** B3
Madre Occidental, Sierra *mts* Mex. **128** B2
Madre Oriental, Sierra *mts* Mex. **129** B2
Madrid Spain **54** C1
Madridejos Spain **54** C2
Madura *i.* Indon. **65** C2
Madura, Selat *sea chan.* Indon. **65** C2
Madurai India **77** B4
Maebashi Japan **71** C3
Mae Hong Son Thai. **66** A2
Mae Sai Thai. **66** A1
Mafeteng Lesotho **99** C2
Mafia Island Tanz. **95** D3
Mafikeng S. Africa **99** C2
Mafinga Tanz. **95** D3
Mafra Brazil **138** C3
Magadan Rus. Fed. **87** M3
Magangue Col. **131** D2
Magdalena *r.* Col. **132**
Magdalena Mex. **128** A1
Magdalena U.S.A. **126** C2
Magdalena, Bahía *b.* Mex. **128** A2
Magdeburg Ger. **49** E1
Magellan, Strait of Chile **137** A6
Magherafelt U.K. **45** C1
Magnitogorsk Rus. Fed. **35** E3
Magnolia U.S.A. **124** B2
Magpie, Lac *l.* Can. **115** D1
Magta' Lahjar Maur. **90** A3
Maguarinho, Cabo *c.* Brazil **135** E3
Magude Moz. **99** D2
Magwe Myanmar *see* Magway
Mahabad Iran **85** C2
Mahajan India **78** B2
Mahajanga Madag. **97** [inset] D1
Mahakam *r.* Indon. **65** C2
Mahalapye Botswana **99** C1

Mahanadi *r.* India **79** C2
Mahanoro Madag. **97** [inset] D1
Maha Sarakham Thai. **67** B2
Mahavavy *r.* Madag. **97** [inset] D1
Mahbubnagar India **77** B3
Mahd adh Dhahab Saudi Arabia **82** B2
Mahdia Guyana **134** D2
Mahé *i.* Seychelles **93**
Mahesana India **78** B2
Mahilyow Belarus **37** D3
Mahón Spain **55** D2
Mahony Lake Can. **112** C1
Mahuva India **78** B2
Maidstone U.K. **47** D4
Maiduguri Nigeria **91** D3
Main *r.* Ger. **49** D2
Maïné-Soroa, Lac *l.*
   Dem. Rep. Congo **94** B3
Main-Donau-Kanal *canal* Ger. **49** E3
Maine *state* U.S.A. **123** G1
Maingkwan Myanmar **66** A1
Mainland *i.* Scotland U.K. **44** C1
Mainland *i.* Scotland U.K. **44** [inset]
Maintirano Madag. **97** [inset] D1
Mainz Ger. **49** D2
Maiquetía Venez. **131** D3
Maitland *N.S.W.* Austr. **105** E2
Maitland *S.A.* Austr. **104** B2
Maíz, Islas del *is* Nic. **130** B3
Maizuru Japan **71** C3
Maja Jezercë *mt.* Albania **58** A2
Majene Indon. **65** C2
Majorca *i.* Spain **55** D2
Majuro *atoll* Marshall Is **110**
Makabana Congo **94** B3
Makale Indon. **65** C2
Makanchi Kazakh. **81** F2
Makarska Croatia **57** C2
Makassar Indon. **65** C2
Makassar, Selat *str.* Indon. **65** C2
Makat Kazakh. **80** C2
Makatini Flats *lowland* S. Africa **99** D2
Makeni Sierra Leone **90** A4
Makgadikgadi *salt pan* Botswana **96** B2
Makhachkala Rus. Fed. **35** D4
Makhado S. Africa **99** C1
Makhambet Kazakh. **80** C2
Makhmur, Barrage El *dam* Morocco **54** B3
Makindu Kenya **95** D3
Makinsk Kazakh. **81** D1
Makiyivka Ukr. **39** E2
Makkah Saudi Arabia *see* Mecca
Makkovik Can. **115** E1
Makó Hungary **51** E3
Makokou Gabon **94** B2
Makongolosi Tanz. **95** D3
Makopong Botswana **98** B2

Makran *reg.* Iran/Pak. **83** D2
Makran Coast Range *mts* Pak. **78** A2
Maksatikha Rus. Fed. **37** E2
Mākū Iran **85** C2
Makum India **66** A1
Makurazaki Japan **71** B4
Makurdi Nigeria **91** C4
Malå Sweden **40** D2
Malabo Equat. Guinea **94** A2
Malacca, Strait of
   Indon./Malaysia **64** A1
Malad City U.S.A. **118** D2
Maladzyechna Belarus **36** C3
Málaga Spain **54** C2
Malaita *i.* Solomon Is **110**
Malakal Sudan **93** B4
Malakula *i.* Vanuatu **110**
Malamala Indon. **65** D2
Malang Indon. **65** C2
Malanje Angola **94** B3
Mälaren *l.* Sweden **41** D4
Malatya Turkey **84** B2
Malawi *country* Africa **97** C1
Malawi, Lake Africa *see*
   Nyasa, Lake
Malaya Vishera Rus. Fed. **37** D2
Malaybalay Phil. **68** B3
Malāyer Iran **85** C2
Malaysia *country* Asia **64** B1
Malbork Pol. **51** D2
Malchin Ger. **49** F1
Maldegem Belgium **48** A2
Malden Island Kiribati **111**
Maldives *country* Indian Ocean **77** B4
Male Maldives **77** B4
Maleas, Akra *pt* Greece **59** B3
Male Atoll Maldives **77** B4
Malé Karpaty *hills* Slovakia **51** D3
Malheur Lake U.S.A. **118** C2
Mali *country* Africa **90** B3
Malili Indon. **65** D2
Malindi Kenya **95** E3
Malin Head Rep. of Ireland **45** C1
Malkara Turkey **59** C2
Mal'kavichy Belarus **36** C3
Mallacoota Austr. **105** D3
Mallacoota Inlet *b.* Austr. **105** D3
Mallaig U.K. **44** B2
Mallery Lake Can. **113** F1
Mallorca *i.* Spain *see* Majorca
Mallow Rep. of Ireland **45** B2
Malmberget Sweden **40** E2
Malmédy Belgium **48** C2
Malmesbury S. Africa **98** A3
Malmö Sweden **41** C4
Malong China **75** A3
Måløy Norway **41** B3
Maloyaroslavets Rus. Fed. **37** E2
Malorya Borisovo Rus. Fed. **37** E2
Malta *country* Europe **91** D1
Malta Latvia **36** C2
Malta *i.* Malta **36**

Malta U.S.A. 118 E1
Maltahöhe Namibia 98 A1
Malton U.K. 46 C2
Maluku is Indon. see Moluccas
Maluku, Laut sea Indon. 63 C3
Malvern U.S.A. 124 B2
Malyn Ukr. 38 C1
Malyy Anyuy r. Rus. Fed. 87 L2
Malyy Lyakhovskiy, Ostrov i.
   Rus. Fed. 87 L2
Mambéré r. C.A.R. 94 B2
Mamelodi S. Africa 99 C2
Mamoré r. Bol./Brazil 136 B2
Mamou Guinea 90 A3
Mamuju Indon. 65 C2
Man Côte d'Ivoire 90 B4
Manacapuru Brazil 134 C3
Manacor Spain 55 D2
Manado Indon. 63 C2
Managua Nic. 130 B3
Manakara Madag. 97 [inset] D2
Manākhah Yemen 82 B3
Manama Bahrain 83 C2
Manam Island P.N.G. 63 D3
Mananara Avaratra Madag.
   97 [inset] D1
Mananjary Madag. 97 [inset] D2
Manantali, Lac de i. Mali 90 A3
Manas Hu i. China 81 F2
Manatuto East Timor 63 D2
Manaus Brazil 134 C3
Manavgat Turkey 84 B2
Manchester U.K. 46 B3
Manchester U.S.A. 123 F2
Mandabe Madag. 97 [inset] D2
Mandal Norway 41 B4
Mandalay Myanmar 66 A1
Mandalgovi Mongolia 72 D2
Mandan U.S.A. 120 C1
Mandla India 79 C2
Mandritsara Madag. 97 [inset] D1
Mandsaur India 78 B2
Mandurah Austr. 102 A3
Mandya India 77 B3
Manevychi Ukr. 38 C1
Manfredonia Italy 57 C2
Mangai Dem. Rep. Congo 94 B3
Mangakino N.Z. 106 C2
Mangalia Romania 38 C3
Mangalore India 77 B3
Mangaung S. Africa 99 C2
Manggar Indon. 64 B2
Mangnai China 72 C2
Mangochi Malawi 97 C1
Mangystau Kazakh. 80 C2
Manhattan U.S.A. 121 D3
Manhiça Moz. 97 C2
Manica Moz. 97 C1
Manicoré Brazil 139 D2
Mania r. Madag. 97 [inset] D1
Maniago Italy 56 B1
Manicoré Brazil 134 C3

Manicouagan r. Can. 115 D2
Manicouagan, Petit Lac i. Can.
   115 D1
Manicouagan, Réservoir resr
   Can. 115 D1
Manifah Saudi Arabia 83 B2
Manihiki atoll Cook Is 111
Manila Phil. 68 B2
Manilla Austr. 105 E2
Manisa Turkey 59 C3
Manistee U.S.A. 122 C2
Manitoba prov. Can. 113 F2
Manitoba, Lake Can. 113 F2
Manitou Islands U.S.A. 122 C1
Manitoulin Island Can. 114 B2
Manitowoc U.S.A. 122 C2
Manizales Col. 134 B2
Mankato U.S.A. 121 E2
Mankono Côte d'Ivoire 90 B4
Mankota Can. 118 E1
Manmad India 78 B2
Mannar, Gulf of India/Sri Lanka
   77 B4
Mannheim Ger. 49 D3
Manning Can. 112 D2
Mannville Can. 113 D2
Manokwari Indon. 63 C3
Manono Dem. Rep. Congo 95 C3
Manosque France 53 D3
Manouane, Lac i. Can. 115 C1
Manresa Spain 55 D1
Mansa Zambia 97 D1
Mansel Island Can. 111 G2
Mansel'ky̆a ridge Fin./Rus. Fed.
   42 F2
Mansfield Austr. 105 D3
Mansfield U.K. 46 C3
Mansfield LA U.S.A. 124 B2
Mansfield OH U.S.A. 122 D2
Manta Ecuador 134 A3
Mantes-la-Jolie France 52 C2
Mantiqueira, Serra da mts Brazil
   139 C2
Mantova Italy see Mantua
Mantua Italy 56 B1
Manui i. Indon. 65 D2
Manukau N.Z. 106 B2
Manus Island P.N.G. 63 D3
Many U.S.A. 124 B2
Manych-Gudilo, Ozero i.
   Rus. Fed. 35 D4
Manyoni Tanz. 95 D3
Manzanares Spain 54 C2
Manzanillo Mex. 128 B3
Manzhouli China 73 D1
Manzini Swaziland 99 D2
Mao Chad 91 D3
Maoke, Pegunungan mts Indon.
   63 D3
Maokeng S. Africa 99 C2
Maokui Shan mt. China 69 A1
Maoming China 75 B3
Mapai Moz. 97 C2
Mapane Indon. 65 D2

Mapastepec Mex. 129 C3
Mapimí, Bolsón de des. Mex.
   128 B2
Mapin i. Phil. 68 A3
Mapinhane Moz. 97 C2
Maputo Moz. 99 D2
Maputo r. Moz./S. Africa 99 D2
Maquan He r. China 79 C2
Maquela do Zombo Angola
   94 B3
Maquoketa U.S.A. 121 E2
Mar, Serra do mts Brazil 147
Maraã Brazil 134 C3
Maraba Brazil 135 E3
Maracá, Ilha de i. Brazil 135 D2
Maracaibo Venez. 134 B1
Maracaibo, Lake Venez. 134 B2
Maracaju Brazil 138 A2
Maracaju, Serra de hills Brazil
   138 A2
Maracay Venez. 134 C1
Marādah Libya 91 D2
Maradi Niger 91 C3
Marāgheh Iran 05 C2
Marajó, Baía de est. Brazil
   135 E3
Marajó, Ilha de i. Brazil 135 D3
Marāki Iran 83 C2
Marand Iran 85 C2
Maranoa r. Austr. 105 D1
Marañón r. Peru 134 B3
Marathon Can. 114 B2
Marathon U.S.A. 126 D4
Marbella Spain 54 C2
Marble Bar Austr. 102 A2
Marburg S. Africa 99 D3
Marburg an der Lahn Ger. 49 D2
Marche-en-Famenne Belgium
   48 B2
Mar Chiquita, Lago i. Arg.
   136 B4
Marchtrenk Austria 53 E2
Marcoing France 48 A2
Marcy, Mount U.S.A. 123 F2
Mardan Pak. 78 B1
Mar del Plata Arg. 137 C4
Mardin Turkey 85 C2
Maree, Loch i. U.K. 44 B2
Marettimo, Isola i. Italy 56 B3
Marevo Rus. Fed. 37 D2
Marfa U.S.A. 126 D2
Margaret River Austr. 102 A3
Margarita, Isla de i. Venez.
   131 D3
Margate U.K. 47 D4
Margherita Peak
   Dem. Rep. Congo/Uganda
   95 C2
Märgow, Dasht-e des. Afgh.
   78 A1
Marhanets' Ukr. 39 D2
María Elena Chile 136 B3
Mariana Trench sea feature
   N. Pacific Ocean 142 C4

Marianna *AR* U.S.A. **124** B2
Marianna *FL* U.S.A. **125** C2
Mariánské Lázně Czech Rep. **50** C3
Marias, Islas *is* Mex. **128** B2
Mariato, Punta *pt* Panama **134** A2
Ma'rib Yemen **82** B3
Maribor Slovenia **56** F1
Maridi *watercourse* Sudan **93** A4
Marie Byrd Land *reg.* Antarctica **107** I2
Mariehamn Fin. **41** D3
Mariental Namibia **98** A1
Mariestad Sweden **41** C4
Marietta *GA* U.S.A. **125** C2
Marietta *OH* U.S.A. **122** D3
Marignane France **52** D3
Mariï, Mys *pt* Rus. Fed. **87** L3
Marijampolė Lith. **36** B3
Marília Brazil **138** C2
Marín Spain **54** B1
Mar''ina Horka Belarus **36** C3
Maringá Brazil **138** B2
Marinha Grande Port. **54** B2
Marion *IN* U.S.A. **122** C2
Marion *OH* U.S.A. **122** D2
Marion *SC* U.S.A. **125** E2
Marion, Lake U.S.A. **125** D2
Marion Bay Austr. **104** B3
Marlin U.S.A. **127** E2
Marmande France **52** C3
Marmara, Sea of *g.* Turkey *see* Marmara, Denizi
Marmara Denizi *g.* Turkey **59** C2
Marmaris Turkey **59** C3
Marne *r.* France **48** A3
Marne-la-Vallée France **52** C2
Maroantsetra Madag. **97** [inset] D1
Maromokotro *mt.* Madag. **97** [inset] D1
Marondera Zimbabwe **97** C1
Maroni *r.* Fr. Guiana **135** D2
Marotiri *i.* Fr. Polynesia **111**
Maroua Cameroon **94** B1
Marovoay Madag. **97** [inset] D1
Marquesas Islands Fr. Polynesia **111**
Marquette U.S.A. **122** C1
Marquion France **48** A2
Marra, Jebel *mt.* Sudan **93** A3
Marrakech Morocco **90** B1

Marra Plateau Sudan **93** A3
Marree Austr. **104** B1
Marresale Rus. Fed. **34** F2
Marrupa Moz. **97** C1
Marsá al'Alam Egypt **92** B2
Marsabit Kenya **95** D2
Marsala Italy **56** B3
Marsá Maṭrūḥ Egypt **92** A1
Marsberg Ger. **49** D2
Marsden Austr. **105** D2
Marseille France **53** D3
Marshall *AR* U.S.A. **124** B1
Marshall *MO* U.S.A. **121** E3
Marshall *TX* U.S.A. **127** F2
Marshall Islands *country* N. Pacific Ocean **100**
Marshalltown U.S.A. **121** E2
Marshfield U.S.A. **122** B2
Marsh Harbour Bahamas **125** E3
Marsh Island U.S.A. **124** B3
Märsta Sweden **36** A2
Martapura *Kalimantan Selatan* Indon. **65** C2
Martapura *Sumatera Selatan* Indon. **64** B2
Martha's Vineyard *i.* U.S.A. **123** F2
Martigny Switz. **53** D2
Martin Slovakia **51** D3
Martin U.S.A. **125** C1
Martínez Mex. **129** C2
Martinique *terr.* West Indies **131** D3
Martinsburg U.S.A. **123** E3
Marton N.Z. **106** C3
Martos Spain **54** C2
Martuk Kazakh. **80** C1
Mary Turkm. **80** D3
Maryborough Austr. **103** E2
Marydale S. Africa **98** B2
Maryland *state* U.S.A. **123** E3
Marysville U.S.A. **121** D3
Maryville *MO* U.S.A. **121** E2
Maryville *TN* U.S.A. **125** D1
Masai Steppe *plain* Tanz. **95** D3
Masaka Uganda **95** D3
Masamba Indon. **65** D2
Masan S. Korea **69** B2
Masasi Tanz. **95** D4
Masbate Phil. **68** B2
Masbate *i.* Phil. **68** B2
Mascara Alg. **55** D2
Maseru Lesotho **99** C2
Mashhad Iran **80** C3
Masibambane S. Africa **99** C2
Masilah, Wādī al *watercourse* Yemen **83** C3
Masilo S. Africa **99** C2
Masindi Uganda **95** D2
Maṣīrah, Jazīrat *i.* Oman **83** C2
Maṣīrah, Khalīj *b.* Oman **83** C3
Masjed Soleymān Iran **85** C2
Mask, Lough *l.* Rep. of Ireland **45** B2

Masoala, Tanjona *c.* Madag. **97** [inset] E1
Mason City U.S.A. **121** E2
Masqaṭ Oman *see* Muscat
Massa Italy **56** B2
Massachusetts *state* U.S.A. **123** F2
Massachusetts Bay U.S.A. **123** F2
Massango Angola **94** B3
Massawa Eritrea **92** B3
Massena U.S.A. **123** F2
Masset Can. **112** B2
Massif Central *mts* France **52** C2
Massillon U.S.A. **122** D2
Massina Mali **90** B3
Massinga Moz. **97** C2
Massingir Moz. **99** D1
Mastābah Saudi Arabia **82** A2
Masterton N.Z. **106** C3
Mastung Pak. **78** A2
Mastūrah Saudi Arabia **82** A2
Masty Belarus **36** B3
Masuda Japan **71** B4
Masvingo Zimbabwe **97** C2
Matadi Dem. Rep. Congo **94** B3
Matagalpa Nic. **130** B3
Matagami Can. **114** C2
Matagami, Lac *l.* Can. **114** C2
Matagorda Island U.S.A. **127** E3
Matala Angola **96** A1
Matam Senegal **90** A3
Matamoros *Coahuila* Mex. **128** B2
Matamoros *Tamaulipas* Mex. **129** C2
Matandu *r.* Tanz. **95** D3
Matane Can. **115** D2
Matanzas Cuba **130** B2
Matará Spain **55** D1
Mataranka Austr. **102** C1
Mataró Spain **55** D1
Mataura N.Z. **106** A4
Mata'utu Wallis and Futuna Is **101**
Matawai N.Z. **106** C2
Mategua Bol. **136** B2
Matehuala Mex. **129** B2
Matera Italy **57** C2
Mathis U.S.A. **127** E3
Mathura India **79** B2
Mati Phil. **68** B3
Matías Romero Mex. **130** A3
Matlock U.K. **46** C3
Mato Grosso, Planalto do *plat.* Brazil **138** B1
Matola Moz. **99** D2
Matsue Japan **71** B3
Matsumae Japan **70** D2
Matsusaka Japan **71** C4
Matsu Tao *i.* Taiwan **75** C3
Matsuyama Japan **71** B4
Mattagami *r.* Can. **114** D1
Matterhorn *mt.* Italy/Switz. **56** A1

Matterhorn *mt.* U.S.A. **118** C2
Mattoon U.S.A. **122** C3
Matwabeng S. Africa **99** C1
Maubeuge France **48** A2
Maui *i.* U.S.A. **120**
Maumere Indon. **65** D2
Maun Botswana **96** B1
Maunatlala Botswana **99** C1
Maurice, Lake *salt flat* Austr. **102** C2
Mauritania *country* Africa **90** A3
Mauritius *country* Indian Ocean **89**
Mawān, Khashm *h.* Saudi Arabia **82** B2
Mawanza Dem. Rep. Congo **94** B3
Mawkmai Myanmar **66** A1
Mawlaik Myanmar **66** A1
Mawlamyaing Myanmar **66** A2
Mawqaq Saudi Arabia **82** B2
Mawza Yemen **82** B3
Maxia, Punta *mt.* Italy **56** A3
Maya *r.* Rus. Fed. **87** K2
Mayaguana *i.* Bahamas **131** C2
Mayamey Iran **85** D2
Maybole U.K. **44** B3
Mayenne France **52** B2
Mayenne *r.* France **52** B2
Mayerthorpe Can. **112** D2
Mayo Can. **112** B1
Mayoko Congo **94** B3
Mayotte *terr.* Africa **97** D1
Maysky Rus. Fed. **87** K3
Maysville U.S.A. **122** C3
Mayumba Gabon **94** B3
Mayya Rus. Fed. **39** D3
Mazabuka Zambia **95** D3
Mazar China **80** E1
Mazara del Vallo Italy **56** B3
Mazār-e Sharīf Afgh. **78** A1
Mazatán Mex. **128** A2
Mazatenango Guat. **130** A3
Mazatlán Mex. **128** B2
Mažeikiai Lith. **36** B2
Mazunga Zimbabwe **97** B2
Mazyr Belarus **36** C2
Mbabane Swaziland **99** C2
Mbaïki C.A.R. **94** B2
Mbala Zambia **95** D3
Mbale Uganda **95** D2
Mbalmayo Cameroon **94** B2
Mbandaka Dem. Rep. Congo **94** B3
M'banza Congo Angola **94** B3
Mbeya Tanz. **95** D3
Mbinga Tanz. **95** D4
Mbomo Congo **94** B2
Mbouda Cameroon **94** B2
Mbour Senegal **90** A3

Mbuji-Mayi Dem. Rep. Congo **94** C3
McAlester U.S.A. **127** E2
McAllen U.S.A. **127** E3
McBride Can. **112** C2
McCall U.S.A. **118** C2
McClintock Channel Can. **110** F2
McClure Strait Can. **110** E2
McComb U.S.A. **124** B2
McConaughy, Lake U.S.A. **120** C2
McCook U.S.A. **120** C2
McDermitt U.S.A. **118** C2
McDonald Peak U.S.A. **118** D1
McGrath U.S.A. **110** B2
McGuire, Mount U.S.A. **118** D1
M'Chounèche Alg. **55** E3
McKinley, Mount U.S.A. **110** B2
McLennan Can. **112** D2
McLeod Lake Can. **112** C2
McMinnville *OR* U.S.A. **118** B1
McMinnville *TN* U.S.A. **125** C1
McPherson U.S.A. **121** D3
McTavish Arm *b.* Can. **112** D1
Mdantsane S. Africa **99** C3
Mead, Lake *resr* U.S.A. **119** D3
Meadow Lake Can. **113** E2
Meadville U.S.A. **123** D2
Meaken-dake *vol.* Japan **70** D2
Mealy Mountains Can. **115** E1
Meander River Can. **112** D2
Meaux France **48** A3
Mecca Saudi Arabia **82** A2
Mechelen Belgium **48** B2
Mechernich Ger. **48** C2
Meckenheim Ger. **48** C2
Mecklenburger Bucht *b.* Ger. **41** C5
Meda Port. **54** B1
Medan Indon. **64** A1
Médanos, Punta *pt* Arg. **137** B5
Medawachchiya Sri Lanka **77** C4
Médéa Alg. **55** D2
Medellín Col. **134** B2
Medenine Tunisia **91** D1
Medford U.S.A. **118** B2
Medgidia Romania **59** C3
Mediaș Romania **38** D2
Medicine Bow Mountains U.S.A. **120** B2
Medicine Bow Peak U.S.A. **120** B2
Medicine Hat Can. **113** D2
Medicine Lodge U.S.A. **121** D3
Medina Brazil **139** D1
Medina Saudi Arabia **82** A2
Medinaceli Spain **54** C1
Medina del Campo Spain **54** C1
Medina de Rioseco Spain **54** C1
Mediterranean Sea **55** C2
Medjedel Alg. **55** D2
Medley Can. **113** D2
Mednogorsk Rus. Fed. **35** E3

Medvezh'i, Ostrova *is* Rus. Fed. **87** M2
Medvezh'yegorsk Rus. Fed. **34** C2
Meekatharra Austr. **102** A2
Meeker U.S.A. **120** B2
Meerut India **79** B2
Megalopoli Greece **59** B3
Meghasani *mt.* India **79** C2
Megisti *i.* Greece **59** C3
Mehamn Norway **40** F1
Meharry, Mount Austr. **102** A2
Mehrān watercourse Iran **83** C2
Mehrān Iran **83** C2
Meia Ponte *r.* Brazil **138** C1
Meiganga Cameroon **94** B2
Meihekou China **69** B1
Meiktila Myanmar **66** A1
Meiningen Ger. **49** E2
Meißen Ger. **49** F2
Meizhou China **75** B3
Mek'elē Eth. **93** B3
Mekerrhane, Sebkha *salt pan* Alg. **90** C2
Meknès Morocco **90** B1
Mekong *r.* Asia **67** B2
Mekong, China **66** B1
Mekong, Mouths of the Vietnam **67** B3
Melaka Malaysia **64** B1
Melanesia *is* Pacific Ocean **142** D5
Melbourne Austr. **105** C3
Melbourne U.S.A. **125** D3
Mele, Capo *c.* Italy **56** A2
Melenki Rus. Fed. **37** F2
Mélèzes, Rivière aux *r.* Can. **115** C1
Mélfi Chad **91** D3
Melfi Italy **56** C2
Melfort Can. **113** E2
Melilla N. Africa **54** C3
Melitopol' Ukr. **39** E2
Melle Ger. **49** D1
Mellerud Sweden **41** C4
Mellrichstadt Ger. **49** E2
Mellum *i.* Ger. **48** D1
Melo Uru. **136** C4
Melton Mowbray U.K. **47** C3
Melun France **52** C2
Melville Can. **110** F3
Melville, Cape Austr. **103** D1
Melville, Lake Can. **115** E1
Melville Island Austr. **102** C1
Melville Island Can. **110** E1
Melville Peninsula Can. **111** G2
Memboro Indon. **65** C2
Memmingen Ger. **50** C3
Memphis *tourist site* Egypt **84** B3
Memphis *TN* U.S.A. **124** B1
Memphis *TX* U.S.A. **127** D2
Mena Ukr. **39** D1
Mena U.S.A. **124** B2
Mènaka Mali **90** C3
Mènam Khong *r.* Asia *see* Mekong

Mende France **53** C3
Mendefera Eritrea **92** B3
Mendi Eth. **95** D2
Mendip Hills U.K. **47** B4
Mendoza Arg. **137** B4
Menemen Turkey **59** C3
Mengala Indon. **64** B2
Mengzi China **75** A3
Menindee Austr. **104** C2
Menindee, Lake Austr. **104** C2
Meningie Austr. **104** B3
Menominee U.S.A. **122** C1
Menongue Angola **96** A1
Menorca i. Spain see **Minorca**
Mentawai, Kepulauan is Indon. **64** A2
Mentok Indon. **64** B2
Menzies Austr. **102** B2
Meppel Neth. **48** C1
Meppen Ger. **48** C1
Mepuze Moz. **99** D1
Meqheleng S. Africa **99** C2
Merano Italy **56** B1
Merauke Indon. **63** D3
Merbein Austr. **104** C2
Merced U.S.A. **119** B3
Mercedes Arg. **136** C3
Mercy, Cape Can. **111** H2
Meredith, Lake U.S.A. **127** D1
Merefa Ukr. **39** E2
Merga Oasis Sudan **92** A3
Mergui Archipelago is Myanmar **67** A2
Meriç r. Greece/Turkey **59** C2
Mérida Mex. **129** D2
Mérida Spain **54** B2
Mérida Venez. **134** B2
Meridian U.S.A. **124** C2
Mérignac France **52** B3
Merimbula Austr. **105** D3
Mérouana Alg. **55** E2
Merowe Sudan **92** B3
Merredin Austr. **102** A3
Merrick h. U.K. **44** B3
Merrillville U.S.A. **122** C2
Merrygoen Austr. **105** D2
Mersch Lux. **48** C3
Merseburg (Saale) Ger. **49** E2
Mersin Turkey **84** B2
Mersing Malaysia **64** B1
Mers-les-Bains France **47** D4
Merta India **78** B2
Merthyr Tydfil U.K. **47** B4
Mertola Port. **54** B2
Mertvyy Kultuk, Sor dry lake Kazakh. **80** C2
Meru vol. Tanz. **95** D3
Merzig Ger. **48** C3
Mesa U.S.A. **126** B2
Mesagne Italy **57** C2
Meschede Ger. **49** D2
Meshchovsk Rus. Fed. **37** E3
Meshkovskaya Rus. Fed. **39** F2
Mesimeri Greece **59** B2

Mesolongi Greece **59** B3
Messalo r. Moz. **97** D1
Messina Italy **56** C3
Messina, Stretta di str. Italy **57** C3
Messiniakos Kolpos b. Greece **59** B3
Meta r. Col./Venez. **134** C2
Metán Arg. **136** B3
Methoni Greece **59** B3
Metkovic Croatia **57** C2
Metu Eth. **93** B4
Metz France **53** D2
Meuse r. Belgium/France **48** B2
Mexia U.S.A. **127** E2
Mexicali Mex. **128** A1
Mexico country Central America **128** B2
Mexico U.S.A. **121** E3
Mexico, Gulf of Mex./U.S.A. **130** A2
Mexico City Mex. **129** C3
Meymaneh Afgh. **78** A1
Mezen' Rus. Fed. **34** D2
Mezen' r. Rus. Fed. **34** D2
Mezhdusharskiy, Ostrov i. Rus. Fed. **34** E1
Mezőtúr Hungary **51** E3
Mfuwe Zambia **97** D1
Mhow India **78** B2
Miahuatlán Mex. **129** C3
Miajadas Spain **54** B2
Miami FL U.S.A. **125** D3
Miami OK U.S.A. **127** F1
Miami Beach U.S.A. **125** D3
Miandoab Iran **85** C2
Miandrivazo Madag. **97** [inset] D1
Miâneh Iran **85** C2
Mianwali Pak. **78** B1
Mianyang China **74** A2
Miarinarivo Madag. **97** [inset] D1
Miass Rus. Fed. **35** F3
Mica Creek Can. **112** D2
Michalovce Slovakia **51** E3
Michigan state U.S.A. **122** C1
Michigan, Lake U.S.A. **122** C2
Michigan City U.S.A. **122** C2
Michipicoten Island Can. **114** B2
Michipicoten River Can. **114** B2
Michurinsk Rus. Fed. **37** F3
Micronesia is Pacific Ocean **142** D4
Micronesia, Federated States of country N. Pacific Ocean **63** D2
Middelburg Neth. **48** A2
Middelburg E. Cape S. Africa **99** C3
Middle Alkali Lake U.S.A. **118** B2
Middle Andaman i. India **67** A2
Middle Loup r. U.S.A. **120** D2
Middlesboro U.S.A. **122** D3
Middlesbrough U.K. **46** C2
Middletown NY U.S.A. **123** F2

Middletown OH U.S.A. **122** D3
Midi Yemen **82** B3
Midland Can. **114** C2
Midland TX U.S.A. **127** D2
Midleton Rep. of Ireland **45** B3
Miðvágur Faroe Is **42** B1
Midzhur mt. Bulg./S.M. **58** B2
Mielec Pol. **51** E2
Miercurea-Ciuc Romania **38** C2
Mieres Spain **54** B1
Mieste Ger. **49** E1
Migriggyangzham Co l. China **79** D1
Miguel Alemán, Presa resr Mex. **129** C3
Miguel Auza Mex. **128** B2
Miguel Hidalgo, Presa resr Mex. **128** B2
Migyaunglaung Myanmar **67** A2
Mikhaylov Rus. Fed. **37** E3
Mikhaylovka Rus. Fed. **70** B2
Mikhaylovskiy Rus. Fed. **81** E1
Mikkeli Fin. **41** F3
Mikuni-sanmyaku mts Japan **71** C3
Mila Alg. **55** E2
Miladhunmadulu Atoll Maldives **77** B4
Milan Italy **56** A1
Milano Italy see **Milan**
Milas Turkey **59** C3
Milbank U.S.A. **121** D1
Mildenhall U.K. **47** D3
Mildura Austr. **104** C2
Mile China **75** A3
100 Mile House Can. **112** C2
Miles City U.S.A. **120** B1
Milford UT U.S.A. **119** D3
Milford Haven U.K. **47** A4
Milford Sound N.Z. **106** A3
Miliana Alg. **55** D2
Milk, Wadi el watercourse Sudan **92** B3
Mil'kovo Rus. Fed. **87** M3
Milk River Can. **113** D3
Millau France **52** C3
Milledgeville U.S.A. **125** D2
Mille Lacs lakes U.S.A. **121** E1
Mille Lacs, Lac des l. Can. **114** A2
Millennium Island atoll Kiribati see **Caroline Island**
Miller U.S.A. **121** D2
Millerovo Rus. Fed. **39** F2
Millers Creek Austr. **104** B2
Millicent Austr. **104** C3
Millmerran Austr. **105** E1
Mills Lake Can. **112** D1
Milos i. Greece **59** B3
Miloslavskoye Rus. Fed. **37** E3
Milove Ukr. **39** F2
Milparinka Austr. **104** C1
Milton N.Z. **106** A4
Milton Keynes U.K. **47** C3

208

Milwaukee U.S.A. **122** C2
Milwaukee Deep *sea feature*
  Caribbean Sea **144** B4
Mimizan France **52** B3
Mimongo Gabon **94** B3
Mináb Iran **83** C2
Minahasa, Semenanjung *pen.*
  Indon. **65** D1
Mina Jebel Ali U.A.E. **83** C2
Minas Indon. **64** B1
Minas Uru. **137** C4
Minas Novas Brazil **139** D1
Minatitlán Mex. **129** C3
Minbu Myanmar **66** A1
Mindanao *i.* Phil. **68** B3
Minden Ger. **49** D1
Minden *LA* U.S.A. **124** B2
Mindoro *i.* Phil. **68** B2
Mindoro Strait Phil. **68** A2
Minehead U.K. **47** B4
Mineiros Brazil **138** B1
Mineral Wells U.S.A. **127** C2
Minfeng China **79** C1
Minga Dem. Rep. Congo **95** C4
mingäçevir Azer. **85** C1
Mingan Can. **115** D1
Mingary Austr. **104** C2
Mingguang China **74** B2
Mingin Myanmar **66** A1
Mingoyo Tanz. **95** D4
Minhe China **74** A2
Minicoy *atoll* India **77** B4
Minilya Austr. **102** A2
Minipi Lake Can. **115** D1
Minna Nigeria **91** D4
Minneapolis U.S.A. **121** E2
Minnedosa Can. **113** F2
Minnesota *r.* U.S.A. **121** E2
Minnesota *state* U.S.A. **121** E1
Miño *r.* Port./Spain **54** B3
Minorca *i.* Spain **55** D1
Minot U.S.A. **120** C1
Minsk Belarus **36** C2
Minto, Lac *l.* Can. **114** C1
Minutang India **66** A1
Minxian China **74** A2
Mirabela Brazil **139** D1
Miramichi Can. **115** D2
Mirampelou, Kolpos *b.* Greece
  59 C3
Miranda Brazil **138** A2
Miranda *r.* Brazil **138** A1
Miranda de Ebro Spain **54** C1
Mirandela Port. **54** B1
Mirandópolis Brazil **138** B2
Mirbāṭ Oman **83** C3
Miri Malaysia **65** C1
Mirim, Lagoa *l.* Brazil **137** C4
Mirjāveh Iran **83** D2
Mirnyy Rus. Fed. **87** J2
Mirpur Khas Pak. **78** A2
Mirtoö Pelagos *sea* Greece
  59 B3
Miryang S. Korea **69** B2

Mirzapur India **79** C2
Mishan China **70** B1
Miskitos, Cayos *is* Nic. **130** B3
Miskolc Hungary **51** E3
Misoöl *i.* Indon. **63** C3
Misrātah Libya **91** D1
Missinaibi *r.* Can. **114** B1
Missinaibi Lake Can. **114** B2
Mission Can. **112** C3
Missia Lake Can. **114** B1
Mississippi *r.* U.S.A. **124** C3
Mississippi *state* U.S.A. **124** C2
Mississippi Delta U.S.A. **124** C3
Missoula U.S.A. **118** D1
Missouri *r.* U.S.A. **121** E3
Missouri *state* U.S.A. **121** E3
Mistassibi *r.* Can. **115** C2
Mistassini, Lac *l.* Can. **114** C1
Mistastin Lake Can. **115** D1
Mistelbach Austria **51** D3
Mistinibi, Lac *l.* Can. **115** D1
Mitchell *r.* Austr. **103** D1
Mitchell *r.* Austr. **103** D1
Mitchell U.S.A. **121** D2
Mithi Pak. **78** A2
Mito Japan **71** D3
Mitole Tanz. **95** D3
Mittagong Austr. **105** E2
Mitú Col. **134** D2
Mitumba, Chaine *des mts*
  Dem. Rep. Congo **95** C3
Mitumba, Monts *mts*
  Dem. Rep. Congo **95** C3
Mitzic Gabon **94** B2
Miyah, Wādī al *watercourse*
  Saudi Arabia **82** B2
Miyake-jima *i.* Japan **71** C4
Miyako Japan **70** D3
Miyakonojō Japan **71** B4
Miyazaki Japan **71** B4
Miẓçãh Libya **91** D1
Mizen Head Rep. of Ireland
  45 B3
Mizhhir"ya Ukr. **38** B2
Mjölby Sweden **41** D4
Mjøsa *l.* Norway **41** C3
Mladá Boleslav Czech Rep.
  50 C2
Mladenovac S.M. **58** B2
Mława Pol. **51** E2
Mlungisi S. Africa **99** C3
Mlyniv Ukr. **38** C1
Mmabatho S. Africa **99** C2
Mmathethe Botswana **99** C2
Mo Norway **42** E1
Moab U.S.A. **119** E3
Moamba Moz. **99** D2
Moba Dem. Rep. Congo **95** C3
Mobayi-Mbongo
  Dem. Rep. Congo **94** C2
Moberly U.S.A. **121** E3
Mobile U.S.A. **124** C2

Mobile Bay U.S.A. **124** C2
Mobridge U.S.A. **120** C1
Moçambique Moz. **97** D1
Môc Châu Vietnam **66** B1
Mocha Yemen **82** B3
Mochudi Botswana **99** C1
Mocimboa da Praia Moz. **97** D1
Möckmühl Ger. **49** D3
Mocoa Col. **134** B2
Mococa Brazil **138** C2
Moctezuma *Chihuahua* Mex.
  128 B1
Moctezuma *Sonora* Mex. **128** B2
Mocuba Moz. **97** C1
Modane France **53** D2
Modder *r.* S. Africa **98** B2
Modena Italy **56** B2
Modesto U.S.A. **119** B3
Modimolle S. Africa **99** C1
Moe Austr. **105** D3
Moers Ger. **48** C2
Moffat U.K. **44** C3
Mogadishu Somalia **93** C4
Mogalakwena *r.* S. Africa **99** C1
Mogaung Myanmar **66** A1
Mogi-Mirim Brazil **138** C2
Mogocha Rus. Fed. **87** J1
Mogok Myanmar **66** A1
Mohács Hungary **51** D3
Mohale's Hoek Lesotho **99** C3
Mohammadia Alg. **55** D2
Mohawk *r.* U.S.A. **123** F2
Mohoro Tanz. **95** D3
Mohyliv Podil's'kyy Ukr. **38** C2
Moijabana Botswana **99** C1
Moineşti Romania **38** C2
Moi i Rana Norway **40** C2
Moissac France **52** C3
Mojave U.S.A. **119** C3
Mojave Desert U.S.A. **119** C3
Mojiang China **66** B1
Moji das Cruzes Brazil **139** C2
Mokau N.Z. **106** B2
Mokhotlong Lesotho **99** C2
Mokopane S. Africa **99** C1
Mokp'o S. Korea **69** B3
Molango Mex. **129** C2
Molde Norway **40** B3
Moldova *country* Europe **38** C2
Moldoveanu, Vârful *mt.* Romania
  38 B2
Moldovei Centrale, Podişul *plat.*
  Moldova **38** C2
Molepolole Botswana **99** C1
Molfetta Italy **57** C2
Molínsco U.S.A. **121** E2
Mölln Ger. **49** F1
Mollendo Peru **134** B4
Molong Austr. **105** D2
Molopo *watercourse*
  Botswana/S. Africa **98** B2
Moloundou Cameroon **94** B2
Molucca Sea Indon. *see*
  Maluku, Laut

Momba Austr. **104** C2
Mombasa Kenya **95** D3
Mombuca, Serra de *hills* Brazil
138 B1
Momi, Ra's *pt* Yemen **83** C3
Men *i.* Denmark **41** C4
Monaco *country* Europe **53** D3
Monadhliath Mountains U.K.
44 B2
Monaghan Rep. of Ireland **45** C1
Monastyrshchina Rus. Fed.
37 D3
Monastyryshche Ukr. **38** C2
Monbetsu Japan **70** D2
Moncalieri Italy **56** A1
Moncheorsk Rus. Fed. **40** G2
Mönchengladbach Ger. **48** C2
Monclova Mex. **128** B2
Moncouche, Lac *l.* Can. **123** F1
Moncton Can. **115** D2
Mondo S. Africa **90** C2
Mondovì Italy **56** A2
Monemvasia Greece **59** B3
Moneron, Ostrov *i.* Rus. Fed.
70 D1
Monfalcone Italy **56** B1
Monforte Spain **54** B1
Mongolia *country* Asia **72** C1
Mongu Zambia **96** B3
Monitor Range *mts* U.S.A.
119 C3
Mono Lake U.S.A. **119** C3
Monopoli Italy **57** C2
Monroe *LA* U.S.A. **124** B2
Monroeville U.S.A. **124** C2
Monrovia Liberia **90** A4
Mons Belgium **48** A2
Montalto *mt.* Italy **57** C3
Montana Bulg. **58** B2
Montana *state* U.S.A. **116** C2
Montargis France **52** C3
Montauban France **52** C3
Montauk Point U.S.A. **123** F2
Mont-aux-Sources *mt.* Lesotho
99 C2
Montbard France **53** C2
Mont Blanc *mt.* France/Italy
53 D2
Mont-de-Marsan France **52** B3
Monte Alegre Brazil **135** D3
Monte-Carlo Monaco **53** D3
Monte Caseros Arg. **136** C4
Montélimar France **53** C3
Montemorelos Mex. **129** C2
Montendre France **52** B2
Montenegro *aut. rep.* S.M. *see*
Crna Gora
Montepuez Moz. **97** C1
Monterey U.S.A. **119** B3
Monterey Bay U.S.A. **119** B3
Monteria Col. **134** B2
Montero Bol. **136** B2
Monterrey Mex. **129** B2

Monte Santo Brazil **135** F4
Monte Santu, Capo di *c.* Italy
56 A2
Montes Claros Brazil **139** D1
Montevideo Uru. **137** C4
Montevideo U.S.A. **121** D2
Montgomery U.S.A. **125** C2
Monthey Switz. **53** D2
Monticello *AR* U.S.A. **124** B2
Monticello *UT* U.S.A. **119** E3
Montilla Spain **54** C2
Mont-Laurier Can. **114** C2
Montluçon France **52** C2
Montmagny Can. **115** D2
Montpelier *ID* U.S.A. **118** D2
Montpelier *VT* U.S.A. **123** F2
Montpellier France **53** C3
Montréal Can. **115** C2
Montreal Lake Can. **113** E2
Montreal Lake *l.* Can. **113** E2
Montreux Switz. **53** D2
Montrose U.K. **44** C2
Montrose U.S.A. **120** B3
Montserrat *terr.* West Indies
131 D3
Monywa Myanmar **66** A1
Monza Italy **56** A1
Monzón Spain **55** D1
Mookane Botswana **99** C1
Moonie Austr. **105** D1
Moonie *r.* Austr. **105** D1
Moonta Austr. **104** B2
Moore, Lake *salt flat* Austr.
102 A2
Moorhead U.S.A. **121** D1
Moose *r.* Can. **114** B1
Moosehead Lake U.S.A. **123** G1
Moose Jaw Can. **110** E3
Moose Lake U.S.A. **121** E1
Moosonee Can. **114** B1
Mootwingee Austr. **104** C2
M'Ooukal Alg. **55** E3
Mopti Mali **90** B3
Moquegua Peru **134** B4
Mora Sweden **41** C3
Mora U.S.A. **121** E1
Moradabad India **79** B2
Moramanga Madag. **97** [inset] D1
Mo'ramba *r.* Europe **58** A1
Moray Firth *b.* U.K. **44** B2
Morbi India **78** B2
Mordaga China **73** E1
Morden Can. **113** F3
Morecambe U.K. **46** B2
Morecambe Bay U.K. **46** B2
Moree Austr. **105** D1
Morehead U.S.A. **125** D3
Morehead City U.S.A. **125** E2
Morelia Mex. **129** B3
Morella Spain **55** C1
Morena, Sierra *mts* Spain **54** B2
Moreni Romania **38** C3
Moresby, Mount Can. **112** B2
Moresby Island Can. **112** B2
Moreton Island Austr. **105** E1

Morgan City U.S.A. **124** B3
Morganton U.S.A. **125** D1
Morgantown U.S.A. **123** E3
Morges Switz. **53** D2
Morice Lake Can. **112** C2
Morioka Japan **70** D3
Morisset Austr. **105** E2
Morlaix France **52** B2
Mornington Island Austr. **103** C1
Morocco *country* Africa **90** B1
Morogoro Tanz. **95** D3
Moro Gulf Phil. **68** B3
Morokweng S. Africa **98** B2
Morombe Madag. **97** [inset] D2
Mörön Mongolia **72** C1
Morondava Madag. **97** [inset] D2
Moroni Comoros **97** C1
Morotai *i.* Indon. **63** C2
Moroto Uganda **95** D2
Morozovsk Rus. Fed. **39** F2
Morpeth U.K. **46** C2
Morrinhos Brazil **138** C1
Morris Can. **113** F3
Morris U.S.A. **121** D1
Morristown U.S.A. **125** D1
Morshanka Rus. Fed. **37** F3
Mortlake Austr. **104** C3
Moruya Austr. **105** E3
Morvern *reg.* U.K. **44** B2
Morwell Austr. **105** D3
Mosbach Ger. **49** D3
Moscow Rus. Fed. **37** E2
Moscow U.S.A. **118** C1
Mosel *r.* Ger. **48** C2
Moselle *r.* France **53** D2
Moses Lake U.S.A. **118** C1
Mosfellsbær Iceland **40** [inset]
Mosgiel N.Z. **106** B4
Moshi Tanz. **95** D3
Mosjøen Norway **40** C2
Moskva Rus. Fed. *see* Moscow
Mosquitos, Golfo de los *b.*
Panama **130** B4
Moss Norway **41** C4
Mossel Bay S. Africa **98** B3
Mossendjo Congo **94** B3
Mossgiel Austr. **104** C2
Mossman Austr. **103** D1
Mossoró Brazil **135** F3
Moss Vale Austr. **105** E2
Most Czech Rep. **50** C2
Mostaganem Alg. **90** C1
Mostar Bos.-Herz. **57** C2
Mostardas Brazil **136** C4
Mostovskoy Rus. Fed. **39** F3
Mosul *Iraq* **85** C2
Motala Sweden **41** D4
Motherwell U.K. **44** C3
Motokwe Botswana **98** B1
Motril Spain **54** C2
Mottama, Gulf of Myanmar
66 A2
Motul Mex. **129** D2

Motu One *atoll* Fr. Polynesia **111**
Moudros Greece **59** C3
Mouila Gabon **94** B3
Moulamein Austr. **104** C3
Moulins France **53** C2
Moultrie U.S.A. **125** D2
Moultrie, Lake U.S.A. **125** E2
Moundou Chad **91** B4
Mountain Grove U.S.A. **121** E3
Mountain Home *AR* U.S.A. **124** E1
Mountain Home *ID* U.S.A. **118** C2
Mount Barker Austr. **104** B3
Mount Desert Island U.S.A. **123** G2
Mount Fletcher S. Africa **99** C3
Mount Frere S. Africa **99** C3
Mount Gambier Austr. **104** C3
Mount Hagen P.N.G. **63** D3
Mount Hope Austr. **105** D2
Mount Isa Austr. **103** C2
Mount Magnet Austr. **102** A2
Mount Manara Austr. **104** C2
Mount Maunganui N.Z. **106** C2
Mount Pleasant *IA* U.S.A. **121** E2
Mount Pleasant *MI* U.S.A. **122** D2
Mount Pleasant *TX* U.S.A. **127** F2
Mount Shasta U.S.A. **118** B2
Mount Vernon *IL* U.S.A. **122** C4
Mount Vernon *OH* U.S.A. **122** D2
Mount Vernon *WA* U.S.A. **118** B1
Moura Austr. **103** D2
Mourdi, Dépression du *depr.* Chad **91** E3
Mouscron Belgium **48** A2
Moussoro Chad **91** B3
Moutong Indon. **65** D1
Mouydir, Monts du *plat.* Alg. **90** C2
Moy r. Rep. of Ireland **45** B3
Moyale Eth. **93** B4
Moyeni Lesotho **99** C3
Mo'ynoq Uzbek. **80** C2
Mozambique *country* Africa **97** C2
Mozambique Channel Africa **97** D2
Mozhaysk Rus. Fed. **37** E2
Mpanda Tanz. **95** D3
Mpika Zambia **97** C1
Mporokoso Zambia **95** D3
Mpumalanga *prov.* S. Africa **99** C2
Mrauk-U Myanmar **66** A1
Mrkonjić-Grad Bos.-Herz. **58** A2
Mshinskaya Rus. Fed. **36** C2
M'Sila Alg. **55** D2
Msta r. Rus. Fed. **37** D2
Mstinskiy Most Rus. Fed. **37** D2

Mstsislaw Belarus **37** D3
Mtsensk Rus. Fed. **37** E3
Mtwara Tanz. **95** E4
Muanda Dem. Rep. Congo **94** B3
Muang Hinboun Laos **75** A4
Muang Khōng Laos **67** B2
Muang Ngoy Laos **66** B1
Muang Pakbeng Laos **66** B2
Muang Sing Laos **66** B1
Muar Malaysia **64** B1
Muaraboulan Indon. **64** B2
Muaralaung Indon. **65** C2
Muarasiberut Indon. **64** A2
Muaratewweh Indon. **65** C2
Mubende Uganda **95** D2
Mubi Nigeria **91** D3
Muchkapskiy Rus. Fed. **39** F1
Mucuri Brazil **139** E1
Mucuri r. Brazil **139** E1
Mudanjiang China **70** A2
Mudan Jiang r. China **70** A1
Mudanya Turkey **59** C3
Mudgee Austr. **105** D2
Mueda Moz. **97** C1
Mufulira Zambia **97** C1
Mufumbwe Zambia **96** B1
Muğla Turkey **59** C3
Muhammad Qol Sudan **92** B2
Mühlhausen (Thüringen) Ger. **49** E2
Muine Bheag Rep. of Ireland **45** C2
Muite Moz. **97** C1
Mukacheve Ukr. **38** B2
Mukalla Yemen **83** B3
Mukdahan Thai. **66** B2
Mukinbudin Austr. **102** A3
Mukomuko Indon. **64** B2
Mulanje, Mount Malawi **97** C1
Mulde r. Ger. **49** F2
Mulegé Mex. **128** A2
Muleshoe U.S.A. **127** D2
Mulhacén *mt.* Spain **54** C2
Mülheim an der Ruhr Ger. **48** C2
Mulhouse France **53** D2
Muling China **70** B1
Muling He r. China **70** B1
Mull i. U.K. **44** B2
Mullaley Austr. **105** D2
Mullen U.S.A. **120** C2
Muller, Pegunungan *mts* Indon. **65** C1
Mullingar Rep. of Ireland **45** C2
Mull of Galloway c. U.K. **44** B3
Mull of Kintyre *hd* U.K. **44** B3
Mull of Oa *hd* U.K. **44** A3
Mulobezi Zambia **96** B1
Multan Pak. **78** B1
Mumbai India **77** B3
Mumbwa Zambia **96** B1
Muna i. Indon. **65** D2
Muna Mex. **129** D2
Münchberg Ger. **49** E2
München Ger. *see* Munich

Mundrabilla Austr. **102** B3
Mungbere Dem. Rep. Congo **95** C2
Munger India **79** C2
Mungeranie Austr. **104** B1
Mungindi Austr. **105** D1
Munich Ger. **50** C3
Muniz Freire Brazil **139** D2
Münster *Niedersachsen* Ger. **49** E1
Münster *Nordrhein-Westfalen* Ger. **48** C2
Munster *reg.* Rep. of Ireland **45** B2
Münsterland *reg.* Ger. **48** C2
Muong Nhie Vietnam **66** B1
Muonio Fin. **40** E2
Muonioälven r. Fin./Sweden **40** E2
Muqdisho Somalia *see* Mogadishu
Mur r. Austria **51** D3
Muramvya Burundi **95** C3
Murat r. Turkey **85** B2
Muratlı Turkey **59** C2
Murchison *watercourse* Austr. **102** A2
Murcia Spain **55** C2
Mureșul r. Romania **38** B2
Muret France **52** C3
Murfreesboro U.S.A. **125** C1
Murghab r. Afgh. **78** A1
Murghob Tajik. **81** E3
Muriaé Brazil **139** D2
Muriege Angola **94** C3
Müritz l. Ger. **49** F1
Murmansk Rus. Fed. **40** G2
Murom Rus. Fed. **37** F2
Muroran Japan **70** D2
Muros Spain **54** B1
Muroto Japan **71** B4
Murphy U.S.A. **125** D1
Murra Murra Austr. **105** D1
Murray r. Austr. **105** B3
Murray r. Can. **112** C2
Murray U.S.A. **122** C3
Murray, Lake U.S.A. **125** D2
Murray Bridge Austr. **104** B3
Murraysburg S. Africa **98** B3
Murrayville Austr. **104** C3
Murrumbidgee r. Austr. **104** C3
Murrupula Moz. **97** C1
Murrurundi Austr. **105** E2
Murska Sobota Slovenia **57** C1
Murupara N.Z. **106** C2
Mururoa *atoll* Fr. Polynesia **111**
Murwara India **79** C2
Murwillumbah Austr. **105** E1
Murzechirla Turkm. **35** F5
Murzüq Libya **91** D2
Mus Turkey **85** C2
Musala *mt.* Bulg. **58** B2
Musan N. Korea **69** B1
Musaymir Yemen **82** B3

Muscat Oman **83** C2
Muscatine U.S.A. **121** E2
Musgrave Ranges *mts* Austr. **102** A2
Mushie Dem. Rep. Congo **94** B3
Musina S. Africa **99** D1
Muskegee U.S.A. **127** E1
Muskwa *r.* Can. **112** C2
Musoma Tanz. **95** D3
Musselburgh U.K. **44** C3
Mustjala Estonia **36** B2
Muswellbrook Austr. **105** E2
Mût Egypt **92** A2
Mutare Zimbabwe **97** C1
Mutsu Japan **70** D2
Mutuali Moz. **97** C1
Muurola Fin. **40** F2
Mu Us Shamo *des.* China **74** A2
Muyezerskiy Rus. Fed. **40** G3
Muyinga Burundi **95** D3
Muzaffargarh Pak. **78** B1
Muzaffarpur India **79** C2
Muzamane Moz. **99** D1
Múzquiz Mex. **128** B2
Muztag *mt.* China **79** C1
Muz Tag *mt.* China **79** C1
Mwanza Tanz. **95** D3
Mweka Dem. Rep. Congo **94** C3
Mwenda Zambia **95** C4
Mwene-Ditu Dem. Rep. Congo **94** C3
Mwenezi Zimbabwe **97** C2
Mweru, Lake Dem. Rep. Congo/Zambia **95** C3
Mwimba Dem. Rep. Congo **94** C3
Mwinilunga Zambia **96** B1
Myadzyel Belarus **36** C3
Myanmar *country* Asia **66** A1
Myaungmya Myanmar **66** A2
Myeik Myanmar **67** C2
Myingyan Myanmar **66** A1
Myitkyina Myanmar **66** A1
Mykolayiv Ukr. **39** D2
Mykonos Greece **59** C3
Mykonos *i.* Greece **59** C3
Mymensingh Bangl. **79** D2
Myŏnggan N. Korea **69** D1
Myory Belarus **36** C2
Mýrdalsjökull *ice cap* Iceland **40** [inset]
Myrhorod Ukr. **39** D2
Myronivka Ukr. **38** D2
Myrtle Beach U.S.A. **125** E2
Myshkin Rus. Fed. **37** E2
Mysore India **77** B3
My Tho Vietnam **67** B2
Mytilini Greece **59** C3
Mytishchi Rus. Fed. **37** E2
Mzimba Malawi **97** C1
Mzuzu Malawi **97** C1

N

Naas Rep. of Ireland **45** C2
Nababeep S. Africa **98** A2
Naberezhnyye Chelny Rus. Fed. **35** E3
Nabire Indon. **63** D3
Naboomspruit S. Africa **99** C1
Nacala Moz. **97** D1
Nachuge India **67** A2
Nacogdoches U.S.A. **127** E2
Nadiad India **78** B2
Nadvirna Ukr. **38** B2
Nadym Rus. Fed. **34** G2
Næstved Denmark **41** C4
Nafpaktos Greece **59** B3
Nafplio Greece **59** B3
Naga Phil. **68** B2
Nagagami *r.* Can. **114** B1
Nagano Japan **71** C3
Nagaoka Japan **71** C3
Nagaon India **79** D2
Nagar Parkar Pak. **78** B2
Nagasaki Japan **71** A4
Nagaur India **78** B2
Nagercoil India **77** B4
Nagina India **79** C2
Nagoya Japan **71** C3
Nagpur India **79** B2
Nagqu China **79** C2
Nagykanizsa Hungary **51** D3
Nahanni Butte Can. **112** C1
Nahāvand Iran **85** C2
Nahrendorf Ger. **49** E1
Nain Can. **115** D1
Na'īn Iran **85** D2
Nairn U.K. **44** C2
Nairobi Kenya **95** D3
Naivasha Kenya **95** D3
Najafābād Iran **85** D2
Najd *reg.* Saudi Arabia **82** B2
Najin N. Korea **69** C1
Najrān Saudi Arabia **82** B3
Nakatsugawa Japan **71** C3
Nakfa Eritrea **82** C3
Nakhodka Rus. Fed. **70** B2
Nakhon Pathom Thai. **67** B2
Nakhon Ratchasima Thai. **67** B2
Nakhon Sawan Thai. **67** B2
Nakhon Si Thammarat Thai. **67** A3
Nakina Can. **114** B1
Nakonde Zambia **95** C3
Nakskov Denmark **41** C5
Nakuru Kenya **95** D3
Nakusp Can. **112** D2
Nal'chik Rus. Fed. **35** D4
Nālūt Libya **91** D1
Namahadi S. Africa **99** C2
Namakzar-e Shadad *salt flat* Iran **83** C1

Namangan Uzbek. **81** E2
Namaqualand *reg.* S. Africa **98** A2
Nambour Austr. **103** E2
Nambucca Heads Austr. **105** E2
Nam Co *salt l.* China **79** D1
Nam Dinh Vietnam **66** B1
Namib Desert Namibia **96** A2
Namibe Angola **96** A1
Namibia *country* Africa **98** A1
Namjagbarwa Feng *mt.* China **76** D2
Namoi *r.* Austr. **105** D2
Nampa U.S.A. **118** C2
Nampala Mali **90** B3
Namp'o N. Korea **69** B2
Nampula Moz. **97** C1
Namrup India **66** A1
Namsang Myanmar **66** A1
Namsos Norway **40** C3
Namtu Myanmar **66** A1
Namur Belgium **48** B2
Namwala Zambia **96** B1
Namwŏn S. Korea **69** B2
Namya Ra Myanmar **66** A1
Nan Thai. **66** B2
Nanaimo Can. **112** C3
Nananib Plateau Namibia **98** A1
Nanao Japan **71** C3
Nanchang *Jiangxi* China **75** B3
Nanchang *Jiangxi* China **75** B3
Nanchong China **74** A2
Nancy France **53** D2
Nanda Devi *mt.* India **79** C1
Nandan China **75** A3
Nanded India **77** B3
Nandurbar India **78** B2
Nandyal India **77** B3
Nanga Eboko Cameroon **94** B2
Nangahpinoh Indon. **65** C2
Nanga Parbat *mt.* Jammu and Kashmir **78** B1
Nangatayap Indon. **65** C2
Nangong China **74** B2
Nangulangwa Tanz. **95** D3
Nanjing China **74** B2
Nanking China *see* **Nanjing**
Nankova Angola **96** A1
Nan Ling *mts* China **75** B3
Nanning China **75** A3
Nanortalik Greenland **111** I2
Nanpan Jiang *r.* China **75** A3
Nanpara India **79** C2
Nanping China **75** B3
Nansei-shotō *is* Japan *see* **Ryukyu Islands**
Nantes France **52** B2
Nantong China **74** C2
Nantucket Island U.S.A. **123** G2
Nanumea *atoll* Tuvalu **110**
Nanusa, Kepulauan *is* Indon. **68** B3
Nanxiong China **75** B3

212

Nanyang China **74** B2
Nanzhang China **74** B2
Nao, Cabo de la c. Spain **55** D2
Nanococane, Lac l. Can. **115** C1
Napa U.S.A. **119** B3
Napaktulik Lake Can. **113** D1
Napasoq Greenland **111** I2
Napier N.Z. **106** C2
Naples Italy **56** B2
Naples U.S.A. **125** D3
Napo r. Ecuador **134** B4
Napoli Italy see Naples
Nara Mali **90** B3
Naracoorte Austr. **104** C3
Naranjos Mex. **129** C2
Narathiwat Thai. **67** B3
Narbonne France **52** C3
Nares Strait Can./Greenland **111** H1
Narib Namibia **98** A1
Narimanov Rus. Fed. **35** D4
Narmada r. India **78** B2
Narnaul India **78** B2
Narni Italy **56** B2
Narodnyi Ukr. **38** C1
Naro-Fominsk Rus. Fed. **37** E2
Narooma Austr. **105** D3
Narrabri Austr. **105** D2
Narrandera Austr. **105** D2
Narromine Austr. **105** D2
Narva Estonia **36** C2
Narva Bay Estonia/Rus. Fed. **36** C2
Narvik Norway **40** D2
Narvskoye Vodokhranilishche resr Estonia/Rus. Fed. **36** C2
Nar'yan-Mar Rus. Fed. **34** E2
Naryn Kyrg. **81** E2
Nashik India **78** B2
Nashua U.S.A. **123** F2
Nashville U.S.A. **124** C1
Nasir Sudan **93** B4
Nass r. Can. **112** C2
Nassau Bahamas **131** C2
Nasser, Lake resr Egypt **92** B2
Nässjö Sweden **41** C4
Nastapoca r. Can. **114** C1
Nastapoka Islands Can. **114** C1
Nata Botswana **96** B2
Natal Brazil **135** F3
Natal prov. S. Africa see Kwazulu-Natal
Natashquan Can. **115** D1
Natashquan r. Can. **115** D1
Natchez U.S.A. **124** B2
Natchitoches U.S.A. **124** B2
Natitingou Benin **90** C3
Natividade Brazil **135** E4
Natori Japan **70** D3
Natuashish Can. **115** D1
Natuna, Kepulauan is Indon. **64** B1
Natuna Besar i. Indon. **64** B1
Nauchas Namibia **98** A1

Nauen Ger. **49** F1
Naujoji Akmenė Lith. **36** B2
Naumburg (Saale) Ger. **49** E2
Nauru country S. Pacific Ocean **100**
Naustdal Norway **42** E1
Navahrudak Belarus **36** C3
Navalmoral de la Mata Spain **54** B2
Navan Rep. of Ireland **45** C2
Navapolatsk Belarus **36** C2
Navarin, Mys c. Rus. Fed. **87** N2
Navarino, Isla i. Chile **137** B6
Navashino Rus. Fed. **37** F2
Naver r. U.K. **44** B1
Navlya Rus. Fed. **37** D3
Năvodari Romania **38** C3
Navoiy Uzbek. **81** D2
Navojoa Mex. **128** B2
Navolato Mex. **128** B2
Nawabshah Pak. **78** A2
Nawnghkio Myanmar **66** A1
Nawngleng Myanmar **66** A1
Naxçıvan Azer. **85** C2
Naxos i. Greece **59** C3
Nayoro Japan **70** D2
Nazareth Israel **84** B2
Nazas Mex. **128** B2
Nazas r. Mex. **128** B2
Nazca Peru **134** B4
Nazilli Turkey **59** C3
Nazrēt Eth. **93** B4
Nazwá Oman **83** C2
Nchelenge Zambia **95** C3
Ncojane Botswana **98** B1
N'dalatando Angola **94** B3
Ndélé C.A.R. **94** C2
Ndendé Gabon **94** B3
Ndjamena Chad **91** D3
Ndola Zambia **97** B1
Neagh, Lough l. U.K. **45** C1
Neale, Lake salt flat Austr. **102** C2
Neath U.K. **47** B4
Nebine Creek r. Austr. **105** D1
Neblina, Pico da mt. Brazil **134** C2
Nebraska state U.S.A. **120** C2
Nebraska City U.S.A. **121** D2
Nebrodi, Monti mts Italy **56** B3
Necochea Arg. **137** C4
Nedluuc, Lac l. Can. **115** C1
Nédroma Alg. **55** C2
Needles U.S.A. **119** D4
Neemuch India **78** B2
Nefteksamsk Rus. Fed. **35** E3
Nefteyugansk Rus. Fed. **34** G2
Negage Angola **94** B3
Negēlē Eth. **93** B4
Negra, Punta pt Peru **134** A3
Negrais, Cape Myanmar **67** A2
Negro r. Arg. **137** B5
Negro r. Brazil **138** D1
Negro r. S. America **134** D3

Negro r. Uru. **136** C4
Negro, Cabo c. Morocco **54** B3
Negros i. Phil. **68** B3
Nehbandān Iran **83** D1
Nehe China **73** E1
Neijiang China **75** A3
Neiljanini Lake Can. **113** F2
Nek'emtē Eth. **93** B4
Nekrasovskoye Rus. Fed. **37** F2
Nelidovo Rus. Fed. **37** D2
Nellore India **77** B3
Nelson Can. **112** D3
Nelson r. Can. **113** F2
Nelson N.Z. **106** B3
Nelson, Cape Austr. **104** C3
Nelson Bay Austr. **105** E2
Nelson Reservoir U.S.A. **118** E1
Nelspruit S. Africa **99** D2
Néma Maur. **90** B3
Neman Rus. Fed. **36** B2
Nemda r. Rus. Fed. **37** F2
Nemours France **52** C2
Nemuro Japan **70** D2
Nemyriv Ukr. **38** C2
Nenagh Rep. of Ireland **45** B2
Nene r. U.K. **47** D3
Nenjiang China **73** E1
Neosho U.S.A. **124** C1
Nepal country Asia **79** C2
Nepalganj Nepal **79** C2
Nephi U.S.A. **119** D3
Nephin h. Rep. of Ireland **45** B1
Nephin Beg Range hills Rep. of Ireland **45** B1
Nepisiguit r. Can. **115** D2
Nepomuk Czech Rep. **49** F3
Nérac France **52** C3
Nerang Austr. **105** E1
Nerchinsk Rus. Fed. **73** D1
Nerekhta Rus. Fed. **37** F2
Neris r. Lith. **36** B3
Nerl' r. Rus. Fed. **37** E2
Nerópolis Brazil **138** C1
Neryungri Rus. Fed. **87** K3
Ness, Loch l. U.K. **44** B2
Ness City U.S.A. **120** D3
Nestos r. Greece **59** B2
Netherlands country Europe **48** B1
Netherlands Antilles terr. West Indies **131** D3
Neubrandenburg Ger. **49** F1
Neuchâtel Switz. **53** D2
Neuenhagen Berlin Ger. **49** F1
Neufchâteau Belgium **48** B3
Neufchâteau France **53** D2
Neuhof Ger. **49** D2
Neumarkt in der Oberpfalz Ger. **49** E3
Neumünster Ger. **50** B2
Neunkirchen Ger. **48** C3

Neuquén Arg. **137** B4
Neuquén r. Arg. **137** B4
Neuruppin Ger. **49** F1
Neuss Ger. **48** C2
Neustadt am Rübenberge Ger. **49** D1
Neustadt an der Aisch Ger. **49** E3
Neustadt an der Weinstraße Ger. **48** D3
Neustrelitz Ger. **49** F1
Neutraubling Ger. **49** F3
Neuwied Ger. **48** C2
Nevada U.S.A. **121** E3
Nevada state U.S.A. **119** C3
Nevada, Sierra mts Spain **54** C2
Nevada, Sierra mts U.S.A. **119** B2
Nevel' Rus. Fed. **36** C2
Nevers France **53** D2
Nevertire Austr. **105** D2
Nevesinje Bos.-Herz. **57** C2
Nevinnomyssk Rus. Fed. **35** D4
New Albany U.S.A. **122** C3
New Amsterdam Guyana **135** D2
Newark NJ U.S.A. **123** F2
Newark OH U.S.A. **122** D2
Newark-on-Trent U.K. **46** C3
New Bedford U.S.A. **123** F2
New Bern U.S.A. **125** E1
Newberry U.S.A. **122** C1
New Boston U.S.A. **127** F2
New Braunfels U.S.A. **127** E3
Newbridge Rep. of Ireland **45** C2
New Britain i. P.N.G. **142** D5
New Brunswick prov. Can. **115** D2
Newbury U.K. **47** C4
New Caledonia terr. S. Pacific Ocean **100**
Newcastle Austr. **105** E2
Newcastle S. Africa **99** C2
Newcastle U.K. **45** D1
New Castle U.S.A. **123** D2
Newcastle U.S.A. **120** C2
Newcastle-under-Lyme U.K. **46** B3
Newcastle upon Tyne U.K. **46** C2
Newcastle West Rep. of Ireland **45** B2
New Delhi India **78** B2
New England Range mts Austr. **105** E2
Newfoundland i. Can. **115** E2
Newfoundland and Labrador prov. Can. **115** E1
New Glasgow Can. **115** D2
New Guinea i. Indon./P.N.G. **63** D3
New Halfa Sudan **82** A3
New Hampshire state U.S.A. **123** F2
New Haven U.S.A. **123** F2

New Hazelton Can. **112** C2
New Iberia U.S.A. **124** B2
New Ireland i. P.N.G. **110**
New Jersey state U.S.A. **123** F3
New Liskeard Can. **114** C2
Newman Austr. **102** A2
New Mexico state U.S.A. **126** C2
New Orleans U.S.A. **124** B3
New Philadelphia U.S.A. **122** D2
New Plymouth N.Z. **106** B2
Newport England U.K. **47** C4
Newport Wales U.K. **47** B4
Newport AR U.S.A. **124** B1
Newport OR U.S.A. **118** B2
Newport RI U.S.A. **123** F2
Newport VA U.S.A. **123** F2
Newport WA U.S.A. **118** C1
Newport News U.S.A. **123** E3
New Providence i. Bahamas **125** E3
Newquay U.K. **47** A4
New Roads U.S.A. **124** B2
New Ross Rep. of Ireland **45** C2
Newry U.K. **45** C1
New Siberia Islands Rus. Fed. **87** L1
New South Wales state Austr. **105** D2
Newton IA U.S.A. **121** E2
Newton KS U.S.A. **121** D3
Newton Abbot U.K. **47** B4
Newton Stewart U.K. **44** B3
Newtown Rep. of Ireland **45** B2
Newtown U.K. **47** B3
New Town U.S.A. **120** C1
Newtownabbey U.K. **45** D1
Newtownards U.K. **45** D1
New Ulm U.S.A. **121** E2
New York U.S.A. **123** F2
New York state U.S.A. **123** E2
New Zealand country Oceania **106**
Neya Rus. Fed. **37** F2
Neya r. Rus. Fed. **37** F2
Neyrīz Iran **85** D3
Neyshābūr Iran **80** C3
Nezahualcóyotl Mex. **129** C3
Nezahualcóyotl, Presa resr Mex. **129** C3
Ngabang Indon. **65** B1
Nganga Ringco salt l. China **79** C1
Ngangla Kangri mt. China **79** C1
Nganglong Kangri mts China **79** C1
Ngangzê Co salt l. China **79** C1
Ngao Thai. **66** A2
Ngaoundéré Cameroon **94** B2
Ngaruawahia N.Z. **106** C2
Ngo Congo **94** B3
Ngoc Linh mt. Vietnam **67** B2
Ngoring Hu l. China **72** C2
Ngourti Niger **91** D3

Nguigmi Niger **91** D3
Ngulu atoll Micronesia **63** D2
Nguru Nigeria **91** D3
Ngwelezana S. Africa **99** D2
Nhamalabué Moz. **97** C1
Nha Trang Vietnam **67** B2
Nhill Austr. **104** C3
Nhlangano Swaziland **99** D2
Nhulunbuy Austr. **103** C1
Niagara Falls Can. **123** E2
Niamey Niger **90** C3
Niangara Dem. Rep. Congo **95** C2
Niangay, Lac l. Mali **90** B3
Nias i. Indon. **64** A1
Nicaragua country Central America **130** B3
Nicaragua, Lake Nic. **130** B3
Nice France **53** D3
Nicobar Islands India **77** D4
Nicosia Cyprus **84** B2
Nicoya, Golfo de b. Costa Rica **130** B4
Nidzica Pol. **51** E2
Niebüll Ger. **50** B2
Niederaula Ger. **49** D2
Niefang Equat. Guinea **94** B2
Niemegk Ger. **49** F1
Nienburg (Weser) Ger. **49** D1
Nieuw Nickerie Suriname **135** D2
Nieuwoudtville S. Africa **98** A3
Nieuwpoort Belgium **48** A2
Niğde Turkey **84** B2
Niger country Africa **91** D3
Niger, Mouths of the Nigeria **91** C4
Nigeria country Africa **91** C4
Nighthawk Lake Can. **114** B2
Nigrita Greece **59** B2
Niigata Japan **71** C3
Niihama Japan **71** B4
Nii-jima i. Japan **71** C4
Niitsu Japan **71** C3
Nijmegen Neth. **48** B2
Nijverdal Neth. **48** C1
Nikel' Rus. Fed. **40** G2
Nikol'skoye Rus. Fed. **87** N3
Nikopol' Ukr. **39** D2
Nikshahr Iran **83** D2
Nikšić S.M. **58** A2
Nile r. Africa **92** B1
Niles U.S.A. **122** C2
Nîmes France **53** C3
Nimmitabel Austr. **105** D3
Nimule Sudan **93** B4
Nindigully Austr. **105** D1
Nine Degree Channel India **77** B4
Ninety Mile Beach Austr. **105** D3
Ninety Mile Beach N.Z. **106** B1
Ningbo China **75** C3
Ningde China **75** B3
Ninghai China **75** C3
Ninging India **66** A1

Jingjing Shan mts China 72 C2
Jingxia Huizu Zizhiqu aut. reg.
China 74 A2
Jingyang China 74 B2
Jinh Binh Vietnam 66 B1
Jinh Hoa Vietnam 67 B2
Jinhoe Japan 70 D2
Jiobrara r. U.S.A. 121 D2
Jiono Mali 90 B3
Jioro Mali 90 B3
Jiort France 52 B2
Jipigon Can. 114 B2
Jipigon, Lake Can. 114 B2
Jipishish Lake Can. 115 D1
Jipissing, Lake Can. 114 C2
Jipton U.S.A. 119 C3
Jiquelândia Brazil 135 E4
Jirmal India 77 B3
Jiš S.M. 58 B2
Jišava r. S.M. 58 B2
Jishino-omote Japan 71 B4
Jioro Mali 90 B3
Jitr r. U.K. 44 C2
Jitra Slovakia 51 D3
Jiua tom b. Pacific Ocean 101
Jivala Fin. 40 E3
Jivelles Belgium 48 B2
Jizamabad India 77 B3
Jizhnevartovsk Rus. Fed. 35 E3
Jizhniy Novgorod Rus. Fed.
35 D3
Jizhniy Odes Rus. Fed. 34 E2
Jizhniy Tagil Rus. Fed. 34 C3
Jiznyn Ukr. 39 D1
Jiazidja i. Comoros 97 C1
Jombe Tanz. 95 D3
Jkongsamba Cameroon 94 A2
Jkwenkwezi S. Africa 99 C3
Jobeoka Japan 71 B4
Jocundra Austr. 104 C1
Jogales Mex. 128 A1
Jogales U.S.A. 126 B2
Jogent-le-Rotrou France 52 C2
Joginsk Rus. Fed. 37 E2
Johfelden Ger. 48 C3
Joirmoutier, Île de i. France
52 B2
Joirmoutier-en-l'Île France
52 B2
Joisseville France 48 C3
Jojkha India 78 B2
Jokia Fin. 41 E3
Jok Kundi Pak. 78 A2
Jola C.A.R. 94 B2
Jomonde S. Africa 99 C3
Jong Khai Thai. 66 B2
Jonning Austr. 104 B2
Jonoava Mex. 128 B2
Jonsan S. Korea 69 B2
Jonthaburi Thai. 67 B2
Jonzwakazi S. Africa 98 B3
Joranda Can. 123 E1

Nordaustlandet i. Svalbard 86 D1
Norden Ger. 48 C1
Nordenshel'da, Arkhipelag is
Rus. Fed. 87 I1
Norderney Ger. 48 C1
Norderstedt Ger. 49 E1
Nordfjordeid Norway 41 B3
Nordhausen Ger. 49 E2
Nordholz Ger. 49 D1
Nordhorn Ger. 48 C1
Nordkapp c. Norway see
North Cape
Nordli Norway 40 C3
Nordmaling Sweden 40 D3
Norðoyar i. Faroe Is 42 B1
Nore r. Rep. of Ireland 45 C2
Norfolk NE U.S.A. 121 D2
Norfolk VA U.S.A. 123 F3
Norfolk Island terr.
S. Pacific Ocean 100
Noril'sk Rus. Fed. 86 H2
Norkyung China 79 C2
Norman U.S.A. 127 E1
Normandès, Îles is English Chan.
see Channel Islands
Normandy reg. France 52 B2
Normanton Austr. 103 D1
Norman Wells Can. 112 C1
Norrköping Sweden 41 D4
Norrtälje Sweden 41 D4
Norseman Austr. 102 B3
Norsjö Sweden 40 D3
Norte, Punta c. Arg. 147
Northallerton U.K. 46 C2
Northampton Austr. 102 A2
Northampton U.K. 47 C3
North Andaman i. India 67 A2
North Battleford Can. 110 E3
North Bay Can. 114 C2
North Belcher Islands Can.
114 C1
North Berwick U.K. 44 C2
North Cape Norway 40 F1
North Cape N.Z. 106 B1
North Caribou Lake Can. 114 A1
North Carolina state U.S.A.
125 E1
North Channel lake channel Can.
114 B2
North Channel U.K. 45 C1
North Cowichan Can. 112 C3
North Dakota state U.S.A.
120 C1
North Downs hills U.K. 47 C4
Northeim Ger. 49 D2
Northern Cape prov. S. Africa
98 A2
Northern Indian Lake Can.
113 F2
Northern Ireland prov. U.K.
45 C1
Northern Mariana Islands terr.
N. Pacific Ocean 63 D1

Northern Territory admin. div.
Austr. 102 C1
Northfield U.S.A. 121 E2
North Foreland c. U.K. 47 D4
North Frisian Islands Ger. 50 B2
North Geomagnetic Pole
146 B2
North Island N.Z. 106 B2
North Korea country Asia 69 B1
North Knife Lake Can. 113 F2
North Lakhimpur India 66 A1
North Magnetic Pole
146 K1
North Nahanni r. Can. 112 C1
North Platte U.S.A. 120 C2
North Platte r. U.S.A. 120 C2
Pole Arctic Ocean 146
North Ronaldsay i. U.K. 44 C1
North Sea Europe 42 D2
North Spirit Lake Can. 114 A1
North Stradbroke Island Austr.
105 E1
North Taranaki Bight b. N.Z.
106 B2
North Twin Island Can. 114 C1
North Tyne r. U.K. 46 B2
North Uist i. U.K. 44 A2
Northumberland Strait Can.
115 D2
North West prov. S. Africa 98 C2
North West Cape Austr. 102 A2
North West River Can. 115 E1
Northwest Territories admin. div.
Can. 110 E2
North York Moors moorland U.K.
46 C2
Norton U.S.A. 122 D3
Norton Zimbabwe 97 C1
Norton Sound sea chan. U.S.A.
110 B2
Norwalk U.S.A. 122 D2
Norway country Europe 41 B3
Norwegian Sea N. Atlantic Ocean
40 B2
Norwich U.K. 47 D3
Norwich CT U.S.A. 123 F2
Noshiro Japan 70 D2
Noshka Ukr. 39 D1
Nosop watercourse Africa 98 B2
Nosovaya Rus. Fed. 34 E2
Noşratābād Iran 83 C2
Nossen Ger. 49 F2
Noted r. Pol. 51 D2
Noto-hantō pen. Japan 71 C3
Notre Dame, Monts mts Can.
115 D2
Notre Dame Bay Can. 115 E2
Nottaway r. Can. 114 C1
Nottingham U.K. 46 C3
Nouâdhibou Maur. 90 A2
Nouakchott Maur. 90 A3
Nouâmghâr Maur. 90 A3
Nouméa New Caledonia 100
Nouna Burkina 90 B3

Nouvelle Calédonie *i.*
S. Pacific Ocean **110**
Nova Esperança Brazil **138** B2
Nova Friburgo Brazil **139** D2
Nova Gradiška Croatia **57** C1
Nova Granada Brazil **138** C2
Nova Iguaçu Brazil **139** D2
Nova Kakhovka Ukr. **39** D2
Nova Lima Brazil **139** D1
Nova Londrina Brazil **138** B2
Nova Odesa Ukr. **39** D2
Nova Paraíso Brazil **134** C2
Nova Scotia *prov.* Can. **115** D2
Nova Venécia Brazil **139** D1
Novaya Sibir', Ostrov *i.* Rus. Fed.
87 L1
Novaya Zemlya *is* Rus. Fed.
34 E1
Nové Zámky Slovakia **51** D3
Novhorod-Sivers'kyy Ukr. **39** D1
Novi Ligure Italy **56** A2
Novi Pazar S.M. **58** B2
Novi Sad S.M. **58** A1
Novoaleksandrovsk Rus. Fed.
39 F2
Novoanninskiy Rus. Fed. **39** F1
Novo Aripuanã Brazil **134** C3
Novoazovs'k Ukr. **39** E2
Novocherkassk Rus. Fed. **39** F2
Novodvinsk Rus. Fed. **34** D2
Novo Hamburgo Brazil **136** C3
Novohrad-Volyns'kyy Ukr. **38** C1
Novokhopersk Rus. Fed. **37** F3
Novokubansk Rus. Fed. **39** F2
Novokuznetsk Rus. Fed. **81** F1
Novo Mesto Slovenia **50** D1
Novomikhaylovskiy Rus. Fed.
39 E3
Novomoskovsk Rus. Fed. **37** E3
Novomoskovs'k Ukr. **39** E2
Novomyrhorod Ukr. **39** D2
Novonikolayevskiy Rus. Fed.
39 F1
Novooleksiyivka Ukr. **39** D2
Novopokrovskaya Rus. Fed.
39 F2
Novopskov Ukr. **39** E2
Novorossiysk Rus. Fed. **39** E3
Novorzhev Rus. Fed. **36** C2
Novosergiyevka Rus. Fed. **35** E3
Novoshakhtinsk Rus. Fed. **39** E2
Novosibirskiye Ostrova *is*
Rus. Fed. *see*
New Siberia Islands
Novosokol'niki Rus. Fed. **37** D2
Novotroyits'ke Ukr. **39** D2
Novoukrayinka Ukr. **39** D2
Novovolyns'k Ukr. **38** B1
Novozybkov Rus. Fed. **37** D3
Nový Jičín Czech Rep. **51** D3
Novyy Bor Rus. Fed. **34** E2
Novyy Oskol Rus. Fed. **39** E1
Novyy Port Rus. Fed. **34** G2

Novyy Urengoy Rus. Fed. **34** G2
Nowogard Pol. **50** D2
Nowra Austr. **105** E2
Now Shahr Iran **85** D2
Nowshera Pak. **78** B1
Nowy Sącz Pol. **51** E3
Nowy Targ Pol. **51** E3
Noyabr'sk Rus. Fed. **35** G2
Noyon France **52** C2
Nsanje Malawi **97** C1
Nu'aym *reg.* Oman **83** C2
Nubian Desert Sudan **92** B2
Nudo Coropuna *mt.* Peru **134** B4
Nueltin Lake Can. **113** F1
Nueva Rosita Mex. **129** B2
Nuevo Casas Grandes Mex.
128 B1
Nuevo Laredo Mex. **129** C2
Nugaal *watercourse* Somalia
93 C4
Nuits-St-Georges France **53** C2
Nu Jiang *r.* China/Myanmar *see*
Salween
Nu Jiang *r.* China/Myanmar *see*
Salween
Nuku'alofa Tonga **101**
Nuku Hiva *i.* Fr. Polynesia **111**
Nukulaelae *atoll* Tuvalu **110**
Nukunonu *atoll* Tokelau **111**
Nukus Uzbek. **80** C2
Nullagine Austr. **102** B2
Nullarbor Plain Austr. **102** B3
Numan Nigeria **91** D4
Numazu Japan **71** C3
Numedal *val.* Norway **41** B3
Numfoor *i.* Indon. **63** C3
Numurkah Austr. **105** D3
Nunap Isua *c.* Greenland *see*
Farewell, Cape
Nunavik *reg.* Can. **111** H3
Nunavut *admin. div.* Can. **110** G2
Nuneaton U.K. **47** C3
Nunivak Island U.S.A. **87** O3
Nuoro Italy **56** A2
Nuqrah Saudi Arabia **82** B2
Nuremberg Ger. **49** F3
Nurioopta Austr. **104** B2
Nurmes Fin. **40** F3
Nürnberg Ger. *see* Nuremberg
Nu Shan *mts* China **66** A1
Nushki Pak. **78** A2
Nuuk Greenland **111** I2
Nuussuaq Greenland **111** I2
Nuussuaq *pen.* Greenland **111** I2
Nuwaybi' al Muzayyinah Egypt
84 B3
Nuweveldberge *mts* S. Africa
98 B3
Nyagan' Rus. Fed. **34** G2
Nyainqêntanglha Feng *mt.* China
79 D1
Nyainqêntanglha Shan *mts* China
79 D2

Nyala Sudan **93** A3
Nyandoma Rus. Fed. **34** D2
Nyanga *r.* Gabon **94** B3
Nyasa, Lake Africa **97** C1
Nyborg Denmark **41** C4
Nyborg Norway **40** F1
Nybro Sweden **41** D4
Nyeri Kenya **95** D3
Nyima China **79** C1
Nyingchi China **72** C3
Nyíregyháza Hungary **51** E3
Nykøbing Denmark **41** C5
Nyköping Sweden **41** D4
Nymagee Austr. **105** D2
Nynäshamn Sweden **41** D4
Nyngan Austr. **105** D2
Nyoman *r.* Belarus/Lith. **36** B3
Nyřany Czech Rep. **49** F3
Nyrob Rus. Fed. **34** E2
Nyssa U.S.A. **118** C2
Nyunzu Dem. Rep. Congo **95** C3
Nyzhn'ohirs'kyy Ukr. **39** D2
Nzega Tanz. **95** D3
Nzérékoré Guinea **90** B4
N'zeto Angola **94** B3

Oahe, Lake U.S.A. **120** C2
Oahu *i.* U.S.A. **120**
Oakbank Austr. **104** C2
Oakey Austr. **105** E1
Oak Harbor U.S.A. **118** B1
Oak Hill U.S.A. **122** D3
Oakland U.S.A. **119** B3
Oakover *r.* Austr. **102** B2
Oakridge U.S.A. **118** B2
Oak Ridge U.S.A. **125** D1
Oamaru N.Z. **106** B3
Oas Phil. **68** B2
Oaxaca Mex. **129** C3
Ob' *r.* Rus. Fed. **34** F2
Obala Cameroon **94** B2
Oban U.K. **44** B2
O Barco Spain **54** B1
Oberá Arg. **138** A3
Oberon Austr. **105** D2
Oberpfälzer Wald *mts* Ger. **49** F3
Obi *i.* Indon. **63** C3
Óbidos Brazil **135** D3
Obihiro Japan **70** D2
Obluch'ye Rus. Fed. **73** E1
Obninsk Rus. Fed. **37** E2
Obo C.A.R. **95** C2
Obock Djibouti **93** C3
Obouya Congo **94** B3
Obregón, Presa *resr* Mex. **128** B2
Obshchiy Syrt *hills* Rus. Fed.
35 E3
Obskaya Guba *sea chan.*
Rus. Fed. **34** G2

ꞏbuasi Ghana 90 B4
ꞏbukhiv Ukr. 38 D1
ꞏb''yachevo Rus. Fed. 34 D2
ꞏcala U.S.A. 125 D3
ꞏcampo Mex. 128 B2
ꞏcaña Spain 54 C2
ꞏccidental, Cordillera mts Col. 134 B2
ꞏccidental, Cordillera mts Peru 134 B4
ꞏcean City U.S.A. 123 E3
ꞏcean Falls Can. 112 C2
ꞏceanside U.S.A. 119 C4
ꞏchakiv Ukr. 39 D2
ꞏdesa U.S.A. 125 D3
ꞏcher Rus. Fed. 34 E3
ꞏchsenfurt Ger. 49 E3
ꞏconee r. U.S.A. 125 D2
ꞏcussi enclave East Timor 63 C4
ꞏda, Jebel mt. Sudan 92 B2
ꞏdate Japan 70 D2
ꞏdawara Japan 71 C3
ꞏdda Norway 41 B3
ꞏdemiş Turkey 59 C3
ꞏdense Denmark 11 G4
ꞏdenwald reg. Ger. 49 D3
ꞏderbucht b. Ger. 50 C2
ꞏdessa Ger. 38 D2
ꞏdessa U.S.A. 127 C3
ꞏdcussi pen. Japan 70 C3
ꞏdra r. Ger. 50 E1
ꞏdeiras Brazil 135 D3
ꞏdulde Ger. 48 D2
ꞏdelrichs U.S.A. 120 C2
ꞏdelsnitz Ger. 49 F2
ꞏdenkerk Neth. 48 B1
ꞏdfanto r. Italy 57 C2
ꞏdffenbach am Main Ger. 49 D2
ꞏdffenburg Ger. 50 B3
ꞏdgaden reg. Eth. 93 C4
ꞏdga-hanto pen. Japan 70 C3
ꞏdgaki Japan 71 C3
ꞏdgallala U.S.A. 122 C2
ꞏdgbomosho Nigeria 90 C4
ꞏdgilvie r. Can. 110 C2
Ogilvie Mountains Can. 110 C2
Oglethorpe, Mount U.S.A. 125 D2
Ogoki r. Can. 114 B1
Ogoki Reservoir Can. 114 B1
Ogre Latvia 36 B2
Ogulin Croatia 56 C1
Ohio r. U.S.A. 123 C3
Ohio state U.S.A. 122 D2
Ohrdruf Ger. 49 E2
Ohrid Macedonia 59 B4
Oiapoque Brazil 135 D2
Oil City U.S.A. 123 E2
Oise r. France 48 A3
Oita Japan 71 B4
Ojinaga Mex. 128 B2
Ojos del Salado, Nevado mt. Arg./Chile 136 B3

Oka r. Rus. Fed. 37 F2
Okahandja Namibia 96 A2
Okanagan Lake Can. 112 D3
Okanogan U.S.A. 118 C1
Okanogan r. U.S.A. 118 C1
Okara Pak. 78 B1
Okavango r. Botswana/Namibia 96 B1
Okavango Delta swamp Botswana 96 B1
Okayama Japan 71 B4
Okazaki Japan 71 C4
Okeechobee, Lake U.S.A. 125 D3
Okefenokee Swamp U.S.A. 125 D2
Okehampton U.K. 47 A4
Okha Rus. Fed. 87 L3
Okhotka r. Rus. Fed. 87 L3
Okhotsk Rus. Fed. 87 L3
Okhotsk, Sea of Japan/Rus. Fed. 87 L4
Okhtyrka Ukr. 39 D1
Okinawa i. Japan 73 E3
Oki-shoto is Japan 71 B3
Oklahoma state U.S.A. 127 E1
Oklahoma City U.S.A. 127 E1
Okmulgee U.S.A. 127 E1
Oko, Wadi watercourse Sudan 82 A2
Okovskiy Les for. Rus. Fed. 37 D3
Okoyo Congo 94 B3
Øksfjord Norway 40 E1
Oktwin Myanmar 66 A2
Oktyabr'skiy Arkhangel'skaya Oblast' Rus. Fed. 34 D2
Oktyabr'skiy Kamchatskaya Oblast' Rus. Fed. 87 M3
Oktyabr'skiy Respublika Bashkortostan Rus. Fed. 35 E3
Oktyabr'skoye Rus. Fed. 34 F2
Oktyabr'skoy Revolyutsii, Ostrov i. Rus. Fed. 87 I1
Okulovka Rus. Fed. 37 D2
Okushiri-tō i. Japan 70 C2
Ólafsvík Iceland 40 [inset]
Öland i. Sweden 41 D4
Olary Austr. 104 C2
Olavarría Arg. 137 B4
Olbernhau Ger. 49 F2
Olbia Italy 56 A2
Oldenburg Ger. 49 D1
Oldenburg in Holstein Ger. 50 C2
Oldenzaal Neth. 48 C1
Old Head of Kinsale hd Rep. of Ireland 45 B3
Oldham U.K. 46 B3
Old Wives Lake Can. 113 C2
Olean U.S.A. 123 E2
Olecko Pol. 51 E2
Olekminsk Rus. Fed. 87 K2
Oleksandriya Ukr. 39 D2

Ølen Norway 42 E2
Olenegorsk Rus. Fed. 40 G2
Olenek Rus. Fed. 87 J2
Olenino Rus. Fed. 37 D2
Olevs'k Ukr. 38 C1
Olhão Port. 54 B2
Olifants r. Moz./S. Africa 99 D1
Olifants watercourse Namibia 98 A2
Olifants S. Africa 99 D1
Olifants r. S. Africa 98 A3
Olifantshoek S. Africa 98 B2
Olinda Brazil 135 F3
Oliva Spain 55 C2
Olivenza Spain 54 B2
Olïague Chile 136 B3
Olney U.S.A. 122 C3
Olomouc Czech Rep. 51 D3
Olongapo Phil. 68 B2
Oloron-Ste-Marie France 52 B3
Olot Spain 55 D1
Olovyannaya Rus. Fed. 73 D1
Olpe Ger. 48 C2
Olsztyn Pol. 51 F2
Olt r. Romania 38 C3
Oltu Turkey 85 F1
Olympia tourist site Greece 59 B3
Olympia U.S.A. 118 B1
Olympus, Mount Greece 59 B2
Olympus, Mount U.S.A. 118 B1
Olyutorskiy, Mys c. Rus. Fed. 87 N3
Omagh U.K. 45 C1
Omaha U.S.A. 122 D2
Oman country Asia 83 C2
Oman, Gulf of Asia 83 C2
Omaruru Namibia 96 A2
Omatako watercourse Namibia 96 B1
Omdurman Sudan 92 D3
Ometepec Mex. 129 C3
Om Hajer Eritrea 82 A3
Omineca Mountains Can. 112 C2
Ōmiya Japan 71 C3
Ommen Neth. 48 C1
Omolon r. Rus. Fed. 87 M2
Omsk Rus. Fed. 81 E1
Omsukchan Rus. Fed. 87 M2
Omu, Vârful mt. Romania 38 C2
Onancock U.S.A. 123 E3
Onaping Lake Can. 122 D1
Oncócua Angola 96 A1
Onderstedorings S. Africa 98 B3
Ondjiva Angola 96 A1
Onega Rus. Fed. 34 C2
Onega r. Rus. Fed. 34 C2
Onega, Lake Rus. Fed. 34 C2
Oneida Lake U.S.A. 123 E2
O'Neill U.S.A. 121 D2
Oneşti Romania 38 C2
Onezhskoye Ozero l. Rus. Fed. see Onega, Lake
Ongjin N. Korea 69 B2

Ongole India 77 C3
Onilahy r. Madag. 97 [inset] D2
Onitsha Nigeria 91 C4
Onotoa atoll Kiribati 110
Onseepkans S. Africa 98 A2
Onslow Austr. 102 A2
Onslow Bay U.S.A. 125 E2
Ontario prov. Can. 114 A1
Ontario U.S.A. 118 C2
Ontario, Lake Can./U.S.A. 123 E2
Oodnadatta Austr. 104 B1
Oostende Belgium see Ostend
Oosterhout Neth. 48 B2
Oosterschelde est. Neth. 48 A2
Oost-Vlieland Neth. 48 B1
Ootsa Lake l. Can. 112 C2
Opataca, Lac l. Can. 114 C1
Opava Czech Rep. 51 D3
Opelika U.S.A. 125 C2
Opelousas U.S.A. 124 B2
Opinaca, Réservoir resr Can. 114 C1
Opiscotéo, Lac l. Can. 115 D1
Opochka Rus. Fed. 36 C2
Opole Pol. 51 D2
Optiki N.Z. 106 C2
Oppdal Norway 41 B3
Opunake N.Z. 106 B2
Opuwo Namibia 96 A1
Oradea Romania 38 B2
Oran Alg. 90 B1
Orán Arg. 136 B3
Orang N. Korea 69 B1
Orange Austr. 105 D2
Orange France 53 C3
Orange r. Namibia/S. Africa 98 A2
Orange U.S.A. 127 F2
Orange, Cabo c. Brazil 146
Orangeburg U.S.A. 125 D2
Orangeville Can. 123 D2
Orange Walk Belize 129 D3
Oranienburg Ger. 49 F1
Oranjemund Namibia 98 A2
Orapa Botswana 96 B2
Orăștie Romania 38 B2
Orbetello Italy 56 B2
Orbost Austr. 105 D3
Ord, Mount Austr. 102 B1
Ordes Spain 54 B1
Ordos China 74 B2
Ordu Turkey 84 B1
Ordzhonikidze Ukr. 39 D2
Örebro Sweden 41 D4
Oregon state U.S.A. 118 B2
Oregon City U.S.A. 118 B1
Orel Rus. Fed. 37 E3
Orem U.S.A. 118 D2
Orenburg Rus. Fed. 35 E3
Orepuki N.Z. 106 A4
Øresund str. Denmark/Sweden 41 C4
Orford Ness hd U.K. 47 D3

Orhaneli Turkey 59 C3
Orhangazi Turkey 59 C2
Orhon Gol r. Mongolia 87 J3
Oriental, Cordillera mts Bol. 136 B2
Oriental, Cordillera mts Col. 134 B2
Oriental, Cordillera mts Peru 134 B4
Orihuela Spain 55 C2
Orikhiv Ukr. 39 E2
Orillia Can. 114 C2
Orinoco r. Col./Venez. 134 C2
Orinoco Delta Venez. 134 C2
Orissaare Estonia 36 B2
Oristano Italy 56 A3
Orivesi l. Fin. 40 F3
Oriximiná Brazil 135 D3
Orizaba Mex. 129 C3
Orizaba, Pico de vol. Mex. 129 C3
Orkanger Norway 40 B3
Örkelljunga Sweden 41 C4
Orkla r. Norway 40 B3
Orkney Islands Scotland U.K. 44 C1
Orlando U.S.A. 125 D3
Orléans France 52 C2
Ormara Pak. 78 A2
Ormoc Phil. 68 B2
Ormskirk U.K. 46 B3
Örnsköldsvik Sweden 40 D3
Orodara Burkina 90 B3
Orofino U.S.A. 118 C1
Orona atoll Kiribati 111
Oroquieta Phil. 68 B3
Orosei, Golfo di b. Italy 56 A2
Orosháza Hungary 51 E3
Oroville U.S.A. 119 B3
Orsha Belarus 37 D3
Orsk Rus. Fed. 35 E3
Ørsta Norway 41 B3
Ortegal, Cabo c. Spain 54 B1
Orthez France 52 B3
Ortigueira Spain 54 B1
Ortonville U.S.A. 121 D1
Orulgan, Khrebet mts Rus. Fed. 87 K2
Orümiyeh, Daryächeh-ye salt l. Iran see Urmia, Lake
Oruro Bol. 136 B2
Orvieto Italy 56 B2
Osage r. U.S.A. 121 E3
Osaka Japan 71 C4
Oschersleben (Bode) Ger. 49 E1
Oschiri Italy 56 A2
Osetr r. Rus. Fed. 37 E3
Osh Kyrg. 81 E2
Oshakati Namibia 96 A1
Oshawa Can. 114 C2
Ō-shima i. Japan 70 C4
Ō-shima i. Japan 71 C4
Oshkosh U.S.A. 122 C2
Oshnovïyeh Iran 85 C2

Oshogbo Nigeria 90 C4
Oshwe Dem. Rep. Congo 94 B3
Osijek Croatia 57 C1
Osilinka r. Can. 112 C2
Osimo Italy 56 B2
Osizweni S. Africa 99 D2
Oskaloosa U.S.A. 121 E2
Oskarshamn Sweden 41 D4
Oskol r. Rus. Fed. 37 E3
Oslo Norway 41 C4
Oslofjorden sea chan. Norway 41 C4
Osmancık Turkey 84 B1
Osmaniye Turkey 84 B2
Osnabrück Ger. 48 D1
Osorno Chile 137 A5
Osorno Spain 54 C1
Osoyoos Can. 112 D3
Osøyri Norway 42 E1
Oss Neth. 48 B2
Ossa, Mount Austr. 103 D4
Ostashkov Rus. Fed. 37 D2
Oste r. Ger. 49 D1
Ostend Belgium 48 A2
Osterburg (Altmark) Ger. 49 E1
Österdalälven l. Sweden 41 C3
Osterholz-Scharmbeck Ger. 49 D1
Osterode am Harz Ger. 49 E2
Östersund Sweden 40 C3
Ostfriesland reg. Ger. 48 C1
Östhammar Sweden 41 D3
Ostrava Czech Rep. 51 D3
Ostróda Pol. 51 D2
Ostrogozhsk Rus. Fed. 37 E3
Ostrołęka Pol. 51 E2
Ostrov Czech Rep. 49 F2
Ostrov Rus. Fed. 36 C2
Ostrowiec Świętokrzyski Pol. 51 E2
Ostrów Mazowiecka Pol. 51 E2
Ostrów Wielkopolski Pol. 51 D2
Osüm r. Bulg. 58 B2
Ōsumi-kaikyō sea chan. Japan 71 B4
Ōsumi-shotō is Japan 71 B4
Osuna Spain 54 C2
Oswego U.S.A. 123 E2
Oswestry U.K. 46 B3
Otago Peninsula N.Z. 106 B4
Otaki N.Z. 106 C3
Otaru Japan 70 D2
Otavi Namibia 96 A1
Othello U.S.A. 118 C1
Otjiwarongo Namibia 96 A1
Otoro, Jebel mt. Sudan 93 B3
Otra r. Norway 41 B4
Otranto, Strait of Albania/Italy 59 A2
Ōtsu Japan 71 C3
Otta Norway 41 B3
Ottawa Can. 114 C2
Ottawa IL U.S.A. 122 C2
Ottawa KS U.S.A. 121 E3

Ottawa *KS* U.S.A. **121** D3
Ottawa Islands Can. **114** B1
Ottignies Belgium **48** B2
Ottumwa U.S.A. **121** E2
Otway, Cape Austr. **104** C3
Ouachita r. U.S.A. **124** E2
Ouachita, Lake U.S.A. **124** B2
Ouachita Mountains U.S.A. **124** B2
Ouadda C.A.R. **94** C2
Ouaddaï reg. Chad **91** D3
Ouagadougou Burkina **90** B3
Ouahigouya Burkina **90** B3
Oualâta Maur. **90** B3
Oued Tiélat Alg. **55** C2
Ouessant, Île d' i. France **52** A2
Ouesso Congo **94** B2
Ouistreham France **47** C5
Oujda Morocco **90** B1
Ouled Farès Alg. **55** D2
Oulu r. Fin. **40** F3
Oulujärvi l. Fin. **40** F3
Oulx Italy **56** A1
Oum-Chalouba Chad **91** E3
Oum-Hadjer Chad **91** D3
Ounianga Kébir Chad **91** E3
Oupeye Belgium **48** D2
Our r. Lux. **48** D3
Ourense Spain **54** B1
Ourinhos Brazil **138** C2
Ouro Preto Brazil **139** D2
Ourthe r. Belgium **48** C2
Ouse r. U.K. **46** C3
Outardes Quatre, Réservoir resr
   Can. **115** D2
Outardes Quatre, Réservoir resr
   Can. **115** D2
Outer Hebrides is U.K. **44** A2
Outjo Namibia **96** A2
Outokumpu Fin. **40** F3
Ouyen Austr. **104** C3
Ovar Port. **54** B1
Överkalix Sweden **40** E2
Overton U.S.A. **119** D3
Övertorneå Sweden **40** E2
Oviedo Spain **54** B1
Ovruch Ukr. **38** C1
Owando Congo **94** B3
Owase Japan **71** C4
Owatonna U.S.A. **121** E2
Owensboro U.S.A. **122** C3
Owens Lake U.S.A. **119** C3
Owen Sound Can. **114** B2
Owerri Nigeria **91** C4
Owyhee U.S.A. **118** C2
Owyhee r. U.S.A. **118** C2
Oxelösund Sweden **36** A2
Oxford N.Z. **106** B3
Oxford U.K. **47** C4
Oxford U.S.A. **124** C2

Oxford Lake Can. **113** F2
Oxley Austr. **104** C2
Oxnard U.S.A. **119** C4
Oyama Japan **71** C3
Oyem Gabon **94** B2
Oyen Can. **113** D2
Oyonnax France **53** D2
Ozark U.S.A. **125** C2
Ozark Plateau U.S.A. **121** E3
Ozarks, Lake of the U.S.A.
   121 E3
Ozernovskiy Rus. Fed. **87** M3
Ozery Rus. Fed. **37** E3
Ozinki Rus. Fed. **35** D3

P

Paamiut Greenland **111** I2
Paarl S. Africa **98** A3
Pabianice Pol. **51** D2
Pabna Bangl. **79** C2
Pab Range mts Pak. **78** A2
Pachino Italy **56** C3
Pachuca Mex. **129** C2
Pacific Ocean **142**
Padang Indon. **64** B2
Padangpanjang Indon. **64** B2
Padangsidimpuan Indon. **64** A1
Paderborn Ger. **49** D2
Padova Italy *see* Padua
Padre Island U.S.A. **127** E3
Padstow U.K. **47** B4
Paducah *KY* U.S.A. **122** C3
Paducah *TX* U.S.A. **127** D2
Paegam N. Korea **69** B1
Paengnyŏng-do i. S. Korea **69** A2
Paeroa N.Z. **106** C2
Pafos Cyprus *see* Paphos
Pag Croatia **56** C2
Pagadian Phil. **68** B3
Pagai Selatan i. Indon. **64** B2
Pagai Utara i. Indon. **64** B2
Pagan i. N. Mariana Is **63** D1
Pagatan Indon. **65** C2
Page U.S.A. **126** B1
Pagėgiai Lith. **36** B2
Pagosa Springs U.S.A. **120** B3
Paide Estonia **36** C2
Päijänne l. Fin. **41** F3
Paikū Co l. China **79** C2
Painted Desert U.S.A. **126** B1
Paisley U.K. **44** B3
Pajala Sweden **40** E2
Pakaraima Mountains S. America
   146
Pakistan country Asia **78** A2
Pakokku Myanmar **66** A1
Paks Hungary **51** D3
Pakwash Lake Can. **114** A1
Pakxan Laos **66** B2
Pakxé Laos **67** B2
Pala Chad **91** D4

Palabuhanratu, Teluk b. Indon.
   64 B2
Palaikastro Greece **59** C3
Palaiochora Greece **59** B3
Palamakoloi Botswana **98** B1
Palamós Spain **55** D1
Palana Rus. Fed. **87** M3
Palangkaraya Indon. **65** C2
Palanpur India **78** B2
Palapye Botswana **99** C1
Palatka Rus. Fed. **87** M2
Palatka U.S.A. **125** D3
Palau country N. Pacific Ocean
   63 C2
Palau Islands Palau **67**
Palaw Myanmar **67** A2
Palawan i. Phil. **68** A3
Paldiski Estonia **36** C2
Palekh Rus. Fed. **37** F2
Palembang Indon. **64** B2
Palencia Spain **54** C1
Palenque Mex. **129** C3
Palermo Italy **56** B3
Palestine U.S.A. **127** E2
Paletwa Myanmar **66** A1
Pali India **78** B2
Palikir Micronesia **100**
Palinuro, Capo c. Italy **56** C2
Palioúri, Akra pt Greece **59** B3
Paliseul Belgium **48** B3
Paljakka h. Fin. **40** F3
Palk Strait India/Sri Lanka **77** B4
Palliser, Îles is Fr. Polynesia **111**
Palma del Río Spain **54** B2
Palma de Mallorca Spain **55** D2
Palmas Brazil **135** C4
Palmeira Brazil **138** C3
Palmer U.S.A. **110** C2
Palmer Land reg. Antarctica
   107 K3
Palmerston atoll Cook Is **111**
Palmerston North N.Z. **106** C3
Palmi Italy **57** C3
Palmira Col. **134** B2
Palmyra Atoll terr.
   N. Pacific Ocean **101**
Palopo Indon. **65** D2
Palos, Cabo de c. Spain **55** C2
Paltamo Fin. **40** F3
Palu Indon. **65** C2
Palyavaam r. Rus. Fed. **87** N2
Pamiers France **52** C3
Pamir mts Asia **81** D3
Pamlico Sound sea chan. U.S.A.
   125 E1
Pampas reg. Arg. **137** B4
Pamplona Col. **134** B2
Pamplona Spain **55** C1
Pamukova Turkey **59** D2
Panaitan i. Indon. **64** B2
Panaji India **77** B3
Panama country Central America
   130 B4

Panama, Gulf of Panama 130 C4
Panama Canal Panama 130 C4
Panama City Panama 130 C4
Panama City U.S.A. 125 C2
Panamint Range *mts* U.S.A. 119 C3
Panarik Indon. 64 B1
Pancevo S.M. 58 B2
Panda Moz. 99 D1
Panevėžys Lith. 36 B2
Pangkalanbuun Indon. 65 C2
Pangkalpinang Indon. 64 B2
Pangnirtung Can. 111 H2
Pangody Rus. Fed. 34 G2
Panipat India 78 B2
Panjgur Pak. 78 A2
Pan Ling *mts* China 69 C1
Panna India 79 C2
Pannawonica Austr. 102 A2
Panorama Brazil 138 B2
Panshi China 69 B1
Pantanal *reg.* Brazil 136 C2
Paola Mex. 129 C2
Panzhihua China 66 B1
Paola Italy 57 C3
Pápa Hungary 51 D3
Papakura N.Z. 106 B2
Papantla Mex. 129 C2
Papeete Fr. Polynesia 101
Papenburg Ger. 48 C1
Paphos Cyprus 84 B2
Papua, Gulf of P.N.G. 63 D3
Papua New Guinea *country* Oceania 63 D3
Para *r.* Rus. Fed. 37 F3
Paraburdoo Austr. 102 A2
Paracatu Brazil 138 C1
Paracatu *r.* Brazil 139 C1
Parachilna Austr. 104 B2
Paracín S.M. 58 B2
Pará de Minas Brazil 139 D1
Paradise U.S.A. 119 B3
Paragould U.S.A. 124 B1
Paraguai *r.* Brazil 135 D4
Paraguay *r.* Arg./Para. 136 C3
Paraguay *country* S. America 136 C3
Parakou Benin 90 C4
Paramaribo Suriname 135 D2
Paraná Arg. 136 B4
Paraná *r.* S. America 138 B2
Paranaguá Brazil 138 C3
Paranaíba Brazil 138 B1
Paranaíba *r.* Brazil 138 B2
Paranapanema *r.* Brazil 138 B2
Paranapiacaba, Serra *mts* Brazil 138 B2
Paranavaí Brazil 138 B2
Paraparaumu N.Z. 106 B3
Parati Brazil 139 D2
Paraúna Brazil 138 B1
Paray-le-Monial France 53 C2
Parbhani India 77 B3

Parchim Ger. 49 E1
Pardo *r.* Bahia Brazil 139 E1
Pardo *r.* Mato Grosso do Sul Brazil 138 B2
Pardo *r.* São Paulo Brazil 138 C2
Pardubice Czech Rep. 51 D2
Parecis, Serra dos *hills* Brazil 134 C4
Parent, Lac Can. 114 C2
Parepare Indon. 65 C2
Parfino Rus. Fed. 37 D2
Parga Greece 59 B3
Pargas Fin. 36 B1
Parima, Serra *mts* Brazil 134 C2
Parintins Brazil 135 D3
Paris France 52 C2
Paris TN U.S.A. 124 C1
Paris TX U.S.A. 127 E2
Parkano Fin. 41 E3
Parker U.S.A. 126 B2
Parkersburg U.S.A. 122 D3
Parkes Austr. 105 D2
Park Rapids U.S.A. 121 D1
Parma Italy 56 B2
Parnaíba Brazil 135 E3
Parnassos *mt.* Greece 59 B3
Parnassus N.Z. 106 B3
Parnon *mts* Greece 59 B3
Pärnu Estonia 36 B2
Paroo *watercourse* Austr. 104 C2
Paropamisus *mts* Afgh. 78 A1
Paros *i.* Greece 59 C3
Parras Mex. 128 B2
Parry Channel Can. 108 D1
Parry Islands Can. 110 E1
Parry Sound Can. 114 B2
Parsons U.S.A. 121 D3
Parthenay France 52 B2
Partry Mountains Rep. of Ireland 45 B2
Paru *r.* Brazil 135 D3
Pasadena U.S.A. 119 C4
Pascagoula U.S.A. 124 C2
Pascani Romania 38 C2
Pasco U.S.A. 118 C1
Pasewalk Ger. 50 C2
Pasfield Lake Can. 113 E2
Pasni Pak. 78 A2
Paso Río Mayo Arg. 137 A5
Paso Robles U.S.A. 119 B3
Passau Ger. 50 C3
Passo Fundo Brazil 136 C3
Passos Brazil 139 C2
Pastavy Belarus 36 C2
Pastaza *r.* Peru 134 B3
Pasto Col. 134 B2
Pasuruan Indon. 65 C2
Pasvalys Lith. 36 B2
Patan Nepal 79 C2
Patea N.Z. 106 B2
Paterson U.S.A. 123 F2
Pathfinder Reservoir U.S.A. 120 B2

Pati Indon. 65 C2
Patmos *i.* Greece 59 C3
Patna India 79 C2
Patnos Turkey 85 C2
Pato Branco Brazil 138 B3
Patos, Lagoa dos *l.* Brazil 136 C4
Patos de Minas Brazil 139 C1
Patquía Arg. 136 B4
Patras Greece 59 B3
Patrocínio Brazil 138 C1
Pattani Thai. 67 B3
Pattaya Thai. 67 B2
Patterson, Mount Can. 112 B1
Pattullo, Mount Can. 112 C2
Pátzcuaro Mex. 128 B3
Pau France 52 B3
Pauillac France 52 B2
Paulo Afonso Brazil 135 F3
Paulpietersburg S. Africa 99 D2
Pauls Valley U.S.A. 127 E2
Paungde Myanmar 66 A2
Pavão Brazil 139 D1
Pavia Italy 56 A1
Pāvilosta Latvia 36 B2
Pavlikeni Bulg. 58 C2
Pavlodar Kazakh. 81 E1
Pavlohrad Ukr. 39 E2
Pavlovo Rus. Fed. 37 F2
Pavlovsk Rus. Fed. 39 F1
Pavlovskaya Rus. Fed. 39 E2
Payakumbuh Indon. 64 B2
Payette U.S.A. 118 C2
Payette *r.* U.S.A. 118 C2
Payne, Lac *l.* Can. 114 C1
Paysandú Uru. 136 C4
Pazardzhik Bulg. 58 B2
Pazin Croatia 56 B1
Peace *r.* Can. 112 D2
Peace River Can. 112 D2
Peale, Mount U.S.A. 119 E3
Pearl *r.* U.S.A. 124 C2
Pearsall U.S.A. 127 E3
Pebane Moz. 97 C3
Peć S.M. 58 B2
Peçanha Brazil 139 D1
Pechora Rus. Fed. 34 E2
Pechora *r.* Rus. Fed. 34 E2
Pechory Rus. Fed. 36 C2
Pecos U.S.A. 127 D2
Pecos *r.* U.S.A. 127 D2
Pécs Hungary 51 D3
Pedra Azul Brazil 139 D1
Pedregulho Brazil 138 C2
Pedreiras Brazil 135 E3
Pedro, Point Sri Lanka 77 C4
Pedro Afonso Brazil 135 E3
Pedro Gomes Brazil 138 B1
Pedro Juan Caballero Para. 136 C3
Peebles U.K. 44 C3
Pee Dee *r.* U.S.A. 125 E2
Peel *r.* Can. 110 C2
Peel Isle of Man 46 A2

egasus Bay N.Z. **106** B3
egg Ger. **49** E3
egu Myanmar **66** A2
egu Yoma *mts* Myanmar **66** A2
eine Ger. **49** E1
eipus, Lake Estonia/Rus. Fed. **36** C2
eixe *r.* Brazil **138** B2
eixoto de Azevedo Brazil **136** C2
ekalongan Indon. **65** B2
ekan Malaysia **64** B1
ekanbaru Indon. **64** B1
eking China *see* Beijing
elee Island Can. **114** B2
elee Indon. **65** D2
elkosenniemi Fin. **40** F2
elleluhu Islands P.N.G. **63** D3
ello Fin. **40** E2
elly *r.* Can. **112** B1
elly Mountains Can. **112** B1
elotas Brazil **136** C4
elotas, Rio das *r.* Brazil **136** C3
emadumcook Lake U.S.A. **120** O1
ematangsiantar Indon. **64** A1
emba Moz. **97** D1
emba Zambia **96** B1
emba Island Tanz. **95** D3
emberton Can. **112** C2
embina *r.* Can. **121** D1
embroke Can. **114** C2
embroke U.K. **47** A4
eña Nevada, Cerro *mt.* Mex. **129** C2
enápolis Brazil **138** A2
eñarroya *mt.* Spain **55** C1
enarroya–Pueblonuevo Spain **54** B2
eñas, Cabo de *c.* Spain **54** B1
enas, Golfo de g. Chile **137** A5
endleton U.S.A. **118** C1
end Oreille Lake U.S.A. **118** C1
englai China **74** C2
engshui China **75** A3
enicuík U.K. **44** C3
eninsular Malaysia Malaysia **64** B1
ennines *hills* U.K. **46** B2
ennsylvania *state* U.S.A. **123** E2
enobscot *r.* U.S.A. **123** G2
enola Austr. **104** C3
enong Austr. **102** C3
enrhyn *atoll* Cook Is **111**
enrith U.K. **46** B2
ensacola U.S.A. **124** C2
ensacola Mountains Antarctica **107** K1
ensiangan Malaysia **65** C1
enticton Can. **112** D3
entland Firth *sea chan.* U.K. **44** C1
enza Rus. Fed. **35** D3
enzance U.K. **47** A4

Peoria U.S.A. **122** C2
Percy Isles Austr. **103** E2
Pereira Col. **134** B2
Pereira Barreto Brazil **138** B2
Peremyshlyany Ukr. **38** B2
Pereslavl'–Zalesskiy Rus. Fed. **37** E2
Pereyaslav-Khmel'nyts'kyy Ukr. **39** D1
Pergamino Arg. **137** B4
Perhonjoki *r.* Fin. **40** E3
Perico Arg. **136** B3
Pericos Mex. **128** B2
Périgueux France **52** C2
Perito Moreno Arg. **137** A5
Perleberg Ger. **49** E1
Perm' Rus. Fed. **34** E3
Pernatty Lagoon *salt flat* Austr. **104** B2
Pernik Bulg. **84** A1
Péronne France **52** C2
Perote Mex. **129** C3
Perpignan France **52** C3
Perry *FL* U.S.A. **125** D2
Perry *GA* U.S.A. **125** D2
Perryton U.S.A. **127** D1
Perryville U.S.A. **121** F3
Pershotravens'k Ukr. **39** E2
Perth Austr. **102** A3
Perth U.K. **44** C2
Pertusato, Capo *c.* France **56** A2
Peru *country* S. America **134** B3
Perugia Italy **56** B2
Péruwelz Belgium **48** A2
Pervomays'k Ukr. **38** D2
Pervomays'ke Ukr. **39** D2
Pervomayskiy Rus. Fed. **37** E3
Pervomays'kyy Ukr. **39** E2
Pesaro Italy **56** B2
Pescara Italy **56** B2
Pescara *r.* Italy **56** B2
Peschanokopskoye Rus. Fed. **39** F2
Peshawar Pak. **78** B1
Peshkopi Albania **58** B2
Pesnica Slovenia **56** C1
Pessac France **52** B3
Pestovo Rus. Fed. **37** E2
Petatlán Mex. **128** B3
Petenwell Lake U.S.A. **122** C2
Peterborough Austr. **104** B2
Peterborough Can. **114** C2
Peterborough U.K. **47** C3
Peterhead U.K. **44** D2
Petermann Ranges *mts* Austr. **102** B2
Peter Pond Lake Can. **113** E2
Petersburg *AK* U.S.A. **112** B2
Petersburg *VA* U.S.A. **123** E2
Petershagen Ger. **49** D1
Petit Mécatina *r.* Can. **115** E1
Peto Mex. **129** D2
Petoskey U.S.A. **122** D1
Petra *tourist site* Jordan **84** B2

Petra Velikogo, Zaliv *b.* Rus. Fed. **70** B2
Petrich Bulg. **59** B2
Petrolina Brazil **135** E3
Petropavlovsk Kazakh. **81** D1
Petropavlovsk-Kamchatskiy Rus. Fed. **87** M3
Petroşani Romania **38** B2
Petrovskoye Rus. Fed. **37** F3
Petrozavodsk Rus. Fed. **34** C2
Petrusburg S. Africa **99** C2
Petrusville S. Africa **98** B3
Petukhovo Rus. Fed. **35** F3
Petushki Rus. Fed. **37** E2
Peureula Indon. **64** A1
Pevek Rus. Fed. **87** N2
Pforzheim Ger. **50** B3
Pfungstadt Ger. **49** D3
Phahameng S. Africa **99** C2
Phalaborwa S. Africa **99** D1
Phalodi India **78** B2
Phang Hoei, San Khao *mts* Thai. **67** B2
Phangnga Thai. **67** A3
Phan Rang Vietnam **67** B2
Phan Thiết Vietnam **67** B2
Phatthalung Thai. **67** B3
Phayao Thai. **66** A2
Phelps Lake Can. **113** E2
Phenix City U.S.A. **125** C2
Phet Buri Thai. **67** A2
Phichit Thai. **66** B2
Philadelphia U.S.A. **123** F3
Philip U.S.A. **120** C2
Philippeville Belgium **48** B2
Philippines *country* Asia **68** B2
Philippine Sea N. Pacific Ocean **63** C1
Philip Smith Mountains U.S.A. **110** C2
Phillip Island Austr. **105** D3
Phillipsburg U.S.A. **121** D3
Phiritona S. Africa **99** C2
Phitsanulok Thai. **66** B2
Phnom Penh Cambodia **67** B2
Phoenix U.S.A. **126** B2
Phoenix Islands Kiribati **111**
Phôngsali Laos **66** B1
Phrae Thai. **66** B2
Phuket Thai. **67** A3
Phumĭ Sâmrâŏng Cambodia **67** B2
Phyu Myanmar **66** A2
Piacenza Italy **56** A1
Pianosa, Isola *i.* Italy **53** E3
Piatra Neamţ Romania **38** C2
Piauí *r.* Brazil **135** E3
Pibor *r.* Sudan **93** B4
Pibor Post Sudan **93** B4
Picayune U.S.A. **124** C2
Pichanal Arg. **136** B3
Pichilingue Mex. **128** A2
Pickle Lake Can. **114** A1
Picos Brazil **135** E3

Pico Truncado Arg. **137** B5
Picton Austr. **105** E2
Picton Bulg. **105** E2
Picton N.Z. **106** B3
Piedras Negras Mex. **129** B2
Pieksämäki Fin. **41** F3
Pielinen *l.* Fin. **40** F3
Pierre U.S.A. **120** C2
Pierrelatte France **53** C3
Pietermaritzburg S. Africa **99** D2
Pietersburg S. Africa *see* Polokwane
Pietrosa *mt.* Romania **38** B2
Pigeon Lake Can. **112** D2
Pigüé Arg. **137** B4
Pijijiapan Mex. **129** C3
Pikes Peak U.S.A. **120** C3
Piketberg S. Africa **98** A3
Pikeville U.S.A. **122** D3
Piła Pol. **51** D2
Pilar Arg. **137** C4
Pilar Para. **136** C3
Pilliga Austr. **105** D2
Pilões, Serra dos *mts* Brazil **138** C1
Pimenta Bueno Brazil **134** C4
Pinamar Arg. **137** C4
Pınarbaşı Turkey **84** B2
Pinar del Río Cuba **130** B2
Pińczów Pol. **51** F2
Pindaré *r.* Brazil **135** C2
Pindos *mts* Greece *see* Pindus Mountains
Pindus Mountains Greece **59** B3
Pine Bluff U.S.A. **124** B2
Pine Creek Austr. **102** C1
Pinedale U.S.A. **120** B2
Pinega Rus. Fed. **34** D2
Pinehouse Lake Can. **113** C2
Pineios *r.* Greece **59** B3
Pine Point Can. **112** D1
Pine Ridge U.S.A. **120** C2
Pinetown S. Africa **99** D2
Pingdingshan China **74** B2
Pingliang China **74** A2
P'ingtung Taiwan **75** C3
Pingxiang *Guangxi* China **75** A3
Pingxiang *Jiangxi* China **75** B3
Pinheiro Brazil **135** E3
Pinneberg Ger. **49** D1
Pinotepa Nacional Mex. **129** C3
Pinsk Belarus **36** C3
Pioche U.S.A. **119** D3
Pionki Pol. **51** E2
Piotrków Trybunalski Pol. **51** D2
Pipestone U.S.A. **121** D2
Pipmuacan, Réservoir *resr* Can. **115** C2
Piquiri *r.* Brazil **138** B2
Piracanjuba Brazil **138** C1
Piracicaba Brazil **138** C2
Piraçununga Brazil **138** C2
Piraeus Greece **59** B3
Piraí do Sul Brazil **138** B3
Pirajuí Brazil **138** C2

Piranhas Brazil **138** B1
Piranhas *r.* Brazil **135** F3
Pirapora Brazil **139** D1
Pires do Rio Brazil **138** C1
Piripiri Brazil **135** E3
Pirmasens Ger. **48** C3
Pirna Ger. **49** F2
Pisa Italy **56** B2
Pisagua Chile **136** A2
Pisco Peru **134** B4
Písek Czech Rep. **50** C3
Pishin Iran **83** D2
Pisté Mex. **129** D2
Pisticci Italy **57** C2
Pistoia Italy **56** B2
Pisuerga *r.* Spain **54** C1
Pit *r.* U.S.A. **118** B2
Pitanga Brazil **138** B2
Pitcairn Island Pitcairn Is **111**
Pitcairn Islands *terr.* S. Pacific Ocean **101**
Piteå Sweden **40** E2
Piteälven *r.* Sweden **40** E2
Piteşti Romania **38** B3
Pithoragarh India **79** C2
Pitlochry U.K. **44** C2
Pitt Island Can. **112** C2
Pittsburg U.S.A. **121** E3
Pittsburgh U.S.A. **123** E2
Pittsfield U.S.A. **123** F2
Piumhí Brazil **139** C2
Piura Peru **134** A3
Pivdennyy Buh *r.* Ukr. **38** D2
Placerville U.S.A. **119** B3
Plainview U.S.A. **127** D2
Planaltina Brazil **138** C1
Plaquemine U.S.A. **124** B2
Plasencia Spain **54** B1
Plasy Czech Rep. **49** F3
Platte *r.* U.S.A. **121** D2
Plattsburgh U.S.A. **123** F2
Plau Ger. **49** F1
Plauen Ger. **49** F2
Plauer See *l.* Ger. **49** F1
Plavsk Rus. Fed. **37** E3
Plây Cu Vietnam **87** B2
Playgreen Lake Can. **113** F2
Plaza Huincul Arg. **137** B4
Pleasanton U.S.A. **127** E3
Pleasant Point N.Z. **106** B3
Pledger Lake Can. **114** B1
Plenty, Bay of *g.* N.Z. **106** C2
Plesetsk Rus. Fed. **34** D2
Plétipi, Lac *l.* Can. **115** C1
Plettenberg Ger. **48** C2
Plettenberg Bay S. Africa **98** B3
Pleven Bulg. **58** B2
Ploče Croatia **57** C2
Płock Pol. **51** D2
Pločno *mt.* Bos.-Herz. **57** C2
Ploemeur France **52** B2
Ploieşti Romania **38** C3
Ploskoye Rus. Fed. **37** F2

Plouzané France **52** B2
Plovdiv Bulg. **58** B2
Plungė Lith. **36** B2
Plyeshchanitsy Belarus **36** C3
Plymouth Montserrat **131** D3
Plymouth U.K. **47** A4
Plyussa Rus. Fed. **36** C2
Plzeň Czech Rep. **50** C3
Pô Burkina **90** B3
Po *r.* Italy **56** B1
Pobeda Peak China/Kyrg. **81** F2
Pocahontas U.S.A. **124** B1
Pocatello U.S.A. **118** D2
Pochayiv Ukr. **38** C1
Pochep Rus. Fed. **37** D3
Pochinok Rus. Fed. **37** D3
Pochutla Mex. **129** C3
Pocomoke City U.S.A. **123** E3
Poços de Caldas Brazil **139** C2
Podbořany Czech Rep. **49** F2
Poddor'ye Rus. Fed. **37** D2
Podgorenskiy Rus. Fed. **39** E1
Podgorica S.M. **58** A2
Podkamennaya Tunguska *r.* Rus. Fed. **87** I2
Podol'sk Rus. Fed. **37** E2
Pofadder S. Africa **98** A2
Pogar Rus. Fed. **37** D3
Pogradec Albania **59** B2
P'ohang S. Korea **69** B2
Pohnpei *atoll* Micronesia **110**
Poiana Mare Romania **38** B3
Poie Dem. Rep. Congo **94** C3
Pointe-Noire Congo **94** B3
Point Lake Can. **113** D1
Poitiers France **52** C2
Pokaran India **78** B2
Pokhara Nepal **79** C2
Pokrovsk Rus. Fed. **87** K2
Pokrovskoye Rus. Fed. **39** E2
Polacca U.S.A. **126** B1
Pola de Lena Spain **54** B1
Poland *country* Europe **51** D2
Polatsk Belarus **36** C2
Pol-e Khomri Afgh. **78** A1
Police Pol. **50** C2
Policoro Italy **57** C2
Polillo Islands Phil. **68** B2
Polis'ke Ukr. **38** C1
Pollino, Monte *mt.* Italy **57** C3
Polohy Ukr. **39** E2
Polokwane S. Africa **99** C1
Polonne Ukr. **38** C1
Polson U.S.A. **118** D1
Poltava Ukr. **39** D2
Poltavka Rus. Fed. **70** B2
Poltavskaya Rus. Fed. **39** E2
Põlva Estonia **36** C2
Polyarnyy Rus. Fed. **40** G2
Polyarnyye Zori Rus. Fed. **40** G2
Polygyros Greece **59** B2
Polykastro Greece **84** A1
Polynesia *is* Pacific Ocean **142** E6
Pomezia Italy **56** B2

omokaira reg. Fin. **40** F2
omorie Bulg. **58** C2
omorska, Zatoka b. Pol. **50** C2
ompéu Brazil **139** D1
onca City U.S.A. **127** E1
once Puerto Rico **131** D3
ondicherry India **77** B3
ond Inlet Can. **111** G2
onferrada Spain **54** B1
ongo watercourse Sudan **93** A4
ongola r. S. Africa **99** D2
onta Grossa Brazil **138** B3
ontalina Brazil **138** C1
ont-à-Mousson France **53** D2
onta Porã Brazil **138** A2
ontarlier France **53** D3
ontianak Indon. **64** B2
ontivy France **52** B2
ontoetoe Suriname **135** D2
ontoise France **43** D4
onton Can. **113** F2
ontypool U.K. **47** D4
onziane, Isole is Italy **56** B2
oochera Austr. **104** A2
oole U.K. **47** C4
oona India see Pune
ooncarie Austr. **104** C2
oopó, Lago de r. Bol. **136** B2
opayán Col. **134** B3
opilfish Austr. **104** C2
oplar r. Can. **113** F2
oplar Bluff U.S.A. **121** E3
opocatépetl, Volcán vol. Mex. **121**
opokabaka Dem. Rep. Congo **94** B3
opovo Bulg. **58** D2
oprad Slovakia **51** E3
orangatu Brazil **135** E4
orbandar India **78** A2
ori Fin. **41** E3
orirua N.Z. **106** B3
orkhov Rus. Fed. **36** C2
oronaysk Rus. Fed. **73** F1
oros Greece **59** B3
orsgrunn Norway **41** B4
ortadown U.K. **45** C1
ortaferry U.K. **45** D1
ortage U.S.A. **122** C2
ortage la Prairie Can. **113** F3
ort Alberni Can. **112** C3
ortalegre Port. **54** B2
ortales U.S.A. **127** D2
ort Alice Can. **112** C2
ort Angeles U.S.A. **118** B1
ort Arthur U.S.A. **127** F3
ort Askaig U.K. **44** A3
ort Augusta Austr. **104** B2

Port-au-Prince Haiti **131** C3
Port aux Choix Can. **115** E1
Port Blair India **67** A2
Port Campbell Austr. **104** C3
Port Chalmers N.Z. **106** B4
Port Charlotte U.S.A. **125** D3
Port-de-Paix Haiti **131** C3
Port Edward Can. **112** B2
Porteirinha Brazil **139** D1
Port Elgin Can. **114** B2
Port Elizabeth S. Africa **99** C3
Port Ellen U.K. **44** A3
Port Erin Isle of Man **46** A2
Port Fairy Austr. **104** C3
Port Fitzroy N.Z. **106** C2
Port-Gentil Gabon **94** A3
Port Harcourt Nigeria **91** C4
Port Hardy Can. **112** C2
Port Hedland Austr. **102** A2
Porthmadog U.K. **46** A3
Port Hope Simpson Can. **115** E1
Port Huron U.S.A. **122** D2
Portimão Port. **54** B2
Portland N.S.W. Austr. **105** D2
Portland Vic. Austr. **104** C3
Portland ME U.S.A. **123** F2
Portland OR U.S.A. **118** B1
Portland Canal inlet Can. **112** B2
Portlaoise Rep. of Ireland **45** C2
Port Lavaca U.S.A. **127** E3
Port Lincoln Austr. **104** B2
Port Louis Mauritius **09**
Port Macquarie Austr. **105** E2
Port McNeill Can. **112** C2
Port Menier Can. **115** D2
Port Moresby P.N.G. **63** D3
Port Ness U.K. **44** A1
Port Nolloth S. Africa **98** A2
Porto Port. see Oporto
Porto Alegre Brazil **138** C4
Porto Esperidião Brazil **134** D4
Portoferraio Italy **56** B2
Porto Franco Brazil **135** E3
Port of Spain Trin. and Tob. **131** D3
Portogruaro Italy **56** B1
Porto Murtinho Brazil **136** C3
Porto Nacional Brazil **135** E4
Porto-Novo Benin **90** C4
Porto Primavera, Represa resr Brazil **138** B2
Porto Santana Brazil **135** D3
Porto Seguro Brazil **139** E1
Porto Tolle Italy **56** B2
Porto Torres Italy **56** A2
Porto-Vecchio France **53** D3
Porto Velho Brazil **134** C2
Portoviejo Ecuador **134** A3
Portpatrick U.K. **44** B1
Port Phillip Bay Austr. **104** C3
Port Pirie Austr. **104** B2
Portree U.K. **44** A2
Portrush U.K. **45** C1
Port Said Egypt **92** B1
Port Shepstone S. Africa **99** D3

Portsmouth U.K. **47** C4
Portsmouth NH U.S.A. **123** F2
Portsmouth OH U.S.A. **122** D3
Portsmouth VA U.S.A. **123** E3
Portstewart U.K. **45** C1
Port St Joe U.S.A. **125** C3
Port St Johns S. Africa **99** C3
Port Sudan Sudan **92** B3
Port Sulphur U.S.A. **124** C3
Port Talbot U.K. **47** C4
Portugal country Europe **54** B2
Port-Vendres France **53** C3
Port Vila Vanuatu **100**
Porvoo Fin. **41** F3
Posadas Arg. **136** C3
Poshekhon'ye Rus. Fed. **37** E2
Posio Fin. **40** F2
Poso Indon. **65** D2
Posse Brazil **135** E4
Pößneck Ger. **49** E2
Post U.S.A. **127** D2
Poste-de-la-Baleine Can. see Kuujjuarapik
Postmasburg S. Africa **98** B2
Poteau U.S.A. **127** F1
Potenza Italy **57** C2
P'ot'i Georgia **89** C1
Potiskum Nigeria **91** D3
Potomac, South Branch r. U.S.A. **123** E3
Potosí Bol. **136** B2
Pototan Phil. **88** B2
Potrero del Llano Mex. **126** D3
Potsdam Ger. **49** F1
Potsdam U.S.A. **123** F2
Pottstown U.S.A. **123** E2
Pottsville U.S.A. **123** E2
Pouch Cove Can. **115** E2
Poughkeepsie U.S.A. **123** F2
Pouso Alegre Brazil **138** C3
Poŭthĭsăt Cambodia **67** D2
Povlen mt. S.M. **58** A2
Póvoa de Varzim Port. **54** B1
Povorino Rus. Fed. **39** F1
Powell U.S.A. **120** B2
Powell, Lake resr U.S.A. **119** D3
Powell River Can. **112** C3
Poxoréu Brazil **138** B1
Poza Rica Mex. **129** C2
Požega Croatia **57** C1
Požega S.M. **58** B2
Pozm Tīāb Iran **83** D2
Poznań Pol. **51** D2
Pozoblanco Spain **54** C2
Pozzuoli Italy **56** B2
Prabumulih Indon. **64** B3
Prachatice Czech Rep. **50** C3
Prachuap Khiri Khan Thai. **67** A2
Prado Brazil **139** E1
Prague Czech Rep. see Praha
Praha Czech Rep. see Prague
Praia Cape Verde **88**
Prairie Dog Town Fork r. U.S.A. **127** D2

Prairie du Chien U.S.A. **122** B2
Prata Brazil **138** C1
Prato Italy **53** E3
Pratt U.S.A. **121** D3
Praya Indon. **65** C2
Preăh Vihéar Cambodia **67** B2
Prechistoye Rus. Fed. **37** F2
Preiļi Latvia **36** C2
Premer Austr. **105** D2
Premnitz Ger. **49** F1
Prenzlau Ger. **49** F1
Preparis Island Cocos Is **67** A2
Preparis North Channel Cocos Is **67** A2
Preparis South Channel Cocos Is **67** A2
Přerov Czech Rep. **51** D3
Prescott U.S.A. **126** B2
Presidencia Roque Sáenz Peña Arg. **136** B3
Presidente Dutra Brazil **135** E3
Presidente Epitácio Brazil **138** B2
Presidente Prudente Brazil **138** B2
Presidio U.S.A. **126** D3
Prešov Slovakia **51** E3
Presque Isle U.S.A. **123** G1
Přeštice Czech Rep. **49** F3
Preston U.K. **46** B3
Preto r. Brazil **139** C1
Pretoria S. Africa **99** C2
Preveza Greece **59** B3
Prey Vêng Cambodia **67** B2
Priboj S.M. **58** B2
Price U.S.A. **119** D3
Price U.S.A. **119** D3
Prienai Lith. **36** B3
Prieska S. Africa **98** B2
Prievidza Slovakia **51** D3
Prijedor Bos.-Herz. **57** C2
Prikaspiyskaya Nizmennost' *lowland* Kazakh./Rus. Fed. *see* Caspian Lowland
Prilep Macedonia **59** B2
Primorsko-Akhtarsk Rus. Fed. **39** E2
Primrose Lake Can. **113** C2
Prince Albert Can. **110** D3
Prince Albert Peninsula Can. **110** E2
Prince Alfred, Cape Can. **110** D2
Prince Charles Island Can. **111** G2
Prince Charles Mountains Antarctica **107** E2
Prince Edward Island *prov.* Can. **115** D2
Prince George Can. **112** C2
Prince of Wales Island Can. **110** F2
Prince of Wales Island U.S.A. **112** B2
Prince Patrick Island Can. **110** E1

Prince Rupert Can. **112** B2
Princess Charlotte Bay Austr. **103** D1
Princess Royal Island Can. **112** C2
Príncipe *i.* São Tomé and Príncipe **94** A2
Priozersk Rus. Fed. **41** G3
Pripet r. Belarus *see* Prypyats'
Pripet Marshes Belarus/Ukr. **36** B3
Pritzwalk Ger. **49** F1
Privolzhsk Rus. Fed. **37** F2
Prizren S.M. **58** B2
Professor van Blommestein Meer *resr* Suriname **135** D2
Progreso Mex. **129** D2
Prokhladnyy Rus. Fed. **85** C1
Prokuplje S.M. **58** B2
Proletarsk Rus. Fed. **39** E2
Prophet r. Can. **110** D3
Prophet River Can. **112** C2
Proserpine Austr. **103** D2
Protvino Rus. Fed. **37** E3
Provence *reg.* France **53** D3
Providence U.S.A. **123** F2
Providencia, Isla de *i.* Caribbean Sea **130** B3
Provideniya Rus. Fed. **87** O2
Provo U.S.A. **118** D2
Provost Can. **113** C2
Prudentópolis Brazil **138** B3
Prudhoe Bay U.S.A. **110** C2
Prüm Ger. **48** C2
Pruszków Pol. **51** E2
Prut r. Europe **38** C2
Pryluky Ukr. **39** D1
Prymors'k Ukr. **39** E2
Pryor U.S.A. **127** E1
Prypyats' r. Belarus **36** C3
Przemyśl Pol. **51** E3
Psara i. Greece **59** C3
Pshekha r. Rus. Fed. **39** E3
Pskov Rus. Fed. **36** C2
Pskov, Lake Estonia/Rus. Fed. **36** C2
Ptolemaïda Greece **59** B2
Ptuj Slovenia **57** C1
Pucallpa Peru **134** B3
Pucheng China **75** B3
Puchezh Rus. Fed. **37** F2
Puch'ŏn S. Korea **69** B2
Pudasjärvi Fin. **40** F2
Pudong China **74** C2
Puebla Mex. **129** C3
Pueblo U.S.A. **120** C3
Puente-Genil Spain **54** C2
Puerto Ángel Mex. **129** C3
Puerto Armuelles Panama **130** B4
Puerto Ayacucho Venez. **134** C2
Puerto Barrios Guat. **129** D3
Puerto Cabezas Nic. **130** B3

Puerto Carreño Venez. **134** C2
Puerto Cortés Mex. **128** A2
Puerto Escondido Mex. **129** C3
Puerto Frey Bol. **136** B2
Puerto Inírida Col. **134** C2
Puerto Isabel Bol. **136** C2
Puerto Libertad Mex. **128** A2
Puerto Limón Costa Rica **130** B3
Puertollano Spain **54** C2
Puerto Madryn Arg. **137** B5
Puerto Maldonado Peru **134** C4
Puerto Montt Chile **137** A5
Puerto Natales Chile **137** A6
Puerto Peñasco Mex. **128** A1
Puerto Princesa Phil. **68** A3
Puerto Rico Arg. **138** A3
Puerto Rico *terr.* West Indies **131** D3
Puerto Rico Trench *sea feature* Caribbean Sea **144** B3
Puerto San José Guat. **130** A3
Puerto Vallarta Mex. **128** B2
Pukaki, Lake N.Z. **106** B3
Pukapuka *atoll* Cook Is **111** I3
Pukatawagan Can. **113** E2
Pukchin N. Korea **69** B1
Pukch'ŏng N. Korea **69** B1
Pukekohe N.Z. **106** B2
Puksubaek-san *mt.* N. Korea **69** B1
Pula Croatia **56** B2
Pulkkila Fin. **40** F3
Pullman U.S.A. **118** C1
Pulog, Mount Phil. **68** B2
Puná, Isla *i.* Ecuador **134** A3
Punakaiki N.Z. **106** B3
Pune India **77** B3
P'ungsan N. Korea **69** B1
Púnguè r. Moz. **97** C1
Punta Alta Arg. **137** B4
Punta Arenas Chile **137** A6
Punta Balestrieri *mt.* Italy **56** A2
Punta del Este Uru. **137** C4
Punta Gorda Belize **129** D3
Puntarenas Costa Rica **130** B3
Punto Fijo Venez. **134** B1
Pur r. Rus. Fed. **34** G2
Puri India **79** C3
Purmerend Neth. **48** B1
Purnia India **79** C2
Puruliya India **79** C2
Purus r. Peru **134** C3
Puryŏng N. Korea **69** B1
Pusan S. Korea **69** B2
Pustoshka Rus. Fed. **36** C2
Putao Myanmar **66** A1
Putian China **75** B3
Puting, Tanjung *pt* Indon. **65** C2
Putrajaya Malaysia **64** B1
Puttgarden Ger. **50** C2
Putumayo r. Col. **134** B3
Putusibau Indon. **65** C1
Putyvl' Ukr. **39** D1
Puvurnituq Can. **114** C1

Puyang China **74** B2
Pwllheli U.K. **46** A3
Pyapon Myanmar **66** A2
Pyasina r. Rus. Fed. **86** H2
Pyatigorsk Rus. Fed. **35** D4
P'yatykhatky Ukr. **39** D2
Pyè Myanmar **66** A2
Pyetrykaw Belarus **36** C3
Pyhäjärvi l. Fin. **41** E3
Pyhäjoki r. Fin. **40** E3
Pyhäsalmi Fin. **40** F3
Pyinmana Myanmar **66** A2
Pyöksŏng N. Korea **69** B2
P'yŏnggang N. Korea **69** B2
P'yŏngsan N. Korea **69** B2
P'yŏngyang N. Korea **69** B2
Pyramid Lake U.S.A. **118** C2
Pyramids of Giza tourist site
    Egypt **84** B3
Pyrenees mts Europe **55** D1
Pyrgos Greece **59** B3
Pyryatyn Ukr. **39** D1
Pyrzyce Pol. **50** C2
Pytalovo Rus. Fed. **35** C2
Pyxaria mt. Greece **59** B3

Q

Qaanaaq Greenland see Thule
Qacha's Nek Lesotho **99** C3
Qagan Nur China **74** B1
Qaidam Pendi basin China **72** C2
Qalansiyah Yemen **83** C3
Qal'at Bishah Saudi Arabia **82** B2
Qamanirjuaq Lake Can. **111** F3
Qamar, Ghubbat al b. Yemen
    83 C3
Qarshi Uzbek. **81** I3
Qaryat al Ulyā Saudi Arabia
    83 B2
Qasigiannguit Greenland **111** I3
Qassimiut Greenland **111** I3
Qatar country Asia **83** C2
Qattara Depression Egypt **92** A2
Qausuittuq Can. see Resolute
Qazax Azer. **85** C1
Qazimämmäd Azer. **85** C1
Qazvin Iran **85** C2
Qeqertarsuaq i. Greenland
    111 I2
Qeqertarsuatsiaat Greenland
    111 I2
Qeqertarsuup Tunua b.
    Greenland **111** I2
Qeshm Iran **83** C2
Qianjiang Chongqing China **75** A3
Qian Shan mts China **69** A1
Qiemo China **81** F3
Qijiang China **75** A3
Qijiaojing China **72** C2
Qikiqtarjuaq Can. **111** H2

Qilian Shan mts China **72** C2
Qillak i. Greenland **111** J2
Qimusseriarsuaq b. Greenland
    111 H1
Qinā Egypt **92** B2
Qingdao China **74** C2
Qinghai prov. China **79** D1
Qinghai Hu salt l. China **72** C2
Qinghai Nanshan mts China
    72 C2
Qingyang Guangdong China
    75 B3
Qingyuan Liaoning China **69** A1
Qingzang Gaoyuan plat. China
    see Tibet, Plateau of
Qingzhou China **74** B2
Qinhuangdao China **74** B2
Qin Ling mts China **74** A2
Qinzhou China **75** A3
Qionghai China **75** B4
Qionglai Shan mts China **74** A2
Qiqihar China **72** E1
Qitaihe China **70** B1
Qixian China **74** B2
Uögir Feng mt.
    China/Jammu and Kashmir
    see K2
Qom Iran **85** D2
Qomolangma Feng mt.
    China/Nepal see Everest, Mount
Qo'ng'irot Uzbek. **80** C2
Qo'qon Uzbek. **81** E2
Qoraqalpog'iston Uzbek. **80** C2
Quakenbrück Ger. **48** D1
Quang Ngai Vietnam **67** B2
Quang Tri Vietnam **66** B2
Quanzhou Fujian China **75** B3
Quanzhou Guangxi China **75** B3
Quartu Sant'Elena Italy **56** A3
Quartzsite U.S.A. **126** B2
Quba Azer. **85** C1
Queanbeyan Austr. **105** D3
Québec Can. **115** C2
Québec prov. Can. **114** C1
Quedlinburg Ger. **49** E2
Queen Charlotte Can. **112** B2
Queen Charlotte Islands Can.
    112 B2
Queen Charlotte Sound
    sea chan. Can. **112** B2
Queen Charlotte Strait Can.
    112 C2
Queen Elizabeth Islands Can.
    110 E1
Queen Maud Gulf Can. **110** F2
Queen Maud Land reg. Antarctica
    107 C2
Queen Maud Mountains
    Antarctica **107** I1
Queensland state Austr. **103** D2
Queenstown Austr. **103** D4
Queenstown N.Z. **106** A4
Queenstown S. Africa **99** C3
Quelimane Moz. **97** C1

Quemado U.S.A. **126** C2
Querétaro Mex. **129** B2
Querfurt Ger. **49** E2
Quesnel Can. **112** C2
Quesnel Lake Can. **112** C2
Quetta Pak. **78** A1
Quezaltenango Guat.
    129 C3
Quezon City Phil. **68** B2
Quibala Angola **96** A1
Quibdó Col. **134** B2
Quiberon France **52** B2
Quilmes Arg. **137** C3
Quilon India **77** B4
Quilpie Austr. **103** D2
Quilpué Chile **137** A4
Quimbele Angola **96** B1
Quimper France **52** B2
Quimperlé France **52** B2
Quincy IL U.S.A. **122** B3
Quincy MA U.S.A. **123** F2
Qui Nhon Vietnam **67** B2
Quinto Spain **55** C1
Quionga Moz. **95** C4
Quirindi Austr. **105** E2
Quissico Moz. **97** C2
Quitapa Angola **94** B4
Quito Ecuador **134** B3
Quixadá Brazil **135** F3
Qujing China **75** A3
Qumar He r. China **79** D1
Quoich r. Can. **113** F1
Quorn Austr. **104** B2
Qurayat Oman **83** C2
Qürghonteppa Tajik. **81** D3
Quzhou China **75** B3

R

Raab r. Austria **51** D3
Raahe Fin. **40** E3
Raalte Neth. **48** C1
Raas i. Indon. **65** C2
Raba Indon. **65** C2
Rabat Morocco **90** B1
Rābigh Saudi Arabia **82** A2
Race, Cape Can. **115** E2
Rach Gia Vietnam **67** B3
Racine U.S.A. **122** C2
Radă' Yemen **82** B3
Rădăuti Romania **38** C2
Radcliff U.S.A. **122** C3
Radebeul Ger. **49** F2
Radhanpur India **78** B2
Radisson Can. **114** C1
Radom Pol. **51** E2
Radomsko Pol. **51** D2
Radomyshl' Ukr. **38** C1
Radoviš Macedonia **57** D2
Radviliškis Lith. **36** B2
Raḍwā, Jabal mt. Saudi Arabia
    82 A2

Radyvyliv Ukr. 38 C1
Rae Bareli India 79 C2
Rae-Edzo Can. 112 D1
Rae Lakes Can. 112 D1
Raetihi N.Z. 106 C2
Rafaela Arg. 136 B4
Rafaï C.A.R. 94 C2
Rafḩā' Saudi Arabia 82 B2
Rafsanjān Iran 85 D2
Ragusa Italy 56 B3
Raha Indon. 65 C2
Rahachow Belarus 36 D3
Rahimyar Khan Pak. 78 B2
Raichur India 77 B3
Raigarh India 79 C2
Rainbow Lake Can. 112 D2
Rainier, Mount vol. U.S.A. 118 B1
Rainy Lake Can./U.S.A. 113 F3
Rainy River Can. 113 F3
Raipur India 79 C2
Raisio Fin. 41 E3
Rajahmundry India 77 C3
Rajang r. Malaysia 65 C1
Rajapur India 78 B2
Rajapalaiyam India 77 B4
Rajkot India 78 B2
Rajshahi Bangl. 79 C2
Rakaia r. N.Z. 106 B3
Rakhiv Ukr. 38 B1
Rakitnoye Rus. Fed. 39 E1
Rakovník Czech Rep. 49 F2
Rakvere Estonia 36 C2
Raleigh U.S.A. 125 E1
Ralik Chain is Marshall Is 110
Rambutyo Island P.N.G. 63 D3
Ramgarh India 78 B2
Rāmhormoz Iran 85 C2
Râmnicu Sărat Romania 38 C2
Râmnicu Vâlcea Romania 38 B2
Ramon' Rus. Fed. 37 E3
Ramotswa Botswana 99 C1
Rampur India 79 B2
Ramree Island Myanmar 66 A2
Ramsey Isle of Man 46 A2
Ramsgate U.K. 47 D4
Ramsing India 66 A1
Ranaghat India 79 C2
Ranau Malaysia 65 C1
Rancagua Chile 137 A4
Ranchi India 79 C2
Randers Denmark 41 C4
Rangiora N.Z. 106 B3
Rangitaiki r. N.Z. 106 C2
Rangoon Myanmar 66 A2
Rangpur Bangl. 79 C2
Rankin Inlet Can. 113 F1
Rankin's Springs Austr. 105 D2
Rannoch Moor moorland U.K. 44 B2
Ranong Thai. 67 A3
Ransiki Indon. 63 C3
Rantaupanjang Indon. 65 C2

Rantauprapat Indon. 64 A1
Rantepao Indon. 65 C2
Ranua Fin. 40 F2
Ranyah, Wādī watercourse Saudi Arabia 82 B2
Raoul Island Kermadec Is 111
Rapa i. Fr. Polynesia 111
Rapid City U.S.A. 120 C2
Rapla Estonia 36 B2
Rapur India 78 A2
Rarotonga i. Cook Is 111
Rasa, Punta pt Arg. 137 B5
Ra's al Khaymah U.A.E. 83 C2
Ras Dejen mt. Eth. 93 B3
Raseiniai Lith. 36 B2
Ra's Ghārib Egypt 84 B3
Rasht Iran 85 C2
Ras Koh mt. Pak. 78 A2
Rasony Belarus 36 C2
Rasskazovo Rus. Fed. 37 F3
Rastede Ger. 49 D1
Ratak Chain is Marshall Is 110
Ratangarh India 78 B2
Rat Buri Thai. 67 A2
Rathedaung Myanmar 66 A1
Rathenow Ger. 49 F1
Rathlin Island U.K. 45 C1
Ratlam India 78 B2
Ratnagiri India 77 B3
Ratnapura Sri Lanka 77 C4
Ratne Ukr. 38 B1
Raton U.S.A. 126 C1
Rattray Head U.K. 44 D2
Ratzeburg Ger. 49 E1
Raufarhöfn Iceland 40 [inset]
Raukumara Range mts N.Z. 106 C2
Rauma Fin. 41 E3
Raurkela India 79 C2
Ravalli U.S.A. 118 D1
Rāvānsar Iran 85 C2
Ravenna Italy 56 B2
Ravensburg Ger. 50 B3
Ravi r. Pak. 78 B1
Rawalpindi Pak. 78 B1
Rawicz Pol. 51 D2
Rawlinna Austr. 102 B3
Rawlins U.S.A. 120 B2
Rawson Arg. 137 B5
Raydah Yemen 82 B3
Rayevskiy Rus. Fed. 35 E3
Raymond Can. 118 D1
Raymond Terrace Austr. 105 E2
Raymondville U.S.A. 127 E3
Rayón Mex. 129 C2
Rayong Thai. 67 B2
Rayyis Saudi Arabia 82 A2
Raz, Pointe du pt France 52 B2
Razāzah, Buḩayrat ar l. Iraq 85 C2
Razgrad Bulg. 58 C2
Razim, Lacul lag. Romania 38 C3
Ré, Île de i. France 52 B2

Reading U.K. 47 C4
Reading U.S.A. 123 E2
Rebiana Sand Sea des. Libya 91 E2
Rebun-tō i. Japan 70 D1
Recherche, Archipelago of the is Austr. 102 B3
Rechytsa Belarus 37 D3
Recife Brazil 135 F3
Recklinghausen Ger. 48 C2
Reconquista Arg. 136 C3
Red r. U.S.A. 127 F2
Red Bay Can. 115 F1
Red Bluff U.S.A. 118 B2
Redcar U.K. 46 C2
Red Cliffs Austr. 104 C2
Red Deer Can. 112 D2
Red Deer r. Can. 110 D3
Red Deer Lake Can. 113 E2
Redding U.S.A. 118 B2
Redditch U.K. 47 C3
Redfield U.S.A. 121 D2
Red Lake Can. 114 A1
Red Lakes U.S.A. 121 E1
Redmond U.S.A. 118 B2
Red Oak U.S.A. 121 D2
Red Sea Africa/Asia 82 A2
Redstone r. Can. 112 C1
Reduzum Neth. 48 B1
Red Wing U.S.A. 121 E2
Redwood Falls U.S.A. 121 D2
Ree, Lough l. Rep. of Ireland 45 C2
Reedsport U.S.A. 118 B2
Reefton N.Z. 106 B3
Regen Ger. 49 F3
Regência Brazil 139 E1
Regensburg Ger. 49 F3
Regenstauf Ger. 49 F3
Reggane Alg. 90 C2
Reggio di Calabria Italy 57 C3
Reggio nell'Emilia Italy 56 B2
Reghin Romania 38 B2
Regina Can. 110 F3
Rehoboth Namibia 98 A1
Reichenbach Ger. 49 F2
Reidsville U.S.A. 125 E1
Reigate U.K. 47 C4
Reims France 53 C2
Reina Adelaida, Archipiélago de la is Chile 137 A6
Reinbek Ger. 49 E1
Reindeer r. Can. 113 E2
Reindeer Island Can. 113 F2
Reindeer Lake Can. 113 E2
Reine Norway 40 C2
Reinsfeld Ger. 48 C3
Reitz S. Africa 99 C2
Reivilo S. Africa 98 B2
Reliance Can. 113 E1
Relizane Alg. 55 D2
Remeshk Iran 83 C2
Remiremont France 53 D2
Remscheid Ger. 48 C2

Rendsburg Ger. **50** B2
Renfrew U.K. **22** E1
Rengat Indon. **64** B2
Reni Ukr. **38** C2
Renmark Austr. **104** C2
Rennell i. Solomon Is **110**
Rennes France **52** B2
Rennie Lake Can. **113** E1
Reno r. Italy **56** B2
Reno U.S.A. **119** C3
Renukut India **79** C2
Renwick N.Z. **106** B3
Reo Indon. **65** D2
Republican r. U.S.A. **120** D3
Requena Peru **134** B3
Requena Spain **55** C2
Resistencia Arg. **136** C3
Reşiţa Romania **38** B?
Resolute Can. **110** F2
Resolution Island Can. **111** H2
Rethymno Greece **59** B3
Réunion terr. Indian Ocean **89**
Reus Spain **55** D1
Reutlingen Ger. **50** B3
Revelstoke Can. **112** D2
Revillagigedo, Islas is Mex. **128** A3
Revillagigedo Island U.S.A. **112** B2
Rewa India **79** C2
Rexburg U.S.A. **118** D2
Reykjanestá pt Iceland **40** [inset]
Reykjavík Iceland **40** [inset]
Reynosa Mex. **129** C2
Rēzekne Latvia **36** C2
Rheden r. Ger. see Rhine
Rheine Ger. **48** C1
Rhin r. France see Rhine
Rhine r. France **50** B3
Rhine r. Ger. **48** C2
Rhinelander U.S.A. **122** C1
Rhinluch marsh Ger. **49** F1
Rhode Island state U.S.A. **123** F2
Rhodes Greece **59** C3
Rhodes i. Greece **59** C3
Rhodope Mountains Bulg./Greece **58** B2
Rhône r. France/Switz. **53** C3
Rhourd Alg. **55** E2
Rhyl U.K. **46** B3
Riau, Kepulauan is Indon. **64** B1
Ribadeo Spain **54** B1
Ribas do Rio Pardo Brazil **138** B2
Ribáuè Moz. **97** C1
Ribécourt-Dreslincourt France **48** A3
Ribeira r. Brazil **138** C2
Ribeirão Preto Brazil **138** C2
Riberalta Bol. **136** B2
Ribniţa Moldova **38** C2
Ribnitz-Damgarten Ger. **50** C2

Rice Lake U.S.A. **122** B1
Richards Bay S. Africa **99** D2
Richardson Mountains Can. **110** C2
Richfield U.S.A. **119** D3
Richland U.S.A. **118** C1
Richmond N.S.W. Austr. **105** E2
Richmond Qld Austr. **103** D2
Richmond N.Z. **106** B3
Richmond U.K. **46** C2
Richmond IN U.S.A. **122** D3
Richmond KY U.S.A. **122** D3
Richmond VA U.S.A. **123** E3
Rideau Lakes Can. **114** C2
Ridgecrest U.S.A. **119** C3
Riesa Ger. **49** F2
Rietberg Ger. **49** D2
Rieti Italy **56** B2
Rifle U.S.A. **120** B3
Riga Latvia **36** B2
Riga, Gulf of Estonia/Latvia **41** E4
Rīgān Iran **83** C2
Rigolet Can. **111** J3
Riihimäki Fin. **41** E3
Rijeka Croatia **56** B1
Riley U.S.A. **118** C2
Rimah, wādī al watercourse Saudi Arabia **82** B2
Rimavská Sobota Slovakia **51** E3
Rimini Italy **56** B2
Rimouski Can. **115** D2
Ringebu Norway **41** C3
Ringkøbing Denmark **41** B4
Ringvassøya i. Norway **40** D2
Rinteln Ger. **49** D1
Riobamba Ecuador **134** D3
Rio Branco Brazil **134** C3
Rio Brilhante Brazil **138** B2
Rio Claro Brazil **138** C2
Río Colorado Arg. **137** B4
Río Cuarto Arg. **137** B4
Rio de Janeiro Brazil **139** D2
Rio do Sul Brazil **138** C3
Río Gallegos Arg. **137** B6
Río Grande Arg. **137** B6
Rio Grande Brazil **136** C4
Río Grande Mex. **128** B2
Rio Grande r. Mex./U.S.A. **128** C2
Rio Grande City U.S.A. **127** E3
Riohacha Col. **134** B1
Río Lagartos Mex. **129** D2
Riom France **53** C2
Río Mulatos Bol. **136** B2
Rio Negro Brazil **138** C3
Rio Pardo de Minas Brazil **139** D1
Río Rancho U.S.A. **126** C1
Río Tigre Ecuador **134** B3
Río Verde Brazil **138** B1
Río Verde Mex. **129** C2
Rio Verde de Mato Grosso Brazil **138** B1
Ripky Ukr. **38** D1

Ripoll Spain **55** D1
Ripon U.K. **46** C2
Rishiri-tō i. Japan **70** D1
Riser Norway **41** B4
Ritchie S. Africa **98** B2
Ritchie's Archipelago is India **67** A2
Ritzville U.S.A. **118** C1
Riva del Garda Italy **56** B1
Rivas Nic. **130** B3
Rivera Uru. **136** C4
Riverina reg. Austr. **105** D2
Riversdale S. Africa **98** B3
Riverside U.S.A. **119** C4
Riverton U.S.A. **120** B2
Riverview Can. **115** D2
Rivière-du-Loup Can. **115** D2
Rivne Ukr. **38** C1
Riwaka N.Z. **106** B3
Riyadh Saudi Arabia **82** B2
Rize Turkey **85** C1
Rizhao China **74** B2
Roanne France **53** C2
Roanoke U.S.A. **123** E3
Roanoke r. U.S.A. **125** E1
Roanoke Rapids U.S.A. **125** E1
Robe Austr. **104** B3
Röbel Ger. **49** F1
Robertsfors Sweden **40** E3
Robertsport Liberia **90** A4
Roberval Can. **115** C2
Robinson Range hills Austr. **102** A2
Robinvale Austr. **104** C2
Roblin Can. **113** E2
Robson, Mount Can. **112** D2
Rocca Busambra mt. Italy **56** B3
Rocha Uru. **137** C4
Rochdale U.K. **46** B3
Rochefort Belgium **48** B2
Rochefort France **52** B2
Rochester MN U.S.A. **121** E2
Rochester NY U.S.A. **123** E2
Rockford U.S.A. **122** C2
Rockhampton Austr. **103** E2
Rock Hill U.S.A. **125** D2
Rockingham Austr. **102** A3
Rock Springs MT U.S.A. **120** B1
Rocksprings U.S.A. **127** D3
Rock Springs WY U.S.A. **120** B2
Rocky Ford U.S.A. **120** C3
Rocky Mount U.S.A. **125** E1
Rocky Mountains Can./U.S.A. **116** C2
Rocroi France **48** B3
Rødbyhavn Denmark **50** C2
Rodez France **52** C3
Roding Ger. **49** F3
Rodniki Rus. Fed. **37** F2
Rodos Greece see Rhodes
Rodos i. Greece see Rhodes
Roebourne Austr. **102** A2
Roebuck Bay Austr. **102** B1
Roermond Neth. **48** B2

Roeselare Belgium **48** A2
Roggeveldberge *esc.* S. Africa **98** B3
Rogan Norway **40** D2
Rogue *r.* U.S.A. **118** B2
Rokan *r.* Indon. **64** B1
Rokiškis Lith. **36** C2
Rokycany Czech Rep. **49** F3
Rokytne Ukr. **38** C1
Rolla U.S.A. **121** E3
Roma Austr. **103** D2
Roma Italy *see* Rome
Romain, Cape U.S.A. **125** E2
Roman Romania **38** C2
Roman-Kosh *mt.* Ukr. **39** D3
Romanovka *Respublika Buryatiya* Rus. Fed. **73** D1
Romanovka *Saratovskaya Oblast'* Rus. Fed. **39** F1
Romblon Phil. **68** B2
Rome Italy **56** B2
Rome U.S.A. **125** C2
Romilly-sur-Seine France **53** C2
Romny Ukr. **39** D1
Romorantin-Lanthenay France **52** C2
Romsey U.K. **47** C4
Roncador, Serra de *hills* Brazil **135** D4
Ronda Spain **54** B2
Rondonópolis Brazil **138** B1
Rondu Jammu and Kashmir **78** B1
Rong'an China **75** A3
Rongjiang China **75** A3
Rongklang Range *mts* Myanmar **66** A1
Rønne Denmark **41** C4
Ronne Ice Shelf Antarctica **107** K2
Ronse Belgium **48** A2
Roorkee India **79** B2
Roosendaal Neth. **48** B2
Roosevelt U.S.A. **118** E2
Roosevelt, Mount Can. **112** C2
Roosevelt Island Antarctica **107** J2
Roraima, Mount Guyana **134** C2
Røros Norway **41** C3
Rosario Arg. **137** B3
Rosario *Baja California* Mex. **128** A1
Rosario *Sinaloa* Mex. **128** B2
Rosario *Sonora* Mex. **128** B2
Rosário Oeste Brazil **135** D4
Rosarito Mex. **128** A2
Rosarno Italy **57** C3
Roscoff France **52** B2
Roscommon Rep. of Ireland **45** B2
Roseau Dominica **131** D3
Roseau U.S.A. **121** D1
Roseburg U.S.A. **118** B2

Rosenberg U.S.A. **127** E3
Rosendal Norway **42** E2
Rosengarten Ger. **49** D1
Rosenheim Ger. **50** C3
Rosetown Can. **113** D2
Roshchino Rus. Fed. **36** C1
Rosh Pinah Namibia **98** A2
Roșiori de Vede Romania **38** C3
Roskilde Denmark **41** C4
Roslavl' Rus. Fed. **37** D3
Rossano Italy **57** C3
Rossan Point Rep. of Ireland **45** B1
Ross Ice Shelf Antarctica **107** H1
Rossignol, Lake Can. **115** D2
Rosslare Rep. of Ireland **45** C2
Rosso Maur. **90** A3
Ross-on-Wye U.K. **47** B4
Rossosh' Rus. Fed. **39** E1
Ross River Can. **112** B1
Røssvatnet *l.* Norway **40** C2
Rostāq Iran **85** D3
Rostock Ger. **50** C2
Rostov Rus. Fed. **37** E2
Rostov-na-Donu Rus. Fed. **39** E2
Rosvik Sweden **40** E2
Rota *i.* N. Mariana Is **63** D2
Rote *i.* Indon. **63** C3
Rotenburg (Wümme) Ger. **49** D1
Roth Ger. **49** E3
Rothenburg ob der Tauber Ger. **49** E3
Rotherham U.K. **46** C3
Rothesay U.K. **44** B3
Roto Austr. **105** D2
Rotondo, Monte *mt.* France **53** D3
Rotorua N.Z. **106** C2
Rotorua, Lake N.Z. **106** C2
Rottenmann Austria **50** C3
Rotterdam Neth. **48** B2
Rottweil Ger. **50** B3
Rotuma *i.* Fiji **110**
Roubaix France **53** C1
Rouen France **52** C2
Round Mountain Austr. **105** E2
Round Pond *l.* Can. **115** E2
Round Rock U.S.A. **127** E2
Roundup U.S.A. **118** E1
Rousay *i.* U.K. **44** C1
Rouyn-Noranda Can. **114** C2
Rovaniemi Fin. **40** F2
Roven'ki Rus. Fed. **39** E2
Roven'ky Ukr. **39** E2
Rovereto Italy **56** B1
Rovigo Italy **56** B1
Roxas Phil. **68** B2
Roxas Phil. **68** B2
Roxas Phil. **68** A2
Roxas Phil. **68** B3
Roxby Downs Austr. **104** B2
Roy U.S.A. **126** D1
Royale, Isle *i.* U.S.A. **122** C1

Royan France **52** B2
Roye France **48** A3
Rozdil'na Ukr. **38** D2
Rozdol'ne Ukr. **39** D2
Rtishchevo Rus. Fed. **35** D3
Ruapehu, Mount *vol.* N.Z. **106** C2
Ruapuke Island N.Z. **106** A4
Rub' al Khālī *des.* Saudi Arabia **82** B3
Rubizhne Ukr. **39** E2
Rubtsovsk Rus. Fed. **81** F1
Ruby U.S.A. **110** B2
Ruby Mountains U.S.A. **118** C2
Rudnya Rus. Fed. **37** D3
Rudnyy Kazakh. **80** D1
Rudolstadt Ger. **49** E2
Rufiji *r.* Tanz. **95** D3
Rufino Arg. **137** B4
Rugby U.K. **47** C3
Rugby U.S.A. **120** C1
Rügen *i.* Ger. **50** C2
Ruhnu *i.* Estonia **36** B2
Ruhr *r.* Ger. **48** C2
Rui'an China **75** C3
Ruidoso U.S.A. **126** C2
Ruiz Mex. **128** B2
Rukwa, Lake Tanz. **95** D3
Rum *i.* U.K. **44** A2
Ruma S.M. **58** A1
Rumāh Saudi Arabia **82** B2
Rumbek Sudan **93** A4
Runanga N.Z. **106** B3
Runcorn U.K. **46** B3
Rundu Namibia **96** A1
Ruoqiang China **81** F3
Rupert *r.* Can. **114** C1
Rupert Bay Can. **114** C1
Rusape Zimbabwe **99** C1
Ruse Bulg. **58** C2
Rushville U.S.A. **120** C2
Rushworth Austr. **105** D3
Russell N.Z. **106** B2
Russellville *AL* U.S.A. **124** C2
Russellville *AR* U.S.A. **124** B1
Rüsselsheim Ger. **49** D2
Russian Federation *country* Asia/Europe **86** G2
Ruston U.S.A. **124** B2
Ruteng Indon. **65** D2
Ruvuma *r.* Moz./Tanz. **95** E4
Ruweis U.A.E. **83** C2
Ruzayevka Kazakh. **81** D1
Ruzayevka Rus. Fed. **35** D3
Rwanda *country* Africa **95** C3
Ryazan' Rus. Fed. **37** E3
Ryazhsk Rus. Fed. **37** F3
Rybachiy, Poluostrov *pen.* Rus. Fed. **40** G2
Rybinsk Rus. Fed. **37** E2
Rybinskoye Vodokhranilishche *resr* Rus. Fed. **37** E2
Rybnik Pol. **51** D2
Rybnoye Rus. Fed. **37** E3

Ryl'sk Rus. Fed. **37** D3
Ryōtsu Japan **70** C3
Ryukyu Islands Japan **73** E3
Rzeszów Pol. **51** E2
Rzhaksa Rus. Fed. **37** F3
Rzhev Rus. Fed. **37** D2

S

Saale *r.* Ger. **49** E2
Saalfeld Ger. **49** E2
Saarbrücken Ger. **48** C3
Saaremaa *i.* Estonia **36** B3
Saarenkylä Fin. **40** F3
Saarijärvi Fin. **40** F3
Saarlouis Ger. **48** C3
Sab' Ābār Syria **64** C2
Sabah *state* Malaysia **65** C1
Sabalana *i.* Indon. **65** C2
Sabará Brazil **139** D1
Sabhā Libya **91** D2
Sabinas Mex. **129** B2
Sabinas Hidalgo Mex. **129** B2
Sable, Cape Can. **115** D2
Sable, Cape U.S.A. **125** D3
Sable Island Can. **115** E2
Sabugal Port. **54** B1
Sabyā Saudi Arabia **82** B3
Sabzevār Iran **80** C2
Sachigo Lake Can. **114** A1
Sach'on S. Korea **69** B3
Sachs Harbour Can. **110** D2
Sacramento U.S.A. **119** B3
Sacramento Mountains U.S.A.
126 C2
Sacramento Valley U.S.A. **118** B2
Sada S. Africa **99** C3
Şa'dah Yemen **82** B3
Sadoga-shima *i.* Japan **70** C3
Safford U.S.A. **126** C2
Saffron Walden U.K. **47** D3
Safi Morocco **90** B1
Safonovo *Smolenskaya Oblast'*
Rus. Fed. **37** D2
Safrā' as Sark *esc.* Saudi Arabia
82 B2
Saga China **79** C2
Saga Japan **71** B4
Sagaing Myanmar **66** A1
Sagamihara Japan **71** C3
Sagar India **79** B2
Saginaw U.S.A. **122** D2
Saginaw Bay U.S.A. **122** D2
Sagres Port. **54** B2
Sagua la Grande Cuba **123** G1
Saguenay *r.* Can. **123** D1
Saguntio Spain **55** C2
Sahagún Spain **54** B1
Sahara *des.* Africa **90** C3
Saharan Atlas *mts* Alg. *see*
Atlas Saharien

Saharanpur India **79** B2
Saharsa India **79** C2
Sahel *reg.* Africa **90**
Sahuayo Mex. **128** B2
Şāḩūq *reg.* Saudi Arabia **82** B2
Saïda Morocco **55** C2
Saïdpur Bangl. **79** C2
Saigon Vietnam *see*
Hồ Chí Minh City
Saiha India **66** A1
Saihan Tal China **74** B1
Saiki Japan **71** B4
Saimaa *l.* Fin. **41** F3
St Abb's Head U.K. **44** C3
St Albans U.K. **47** C4
St Alban's Head U.K. **47** B4
St Aldhelm's Head U.K. *see*
St Alban's Head
St Andrews U.K. **44** C2
St Anthony Can. **115** E1
St Anthony U.S.A. **118** D2
St Arnaud Austr. **104** C3
St-Augustin Can. **115** E1
St Augustin *r.* Can. **115** E1
St Augustine U.S.A. **125** D3
St Austell U.K. **47** A4
St-Avertin France **52** C2
St-Avold France **48** C3
St Bees Head U.K. **46** B2
St Bride's Bay U.K. **47** A4
St-Brieuc France **52** B2
St Catharines Can. **114** C2
St Catherine's Point U.K. **47** C4
St Charles U.S.A. **121** E3
St Clair, Lake Can./U.S.A.
114 D2
St Cloud U.S.A. **121** E1
St Croix *r.* U.S.A. **123** B2
St David's Head U.K. **47** A4
St-Denis Réunion **89**
St-Dizier France **53** D2
St-Égrève France **53** D2
St Elias Mountains Can. **110** C2
Ste-Marguerite *r.* Can. **115** D1
Sainte Rose du Lac Can. **113** F2
Saintes France **52** B2
St-Étienne France **53** C2
St-Florent France **56** A2
St-Flour France **52** C2
St Francis U.S.A. **120** C3
St-Gaudens France **52** C3
St George Austr. **105** D1
St George U.S.A. **119** D3
St George Island U.S.A. **125** D3
St-Georges Can. **115** C2
St George's Grenada **131** D3
St George's Channel
Rep. of Ireland/U.K. **45** C3
St Gotthard Pass Switz. **53** D2
St Helena *i.* S. Atlantic Ocean **89**
St Helena and Dependencies
terr. S. Atlantic Ocean **89**
St Helena Bay *b.* S. Africa **98** A3
St Helens U.K. **46** B3

St Helens, Mount *vol.* U.S.A.
118 B1
St Helier Channel Is **47** B5
St-Hubert Belgium **48** B2
St-Hyacinthe Can. **123** F1
St Ignace U.S.A. **122** D1
St Ignace Island Can. **114** B2
St Ives U.K. **47** A4
St James, Cape Can. **112** B2
St-Jean, Lac *l.* Can. **115** C2
St-Jean-sur-Richelieu Can.
114 C2
St-Jérôme Can. **123** F1
St Joe *r.* U.S.A. **118** C1
Saint John Can. **111** H3
St John *r.* U.S.A. **123** G1
St John's Antigua **131** D3
St John's Can. **115** E2
St Johns U.S.A. **126** C2
St Johnsbury U.S.A. **123** F2
St Joseph U.S.A. **121** E3
St Joseph, Lake Can. **114** A1
St Joseph Island Can. **114** B2
St Junien France **52** C2
St Kilda *i.* U.K. **42** B2
St Kitts and Nevis *country*
West Indies **131** D3
St-Laurent, Golfe du *g.* Can. *see*
St Lawrence, Gulf of
St-Laurent-du-Maroni Fr. Guiana
135 D2
St Lawrence *inlet* Can. **115** D2
St Lawrence, Gulf of Can.
115 D2
St Lawrence Island U.S.A.
110 A2
St-Lô France **52** B2
St Louis Senegal **90** A3
St Louis U.S.A. **121** E3
St Louis *r.* U.S.A. **121** E1
St Lucia *country* West Indies
131 D3
St Lucia Estuary S. Africa **99** D2
St-Malo France **52** B2
St-Malo, Golfe de *g.* France
52 B2
St-Martin *i.* West Indies **131** D3
St Martin, Cape S. Africa
98 A3
St Matthias Group *is* P.N.G.
63 D3
St-Nazaire France **52** B2
St-Omer France **52** C1
St Paul U.S.A. **121** E2
St Peter U.S.A. **121** E2
St Peter Port Channel Is **47** B5
St Petersburg Rus. Fed. **37** D2
St Petersburg U.S.A. **125** D3
St-Pierre St Pierre and Miquelon
115 E2
St Pierre and Miquelon *terr.*
N. America **115** E2
St-Pierre-d'Oléron France **52** B2
St-Quentin France **53** C2

St-Siméon Can. **115** D2
St Thomas Can. **114** B2
St-Tropez France **53** D3
St-Tropez, Cap de c. France **53** D3
St Vincent, Gulf Austr. **104** B3
St Vincent and the Grenadines *country* West Indies **131** D3
St-Vith Belgium **48** C2
Saipan *i.* N. Mariana Is **63** D1
Saitama Japan **71** C4
Sajama, Nevado *mt.* Bol. **136** B2
Sak *watercourse* S. Africa **98** B2
Sakai Japan **71** C4
Sakaide Japan **71** B4
Sakakawea, Lake U.S.A. **120** C1
Sakarya *r.* Turkey see Adapazarı
Sakarya *r.* Turkey **59** D2
Sakata Japan **70** C3
Sakchu N. Korea **69** B1
Sakhalin *i.* Rus. Fed. **70** D1
Sakhile S. Africa **99** C2
Şäki Azer. **85** C1
Sakishima-shotō *is* Japan **73** E3
Sakon Nakhon Thai. **66** B2
Sakrivier S. Africa **98** B3
Sakura Japan **71** D3
Saky Ukr. **39** D2
Sal *r.* Rus. Fed. **39** F2
Salaberry-de-Valleyfield Can. **114** C2

Salina, Isola *i.* Italy **56** B3
Salina Cruz Mex. **129** C3
Salinas Brazil **139** D1
Salinas Mex. **128** B2
Salinas U.S.A. **119** B3
Salines, Cap de ses *c.* Spain **55** D2
Salinópolis Brazil **135** E3
Salisbury U.K. **47** C4
Salisbury *MD* U.S.A. **123** E3
Salisbury *NC* U.S.A. **125** D1
Salisbury Plain U.K. **47** B4
Salluit Can. **111** G2
Salmãs Iran **85** C2
Salmon U.S.A. **118** D1
Salmon *r.* U.S.A. **118** C1
Salmon Arm Can. **112** D2
Salmon River Mountains U.S.A. **118** C2
Salmtal Ger. **48** C3
Salo Fin. **41** E3
Sal'sk Rus. Fed. **39** F2
Salt *watercourse* S. Africa **98** B3
Salt *r.* U.S.A. **126** B2
Salta Arg. **136** B3
Saltillo Mex. **129** B2
Salt Lake City U.S.A. **118** D2
Salto Brazil **138** C2
Salto Uru. **136** C4
Salto do Guairá Para. **138** B2
Salton Sea *salt l.* U.S.A. **119** C4
Salvador Brazil **135** F4
Salwah Saudi Arabia **83** C2
Salween *r.* China/Myanmar **66** A1
Salween *r.* China/Myanmar **72** C3
Salyan Azer. **85** C2
Salzburg Austria **50** C3
Salzgitter Ger. **49** E1
Salzkotten Ger. **49** D2
Salzwedel Ger. **49** E1
Samani Japan **70** D2
Samar *i.* Phil. **68** B2
Samara Rus. Fed. **35** E3
Samarinda Indon. **65** C2
Samarqand Uzbek. **81** D3
Sāmarrā' Iraq **85** C2
Samba Dem. Rep. Congo **95** C3
Sambaliung *mts* Indon. **65** C1
Sambalpur India **79** C2
Sambar, Tanjung *pt* Indon. **65** C2
Sambas Indon. **64** B1
Sambava Madag. **97** [inset] E1
Sambir Ukr. **38** B2
Samborombón, Bahía *b.* Arg. **137** C4
Samch'ŏk S. Korea **69** B2
Samdi Dag *mt.* Turkey **85** C2
Same Tanz. **95** D3
Samīrah Saudi Arabia **82** B2
Samoa *country* S. Pacific Ocean **101**
Samoan Islands *is* S. Pacific Ocean **111**

Samos *i.* Greece **59** C3
Samothraki Greece **59** C2
Samothraki *i.* Greece **59** C2
Sampit Indon. **65** C2
Sam Rayburn Reservoir U.S.A. **127** F2
Samsun Turkey **84** B1
Samtredia Georgia **85** C1
Samui, Ko *i.* Thai. **67** B3
Samut Songkhram Thai. see **67** B2
San Mali **90** B3
San'a' Yemen **82** B3
San Ambrosio, Isla *i.* S. Pacific Ocean **133**
Sanandaj Iran **85** C2
San Andrés, Isla de *i.* Caribbean Sea **130** B3
San Andreas U.S.A. **126** C2
San Andrés Tuxtla Mex. **129** C3
San Angelo U.S.A. **127** D2
San Antonio Chile **136** A4
San Antonio U.S.A. **127** E3
San Antonio, Mount U.S.A. **119** C4
San Antonio Abad Spain **55** D2
San Antonio Oeste Arg. **137** B5
San Benedetto del Tronto Italy **56** B2
San Benedicto, Isla *i.* Mex. **128** A3
San Bernardino U.S.A. **119** C4
San Bernardino Mountains U.S.A. **119** C4
San Blas, Cape U.S.A. **125** C3
San Borja Bol. **136** B2
San Buenaventura Mex. **128** B2
San Carlos Phil. **68** B2
San Carlos de Bariloche Arg. **137** A5
San Clemente Island U.S.A. **119** C4
San Cristóbal *i.* Solomon Is **110**
San Cristóbal Venez. **134** B2
San Cristóbal de las Casas Mex. **129** C3
Sancti Spíritus Cuba **130** C2
Sandakan Malaysia **65** C1
Sandane Norway **41** B3
Sandanski Bulg. **59** B2
Sanday *i.* U.K. **44** C1
Sanderson U.S.A. **127** D2
Sandia Peru **134** C4
San Diego U.S.A. **119** C4
Sandıklı Turkey **84** B2
Sandnes Norway **41** B4
Sandnessjøen Norway **40** C2
Sandomierz Pol. **51** E2
Sandoy *i.* Faroe Is **42** B1
Sandpoint U.S.A. **118** C1
Sandu China **75** B3
Sandur Faroe Is **42** B1
Sandusky U.S.A. **122** D2
Sandveld *mts* S. Africa **98** A3

Sandvika Norway **41** C4
Sandviken Sweden **41** D3
Sandwich Bay Can. **115** E1
Sandy Cape Austr. **103** E2
Sandy Lake Can. **114** A1
Sandy Lake *l.* Can. **114** A1
San Estanislao Para. **138** A2
San Felipe *Baja California* Mex. **128** A1
San Felipe *Guanajuato* Mex. **129** B2
San Felipe Venez. **134** C1
San Félix Chile **133**
San Fernando *Baja California* Mex. **128** A2
San Fernando *Tamaulipas* Mex. **129** C2
San Fernando Phil. **68** B2
San Fernando Phil. **68** B2
San Fernando Spain **54** B2
San Fernando Trin. and Tob. **131** D3
San Fernando de Apure Venez. **134** C2
Sanford *FL* U.S.A. **125** D3
San Francisco Arg. **136** B4
San Francisco U.S.A. **119** B3
San Francisco Javier Spain **55** D2
San Gavino Monreale Italy **56** A3
Sangerhausen Ger. **49** E2
Sanggau Indon. **65** C1
Sangha *r.* Congo **94** B3
San Giovanni in Fiore Italy **57** C3
Sangir *i.* Indon. **68** B2
Sangir, Kepulauan *is* Indon. **68** C2
Sangju S. Korea **69** B2
Sangkulirang Indon. **65** C1
Sangli India **77** B3
Sangmélima Cameroon **94** B2
Sango Zimbabwe **97** C2
Sangre de Cristo Range *mts* U.S.A. **120** B3
San Hipólito, Punta *pt* Mex. **128** A2
Sanikiluaq Can. **114** C1
Sanjiang China **75** A3
San Joaquin *r.* U.S.A. **119** B3
San Jorge, Golfo de *g.* Arg. **133** C7
San José Costa Rica **130** B4
San Jose Phil. **68** B2
San Jose Phil. **68** B2
San Jose U.S.A. **119** B3
San Jose, Isla *i.* Mex. **128** A2
San José de Buenavista Phil. **68** B2
San José de Comondú Mex. **128** A2
San José del Cabo Mex. **128** B2
San José del Guaviare Col. **134** B2

San Juan Arg. **136** B4
San Juan *r.* Costa Rica/Nic. **130** B3
San Juan Puerto Rico **131** D3
San Juan *r.* U.S.A. **119** D3
San Juan Bautista Spain **55** D2
San Juan Islands U.S.A. **118** B1
San Juan Mountains U.S.A. **120** B3
San Julián Arg. **137** B5
San Juur *r.* India **79** C2
Sankt Gallen Switz. **53** D2
Sankt Moritz Switz. **53** D2
Sankt-Peterburg Rus. Fed. *see* St Petersburg
Sankt Veit an der Glan Austria **50** C3
Sankt Wendel Ger. **48** C3
Şanlıurfa Turkey **84** B2
San Lorenzo Mex. **126** C3
Sanlúcar de Barrameda Spain **54** B2
San Lucas Mex. **128** B2
San Luis Arg. **137** B4
San Luis de la Paz Mex. **129** B2
San Luisito Mex. **126** B2
San Luis Obispo U.S.A. **119** B3
San Luis Potosí Mex. **129** B2
San Luis Río Colorado Mex. **128** A1
San Marcos U.S.A. **127** E3
San Marino San Marino **56** B2
San Marino *country* Europe **56** B2
San Martín San Marino **56** B2
San Martín de los Andes Arg. **137** A5
San Matías, Golfo *g.* Arg. **107** D5
Sanmenxia China **74** B2
San Miguel El Salvador **130** B3
San Miguel de Tucumán Arg. **136** B3
Sanming China **75** B3
San Nicolás de los Arroyos Arg. **137** B4
San Nicolas Island U.S.A. **119** C4
Sannieshof S. Africa **99** C2
Sanok Pol. **51** E3
San Pablo Phil. **68** B2
San Pedro Arg. **136** B3
San Pedro Mex. **128** A2
San Pedro *watercourse* U.S.A. **126** B2
San Pedro, Sierra de *mts* Spain **54** B2
San Pedro Sula Hond. **130** B3
San Pietro, Isola di *i.* Italy **56** A3
San Quintín, Cabo *c.* Mex. **128** A1
San Rafael Arg. **137** B4
San Remo Italy **56** A2
San Salvador El Salvador **130** B3

San Salvador de Jujuy Arg. **136** B3
San Severo Italy **56** C2
Sanski Most Bos.-Herz. **57** C2
Santa Ana El Salvador **130** B3
Santa Ana Mex. **128** A1
Santa Ana U.S.A. **119** C4
Santa Bárbara Mex. **128** B2
Santa Barbara U.S.A. **119** C4
Santa Bárbara, Serra de *hills* Brazil **138** B2
Santa Clara Cuba **130** C2
Santa Clarita U.S.A. **119** C4
Santa Croce, Capo *c.* Italy **56** C3
Santa Cruz *r.* Arg. **137** B6
Santa Cruz Bol. **136** B2
Santa Cruz U.S.A. **119** B3
Santa Cruz Barillas Guat. **129** C3
Santa Cruz Cabrália Brazil **139** E1
Santa Cruz de Tenerife Canary Is **90** A2
Santa Cruz Island U.S.A. **119** C4
Santa Cruz Islands Solomon Is **110**
Santa Elena, Punta *pt* Ecuador **134** A4
Santa Fé Arg. **136** B4
Santa Fe U.S.A. **126** C1
Santa Helena de Goiás Brazil **138** B1
Santa Isabel *i.* Solomon Is **110**
Santa Luisa, Serra de *hills* Brazil **138** B1
Santa María Brazil **136** C3
Santa María *i.* Mex. **128** B1
Santa María U.S.A. **119** B4
Santa Maria, Cabo de *c.* Moz. **99** D2
Santa Maria, Cabo de *c.* Port. **54** B2
Santa Maria das Barreiras Brazil **135** E3
Santa Maria di Leuca, Capo *c.* Italy **57** C3
Santa Marta Col. **134** B1
Santa Monica U.S.A. **119** C4
Santander Spain **54** C1
Sant'Antioco Italy **56** A3
Sant'Antioco, Isola di *i.* Italy **56** A3
Santarém Brazil **135** D3
Santarém Port. **54** B2
Santa Rita do Araguaia Brazil **138** B1
Santa Rosa Arg. **137** B4
Santa Rosa *CA* U.S.A. **119** B3
Santa Rosa *NM* U.S.A. **126** C2
Santa Rosa de Copán Hond. **130** B3
Santa Rosa Island U.S.A. **119** B4
Santa Rosalía Mex. **128** A2
Santiago Brazil **136** C3

Santiago Chile **137** A4
Santiago Dom. Rep. **131** C3
Santiago Mex. **128** B2
Santiago Panama **130** B4
Santiago Phil. **68** B2
Santiago de Compostela Spain **54** B1
Santiago Ixcuintla Mex. **128** B2
San Jordi, Golf de g. Spain **55** D1
Santo André Brazil **139** C2
Santo Angelo Brazil **136** C3
Santo Antônio, Cabo c. Brazil **146**
Santo Antônio de Jesus Brazil **135** F4
Santo Antônio do Içá Brazil **134** C3
Santo Domingo Dom. Rep. **131** D3
Santo Domingo Pueblo U.S.A. **126** C1
Santorini i. Greece see Thira
Santos Brazil **139** C2
San Valentín, Cerro mt. Chile **137** A5
San Vicente El Salvador **130** B3
San Vicente Mex. **128** A1
San Vincenzo Italy **56** B2
San Vito, Capo c. Italy **56** B3
Sanya China **75** A4
São Bernardo do Campo Brazil **139** C2
São Borja Brazil **136** C3
São Carlos Brazil **138** C2
São Félix Mato Grosso Brazil **135** D4
São Fidélis Brazil **139** D2
São Francisco Brazil **139** D1
São Francisco r. Brazil **135** E4
São Francisco, Ilha de i. Brazil **138** C3
São Francisco do Sul Brazil **138** C3
São Gabriel Brazil **136** C4
São Gonçalo Brazil **139** D2
São João da Barra Brazil **139** D2
São João da Boa Vista Brazil **139** C2
São João da Madeira Port. **54** B1
São Joaquim da Barra Brazil **138** C2
São José do Rio Preto Brazil **138** C2
São José dos Campos Brazil **139** C2
São José dos Pinhais Brazil **138** C3
São Lourenço, Pantanal de marsh Brazil **138** A1
São Luís Brazil **135** E3
São Manuel Brazil **138** C2

São Mateus Brazil **139** E1
São Paulo Brazil **139** C2
São Raimundo Nonato Brazil **135** E3
São Romão Brazil **139** C1
São Roque, Cabo de c. Brazil **146**
São Sebastião, Ilha de i. Brazil **139** C2
São Sebastião do Paraíso Brazil **138** C2
São Simão Brazil **138** C2
São Simão, Barragem de resr Brazil **138** B1
São Tomé i.
   São Tomé and Príncipe **94** A2
São Tomé, Cabo de c. Brazil **139** D2
São Tomé and Príncipe country Africa **94** A2
São Vicente Brazil **139** C2
São Vicente, Cabo de c. Port. **54** B2
Sapporo Japan **70** D2
Saqqez Iran **85** C2
Sarāb Iran **85** C2
Sara Buri Thai. **67** B2
Sarai Rus. Fed. **37** F3
Sarajevo Bos.-Herz. **57** C2
Saranac Lake U.S.A. **123** F2
Sarandë Albania **59** B3
Sarangani Islands Phil. **68** B3
Saransk Rus. Fed. **35** D3
Sarapul Rus. Fed. **35** E3
Sarasota U.S.A. **125** D3
Sarata Ukr. **58** D1
Saratoga Springs U.S.A. **123** F2
Saratok Malaysia **65** C1
Saratov Rus. Fed. **35** D3
Saravan Iran **83** D2
Sarawak state Malaysia **65** C1
Sarayköy Turkey **59** C3
Sardarshahr India **78** B2
Sardegna i. Italy see Sardinia
Sardinia i. Italy **56** A2
Sarektjåkkå mt. Sweden **40** D2
Sar-e Pol Afgh. **78** A1
Sargasso Sea N. Atlantic Ocean **144** B4
Sargodha Pak. **78** B1
Sarh Chad **91** D4
Sarhad reg. Iran **83** D2
Sārī Iran **85** D2
Sarıgöl Turkey **59** C3
Sarıkamış Turkey **85** C1
Sarikei Malaysia **65** C1
Sarir Tibesti des. Libya **91** D2
Sariwŏn N. Korea **69** B2
Sarıyer Turkey **59** C2
Sarkand Kazakh. **81** E2
Şarköy Turkey **59** C2
Sarmi Indon. **63** D3

Sarnia Can. **122** D2
Sarny Ukr. **38** C1
Saronikos Kolpos g. Greece **59** B3
Saros Körfezi b. Turkey **59** C2
Sarova Rus. Fed. **35** D3
Sarrebourg France **53** D2
Sarria Spain **54** B1
Sarrión Spain **55** C1
Sartène France **53** D3
Sárrár Hungary **51** D3
Saryozek Kazakh. **81** E2
Sarysu watercourse Kazakh. **86** G3
Sary-Tash Kyrg. **81** E3
Sasaram India **79** C2
Sasebo Japan **71** A4
Saskatchewan prov. Can. **113** E2
Saskatchewan r. Can. **113** E2
Saskatoon Can. **110** E3
Sasolburg S. Africa **99** C2
Sasovo Rus. Fed. **37** F3
Sassandra Côte d'Ivoire **90** B4
Sassari Italy **56** A2
Sassnitz Ger. **50** C2
Satadougou Mali **90** A3
Satara S. Africa **99** D1
Satna India **79** C2
Satpura Range mts India **78** B3
Satu Mare Romania **38** B2
Satun Thai. **67** B3
Sauclilo Mex. **128** B2
Sauda Norway **41** B4
Sauðárkrókur Iceland **40** [inset]
Saudi Arabia country Asia **82** B2
Saulieu France **53** C2
Sault Sainte Marie Can. **114** D2
Sault Sainte Marie U.S.A. **122** D1
Saumalkol' Kazakh. **81** D1
Saumlakki Indon. **63** C3
Saumur France **52** B2
Saurimo Angola **94** C3
Sava r. Europe **58** C2
Savai'i i. Samoa **111**
Savala r. Rus. Fed. **37** F3
Savannah GA U.S.A. **125** D2
Savannah TN U.S.A. **124** C1
Savannah r. U.S.A. **125** D2
Savannakhét Laos **66** B2
Savant Lake Can. **114** A1
Savașteep Turkey **59** C3
Savona Italy **56** A2
Savonlinna Fin. **41** F3
Savu i. Indon. **65** D3
Savu Sea Indon. see Sawu, Laut
Sawai Madhopur India **78** B2
Sawankhalok Thai. **66** A2
Sawatch Range mts U.S.A. **120** B3
Sawhâj Egypt **92** B2

232

Sawtell Austr. **105** E2
Sawu, Laut sea Indon. **65** D2
Sayhūt Yemen **83** D3
Saynshand Mongolia **73** D2
Sayre U.S.A. **123** E2
Sayula Jalisco Mex. **128** B3
Sayula Veracruz Mex. **129** C3
Scafell Pike h. U.K. **46** E3
Scalea Italy **54** F5
Scapa Flow inlet U.K. **44** C1
Scarborough Can. **114** C2
Scarborough Trin. and Tob. **131** D3
Scarborough U.K. **46** G3
Scarborough Shoal sea feature S. China Sea **68** A2
Scarinish U.K. **44** A2
Scarpanto i. Greece see Karpathos
Schaffhausen Switz. **53** D2
Schagen Neth. **48** B1
Scharendijke Neth. **48** A2
Scheeßel Ger. **49** D1
Schefferville Can. **115** U1
Schell Creek Range mts U.S.A. **119** D3
Schenectady U.S.A. **123** F2
Scheßlitz Ger. **49** E2
Schiermonnikoog i. Neth. **48** C1
Schio Italy **56** D1
Schleiz Ger. **49** E2
Schleswig Ger. **50** B2
Schloss Holte-Stukenbrock Ger. **49** D2
Schlüchtern Ger. **49** D2
Schmallenberg Ger. **49** D2
Schnaverdingen Ger. **49** D1
Schönebeck (Elbe) Ger. **49** E1
Schöningen Ger. **49** E1
Schouten Islands P.N.G. **63** D3
Schwabach Ger. **49** E3
Schwäbische Alb mts Ger. **50** B3
Schwandorf Ger. **49** F3
Schwaner, Pegunungan mts Indon. **65** C2
Schwarzenbek Ger. **49** D2
Schwarzenberg Ger. **49** F2
Schwarzrand mts Namibia **98** A2
Schwarzwald mts Ger. see Black Forest
Schwaz Austria **50** C3
Schwedt an der Oder Ger. **50** C2
Schweinfurt Ger. **49** E2
Schweriner See l. Ger. **49** E1
Schwyz Switz. **53** D2
Sciacca Italy **56** D3
Scilly, Isles of U.K. **43** B4
Scioto r. U.S.A. **122** D3
Scobey U.S.A. **120** B1
Scone Austr. **105** E2
Scotia Sea S. Atlantic Ocean **107** A4
Scotland admin. div. U.K. **44** C2

Scott, Cape Can. **112** C2
Scottburgh S. Africa **99** D3
Scott City U.S.A. **120** C3
Scottsbluff U.S.A. **120** C2
Scottsboro U.S.A. **125** C2
Scourie U.K. **44** B1
Scranton U.S.A. **123** E2
Scunthorpe U.K. **46** G3
Seal r. Can. **113** F2
Seal, Cape S. Africa **98** B3
Sea Lake Austr. **104** C3
Searcy U.S.A. **124** B1
Seascale U.K. **46** E3
Seattle U.S.A. **118** B1
Sebago Lake U.S.A. **123** F2
Sebastián Vizcaíno, Bahía b. Mex. **128** A2
Seboea Romania **38** B2
Sebeși i. Indon. **64** B2
Sebezh Rus. Fed. **36** C2
Sebring U.S.A. **125** D3
Sechelt Can. **112** C3
Secunderabad India **77** B3
Sedalia U.S.A. **121** E3
Sedan France **53** C2
Seddon N.Z. **106** B3
Sedona U.S.A. **126** B2
Seehausen (Altmark) Ger. **49** E1
Seeheim Namibia **98** A2
Sées France **52** C2
Seesen Ger. **49** E2
Seevetal Ger. **49** E1
Sefare Botswana **99** C1
Segamat Malaysia **64** B1
Segezha Rus. Fed. **34** C2
Ségou Mali **90** B3
Segovia Spain **54** C1
Séguédine Niger **91** D2
Séguéla Côte d'Ivoire **90** B4
Seguin U.S.A. **127** E3
Segura r. Spain **55** C2
Segura, Sierra de mts Spain **55** C2
Sehithwa Botswana **96** B3
Seinäjoki Fin. **40** E3
Seine r. France **52** C2
Seine, Baie de b. France **52** B2
Sekondi Ghana **90** B4
Selaru i. Indon. **63** C3
Selatan, Tanjung pt Indon. **65** C2
Selawik U.S.A. **110** B2
Selby U.K. **46** C3
Selebi-Phikwe Botswana **96** B2
Selenga r. Rus. Fed. **67**
Selestat France **53** D2
Selfoss Iceland **40** [inset]
Sélibabi Maur. **90** A3
Seligman U.S.A. **126** B1
Selima Oasis Sudan **92** A2
Sélingué, Lac de l. Mali **90** B3
Selizharovo Rus. Fed. **37** D2
Seljord Norway **41** B4
Selkirk Can. **113** F2
Selkirk U.K. **44** C3
Selkirk Mountains Can. **112** D2

Selma AL U.S.A. **124** C2
Selma CA U.S.A. **119** C3
Sel'tso Rus. Fed. **37** D3
Selvas reg. Brazil **134** B3
Selway r. U.S.A. **118** C1
Selwyn Lake Can. **113** E1
Selwyn Mountains Can. **112** B1
Selwyn Range hills Austr. **103** C2
Semarang Indon. **65** C2
Sematan Malaysia **65** B1
Sembé Congo **94** B2
Semenivka Ukr. **39** D1
Semeru, Gunung vol. Indon. **65** C2
Semikarakorsk Rus. Fed. **39** F2
Semiluki Rus. Fed. **37** E3
Seminoe Reservoir U.S.A. **120** B2
Seminole U.S.A. **127** D2
Seminole, Lake U.S.A. **125** D2
Semipalatinsk Kazakh. **81** F1
Semnān Iran **85** D2
Semporna Malaysia **65** C1
Sena Madureira Brazil **134** C3
Senanga Zambia **96** B1
Sendai Kagoshima Japan **71** B4
Sendai Miyagi Japan **70** D3
Senegal country Africa **90** A3
Sénégal r. Maur./Senegal **90** A3
Senftenberg Ger. **49** C2
Senhor do Bonfim Brazil **135** E4
Senigallia Italy **56** D2
Senj Croatia **56** B2
Senja i. Norway **40** D2
Senlis France **52** C2
Senmonorom Cambodia **67** B2
Sennar Sudan **93** B3
Senneterre Can. **114** C2
Senqu r. Lesotho **99** C3
Sens France **53** C2
Senta S.M. **58** B1
Sentinel Peak Can. **112** C2
Seoni India **79** B2
Seoul S. Korea **69** B2
Sepetiba, Baía de b. Brazil **139** D2
Sepik r. P.N.G. **63** D3
Sepinang Indon. **65** C1
Sept-Îles Can. **115** D1
Seram i. Indon. **63** C3
Seram, Laut sea Indon. **63** C3
Serang Indon. **64** B2
Serbia aut. rep. S.M. see Srbija
Serbia and Montenegro country Europe **58** B2
Seremban Malaysia **64** B1
Serengeti Plain Tanz. **95** D3
Sergiyev Posad Rus. Fed. **37** E2
Seria Brunei **65** C1
Serifos i. Greece **59** B3
Serik Turkey **84** B2
Serov Rus. Fed. **34** F3
Serowe Botswana **99** C1
Sorpa Port. **54** B2

Serpukhov Rus. Fed. **37** E3
Serra da Mesa, Represa *resr* Brazil **135** E4
Serre *r.* France **48** A3
Sèrro Greece **59** B2
Sèrro Brazil **139** D1
Sertãozinho Brazil **138** C2
Sertolovo Rus. Fed. **37** D1
Seruyan *r.* Indon. **65** C2
Sesfontein Namibia **96** A1
Sessa Aurunca Italy **56** B2
Sestri Levante Italy **56** A2
Sestroretsk Rus. Fed. **36** C1
Sète France **53** C3
Sete Lagoas Brazil **139** D1
Setermoen Norway **40** D2
Setesdal *val.* Norway **41** B4
Sétif Alg. **91** C1
Seto-naikai *sea* Japan **71** B4
Settle U.K. **46** B2
Setúbal Port. **54** B2
Setúbal, Baía de *b.* Port. **54** B2
Seul, Lac *l.* Can. **114** A1
Sevan Armenia **80** D2
Sevan, Lake Armenia **80** D2
Sevastopol' Ukr. **39** D3
Seven Islands Bay Can. **115** D1
Sévérac-le-Château France **52** C3
Severn *r.* Can. **114** B1
Severn *r.* Can. **114** B1
Severn S. Africa **98** C2
Severn *r.* U.K. **47** B4
Severnaya Dvina *r.* Rus. Fed. **34** D2
Severnaya Zemlya *is* Rus. Fed. **87** I1
Severnyy Nenetskiy Avtonomnyy Okrug Rus. Fed. **34** D2
Severnyy Respublika Komi Rus. Fed. **34** F2
Severodvinsk Rus. Fed. **34** C2
Severomorsk Rus. Fed. **40** G2
Severskaya Rus. Fed. **39** E3
Sevier *r.* U.S.A. **119** D3
Sevier Lake U.S.A. **119** D3
Sevilla Spain *see* Seville
Seville Spain **54** B2
Seward U.S.A. **110** C2
Seward Peninsula U.S.A. **110** B2
Sextin *r.* Mex. **128** B2
Seyakha Rus. Fed. **34** G1
Seychelles *country* Indian Ocean **89**
Seyðisfjörður Iceland **40** [inset]
Seym *r.* Rus./Ukr. **39** D1
Seymchan Rus. Fed. **87** M2
Seymour Austr. **105** D3
Seymour *IN* U.S.A. **122** C3
Seymour *TX* U.S.A. **127** E2
Sézanne France **53** C2
Sfakia Greece **53** C3
Sfântu Gheorghe Romania **38** C2
Sfax Tunisia **91** D1

's-Gravenhage Neth. *see* The Hague
Sgurr Alasdair *h.* U.K. **44** A2
Shaanxi *prov.* China **74** A2
Shabel'sk Rus. Fed. **39** E2
Shache China **81** E3
Shackleton Range *mts* Antarctica **107** A1
Shaftesbury U.K. **47** B4
Shageluk U.S.A. **110** B2
Shahdol India **79** C2
Shah Fuladi *mt.* Afgh. **78** A1
Shahjahanpur India **79** B2
Shahr-e Kord Iran **85** D2
Shahrezā Iran **85** D2
Shahrisabz Uzbek. **81** D3
Shakhovskaya Rus. Fed. **37** E2
Shakhty Rus. Fed. **39** F2
Shakhun'ya Rus. Fed. **34** D3
Shakotan-misaki *c.* Japan **70** D2
Shalkar Kazakh. **80** C2
Shaluli Shan *mts* China **72** C2
Shamattawa Can. **113** F2
Shamrock U.S.A. **127** D1
Shandan China **72** C2
Shandong *prov.* China **74** B2
Shandong Bandao *pen.* China **74** C2
Shangani *r.* Zimbabwe **97** B1
Shanghai China **74** C2
Shanghai *mun.* China **74** C2
Shangrao China **75** B3
Shangluo China **74** A2
Shangrao China **75** B3
Shangzhou China *see* Shangluo
Shannon *r.* Rep. of Ireland **45** B2
Shannon, Mouth of the Rep. of Ireland **45** B2
Shantou China **75** B3
Shanxi *prov.* China **74** B2
Shaoguan China **75** B3
Shaowu China **75** B3
Shaoxing China **75** C2
Shaoyang China **75** B3
Shaqra' Saudi Arabia **92** C2
Sharhorod Ukr. **38** C2
Sharjah U.A.E. **83** C2
Sharkawshchyna Belarus **36** C2
Shark Bay Austr. **102** A2
Sharm ash Shaykh Egypt **82** A2
Shar'ya Rus. Fed. **34** D3
Shashe *r.* Botswana/Zimbabwe **97** B2
Shashemenē Eth. **93** B4
Shasta, Mount *vol.* U.S.A. **118** B2
Shasta Lake U.S.A. **118** B2
Shatsk Rus. Fed. **37** F3
Shatura Rus. Fed. **37** E2
Shaunavon Can. **113** E3
Shawano U.S.A. **122** C2
Shawnee U.S.A. **127** E1
Shay Gap Austr. **102** B2
Shchekino Rus. Fed. **37** E3
Shchelkovo Rus. Fed. **37** E2

Shchigry Rus. Fed. **37** E3
Shchors Ukr. **39** D1
Shchuchyn Belarus **36** B3
Shebekino Rus. Fed. **39** E1
Sheberghān Afgh. **78** A1
Sheboygan U.S.A. **122** C2
Shebsh *r.* Rus. Fed. **39** E3
Sheelin, Lough *l.* Rep. of Ireland **45** C2
Sheffield U.K. **46** C3
Sheksna Rus. Fed. **37** E2
Sheksninskoye Vodokhranilishche *resr* Rus. Fed. **37** E2
Shelagskiy, Mys *pt* Rus. Fed. **87** N2
Shelburne Can. **115** D2
Shelby U.S.A. **118** D1
Shelbyville *IN* U.S.A. **122** C3
Shelbyville *TN* U.S.A. **125** C1
Shelikhova, Zaliv *g.* Rus. Fed. **87** M2
Shellbrook Can. **113** E2
Shelton U.S.A. **118** B1
Shenandoah *r.* U.S.A. **123** E3
Shendam Nigeria **94** A2
Shendi Sudan **82** A3
Shenyang China **74** C1
Shenzhen China **75** B3
Shepetivka Ukr. **38** C1
Shepparton Austr. **105** D3
Sheppey, Isle of *i.* U.K. **47** D4
Sherbrooke *N.S.* Can. **115** D2
Sherbrooke *Que.* Can. **115** C2
Shereiq Sudan **92** B3
Sheridan U.S.A. **120** B2
Sherman U.S.A. **127** E2
's-Hertogenbosch Neth. **48** B2
Shetland Islands *Scotland* U.K. **44** [inset]
Shetpe Kazakh. **80** C2
Sheyenne *r.* U.S.A. **121** D1
Shibām Yemen **83** B3
Shibetsu Japan **70** E2
Shijiazhuang China **74** B2
Shikarpur Pak. **78** A2
Shikoku *i.* Japan **71** B4
Shikotsu-ko *l.* Japan **70** D2
Shiliguri India **79** C2
Shillong India **79** D2
Shilovo Rus. Fed. **37** F3
Shimbiris *mt.* Somalia **93** C3
Shimla India **71** C3
Shimla India **79** B1
Shimoga India **77** B3
Shimonoseki Japan **71** A4
Shin, Loch *l.* U.K. **44** B1
Shindand Afgh. **78** A1
Shingū Japan **71** C4
Shingwedzi S. Africa **99** D1
Shingwedzi *r.* S. Africa **99** D1
Shinyanga Tanz. **95** D3

Shiono-misaki c. Japan **71** C4
Shiprock U.S.A. **126** C1
Shiquan China **74** A2
Shiquan He r. China *see* Indus
Shiretoko-misaki c. Japan **70** E2
Shiriya-zaki c. Japan **70** D2
Shiv India **78** B2
Shivpuri India **79** B2
Shiyan China **74** B2
Shizuishan China **74** A2
Shizuoka Japan **71** C4
Shklow Belarus **37** D3
Shkodër Albania **57** C2
Shor Barsa-Kel'mes *salt marsh* Uzbek. **85** D1
Shoshone U.S.A. **119** C3
Shoshone Mountains U.S.A. **119** C3
Shoshong Botswana **99** C1
Shostka Ukr. **39** D2
Showak Sudan **82** A3
Show Low U.S.A. **126** B2
Shpola Ukr. **39** D2
Shreveport U.S.A. **124** B2
Shrewsbury U.K. **47** B3
Shu'ab, Ra's *pt* Yemen **83** C3
Shuangjiang China **66** B1
Shuangliao China **69** A1
Shuangyang China **69** B1
Shuangyashan China **70** B1
Shubarkuduk Kazakh. **80** C2
Shubrā al Khaymah Egypt **92** B1
Shumba Zimbabwe **96** B1
Shumen Bulg. **58** C2
Shumilina Belarus **36** C1
Shumyachi Rus. Fed. **37** D3
Shungnak U.S.A. **110** B2
Shuqrah Yemen **82** B3
Shushtar Iran **85** C2
Shuswap Lake Can. **112** D2
Shuya Rus. Fed. **37** F2
Shuyskoye Rus. Fed. **37** F2
Shwebo Myanmar **66** A1
Shymkent Kazakh. **81** D2
Shyroke Ukr. **39** D2
Sia Indon. **63** C3
Siahan Range *mts* Pak. **78** A2
Sialkot Pak. **78** B1
Siargao i. Phil. **68** B3
Siauliai Lith. **36** B2
Šibenik Croatia **57** C2
Siberia *reg.* Rus. Fed. **87** J2
Siberut i. Indon. **64** A2
Sibi Pak. **78** A2
Sibiu Romania **38** B2
Sibolga Indon. **64** A1
Sibsagar India **66** A1
Sibu Malaysia **65** C1
Sibut C.A.R. **94** B2
Sibuyan i. Phil. **68** B2
Sibuyan Sea Phil. **68** B2
Sicamous Can. **112** D2
Sichon Thai. **67** A3
Sichuan *prov.* China **74** A2

Sichuan Pendi *basin* China **75** A3
Sicié, Cap c. France **53** D3
Sicilia i. Italy *see* Sicily
Sicilian Channel Italy/Tunisia **56** B3
Sicily i. Italy **56** B3
Sicuani Peru **134** B4
Siddhapur India **78** B2
Sideros, Akra *pt* Greece **59** C3
Sidi Aïssa Alg. **55** D2
Sidi Ali Alg. **55** D2
Sidi Bel Abbès Alg. **90** B1
Sidikalang Indon. **64** A1
Sidi Okba Alg. **55** D2
Sidlaw Hills U.K. **44** C2
Sidmouth U.K. **47** B4
Sidney Can. **118** B1
Sidney *MT* U.S.A. **120** C1
Sidney *NE* U.S.A. **120** C2
Sidney *OH* U.S.A. **122** D2
Sidney Lanier, Lake U.S.A. **125** D2
Sidoan Indon. **65** D1
Sidon Lebanon **84** B2
Sidrolândia Brazil **138** B2
Siedlce Pol. **51** E2
Siegen Ger. **48** B2
Siémréab Cambodia **67** B2
Siena Italy **56** B2
Sieradz Pol. **51** D2
Sierra Grande Arg. **137** B5
Sierra Leone *country* Africa **90** A4
Sierra Vista U.S.A. **126** B2
Sierre Switz. **55** D2
Sifnos i. Greece **59** B3
Sig Alg. **55** C2
Sigguup Nunaa *pen.* Greenland **111** I2
Sighetu Marmaţiei Romania **38** B2
Sighişoara Romania **38** B2
Sigli Indon. **64** A1
Siglufjörður Iceland **40** [inset]
Sigmaringen Ger. **50** B3
Signy-l'Abbaye France **48** B3
Sigüenza Spain **54** C1
Siguiri Guinea **90** B3
Sigulda Latvia **36** C2
Sihanoukville Cambodia **67** B2
Siilinjärvi Fin. **40** F3
Siirt Turkey **85** C2
Sikar India **78** B2
Sikasso Mali **90** B3
Sikeston U.S.A. **121** F3
Sikhote-Alin' *mts* Rus. Fed. **70** B2
Sikinos i. Greece **59** C3
Sikkim *state* India **79** C2
Silchar India **66** A1
Siletitengiz, Ozero *salt l.* Kazakh. **81** E1
Silgarhi Nepal **79** C2
Silifke Turkey **84** B2

Siling Co *salt l.* China **79** C1
Silistra Bulg. **58** C2
Siljan l. Sweden **41** C3
Sillamäe Estonia **36** C2
Šilobela S. Africa **99** C2
Šilutė Lith. **36** B2
Silvan Turkey **85** C2
Silver City U.S.A. **126** C2
Silverton U.S.A. **120** B3
Simao China **66** B1
Simard, Lac l. Can. **114** C2
Simav Turkey **59** C3
Simav Dağları *mts* Turkey **59** C3
Simba Dem. Rep. Congo **94** C3
Simcoe, Lake Can. **123** D2
Simeulue i. Indon. **64** A1
Simferopol' Ukr. **39** D3
Simleu Silvaniei Romania **38** B2
Şimonhouse Can. **113** E2
Simpson Desert Austr. **103** C2
Simrishamn Sweden **41** C4
Sinabang Indon. **64** A1
Sinai *pen.* Egypt **92** B2
Sinanju N. Korea **69** B2
Sinbo Myanmar **66** A1
Sincelejo Col. **134** B2
Sindor Rus. Fed. **34** E2
Sines Port. **54** B2
Sines, Cabo de c. Port. **54** B2
Singa Sudan **82** A3
Singahi India **70** C2
Singapore Asia **64** B1
Singapore *country* Asia **64** B1
Singaraja Indon. **65** C2
Singida Tanz. **95** D3
Singkang Indon. **68** D2
Singkawang Indon. **64** D1
Singkil Indon. **64** A1
Singleton Austr. **105** E2
Siniscola Italy **56** A2
Sinj Croatia **57** C2
Sinjai Indon. **65** D2
Sinkat Sudan **92** B3
Sinkiang *aut. reg.* China *see* Xinjiang Uygur Zizhiqu
Sinop Turkey **84** B1
Sinp'o N. Korea **69** B1
Sinsheim Ger. **49** D3
Sintang Indon. **65** C1
Sint Anthonis Neth. **48** B2
Sint Maarten i. Neth. Antilles **131** D3
Sint-Niklaas Belgium **48** B2
Sinton U.S.A. **127** E3
Sinŭiju N. Korea **69** A1
Siófok Hungary **51** D3
Sion Switz. **53** D2
Sioux Center U.S.A. **121** D2
Sioux City U.S.A. **121** D2
Sioux Falls U.S.A. **121** D2
Sioux Lookout Can. **114** A1
Siping China **69** A1
Sipiwesk Lake Can. **113** F2
Sīpura i. Indon. **64** A2

Sira r. Norway **41** B4
Sir Edward Pellew Group is Austr. **103** C1
Siri Kit Dam Thai. **66** B2
Sir James MacBrien, Mount Can. **112** C1
Sirjān Iran **85** D3
Şırnak Turkey **85** C2
Sirsa India **78** B2
Sirte Libya **91** D1
Sirte, Gulf of Libya **91** D1
Širvintos Lith. **36** E2
Sisal Mex. **129** C2
Sishen S. Africa **98** B2
Sisian Armenia **85** C2
Sisipuk Lake Can. **113** E2
Sisophon Cambodia **67** B2
Sisteron France **53** D3
Sitapur India **79** C2
Siteki Swaziland **99** D2
Sitka U.S.A. **112** B2
Sittard Neth. **48** B2
Sittwe Myanmar **66** A1
Situbondo Indon. **65** C2
Sivas Turkey **84** B2
Siverek Turkey **84** B2
Sivrihisar Turkey **84** B2
Sīwah Egypt **92** A2
Sīwah, Wāḥāt oasis Egypt **84** A3
Siwalik Range mts India/Nepal **78** B1
Siwa Oasis Egypt see Sīwah, Wāḥāt
Six-Fours-les-Plages France **53** D3
Siyabuswa S. Africa **99** C2
Skadovs'k Ukr. **39** D2
Skagen Denmark **41** C4
Skagerrak str. Denmark/Norway **41** B4
Skagit r. U.S.A. **118** B1
Skagway U.S.A. **112** B2
Skarżysko-Kamienna Pol. **51** E2
Skeena r. Can. **112** C2
Skeena Mountains Can. **112** C2
Skegness U.K. **46** D3
Skellefteå Sweden **40** E3
Skellefteälven r. Sweden **40** E3
Skerries Rep. of Ireland **45** C2
Skiathos i. Greece **59** B3
Skibbereen Rep. of Ireland **45** B3
Skiðadals-jökull glacier Iceland **40** [inset]
Skidday h. U.K. **46** B2
Skien Norway **41** C4
Skierniewice Pol. **51** E2
Skikda Alg. **91** C1
Skodje Norway **42** E1
Skopelos i. Greece **59** B3
Skopin Rus. Fed. **37** E3
Skopje Macedonia **58** B2
Skövde Sweden **41** C4
Skowhegan U.S.A. **123** G2

Skrunda Latvia **36** B2
Skukum, Mount Can. **112** B1
Skukuza S. Africa **99** D1
Skuodas Lith. **36** B2
Skye i. U.K. **44** A2
Skyros Greece **59** B3
Skyros i. Greece **59** B3
Slagelse Denmark **41** C4
Slaney r. Rep. of Ireland **45** C2
Slantsy Rus. Fed. **36** C2
Slatina Croatia **57** C1
Slatina Romania **38** B3
Slave r. Can. **113** D1
Slave Coast Africa **90** C4
Slave Lake Can. **112** D2
Slavgorod Rus. Fed. **81** E1
Slavonski Brod Croatia **57** C1
Slavuta Ukr. **38** C1
Slavutych Ukr. **38** D1
Slavyanka Rus. Fed. **70** B2
Slavyansk-na-Kubani Rus. Fed. **39** E2
Slawno Pol. **51** D2
Sea Head Rep. of Ireland **45** A2
Sleeper Islands Can. **114** C1
Slieve Donard h. U.K. **45** D1
Sligo Rep. of Ireland **45** B1
Sligo Bay Rep. of Ireland **45** B1
Slite Sweden **41** D4
Sliven Bulg. **58** C2
Slobozia Romania **38** C3
Slonim Belarus **36** C3
Sloten Neth. **48** B1
Slough U.K. **47** C4
Slovakia country Europe **51** D3
Slovenia country Europe **56** B1
Slov"yans'k Ukr. **39** E2
Sluch r. Ukr. **38** C1
Słupsk Pol. **51** D2
Slutsk Belarus **36** C3
Slyne Head Rep. of Ireland **45** A2
Smallwood Reservoir Can. **115** D1
Smalyavichy Belarus **36** C3
Smarhon' Belarus **36** C3
Smeaton Can. **113** E2
Smederevo S.M. **58** B2
Smederevska Palanka S.M. **58** B2
Smila Ukr. **39** D2
Smithers Can. **112** C2
Smithfield U.S.A. **125** E1
Smith Mountain Lake U.S.A. **123** E3
Smoky Hills U.S.A. **121** D3
Smola i. Norway **40** B3
Smolensk Rus. Fed. **37** D3
Smolyan Bulg. **58** B2
Smooth Rock Falls Can. **114** B2
Smyrna Turkey see İzmir
Snæfell mt. Iceland **40** [inset]
Snaefell h. Isle of Man **46** A2
Snake r. U.S.A. **118** C1
Snake River Plain U.S.A. **118** D2

Sneek Neth. **48** B1
Sneeuberge mts S. Africa **98** B3
Snežnik mt. Slovenia **56** B1
Snihurivka Ukr. **39** D2
Snøhetta mt. Norway **41** B3
Snowbird Lake Can. **113** E1
Snowdon mt. U.K. **46** A3
Snowdrift r. Can. **113** D1
Snow Lake Can. **113** E2
Snowtown Austr. **104** B2
Snowy r. Austr. **105** D3
Snowy Mountains Austr. **105** D3
Snyder U.S.A. **127** D2
Soalala Madag. **97** [inset] D1
Sobat r. Sudan **93** B4
Sobernheim Ger. **48** C3
Sobinka Rus. Fed. **37** F2
Sobradinho, Barragem de resr Brazil **135** E4
Sobral Brazil **135** E3
Sochi Rus. Fed. **39** E3
Söch'ŏn S. Korea **69** B2
Society Islands Fr. Polynesia **143** E6
Socorro U.S.A. **126** C2
Socorro, Isla i. Mex. **128** A3
Socotra i. Yemen **83** C3
Soc Trăng Vietnam **67** B3
Socuéllamos Spain **54** C2
Sodankylä Fin. **40** F2
Soda Springs U.S.A. **118** D2
Söderhamn Sweden **41** D3
Södertälje Sweden **41** D4
Sodiri Sudan **92** A3
Sodo Eth. **93** B4
Södra Kvarken str. Fin./Sweden **41** D3
Soest Ger. **48** D2
Sofia Bulg. **58** B2
Sofiya Bulg. see Sofia
Sofporog Rus. Fed. **40** G2
Sōfu-gan i. Japan **71** D5
Sog China **72** C2
Sognefjorden inlet Norway **41** A3
Soignies Belgium **48** B2
Soissons France **53** C2
Sokal' Ukr. **38** C1
Söke Turkey **59** C3
Sokhumi Georgia **85** C1
Sokodé Togo **90** C4
Sokol Rus. Fed. **37** F2
Sokolov Czech Rep. **49** F2
Sokoto Nigeria **91** C3
Sokyryany Ukr. **38** C2
Solapur India **77** B3
Soledad U.S.A. **119** B3
Solihull U.K. **47** C3
Solikamsk Rus. Fed. **34** E3
Sol'-Iletsk Rus. Fed. **34** E3
Solingen Ger. **48** C2
Solitaire Namibia **98** A1
Sollefteå Sweden **40** D3
Sollentuna Sweden **41** D4
Solling hills Ger. **49** D2

Solnechnogorsk Rus. Fed. **37** E2
Solok Indon. **64** B2
Solomon Islands country
  S. Pacific Ocean **100**
Solomon Sea S. Pacific Ocean
  142 D5
Solothurn Switz. **53** D2
Soltau Ger. **49** D1
Sol'tsy Rus. Fed. **38** B1
Solway Firth est. U.K. **44** C3
Solwezi Zambia **96** B1
Soma Turkey **59** C3
Somalia country Africa **93** C4
Sombo Angola **94** C3
Sombor S.M. **58** A1
Sombrerete Mex. **128** B2
Somerset U.S.A. **122** D3
Somerset Island Can. **110** F2
Somerset West S. Africa **98** A3
Sömmerda Ger. **49** E2
Son r. India **79** C2
Sønderborg Denmark **41** B5
Sønderborg Denmark **41** B5
Sondershausen Ger. **49** E2
Song Da r. Vietnam see
  Black River
Songea Tanz. **95** D4
Sŏnggan N. Korea **69** B1
Songhua Hu resr China **69** B1
Songkhla Thai. **67** B3
Sŏngnam S. Korea **69** B2
Songnim N. Korea **69** B2
Songo Angola **94** B3
Songo Moz. **97** C1
Sonkovo Rus. Fed. **37** E2
Son La Vietnam **66** B1
Sonmiani Pak. **78** A2
Sonneberg Ger. **49** E2
Sonora r. Mex. **128** A2
Sonora CA U.S.A. **119** B3
Sonora TX U.S.A. **127** D2
Sopo watercourse Sudan **93** A4
Sopron Hungary **51** D3
Sora Italy **56** B2
Sorel Can. **114** C2
Sorell Austr. **103** D4
Soria Spain **54** C1
Soroca Moldova **38** C2
Sorocaba Brazil **138** C2
Sorol atoll Micronesia **63** D2
Sorong Indon. **63** C3
Soroti Uganda **95** D2
Sørøya i. Norway **40** E1
Sorsele Sweden **40** D2
Sorsogon Phil. **68** B2
Sortavala Rus. Fed. **41** G3
Sortland Norway **40** D2
Sösan S. Korea **69** B2
Soshanguve S. Africa **99** C2
Sosna r. Rus. Fed. **37** E3
Sosnogorsk Rus. Fed. **34** E2
Sosnovka Tambovskaya Oblast'
  Rus. Fed. **37** F3
Sosnovyy Bor Rus. Fed. **36** C2
Sosnowiec Pol. **51** D2

Sosyka r. Rus. Fed **39** E2
Soto la Marina Mex. **129** C2
Souanké Congo **94** B3
Sougueur Alg. **55** D2
Souillac France **52** C3
Soul S. Korea see Seoul
Soulac-sur-Mer France **52** B2
Sour el Ghozlane Alg. **55** D2
Souris r. Can. **120** D1
Sousa Brazil **135** F3
Sousse Tunisia **91** D1
South Africa, Republic of coun-
  try Africa **98** B3
Southampton U.K. **47** C4
Southampton, Cape Can.
  113 G1
Southampton Island Can.
  113 G1
South Andaman i. India **67** A2
South Australia state Austr.
  104 A2
South Bend U.S.A. **122** C2
South Carolina state U.S.A.
  125 D2
South China Sea
  N. Pacific Ocean **62** B2
South Dakota state U.S.A.
  120 C2
South Downs hills U.K. **47** C4
South East Cape Austr. **110**
Southend Can. **110** C2
Southend-on-Sea U.K. **47** D4
Southern Alps mts N.Z. **106** B3
Southern Cross Austr. **102** A3
Southern Indian Lake Can.
  113 F2
Southern Pines U.S.A. **125** E1
Southern Uplands hills U.K.
  44 B3
South Geomagnetic Pole
  Antarctica **107** F1
South Georgia i.
  S. Atlantic Ocean **137** E6
South Georgia and South
  Sandwich Islands terr.
  S. Atlantic Ocean **133**
South Henik Lake Can. **113** F1
South Island N.Z. **106** B3
South Korea country Asia **69** B2
South Lake Tahoe U.S.A. **119** B3
South Magnetic Pole Antarctica
  107 G3
South Orkney Islands
  S. Atlantic Ocean **107** A3
South Platte r. U.S.A. **120** C2
South Pole Antarctica **107**
Southport U.K. **46** B3
Southport U.S.A. **125** E2
South Ronaldsay i. U.K. **44** C1
South Sandwich Islands
  S. Atlantic Ocean **147**
South Saskatchewan r. Can.
  113 F2
South Seal r. Can. **113** F2

South Shetland Islands
  Antarctica **107** A3
South Shields U.K. **46** C2
South Taranaki Bight b. N.Z.
  106 B2
South Twin Island Can. **114** C1
South Uist i. U.K. **44** A2
South West Rocks Austr. **105** E2
Southwold U.K. **47** D3
Soverato Italy **57** C3
Sovetsk Rus. Fed. **36** B2
Sovetskiy Khanty-Mansiyskiy
  Avtonomnyy Okrug Rus. Fed.
  34 F2
Sovyets'kyy Ukr. **39** D2
Soweto S. Africa **99** C2
Sōya-misaki c. Japan **70** D1
Sozh r. Europe **39** D1
Sozopol Bulg. **58** C2
Spain country Europe **54** C1
Spalding U.K. **46** C3
Spanish Fork U.S.A. **118** D2
Sparks U.S.A. **119** C3
Sparta U.S.A. **122** B2
Spartanburg U.S.A. **125** D2
Sparti Greece **59** B3
Spartivento, Capo c. Italy **57** C3
Spas-Demensk Rus. Fed. **37** D3
Spas-Klepiki Rus. Fed. **37** F2
Spassk-Dal'niy Rus. Fed. **70** B2
Spatha, Akra pt Greece **59** B3
Spearfish U.S.A. **120** C2
Spencer U.S.A. **127** D2
Spencer Gulf est. Austr. **104** B2
Spennymoor U.K. **46** C2
Spenser Mountains N.Z. **106** B3
Spessart reg. Ger. **49** D3
Spey r. U.K. **44** C2
Speyer Ger. **49** D3
Spiekeroog i. Ger. **40** C1
Spijkenisse Neth. **48** B2
Spirit River Can. **112** D2
Spitsbergen i. Svalbard **86** D1
Spittal an der Drau Austria
  50 C3
Split Croatia **57** C2
Split Lake Can. **113** F2
Split Lake i. Can. **113** F2
Spokane U.S.A. **118** C1
Spoleto Italy **56** B2
Spooner U.S.A. **122** B1
Spree r. Ger. **50** C2
Springbok S. Africa **98** A2
Springdale Can. **115** E2
Springdale U.S.A. **124** B1
Springe Ger. **49** D1
Springer U.S.A. **126** D1
Springerville U.S.A. **126** B2
Springfield CO U.S.A. **120** C3
Springfield IL U.S.A. **122** C3
Springfield MA U.S.A. **123** F2
Springfield MO U.S.A. **121** E3
Springfield OH U.S.A. **122** D3
Springfield OR U.S.A. **118** B2

Springfontein S. Africa **99** C3
Spring Hill U.S.A. **125** D3
Springs Junction N.Z. **106** B3
Spurn Head U.K. **46** D3
Squamish Can. **112** C3
Squillace, Golfo di g. Italy **57** C3
Srbija aut. rep. S.M. **58** D2
Srebrenica Bos.-Herz. **57** C2
Sredets Bulg. **58** C2
Sredinnyy Khrebet mts Rus. Fed. **87** M3
Sredne-Russkaya Vozvyshennost' hills Rus. Fed.
see **Central Russian Upland**
Srednogorie Bulg. **58** B2
Sretensk Rus. Fed. **73** J1
Sri Aman Malaysia **65** C1
Sri Jayewardenepura Kotte
Sri Lanka **77** C4
Srikakulam India **77** D3
Sri Lanka country Asia **77** C4
Srinagar India **78** B1
Sri Pada mt. Sri Lanka **77** C4
Stade Ger. **49** D1
Stadensen Ger. **49** E1
Stadskanaal Neth. **48** C1
Stadtallendorf Ger. **49** D2
Stadthagen Ger. **49** D1
Staffelstein Ger. **49** E2
Stafford U.K. **46** B3
Staines U.K. **47** C4
Stakhanov Ukr. **39** E2
Stalingrad Rus. Fed. see
Volgograd
Stalowa Wola Pol. **51** E2
Stamford U.K. **47** C3
Stamford CT U.S.A. **123** F2
Stamford TX U.S.A. **127** D2
Stampriet Namibia **98** A1
Standish U.S.A. **122** D2
Stanger S. Africa **99** E2
Staňkov Czech Rep. **49** F3
Stanley Falkland Is **137** C6
Stanley U.S.A. **120** C1
Stanovoye Nagor'ye mts
Rus. Fed. **87** J3
Stanovoy Khrebet mts Rus. Fed.
87 K3
Stanthorpe Austr. **105** E1
Starachowice Pol. **51** E2
Stara Planina mts Bulg./S.M. see
Balkan Mountains
Staraya Russa Rus. Fed. **37** D2
Staraya Toropa Rus. Fed. **37** D2
Stara Zagora Bulg. **58** C2
Stargard Szczeciński Pol. **51** D2
Starkville U.S.A. **124** C2
Starobil's'k Ukr. **39** E2
Starodub Rus. Fed. **37** D3
Starogard Gdański Pol. **51** D2
Starokostyantyniv Ukr. **38** C2
Starominskaya Rus. Fed. **39** E2
Staroshcherbinovskaya
Rus. Fed. **39** E2

Starotitarovskaya Rus. Fed.
39 E2
Start Point U.K. **47** B4
Staryya Darohi Belarus **36** C3
Staryy Oskol Rus. Fed. **37** E3
Staßfurt Ger. **49** E2
State College U.S.A. **123** E2
Statesboro U.S.A. **125** D2
Statesville U.S.A. **125** D1
Stavanger Norway **41** B4
Stavropol' Rus. Fed. **35** D4
Stavropol'skaya Vozvyshennost'
hills Rus. Fed. **35** D4
Stawell Austr. **104** C3
Steamboat Springs U.S.A.
120 B2
Steen River Can. **112** D2
Steens Mountain U.S.A. **118** C2
Steenwijk Neth. **48** C1
Stefansson Island Can. **110** E2
Steigerwald mts Ger. **49** E3
Steinbach Can. **113** F3
Steinfurt Ger. **48** C1
Steinhausen Namibia **96** A2
Steinkjer Norway **40** C3
Steinkopf S. Africa **98** A2
Stella S. Africa **98** D2
Stendal Ger. **49** E1
Stephenville Can. **115** E2
Stephenville U.S.A. **127** E2
Sterling S. Africa **98** B3
Sterling CO U.S.A. **120** C2
Sterlitamak Rus. Fed. **35** E3
Steubenville U.S.A. **123** D2
Stevenage U.K. **47** C4
Stevenson Lake Can. **113** F2
Stevens Village U.S.A. **110** C2
Stewart Can. **112** C2
Stewart r. Can. **112** B1
Stewart Island N.Z. **106** A4
Steyr Austria **50** C3
Steytlerville S. Africa **98** B3
Stikine r. Can. **112** B2
Stikine Plateau Can. **112** B2
Stilbaai S. Africa **98** B3
Stillwater U.S.A. **127** E1
Štip Macedonia **57** D2
Stirling U.K. **44** C2
Stjørdalshalsen Norway **40** C3
Stockholm Sweden **41** D4
Stockport U.K. **46** B3
Stockton U.S.A. **119** B3
Stockton-on-Tees U.K. **46** C2
Stôeng Trêng Cambodia **67** B2
Stoke-on-Trent U.K. **46** B3
Stol mt. S.M. **58** B2
Stolberg (Rheinland) Ger. **48** C2
Stolbovoy Rus. Fed. **34** C1
Stolin Belarus **36** C3
Stollberg Ger. **49** F2
Stolzenau Ger. **49** D1
Stonehaven U.K. **44** C2
Stony Rapids Can. **110** E3

Storavan l. Sweden **40** D2
Store Bælt sea chan. Denmark
see **Great Belt**
Støren Norway **40** C3
Storkerson Peninsula Can.
110 E2
Storm Lake U.S.A. **121** D3
Stornoway U.K. **44** A1
Storozhevsk Rus. Fed. **34** E2
Storozhynets' Ukr. **38** C2
Storsjön l. Sweden **40** C3
Storslett Norway **40** D2
Storuman Sweden **40** D2
Stour r. England U.K. **47** C3
Stour r. England U.K. **47** C4
Stout Lake Can. **114** A1
Stowbtsy Belarus **36** C3
Strabane U.K. **45** C1
Strakonice Czech Rep. **50** C3
Stralsund Ger. **50** C2
Stranda Norway **41** B3
Strangford Lough inlet U.K.
45 D1
Stranraer U.K. **44** C3
Strasbourg France **53** D2
Strasburg Ger. **49** F1
Stratford Can. **123** D2
Stratford N.Z. **106** B2
Stratford U.S.A. **127** D1
Stratford-upon-Avon U.K. **47** C3
Strathspey val. U.K. **44** C2
Straubing Ger. **50** C3
Strausberg Ger. **49** F1
Streaky Bay Austr. **104** A2
Streator U.S.A. **122** C2
Strehaia Romania **38** B3
Strÿder Arg. **137** B5
Ströhen Ger. **49** D1
Stromboli, Isola i. Italy **56** C3
Stromness U.K. **44** C1
Strömsund Sweden **40** D3
Stronsay i. U.K. **44** C1
Stroud Austr. **105** E2
Stroud U.K. **47** B4
Struga Macedonia **59** B2
Strugi-Krasnyye Rus. Fed. **36** C2
Struis Bay S. Africa **98** B3
Strumica Macedonia **59** B2
Strydenburg S. Africa **98** B2
Stryy Ukr. **38** B2
Stuart Lake Can. **112** C2
Stull Lake Can. **113** F2
Stupino Rus. Fed. **37** E3
Sturgeon Lake Can. **114** A2
Sturgis SD U.S.A. **120** C2
Sturt Creek watercourse Austr.
102 B1
Sturt Stony Desert Austr.
104 C1
Stutterheim S. Africa **99** C3
Stuttgart Ger. **50** B3
Stuttgart U.S.A. **124** B2
Stykkishólmur Iceland **40** [inset]
Styr r. Belarus/Ukr. **38** C1

Suaçuí Grande r. Brazil 139 D1
Suakin Sudan 92 B3
Suao Taiwan 71 C4
Subotica S.M. 58 A1
Suceava Romania 38 C2
Suck r. Rep. of Ireland 45 D2
Sucre Bol. 136 B2
Sucuriú r. Brazil 138 B2
Suda Rus. Fed. 37 E2
Sudak Ukr. 39 D3
Sudan country Africa 93 A3
Sudbury Can. 114 B2
Sudd swamp Sudan 93 A4
Sudety mts Czech Rep./Pol. 36
Sudogda Rus. Fed. 37 F2
Suðuroy i. Faroe Is 42 B1
Sueca Spain 55 C2
Suez Egypt 82 B2
Suez, Gulf of Egypt 82 B2
Suez Canal Egypt 82 B2
Suffolk U.S.A. 123 E3
Şuḩār Oman 83 C2
Suhl Ger. 49 E2
Suide China 74 B2
Suifenhe China 70 E2
Suihua China 73 E1
Suining China 74 B2
Suiping China 74 B2
Suiyang China 74 B2
Suizhou China 74 B2
Sujangarh India 78 B2
Sujanpur India 78 B1
Sujawal Pak. 78 A2
Sukabumi Indon. 64 B2
Sukadana Indon. 65 B2
Sukaraja Indon. 65 C2
Sukhinichi Rus. Fed. 37 E3
Sukhona r. Rus. Fed. 37 F2
Sukhothai Thai. 66 A2
Sukkur Pak. 78 A2
Sula i. Norway 42 D1
Sula, Kepulauan is Indon. 63 C3
Sulaiman Range mts Pak. 78 A1
Sulawesi i. Indon. see Celebes
Sullana Peru 134 A3
Sullivan U.S.A. 121 E3
Sulphur Springs U.S.A. 127 C2
Sulu Archipelago is Phil. 68 B3
Sulu Sea N. Pacific Ocean 68 A3
Sulzbach-Rosenberg Ger. 49 E3
Sumāil Oman 83 C2
Sumatera i. Indon. see Sumatra
Sumatra i. Indon. 64 A1
Šumava mts Czech Rep. 49 F3
Sumba i. Indon. 65 C2
Sumba, Selat sea chan. Indon.
65 C2
Sumbawa i. Indon. 65 C2
Sumbawanga Tanz. 95 D3
Sumbe Angola 96 A1
Sumburgh U.K. 44 [inset]
Sumburgh Head U.K. 44 [inset]
Sumenep Indon. 65 C2

Sumisu-jima i. Japan 71 D4
Summerside Can. 115 D2
Summit Lake Can. 112 C2
Šumperk Czech Rep. 51 D3
Sumqayıt Azer. 85 C1
Sumter U.S.A. 125 D2
Sumy Ukr. 39 D1
Sunan N. Korea 69 B2
Sunaynah Oman 83 C2
Sunbury Austr. 104 C3
Sunch'ŏn N. Korea 69 B2
Sunch'ŏn S. Korea 69 B3
Sun City S. Africa 99 C2
Sunda, Selat str. Indon. 64 B2
Sundance U.S.A. 120 C2
Sundarbans coastal area
Bangl./India 79 C2
Sunderland U.K. 46 C2
Sundsvall Sweden 41 D3
Sundumbili S. Africa 99 D2
Sungailiat Indon. 64 B2
Sungaipenuh Indon. 64 B2
Sungai Petani Malaysia 64 A1
Sungurlu Turkey 84 B1
Sunndal Norway 42 E1
Sunndalsøra Norway 40 B3
Sunnyside U.S.A. 118 C1
Sunnyvale U.S.A. 119 B3
Sunyani Ghana 90 B4
Superior NE U.S.A. 121 D2
Superior WI U.S.A. 122 B1
Superior, Lake Can./U.S.A.
122 C1
Suponevo Rus. Fed. 37 D3
Süq ash Shuyūkh Iraq 85 C2
Suqian China 74 B2
Şūq Suwayq Saudi Arabia 82 A2
Suqutrā i. Yemen see Socotra
Şūr Oman 83 C2
Şūr, Punta pt Arg. 147
Surab Pak. 78 A2
Surabaya Indon. 65 C2
Surakarta Indon. 65 C2
Surat India 78 B2
Suratgarh India 78 B2
Surat Thani Thai. 67 A3
Surazh Rus. Fed. 37 D3
Surdulica S.M. 58 B2
Surendranagar India 78 B2
Surgut Rus. Fed. 34 I2
Surigao Phil. 68 B3
Surin Thai. 67 B2
Suriname country S. America
135 D2
Surulangun Indon. 64 B2
Susanino Rus. Fed. 37 F2
Susanville U.S.A. 118 B2
Suşehri Turkey 84 B1
Sušice Czech Rep. 49 F3
Sussex U.S.A. 115 C2
Süstedt Ger. 49 D1
Susuman Rus. Fed. 87 L2
Susurluk Turkey 59 C3
Sutak Jammu and Kashmir 79 B1

Sutherland S. Africa 98 B3
Sutton Coldfield U.K. 47 C3
Suttsu Japan 70 D2
Suva Fiji 100
Suwałki Pol. 51 E2
Suwannaphum Thai. 67 B2
Suwannee r. U.S.A. 125 D3
Suwarrow atoll Cook Is 111
Suways, Qanāt as canal Egypt
see Suez Canal
Suwŏn S. Korea 69 B2
Suya Rus. Fed. 37 F2
Suzhou Anhui China 74 B2
Suzhou Jiangsu China 74 C2
Suzu Japan 71 C3
Suzu-misaki pt Japan 71 C3
Svalbard terr. Arctic Ocean 86 C1
Svatove Ukr. 39 E2
Svay Riĕng Cambodia 67 B2
Sveg Sweden 41 C3
Svelgen Norway 42 E1
Švenčionys Lith. 36 C2
Sverdlovsk Rus. Fed. see
Yekaterinburg
Svetlaya Rus. Fed. 70 C1
Svetlogorsk Rus. Fed. 36 B3
Svetlyy Rus. Fed. 36 B3
Svetogorsk Rus. Fed. 41 F3
Svinecea Mare, Vârful mt.
Romania 90 D3
Svir' r. Rus. Fed. 37 E1
Svishtov Bulg. 58 C2
Svitavy Czech Rep. 51 D3
Svitlovods'k Ukr. 39 D2
Svobodnyy Rus. Fed. 73 E1
Svolvær Norway 40 C2
Svyetlahorsk Belarus 37 C3
Swakop watercourse Namibia
98 A1
Swakopmund Namibia 96 A1
Swan Hill Austr. 104 C3
Swan Lake Can. 113 E2
Swan River Can. 113 E2
Swansea U.K. 47 B4
Swatow China see Shantou
Swaziland country Africa 99 D2
Sweden country Europe 41 C3
Sweetwater U.S.A. 127 C2
Sweetwater r. U.S.A. 120 B2
Swellendam S. Africa 98 B3
Świdnica Pol. 51 D2
Świdwin Pol. 51 D2
Świebodzin Pol. 51 D2
Świecie Pol. 51 D2
Swift Current Can. 110 E3
Swindon U.K. 47 C4
Świnoujście Pol. 50 C2
Switzerland country Europe
53 D2
Swords Rep. of Ireland 45 C2
Syanno Belarus 36 C3
Sychevka Rus. Fed. 37 D2

Sydney Austr. **105** E2
Sydney Can. **115** D2
Sydney Mines Can. **115** D2
Syeverodonets'k Ukr. **39** E2
Syktyvkar Rus. Fed. **34** E2
Sylacauga U.S.A. **125** C2
Sylhet Bangl. **79** D2
Sylt *i.* Ger. **50** B2
Symi *i.* Greece **59** C3
Syracuse Italy **56** C3
Syracuse *NY* U.S.A. **123** E2
Syrdar'ya *r.* Asia **81** D2
Syria *country* Asia **84** B2
Syrian Desert Asia **84** B2
Syros *i.* Greece **59** B3
Syzran' Rus. Fed. **35** D3
Szczecin Pol. **50** C2
Szczecinek Pol. **51** D2
Szczytno Pol. **51** E2
Szeged Hungary **51** E3
Székesfehérvár Hungary **51** D3
Szekszárd Hungary **51** D3
Szigetvár Hungary **51** D3
Szolnok Hungary **51** E3
Szombathely Hungary **51** D3

T

Tabas Iran **85** D2
Tābask, Kūh-e *mt.* Iran **85** D3
Tabelbala Alg. **90** B2
Taber Can. **113** D3
Tábor Czech Rep. **50** C3
Tabora Tanz. **95** D3
Tabou Côte d'Ivoire **90** B4
Tabrīz Iran **85** C2
Tabūk Saudi Arabia **82** A2
Täby Sweden **36** A2
Tacheng China **81** F2
Tachov Czech Rep. **50** C3
Tacloban Phil. **68** B2
Tacna Peru **134** B4
Tacoma U.S.A. **118** B1
Tacuarembó Uru. **136** C4
Tacupeto Mex. **120** C2
Tadjoura Djibouti **93** C3
Tadmur Syria **84** B2
Tadoule Lake Can. **113** F2
Taegu S. Korea **69** B2
Taejŏn S. Korea **69** B2
Ta'erqi China **73** E1
Tafalla Spain **55** C1
Tafí Viejo Arg. **136** B3
Taftān, Kūh-e *mt.* Iran **83** D2
Taganrog Rus. Fed. **39** E2
Taganrog, Gulf of Rus. Fed./Ukr. **39** E2
Tagbilaran Phil. **68** B3
Tagum Phil. **68** B3
Tagus *r.* Port. **54** B2

Tagus *r.* Spain **54** B2
Tahan, Gunung *mt.* Malaysia **64** B1
Tahat, Mont *mt.* Alg. **91** C2
Tahe China **73** E1
Tahiti *i.* Fr. Polynesia **111**
Tahlequah U.S.A. **127** F1
Tahoe, Lake U.S.A. **119** B3
Tahoe City U.S.A. **119** B3
Tahoua Niger **91** C3
Tahrūd Iran **83** C2
Tahsis Can. **112** C3
Tai'an China **74** B2
T'aichung Taiwan **75** C3
Taihape N.Z. **106** C2
Tailem Bend Austr. **104** B3
T'ainan Taiwan **75** C3
Taiobeiras Brazil **139** D1
T'aipei Taiwan **75** C3
Taiping Malaysia **64** B1
Taishan China **75** B3
T'aitung Taiwan **75** C3
Taivalkoski Fin. **40** F2
Taivaskero *h.* Fin. **40** E2
Taiwan *country* Asia **75** C3
Taiwan Strait China/Taiwan **75** B3
Taiyuan China **74** B2
Taizhou *Jiangsu* China **74** B2
Taizhou *Zhejiang* China **75** C3
Ta'izz Yemen **82** B3
Tajamulco, Volcán de *vol.* Guat. **129** C3
Tajikistan *country* Asia **81** E3
Taj Mahal *tourist site* India **79** B2
Tajo *r.* Spain *see* Tagus
Tak Thai. **66** A2
Takaka N.Z. **106** B3
Takamatsu Japan **71** B4
Takaoka Japan **71** C3
Takapuna N.Z. **106** B2
Takasaki Japan **71** C3
Takatokwane Botswana **98** B1
Takatshwaane *Ghanzi* Botswana **98** B1
Takayama Japan **71** C3
Takengon Indon. **64** A1
Takêv Cambodia **67** B2
Takhemaret Alg. **55** D2
Takikawa Japan **70** D2
Takla Landing Can. **112** C2
Takla Makan des. China **81** F3
Taklimakan Desert China **81** F3
Taklimakan Shamo des. China *see* Taklimakan Desert
Taku *r.* Can./U.S.A. **112** B2
Takua Pa Thai. **67** A3
Talachyn Belarus **36** C3
Talara Peru **134** A3
Talaud, Kepulauan *is* Indon. **63** C2
Talavera de la Reina Spain **54** C2
Talca Chile **137** A4

Talcahuano Chile **137** A4
Taldom Rus. Fed. **37** E2
Taldykorgan Kazakh. **81** E2
Talia Austr. **104** A2
Talisay Phil. **68** B2
Taliwang Indon. **65** C2
Tall 'Afar Iraq **85** C2
Tallahassee U.S.A. **125** D2
Tallinn Estonia **36** B2
Tallulah U.S.A. **124** B2
Tal'ne Ukr. **38** D2
Talodi Sudan **93** B3
Tāloqān Afgh. **78** A1
Talovaya Rus. Fed. **37** F3
Taloyoak Can. **110** F2
Talsi Latvia **36** B2
Taltal Chile **136** A3
Taltson *r.* Can. **113** D1
Talu Indon. **64** A1
Talwood Austr. **105** D1
Tamala Rus. Fed. **39** F1
Tamale Ghana **90** B4
Tamanrasset Alg. **91** C2
Tamar *r.* U.K. **47** A4
Tambacounda Senegal **90** A3
Tambelan, Kepulauan *is* Indon. **64** B1
Tambey Rus. Fed. **34** G1
Tambov Rus. Fed. **37** F3
Tamiahua, Laguna de *lag.* Mex. **129** C2
Tampa U.S.A. **125** D3
Tampa Bay U.S.A. **125** D3
Tampere Fin. **41** E3
Tampico Mex. **129** C2
Tamworth Austr. **105** E2
Tamworth U.K. **47** C3
Tana *r.* Kenya **95** E3
Tana, Lake Eth. **93** B3
Tanabe Japan **71** C4
Tana Bru Norway **40** F1
Tanahgrogot Indon. **65** C2
Tanahjampea *i.* Indon. **65** D2
Tanami Desert Austr. **102** C1
Tanaro *r.* Italy **56** A1
Tanch'ŏn N. Korea **69** B1
Tandag Phil. **68** B3
Țăndărei Romania **38** C3
Tandil Arg. **137** C4
Tando Adam Pak. **78** A2
Tando Muhammad Khan Pak. **78** A2
Tanezrouft *reg.* Alg./Mali **90** B2
Tanga Tanz. **95** D3
Tanganyika, Lake Africa **95** C3
Tanger Morocco *see* Tangier
Tangermünde Ger. **49** E1
Tanggula Shan *mt.* China **79** D1
Tanggula Shan *mts* China **79** C1
Tangier Morocco **90** B1
Tangra Yumco *salt l.* China **79** C1
Tangshan China **74** B2
Taniantaweng Shan *mts* China **72** C2

Tanimbar, Kepulauan is Indon. 63 C3
Tanjay Phil. 68 B3
Tanjungbalai Indon. 64 A1
Tanjungpandan Indon. 64 B2
Tanjungpinang Indon. 64 B1
Tanjungredeb Indon. 65 C1
Tanjungselor Indon. 65 C1
Tanna i. Vanuatu 110
Tanout Niger 91 C3
Tansen Nepal 79 C2
Tanța Egypt 92 B1
Tanzania country Africa 95 D3
Taoudenni Mali 90 B2
Tapa Estonia 36 C2
Tapachula Mex. 129 C3
Tapajós r. Brazil 135 D3
Tapaktuan Indon. 64 A1
Tapauá Brazil 134 C3
Tapeta Liberia 90 B4
Tapi r. India 78 B2
Tapurucuara Brazil 104 C3
Taquari r. Brazil 138 A1
Taquari, Pantanal do marsh Brazil 138 A1
Taquari, Serra de hills Brazil 138 B1
Taquaritinga Brazil 138 C2
Tarābulus Libya see Tripoli
Tarakan Indon. 65 C1
Taran, Mys of Rus. Fed. 36 A3
Taranaki, Mount vol. N.Z. 106 B2
Tarancón Spain 53 E3
Taranto Italy 57 C2
Taranto, Golfo di g. Italy 57 C2
Tarapoto Peru 134 B3
Tarasovskiy Rus. Fed. 39 F2
Tarauacá Brazil 134 B3
Tarauacá r. Brazil 134 C3
Tarawa atoll Kiribati 111
Taraz Kazakh. 81 E2
Tarazona Spain 55 C1
Tarbagatay, Khrebet mts Kazakh. 81 F2
Tarbert Scotland U.K. 44 B3
Tarbert Scotland U.K. 44 A3
Tarbes France 52 C3
Tarcoola Austr. 104 A2
Taree Austr. 105 E2
Târgovişte Romania 38 C3
Targuist Morocco 54 C3
Târgu Jiu Romania 38 B2
Târgu Mureş Romania 38 C2
Târgu Neamţ Romania 38 C2
Tarif U.A.E. 83 C2
Tarija Bol. 136 B3
Tarim Yemen 83 B3
Tarim Basin China 87 F3
Tarim He r. China 81 F1
Tarim Pendi basin China see Tarim Basin
Taritatu r. Indon. 63 D3
Tarko-Sale Rus. Fed. 34 G2

Tarlac Phil. 68 B2
Tärnaby Sweden 40 D2
Tarnak r. Afgh. 78 A1
Târnăveni Romania 38 B2
Tarnobrzeg Pol. 51 E2
Tarnów Pol. 51 E2
Taroudannt Morocco 90 B1
Tarquinia Italy 56 B2
Tarragona Spain 55 D1
Tàrrega Spain 55 D1
Tarso Turkey 84 B2
Tartagal Arg. 136 B3
Tartu Estonia 36 C2
Tartūs Syria 84 B2
Tarumirim Brazil 139 D1
Tasian, Lac l. Can. 114 C1
Tasiujaq Can. 115 D1
Taskesken Kazakh. 81 F2
Tasman Bay N.Z. 106 B3
Tasmania i. Austr. 110
Tasmania state Austr. 103 D4
Tasman Mountains N.Z. 106 B3
Tasman Sea S. Pacific Ocean 110
Tassili du Hoggar plat. Alg. 91 C2
Tassili n'Ajjer plat. Alg. 91 C2
Tatabánya Hungary 51 D3
Tatarbunary Ukr. 38 C2
Tatarskiy Proliv str. Rus. Fed. 73 F1
Tathlina Lake Can. 112 D1
Tathidh Saudi Arabia 82 B3
Tathlith, Wādī watercourse Saudi Arabia 82 B2
Tathra Austr. 105 D3
Tatkon Myanmar 66 A1
Tatra Mountains mts Slovakia 51 D3
Tatta Pak. 78 A2
Tatui Brazil 138 C2
Tatum U.S.A. 127 D2
Tatvan Turkey 85 C2
Taua Brazil 135 D3
Taubaté Brazil 139 C2
Taubenbischofsheim Ger. 49 D3
Taumarunui N.Z. 106 C2
Taung S. Africa 98 C2
Taung-ngu Myanmar 66 A2
Taungup Myanmar 66 A2
Taunton U.K. 47 B4
Taunus hills Ger. 48 C3
Taupo N.Z. 106 C2
Taupo, Lake N.Z. 106 C2
Tauragė Lith. 36 B2
Tauranga N.Z. 106 C2
Taurus Mountains Turkey 84 B2
Tavas Turkey 59 C3
Tavda Rus. Fed. 34 F3

Tavistock U.K. 47 A4
Tavoy Myanmar 67 A2
Tavşanlı Turkey 59 C3
Taw r. U.K. 47 A4
Tawas City U.S.A. 122 C2
Tawau Malaysia 65 C1
Tawitawi i. Phil. 68 A3
Taxco Mex. 129 C3
Taxiatosh Uzbek. 80 C2
Taxkorgan China 81 E3
Tay r. U.K. 44 C2
Tay, Firth of est. U.K. 44 C2
Tay, Loch l. U.K. 44 B2
Taylor U.S.A. 127 E2
Taylorville U.S.A. 122 C3
Taymā' Saudi Arabia 82 A2
Taymyr, Ozero l. Rus. Fed. 87 I2
Taymyr, Poluostrov pen. Rus. Fed. see Taymyr Peninsula
Taymyr Peninsula Rus. Fed. 87 H2
Tây Ninh Vietnam 67 B2
Taytay Phil. 68 A2
Taz r. Rus. Fed. 34 G2
Taza Morocco 90 B1
Tazin Lake Can. 113 E2
Tazoult Lambèse Alg. 55 E2
T'bilisi Georgia 85 C1
Tbilisskaya Rus. Fed. 39 F2
Tchibanga Gabon 94 B3
Tczew Pol. 51 D2
Te Anau N.Z. 106 A4
Te Anau, Lake N.Z. 106 A4
Teapa Mex. 129 C3
Te Awamutu N.Z. 106 C2
Tébessa Alg. 91 C1
Tebingtinggi Sumatera Utara Indon. 64 A1
Techiman Ghana 90 B4
Tecomán Mex. 128 B3
Tecoripa Mex. 128 B2
Técpan Mex. 129 B3
Tecuala Mex. 128 B2
Tecuci Romania 38 C2
Tedzhen Turkm. 80 D3
Teeli Rus. Fed. 81 G1
Tees r. U.K. 46 C2
Tefenni Turkey 59 C3
Tegal Indon. 64 B2
Tegucigalpa Hond. 130 B3
Teguidda-n-Tessoum Niger 91 C3
Tehek Lake Can. 113 F1
Tehrān Iran 85 D2
Tehuacán Mex. 129 C3
Tehuantepec, Golfo de g. Mex. 129 C3
Tehuantepec, Istmo de isth. Mex. 129 C3
Teifi r. U.K. 47 A3
Tejo r. Port. see Tagus
Tekapo, Lake N.Z. 106 B3
Tekax Mex. 129 C2
Tekirdağ Turkey 59 C2

Te Kuiti N.Z. **106** C2
T'elavi Georgia **85** C1
Tel Aviv–Yafo Israel **84** B2
Telegraph Creek Can. **112** B2
Telémaco Borba Brazil **138** B2
Telford U.K. **47** B3
Telo Indon. **64** A2
Tel'pos-Iz, Gora *mt.* Rus. Fed. **34** E2
Telšiai Lith. **36** B2
Telukbatang Indon. **65** B2
Telukdalam Indon. **64** A1
Teluk Intan Malaysia **64** B1
Temagami Lake Can. **114** C2
Temba S. Africa **99** C2
Tembilahan Indon. **64** B2
Tembo Aluma Angola **94** B1
Temerluh Malaysia **64** B1
Temirtau Kazakh. **81** E1
Temora Austr. **105** D2
Temple U.S.A. **127** E2
Templemore Rep. of Ireland **45** C2
Templin Ger. **49** F1
Tempoal Mex. **129** C2
Temryuk Rus. Fed. **39** E2
Temuco Chile **137** A4
Temuka N.Z. **106** B3
Tenabo Mex. **129** C2
Tenali India **77** C3
Tenasserim Myanmar **67** A2
Tendaho Eth. **93** C3
Tende France **53** D3
Ten Degree Channel India **67** A3
Tendō Japan **70** D3
Ténéré, Erg du *des.* Niger **91** D3
Ténéré du Tafassâsset *des.* Niger **91** D2
Tenerife *i.* Canary Is **90** A2
Ténès Alg. **55** D2
Tengah, Kepulauan *is* Indon. **65** C2
Tengchong China **66** A1
Tenggarong Indon. **65** C2
Tengger Shamo *des.* China **74** A2
Tenke Dem. Rep. Congo **95** C4
Tenkodogo Burkina **90** B3
Tennant Creek Austr. **102** C1
Tennessee *r.* U.S.A. **124** C1
Tennessee *state* U.S.A. **124** C1
Tenosique Mex. **129** C3
Tenteno Indon. **65** D2
Tenterfield Austr. **105** E1
Teodoro Sampaio Brazil **138** B2
Teófilo Otóni Brazil **139** D1
Tepache Mex. **128** B2
Te Paki N.Z. **106** B1
Tepatitlán Mex. **128** B2
Tepelenë Albania **59** B2
Tepic Mex. **128** B2
Teplice Czech Rep. **50** C2
Tequila Mex. **128** B2
Teramo Italy **56** B2
Terebovlya Ukr. **38** C2

Terek *r.* Rus. Fed. **35** D4
Teresina Brazil **135** E3
Teresópolis Brazil **139** D2
Teressa Island India **67** A3
Tergnier France **48** A3
Terme Turkey **84** B1
Termini Imerese Italy **56** B3
Termiz Uzbek. **81** D3
Termoli Italy **56** B2
Ternate Indon. **63** C2
Terneuzen Neth. **48** A2
Terni Italy **56** B2
Ternopil' Ukr. **38** C2
Terpeniya, Mys *c.* Rus. Fed. **73** F1
Terpeniya, Zaliv *g.* Rus. Fed. **73** F1
Terrace Can. **112** C2
Terrace Bay Can. **114** B2
Terra Firma S. Africa **98** B2
Terre Haute U.S.A. **140** B3
Terschelling *i.* Neth. **48** B1
Tertenia Italy **56** A3
Teruel Spain **55** C1
Tervola Fin. **40** E2
Teseney Eritrea **92** B3
Teshio-gawa *r.* Japan **70** D2
Teslin Can. **112** B1
Teslin Lake Can. **112** B1
Tesouro Brazil **138** B1
Tessaoua Niger **91** C3
Tetas, Punta *c.* Chile **147**
Tete Moz. **97** C1
Teteriv *r.* Ukr. **38** D1
Teterow Ger. **49** F1
Tetiyiv Ukr. **38** C2
Tétouan Morocco **90** B1
Tetovo Macedonia **58** B2
Teuco *r.* Arg. **136** B3
Tevere *r.* Italy *see* Tiber
Tewantin Austr. **103** E2
Te Wharau N.Z. **106** C3
Texarkana U.S.A. **127** E2
Texas *state* U.S.A. **127** E2
Texas City U.S.A. **127** F3
Texel *i.* Neth. **48** B1
Teziutlán Mex. **129** C3
Tezpur India **79** D2
Teza *r.* Rus. Fed. **37** F2
Tezpur India **79** D2
Tha-anne *r.* Can. **113** F1
Thabana-Ntlenyana *mt.* Lesotho **99** C2
Thabazimbi S. Africa **99** C1
Thabong S. Africa **99** C2
Thagyettaw Myanmar **67** A2
Thai Binh Vietnam **66** B1
Thailand *country* Asia **67** B2

Thailand, Gulf of Asia **67** B2
Thai Nguyên Vietnam **66** B1
Thakèk Laos **66** B2
Thalang Thai. **67** A3
Thal Desert Pak. **78** B1
Thale (Harz) Ger. **49** E2
Thamaga Botswana **99** C1
Thamar, Jabal *mt.* Yemen **82** B3
Thamarīt Oman **83** C3
Thames *r.* Can. **114** B2
Thames N.Z. **106** C2
Thames *r.* U.K. **47** D4
Thanbyuzayat Myanmar **67** A2
Thandwè Myanmar **66** A2
Thanh Hoa Vietnam **66** B2
Thanjavur India **77** B3
Thanlyin Myanmar **66** A2
Thar Desert India/Pak. **78** A2
Thargomindah Austr. **104** C1
Tharthār, Buḩayrat ath *l.* Iraq **85** C2
Thasos *i.* Greece **59** C2
Thaton Myanmar **66** A2
Thaungdut Myanmar **66** A1
Thayawadi Myanmar **66** A2
Thayetmyo Myanmar **66** A2
Thazi Myanmar **66** A1
The Bahamas *country* West Indies **131** C2
The Cheviot *h.* U.K. **46** B2
The Dalles U.S.A. **118** B1
The Fens *reg.* U.K. **47** C3
The Great Oasis Egypt *see* Khārijah, Wāḩāt al
The Gulf Asia **83** C2
The Hague Neth. **48** B1
Thelon *r.* Can. **113** F1
The Minch *sea chan.* U.K. **44** A1
The Pas Can. **113** E2
Theodore Roosevelt *r.* Brazil **134** C3
Thermaïkos Kolpos *g.* Greece **59** B2
Thermopolis U.S.A. **120** B2
The Rock Austr. **105** D3
Thessalon Can. **114** B2
Thessaloníki Greece **59** B2
Thetford U.K. **47** D3
The Triangle *mts* Myanmar **66** A1
Thévenet, Lac *l.* Can. **115** D1
The Wash *b.* U.K. **46** D3
Thibodaux U.S.A. **124** B3
Thicket Portage Can. **113** F2
Thief River Falls U.S.A. **121** D1
Thiers France **53** C2
Thika Kenya **95** D3
Thiladhunmathi Atoll Maldives **77** B4
Thimphu Bhutan **79** C2
Thionville France **53** D2
Thira *i.* Greece **59** C3
Thirsk U.K. **46** C2
Thisted Denmark **41** B4
Thlewiaza *r.* Can. **113** F1

Thoen Thai. **66** A2
Thohoyandou S. Africa **99** D1
Thomastown Rep. of Ireland
    45 C2
Thomasville U.S.A. **125** D2
Thompson Can. **113** F2
Thompson r. U.S.A. **112** D2
Thompson Falls U.S.A. **118** C1
Thompson Sound Can. **112** C2
Thorshavnheiane reg. Antarctica
    107 C2
Thouars France **52** B2
Three Pagodas Pass
    Myanmar/Thai. **67** A2
Thuin Belgium **48** B2
Thule Greenland **111** H1
Thunder Bay Can. **114** B2
Thung Song Thai. **67** A3
Thüringer Wald mts Ger. **49** E2
Thurles Rep. of Ireland **45** C2
Thurso U.K. **44** C1
Thurso r. U.K. **44** C1
Tianjin China **74** B2
Tianjin mun. China **74** B2
Tianlin China **75** A3
Tianmen China **74** B2
Tianshan China **74** C1
Tianshui China **74** A2
Tianzhu China **74** A2
Tiaret Alg. **55** D2
Tibagi r. Brazil **138** B2
Tibati Cameroon **94** B2
Tiber r. Italy **56** B2
Tiberias, Lake Israel see
    Galilee, Sea of
Tibesti mts Chad **91** D3
Tibet aut. reg. China see
    Xizang Zizhiqu
Tibet, Plateau of China **79** C1
Tibooburra Austr. **104** C1
Tiburón, Isla i. Mex. **128** A2
Tichit Maur. **90** B3
Tichla Western Sahara **90** A2
Ticul Mex. **129** D2
Tidjikja Maur. **90** A3
Tiel Neth. **48** B?
Tieling China **74** C1
Tielt Belgium **48** A2
Tienen Belgium **48** B2
Tien Shan mts China/Kyrg. **72** B2
Tientsin China see Tianjin
Tierp Sweden **41** D3
Tierra Blanca Mex. **129** C3
Tierra del Fuego, Isla Grande
    de i. Arg./Chile **137** B6
Tietê Brazil **138** C2
Tietê r. Brazil **138** B2
Tiflis Georgia see T'bilisi
Tifton U.S.A. **125** D2
Tighina Moldova **38** C2
Tignish Can. **115** D2
Tigre r. Ecuador/Peru **134** B3
Tigris r. Turkey **85** C2
Tijuana Mex. **128** A1

Tikhoretsk Rus. Fed. **39** F2
Tikhvin Rus. Fed. **37** D2
Tikhvinskaya Gryada ridge
    Rus. Fed. **37** D2
Tikokino N.Z. **106** C2
Tikrit Iraq **85** C2
Tiksi Rus. Fed. **87** K2
Tilburg Neth. **48** B2
Tilcha Austr. **104** C1
Tillabéri Niger **90** C3
Tilos i. Greece **59** C3
Tilpa Austr. **104** C2
Timanskiy Kryazh ridge Rus. Fed.
    34 D2
Timaru N.Z. **106** B3
Timashevsk Rus. Fed. **39** E2
Timbedgha Maur. **90** B3
Timber Creek Austr. **102** C1
Timbuktu Mali **90** B3
Timimoun Alg. **90** C2
Timiş r. Romania **38** B2
Timişoara Romania **38** B2
Timmins Can. **114** B2
Timokhino Rus. Fed. **37** E2
Timon Brazil **135** E3
Timor i. East Timor/Indonesia
    63 C3
Timor Sea Austr./Indon. **62** C3
Timrå Sweden **41** D3
Tindouf Alg. **90** B2
Tingri China **79** C2
Tinian i. N. Mariana Is **63** D?
Tinos Greece **59** C3
Tinos i. Greece **59** C3
Tinqueux France **48** A3
Tinrhert, Plateau du Alg. **91** C2
Tinsukia India **66** A1
Tipasa Alg. **55** D2
Tipperary Rep. of Ireland **45** B2
Tirana Albania **59** A2
Tiranë Albania see Tirana
Tiraspol Moldova **38** C2
Tire Turkey **59** C3
Tiree i. U.K. **44** A2
Tirich Mir mt. Pak. **78** B1
Tiruchchirappalli India **77** B3
Tirunelveli India **77** B4
Tirupati India **77** B3
Tiruppur India **77** B3
Tisa r. S.M. **58** B1
Tisdale Can. **113** E2
Tissemsilt Alg. **55** D2
Titicaca, Lake Bol./Peru **136** B?
Titlagarh India **79** C2
Titu Romania **38** C2
Titusville U.S.A. **125** D3
Tiverton U.K. **47** B4
Tivoli Italy **56** B2
Tiwi Oman **83** C2
Tizimin Mex. **129** D2
Tizi Ouzou Alg. **55** D2
Tiznit Morocco **90** B2
Tlacotalpán Mex. **129** C3

Tlapa Mex. **129** C3
Tlaxcala Mex. **129** C3
Tlemcen Alg. **90** B1
Tlokweng Botswana **99** C1
Toad River Can. **112** C2
Toamasina Madag. **97** [inset] D1
Toba, Danau l. Indon. **64** A1
Toba and Kakar Ranges mts Pak.
    78 A1
Tobago i. Trin. and Tob. **131** D3
Tobermory Can. **114** B2
Tobermory U.K. **44** A2
Tobin Lake Can. **113** E2
Toboali Indon. **64** B2
Tobol r. Kazakh./Rus. Fed. **80** D1
Tobol'sk Rus. Fed. **34** F3
Tocantins r. Brazil **135** E3
Tóccoa U.S.A. **125** D2
Tocco r. Italy **56** A1
Tocopilla Chile **136** A3
Todos Santos Mex. **128** A2
Toft U.K. **44** [inset]
Tofua i. Tonga **111**
Togian i. Indon. **65** D2
Togian, Kepulauan is Indon.
    65 D2
Togo country Africa **90** C4
Tok U.S.A. **112** A2
Tokara-rettō is Japan **73** E3
Tokarevka Rus. Fed. **37** F3
Tokelau terr. S. Pacific Ocean
    101
Tokelau is Tokelau **111**
Tokmak Ukr. **39** E2
Tokmok Kyrg. **81** E2
Tokoroa N.Z. **106** C2
Toksun China **81** G2
Tokushima Japan **71** B4
Tōkyō Japan **71** C3
Tôlañaro Madag. **97** [inset] D2
Toledo Brazil **138** B2
Toledo Spain **54** C2
Toledo U.S.A. **122** D2
Toledo, Montes de mts Spain
    54 C2
Toledo Bend Reservoir U.S.A.
    124 B2
Toliara Madag. **97** [inset] D2
Tolitoli Indon. **65** D1
Tolmezzo Italy **56** B1
Tolosa Spain **52** B3
Toluca Mex. **129** C3
Tol'yatti Rus. Fed. **35** D3
Tomah U.S.A. **122** B2
Tomakomai Japan **70** D2
Tomar Port. **54** B2
Tomaszów Lubelski Pol. **51** E2
Tomaszów Mazowiecki Pol.
    51 E2
Tomatlán Mex. **128** B3
Tombador, Serra do mts Brazil
Tombigbee r. U.S.A. **124** C2
Tombos Brazil **139** D2
Tombouctou Mali see Timbuktu
Tombua Angola **96** A1

Tom Burke S. Africa **99** C1
Tomingley Austr. **105** D2
Tomini, Teluk *g.* Indon. **65** D2
Tom Price Austr. **102** A2
Tomsk Rus. Fed. **86** H3
Tomtabacken *h.* Sweden **41** C4
Tonalá Mex. **129** C3
Tonantins Brazil **134** C3
Tender Denmark **50** B2
Tonga *country* S. Pacific Ocean **101**
Tongatapu Group *is* Tonga **111**
Tongcheng China **75** B3
Tongchuan China **74** A2
Tongdao China **75** A3
Tongduch'ŏn S. Korea **69** B2
Tongeren Belgium **48** B2
Tonghae S. Korea **69** B2
Tonghai China **75** A3
Tonghua China **69** B1
Tongjosŏn-man *b.* N. Korea **69** B2
Tongking, Gulf of China/Vietnam **75** A3
Tongliao China **74** C1
Tongling China **75** B3
Tongo Austr. **104** C2
Tongren China **75** A3
Tongshi China *see* Wuzhishan
Tongtian He *r.* China *see* Yangtze
Tongue U.K. **44** B1
T'ongyŏng S. Korea **69** B3
Tongyu China **73** E2
Tonk India **78** B2
Tonle Sap *l.* Cambodia **67** B2
Tonopah U.S.A. **119** C3
Tønsberg Norway **41** C4
Tooleybuc Austr. **104** C3
Toowoomba Austr. **105** E1
Topeka U.S.A. **121** D3
Topolobampo Mex. **128** B2
Topozero, Ozero *l.* Rus. Fed. **40** D2
Toppenish U.S.A. **118** C3
Torbalı Turkey **59** C3
Torbat-e Heydarīyeh Iran **80** C3
Torbat-e Jām Iran **80** C3
Tordesillas Spain **54** C1
Tordesilos Spain **55** C1
Torgau Ger. **49** F2
Torgelow Ger. **49** G1
Torhout Belgium **48** A2
Torino Italy *see* Turin
Tori-shima *i.* Japan **71** D4
Torixoréu Brazil **138** B1
Tor'kovskoye Vodokhranilishche *resr* Rus. Fed. **37** F2
Tormes *r.* Spain **54** B1
Torneälven *r.* Sweden **40** E2
Torngat Mountains Can. **115** D1
Tornio Fin. **40** E2
Toro Spain **54** B1
Toronto Can. **114** C2

Tororo Uganda **95** D2
Toros Dağları *mts* Turkey *see* Taurus Mountains
Torquay U.K. **47** B4
Torre *mt.* Port. **54** B1
Torrecerredo *mt.* Spain **54** C1
Torrelavega Spain **54** C1
Torrens, Lake *salt flat* Austr. **104** B2
Torrent Spain **55** C2
Torreón Mex. **128** B2
Torres Novas Port. **54** B2
Torres Strait Austr. **110**
Torres Vedras Port. **54** B2
Torrevieja Spain **55** C2
Torridon U.K. **44** B2
Tórshavn Faroe Is **42** B1
Tortoli Italy **56** A3
Tortosa Spain **55** D1
Toruń Pol. **51** D2
Tory Island Rep. of Ireland **45** B1
Torzhok Rus. Fed. **37** D2
Tosca S. Africa **98** B2
Toscano, Arcipelago *is* Italy **56** A2
Tosno Rus. Fed. **37** D2
Tostado Arg. **136** B3
Tostedt Ger. **49** D1
Tot'ma Rus. Fed. **37** F2
Tottori Japan **71** B3
Touba Côte d'Ivoire **90** B4
Tougan Burkina **90** B3
Touggourt Alg. **91** C1
Toul France **53** D2
Touliu Taiwan **75** C3
Toulon France **53** D3
Toulouse France **52** C3
Tourcoing France **48** C1
Tournai Belgium **48** A2
Touros Brazil **135** F3
Tours France **52** C2
Toussidé, Pic *mt.* Chad **91** D2
Towada Japan **70** D2
Townsend U.S.A. **118** D1
Townsville Austr. **103** D3
Towori, Teluk *b.* Indon. **65** D2
Toxkan He *r.* China **81** F2
Tōya-ko *l.* Japan **70** D2
Toyama Japan **71** C3
Toyota Japan **71** C3
Tozeur Tunisia **91** C1
Tqvarch'eli Georgia **85** C1
Trâblous Lebanon *see* Tripoli
Trabzon Turkey **84** B1
Trafalgar, Cabo *c.* Spain **54** B2
Trail Can. **112** D3
Trakai Lith. **36** B3
Tralee Rep. of Ireland **45** B2
Tramore Rep. of Ireland **45** C2
Tranås Sweden **41** C4
Trang Thai. **67** A3
Trangan *i.* Indon. **63** C3
Transantarctic Mountains Antarctica **107** H2

Transylvanian Alps *mts* Romania **38** B2
Trapani Italy **56** B3
Traralgon Austr. **105** D3
Trat Thai. **67** B2
Traunstein Ger. **50** C3
Traverse City U.S.A. **122** C2
Třebíč Czech Rep. **51** D3
Trebinje Bos.-Herz. **57** C2
Trebišov Slovakia **51** E3
Trebnje Slovenia **56** C1
Treinta y Tres Uru. **137** C4
Trelew Arg. **137** B5
Trelleborg Sweden **41** C4
Tremblant, Mont *h.* Can. **114** C2
Tremiti, Isole *is* Italy **56** C2
Tremonton U.S.A. **118** D2
Tremp Spain **55** D1
Trenčín Slovakia **51** D3
Trenque Lauquén Arg. **137** B4
Trent *r.* U.K. **46** C3
Trento Italy **56** B1
Trenton Can. **123** E2
Trenton *MO* U.S.A. **121** E2
Trenton *NJ* U.S.A. **123** F2
Tres Arroyos Arg. **137** B4
Três Corações Brazil **139** C2
Três Lagoas Brazil **138** B2
Tres Lagos Arg. **137** A5
Três Marias, Represa *resr* Brazil **139** C1
Três Pontas Brazil **139** C2
Três Ríos Brazil **139** C2
Treviglio Italy **56** A1
Treviso Italy **56** B1
Trevose Head U.K. **47** A4
Tricase Italy **57** D3
Trichur India **77** B3
Trida Austr. **105** C2
Trier Ger. **48** C3
Trieste Italy **56** B1
Triglav *mt.* Slovenia **56** B1
Trincomalee Sri Lanka **77** C4
Trindade Brazil **138** C1
Trinidad Bol. **136** B2
Trinidad *i.* Trin. and Tob. **131** D3
Trinidad U.S.A. **120** C3
Trinidad and Tobago *country* West Indies **131** D3
Trinity Bay Can. **115** E2
Tripoli Greece **59** B3
Tripoli Lebanon **84** B2
Tripoli Libya **91** D1
Tristan da Cunha *i.* S. Atlantic Ocean **144** D8
Trivandrum India **77** B4
Trnava Slovakia **51** D3
Trogir Croatia **57** C2
Troisdorf Ger. **48** C2
Trois Fourches, Cap des *c.* Morocco **54** C2
Trois-Rivières Can. **115** C2
Troitsko-Pechorsk Rus. Fed. **34** E2

Trombetas r. Brazil 135 D3
Trompsburg S. Africa 99 C3
Tromsø Norway 40 D2
Trondheim Norway 40 C3
Trout Lake Can. 112 D2
Trout Lake l. N.W.T. Can. 112 C1
Trout Lake l. Ont. Can. 114 A1
Trowbridge U.K. 47 B4
Troy AL U.S.A. 125 C2
Troy NY U.S.A. 123 F2
Troyes France 53 C2
Trubchevsk Rus. Fed. 37 D3
Trucial Coast U.A.E. 83 C2
Trujillo Hond. 130 B3
Trujillo Peru 134 B3
Trujillo Spain 54 B2
Trujillo Venez. 134 B2
Truman U.S.A. 124 B1
Truro Can. 115 D2
Truro U.K. 47 A4
Truth or Consequences U.S.A. 126 C2
Trutnov Czech Rep. 51 D2
Trysil Norway 41 C3
Tsagaannuur Mongolia 72 B1
Tsaratanana, Massif de mts Madag. 97 [inset] D1
Tsarevo Bulg. 58 C2
Tselina Rus. Fed. 39 F2
Tses Namibia 98 A2
Tsetseng Botswana 98 B1
Tsetserleg Mongolia 72 C1
Tshabong Botswana 98 B2
Tshane Botswana 98 B1
Tschikskoye Vodokhranilishche resr Rus. Fed. 39 E2
Tshela Dem. Rep. Congo 94 B3
Tshikapa Dem. Rep. Congo 94 C3
Tshikapa r. Dem. Rep. Congo 94 C3
Tshitanzu Dem. Rep. Congo 94 C3
Tshuapa r. Dem. Rep. Congo 94 C3
Tshwane S. Africa see Pretoria
Tsimlyanskoye Vodokhranilishche resr Rus. Fed. 35 D4
Tsingtao China see Qingdao
Tsna r. Rus. Fed. 37 F3
Tsu Japan 71 C4
Tsuchiura Japan 71 D3
Tsugarū-kaikyō str. Japan 70 D2
Tsumeb Namibia 96 A1
Tsumis Park Namibia 98 A1
Tsumkwe Namibia 96 B1
Tsuruga Japan 71 C3
Tsuruoka Japan 70 C3
Tsushima is Japan 71 A4
Tsuyama Japan 71 B3
Tswelelang S. Africa 99 C2
Tsyurupyns'k Ukr. 39 D2
Tual Indon. 63 C3
Tuam Rep. of Ireland 45 B2

Tuamotu Archipelago is Fr. Polynesia 143 F6
Tuapse Rus. Fed. 39 E3
Tuatapere N.Z. 106 A4
Tuba City U.S.A. 126 B1
Tubarão Brazil 136 D3
Tübingen Ger. 50 B3
Tobruq Libya 91 E1
Tubuai Islands Fr. Polynesia 111
Tubutama Mex. 128 A1
Tuchitua Can. 112 C1
Tucson U.S.A. 126 B2
Tucumcari U.S.A. 127 D1
Tucupita Venez. 134 C2
Tucuruí Brazil 135 E3
Tucuruí, Represa resr Brazil 135 E3
Tudela Spain 55 C1
Tuela r. Port. 54 B1
Tugela r. S. Africa 99 D2
Tuguegarao Phil. 68 B2
Tui Spain 54 B1
Tukangbesi, Kepulauan is Indon. 63 C3
Tuktoyaktuk Can. 110 D2
Tukums Latvia 36 B2
Tula Mex. 129 C2
Tulancingo Mex. 129 C2
Tulare U.S.A. 119 C3
Tularosa U.S.A. 126 C2
Tulcea Romania 38 C2
Tul'chyn Ukr. 38 C2
Tulemalu Lake Can. 113 F1
Tulia U.S.A. 127 D2
Tull Can. 112 C1
Tullahoma U.S.A. 125 C1
Tullamore Rep. of Ireland 45 C2
Tulle France 52 C2
Tulsa U.S.A. 127 E1
Tuluksak U.S.A. 110 B2
Tumaco Col. 134 B2
Tumahole S. Africa 99 C2
Tumba Sweden 41 D4
Tumba, Lac l. Dem. Rep. Congo 94 B3
Tumbarumba Austr. 105 D3
Tumbes Peru 134 A3
Tumbler Ridge Can. 112 C2
Tumby Bay Austr. 104 B3
Tumen China 69 B1
Tumereng Guyana 134 C2
Tumindao i. Phil. 68 A3
Tumkur India 77 B3
Tummin r. Rus. Fed. 73 F1
Tump Pak. 78 A2
Tumucumaque, Serra hills Brazil 135 D2
Tumut Austr. 105 D3
Tunbridge Wells, Royal U.K. 47 D4
Tunceli Turkey 84 B2
Tuncurry Austr. 105 E2
Tunduru Tanz. 95 D4
Tungsten Can. 112 C1

Tunis Tunisia 91 D1
Tunisia country Africa 91 C1
Tunja Col. 134 B2
Tunnsjøen l. Norway 40 C3
Tupã Brazil 138 C2
Tupaciguara Brazil 138 C1
Tupelo U.S.A. 124 C2
Tupiza Bol. 136 B3
Tura Rus. Fed. 87 I2
Tura r. Rus. Fed. 34 F3
Turabah Saudi Arabia 82 B2
Turana, Khrebet mts Rus. Fed. 87 K3
Turangi N.Z. 106 C2
Turan Lowland Asia 80 C3
Turayf Saudi Arabia 82 A1
Turba Estonia 36 C2
Turbat Pak. 78 A2
Turbo Col. 134 B2
Turda Romania 38 B2
Turfan China see Turpan
Turgay Kazakh. 80 D2
Turgutlu Turkey 59 C3
Turhal Turkey 84 B1
Turia r. Spain 55 C2
Turin Italy 56 A1
Turiya'sk Ukr. 38 B1
Turkana, Lake salt l. Eth./Kenya 93 B4
Turkestan Kazakh. 81 D2
Turkey country Asia/Europe 84 B2
Turkmenabat Turkm. 80 D3
Turkmenbashi Turkm. 80 C2
Turkmenistan country Asia 80 C2
Turks and Caicos Islands terr. West Indies 131 C2
Turku Fin. 41 E3
Turlock U.S.A. 119 B3
Turnagain, Cape N.Z. 106 C3
Turneffe Islands atoll Belize 129 D3
Turnhout Belgium 48 B2
Turnor Lake Can. 113 E2
Turnu Măgurele Romania 58 B2
Turpan China 81 F2
Turugart Pass China/Kyrg. 81 E2
Tuscaloosa U.S.A. 124 C2
Tuskegee U.S.A. 125 C2
Tuticorin India 77 B4
Tutume Botswana 96 B2
Tuvalu country S. Pacific Ocean 100
Tuwayq, Jabal hills Saudi Arabia 82 B2
Tuwayq, Jabal mts Saudi Arabia 82 B2
Tuwwal Saudi Arabia 82 A2
Tuxpan Nayarit Mex. 128 B2
Tuxpan Veracruz Mex. 129 C2
Tuxtla Gutiérrez Mex. 129 C3
Tuy Hoa Vietnam 67 B2
Tuz, Lake salt l. Turkey 84 B2

Tuz Gölü *salt l.* Turkey *see*
Tuz, Lake
Tuz Khurmātū Iraq **85** C2
Tuzla Bos.-Herz. **57** C2
Tuzlov *r.* Rus. Fed. **39** F2
Tver' Rus. Fed. **37** E2
Tweed *r.* U.K. **46** B2
Twee Rivier Namibia **98** A2
Twentynine Palms U.S.A. **119** C4
Twin Falls U.S.A. **118** D2
Twizel N.Z. **106** B3
Two Harbors U.S.A. **121** E1
Tyler U.S.A. **127** E2
Tynda Rus. Fed. **87** K3
Tynset Norway **41** C3
Tyre Lebanon **84** B2
Tyrnavos Greece **59** B3
Tyrrell, Lake *dry lake* Austr.
104 C3
Tyrrhenian Sea France/Italy
56 B2
Tyub-Karagan, Mys *pt* Kazakh.
80 C2
Tyumen' Rus. Fed. **34** F3
Tywi *r.* U.K. **47** A4
Tzaneen S. Africa **99** D1

U

Uamanda Angola **96** B1
Uaupés Brazil **134** C3
Uba Brazil **139** D2
Ubai Brazil **139** D1
Ubangi *r.* C.A.R./Dem. Rep. Congo
94 B3
Ube Japan **71** B4
Úbeda Spain **54** C2
Uberaba Brazil **138** C1
Uberlândia Brazil **138** C1
Ubombo S. Africa **99** D2
Ubon Ratchathani Thai. **67** B2
Uchur *r.* Rus. Fed. **87** K3
Ucluelet Can. **112** C3
Udaipur India **78** B2
Uday *r.* Ukr. **39** D1
Uddevalla Sweden **41** C4
Uddjaure *l.* Sweden **40** C2
Uden Neth. **48** B2
Udhampur India **78** B1
Udine Italy **56** B1
Udomlya Rus. Fed. **37** E2
Udon Thani Thai. **66** B2
Udupi India **77** B3
Ueda Japan **71** C3
Uekuli Indon. **65** D2
Uele *r.* Dem. Rep. Congo **94** C2
Uelen Rus. Fed. **110** A2
Uelzen Ger. **49** E1

Uere *r.* Dem. Rep. Congo **95** C2
Ufa Rus. Fed. **35** E3
Ugalla *r.* Tanz. **95** D3
Uganda *country* Africa **95** D2
Uglegorsk Rus. Fed. **73** F1
Uglich Rus. Fed. **37** E2
Uglovka Rus. Fed. **37** D2
Ugra Rus. Fed. **37** D3
Uherské Hradiště Czech Rep.
51 D3
Uhlava *r.* Czech Rep. **49** F3
Uig U.K. **44** A2
Uíge Angola **95** B3
Ŭijŏngbu S. Korea **69** B2
Uinta Mountains U.S.A. **118** D2
Uísŏng S. Korea **69** B2
Uitenhage S. Africa **99** C3
Uithuizen Neth. **48** C1
Uivak, Cape Can. **115** D1
Ujjain India **78** B2
Ukholovo Rus. Fed. **37** F3
Ukhrul India **66** A1
Ukhta Rus. Fed. **34** E2
Ukiah U.S.A. **119** B3
Ukkusissat Greenland **111** I2
Ukmergė Lith. **36** B2
Ukraine *country* Europe **38** D2
Ulaanbaatar Mongolia *see*
Ulan Bator
Ulaangom Mongolia **72** C1
Ulan Bator Mongolia **72** D1
Ulanhad China *see* Chifeng
Ulanhot China **73** E1
Ulan-Khol Rus. Fed. **35** D4
Ulan-Ude Rus. Fed. **73** D1
Ulan Ul Hu *l.* China **79** D1
Ulchin S. Korea **69** B2
Ülenurme Estonia **36** C2
Ulhasnagar India **77** B3
Uliastai China **73** D1
Uliastay Mongolia **72** C1
Ulithi *atoll* Micronesia **63** D2
Ulladulla Austr. **106** L5
Ullapool U.K. **44** B2
Ullswater *l.* U.K. **46** B2
Ullŭng-do *i.* S. Korea **69** C2
Ulm Ger. **50** B3
Ulsan S. Korea **69** B2
Ulsta U.K. **44** [inset]
Ulster *reg.* Rep. of Ireland/U.K.
45 C1
Ultima Austr. **104** C3
Ulua *r.* Hond. **129** D3
Uludağ *mt.* Turkey **59** C2
Ulundi S. Africa **99** D2
Ulungur Hu *l.* China **81** F2
Uluru *h.* Austr. **102** C2
Ulverston U.K. **46** B2
Ul'yanovsk Rus. Fed. **35** D3
Ulysses U.S.A. **120** C3
Uman' Ukr. **38** D2
Umboi *i.* P.N.G. **63** D3
Umeå Sweden **40** E3
Umeälven *r.* Sweden **40** E3

Umet Rus. Fed. **39** F1
Umingmaktok Can. **110** E2
Umlazi S. Africa **99** D2
Umm Lajj Saudi Arabia **82** A2
Umm Ruwaba Sudan **93** B3
Umm Sa'ad Libya **91** E1
Umnugovĭ Mongolia *see*
Ulan Bator
Umtata S. Africa **99** C3
Umuarama Brazil **138** B2
Una *r.* Bos.-Herz./Croatia **57** C1
Unaí Brazil **138** C1
Unalakleet U.S.A. **110** B2
'Unayzah Saudi Arabia **82** B2
Unecha Rus. Fed. **37** D3
Ungarie Austr. **105** D2
Ungarra Austr. **104** A2
Ungava, Péninsule d' *pen.* Can.
111 H2
Ungava Bay Can. **115** D1
Unggi N. Korea **69** C1
Ungheni Moldova **38** C2
Unguja *i.* Tanz. *see*
Zanzibar Island
União da Vitória Brazil **138** B3
Unini *r.* Brazil **134** C3
Union City U.S.A. **124** C1
Uniondale S. Africa **98** B3
Uniontown U.S.A. **123** E3
United Arab Emirates *country*
Asia **83** C2
United Kingdom *country* Europe
42 C2
United States of America
country N. America **116** D3
Unst *i.* U.K. **44** [inset]
Unstrut *r.* Ger. **49** E2
Upa *r.* Rus. Fed. **37** E3
Upemba, Lac *l.* Dem. Rep. Congo
95 C3
Upington S. Africa **98** B2
Upolu *i.* Samoa **111**
Upper Alkali Lake U.S.A. **118** B2
Upper Arrow Lake Can. **112** D2
Upper Klamath Lake U.S.A.
118 B2
Upper Liard Can. **112** C1
Upper Lough Erne *l.* U.K. **45** C1
Uppsala Sweden **41** D4
'Uqlat aş Şuqūr Saudi Arabia
82 B2
Ural *r.* Kazakh./Rus. Fed. **80** C2
Uralla Austr. **105** E2
Ural Mountains Rus. Fed. **35** F2
Ural'sk Kazakh. **80** C1
Ural'skiy Khrebet *mts* Rus. Fed.
see Ural Mountains
Urambo Tanz. **95** D3
Urana Austr. **105** D3
Uray Rus. Fed. **34** F2
Urengoy Rus. Fed. **34** G2
Urganch Uzbek. **80** C2
Urk Neth. **48** B1
Urla Turkey **59** C3
Urmia, Lake *salt l.* Iran **85** C2

Iroševac S.M. **58** B2
Iruáchic Mex. **128** B2
Iruaçu Brazil **135** E4
Iruapan Mex. **128** B3
Irucara Brazil **135** D3
Iruçuí Brazil **135** E3
Iruguaí r. Brazil **138** B3
Iruguaiana Brazil **136** C3
Iruguay r. Arg./Uru. **133**
  137 C4
Irumqi China **81** F2
Irup r. Rus. Fed. **39** F2
Iryupinsk Rus. Fed. **39** F1
Irziceni Romania **38** C3
Isa Japan **71** B4
Ise r. Rus. Fed. **37**
Isak Turkey **59** C3
Isakos Namibia **98** A1
Ishtobe Kazakh. **81** E2
Ishuaia Arg. **137** B6
Isinsk Rus. Fed. **34** E2
Iskhodni Belarus **36** C3
Isman' Rus. Fed. **37** E3
Isogorsk Rus. Fed. **34** D2
Issel Franco **52** C2
Issuriysk Rus. Fed. **70** B2
Ist'-Donetskiy Rus. Fed. **39** F2
Istica, Isola di i. Italy **56** B3
Ist'-Ilimsk Rus. Fed. **87** I3
Istka Pol. **51** D2
Ist'-Kamchatsk Rus. Fed. **07** M3
Ist'-Kamenogorsk Kazakh.
  81 F2
Ist'-Kara Rus. Fed. **34** F2
Ist' Kulom Rus. Fed. **34** F2
Ist'-Kut Rus. Fed. **87** J3
Ist'-Labinsk Rus. Fed. **39** E2
Ist'-Luga Rus. Fed. **36** C2
Ist'-Nera Rus. Fed. **87** L2
Ist'-Omchug Rus. Fed. **87** L2
Ist'-Ordynskiy Rus. Fed. **87** I3
Ist'-Port Rus. Fed. **34** H2
Ist'-Tsil'ma Rus. Fed. **34** E2
Istyurt Plateau Kazakh./Uzbek.
  80 C2
Istyuzhna Rus. Fed. **37** E2
Isvyaty Rus. Fed. **37** D2
Itah state U.S.A. **119** D3
Itah Lake U.S.A. **118** D2
Itena Lith. **36** C2
Itica U.S.A. **123** E2
Itiel Spain **55** C2
Itikuma Lake Can. **112** D2
Itrecht Neth. **48** B1
Itrera Spain **54** B2
Itsjoki Fin. **40** F2
Itsunomiya Japan **71** C3
Ittaradit Thai. **66** B2
Iummamnaq Greenland see
  Dundas
Iusikaupunki Fin. **41** E3
Ivalde U.C.A. **127** E3
Ivarovo Rus. Fed. **39** F1

Uvs Nuur salt l. Mongolia **72** C1
Uwajima Japan **71** B4
'Uwayriḍ, Ḥarrat al lava field
  Saudi Arabia **82** A2
Uweinat, Jebel mt. Sudan **92** A2
Uyar Rus. Fed. **87** I3
Uyo Nigeria **91** C4
Uyuni Bol. **136** B3
Uyuni, Salar de salt flat Bol.
  136 B3
Uzbekistan country Asia **80** D2
Uzerche France **52** C2
Uzès France **53** C3
Uzh r. Ukr. **38** D1
Uzhhorod Ukr. **38** B2
Užice S.M. **58** A2
Uzlovaya Rus. Fed. **37** E3
Uzunköprü Turkey **59** C2

V

Vaal r. S. Africa **99** D3
Vaal Dam S. Africa **99** C2
Vaasa Fin. **40** E3
Vác Hungary **51** D3
Vacaria Brazil **138** C3
Vacaria, Serra hills Brazil **138** B2
Vacaville U.S.A. **119** B3
Vacha Rus. Fed. **37** F2
Vadodara India **78** B2
Vadsø Norway **40** F1
Vaduz Liechtenstein **53** D2
Vágar i. Faroe Is **42** B1
Vágur Faroe Is **42** B1
Váh r. Slovakia **51** D3
Vaiaku Tuvalu **100**
Vaida Estonia **36** B2
Vail U.S.A. **120** B3
Valday Rus. Fed. **37** D2
Valdayskaya Vozvyshennost' hills
  Rus. Fed. **37** D2
Valdecañas, Embalse de resr
  Spain **54** B2
Val-de-Meuse France **53** D2
Valdepeñas Spain **54** C2
Val-de-Reuil France **47** D5
Valdés, Península pen. Arg.
  137 B5
Valdez U.S.A. **112** A1
Valdivia Chile **137** A4
Val-d'Or Can. **114** C2
Valdosta U.S.A. **125** D2
Valemount Can. **112** D2
Valence France **53** C3
Valencia Spain **55** C2
Valencia Venez. **134** C1
Valencia, Golfo de g. Spain
  55 D2
Valenciennes France **48** A2
Valentine U.S.A. **120** C2
Valenzuela Phil. **68** B2
Valera Venez. **134** B2

Valjevo S.M. **58** A2
Valka Latvia **36** C2
Valkeakoski Fin. **41** E3
Valkenswaard Neth. **48** B2
Valky Ukr. **39** E2
Valkyrie Dome ice feature
  Antarctica **107** D2
Valladolid Mex. **129** D2
Valladolid Spain **54** C1
Vall de Uxó Spain **55** C2
Valle Norway **41** B4
Valledupar Col. **134** B1
Valle Hermoso Mex. **129** C2
Vallejo U.S.A. **119** B3
Vallenar Chile **136** A3
Valletta Malta **91** D1
Valley City U.S.A. **121** D1
Valley Falls U.S.A. **118** B3
Valleyview Can. **112** D2
Valls Spain **55** D1
Val Marie Can. **120** B1
Valmiera Latvia **36** C2
Valognes France **47** C5
Valozhyn Belarus **36** C3
Valparaíso Brazil **138** B2
Valparaíso Chile **136** A3
Vals, Tanjung c. Indon. **63** D3
Valsad India **78** B2
Valspan S. Africa **98** B2
Valuyki Rus. Fed. **39** E1
Valverde del Camino Spain
  54 B2
Van Turkey **85** C2
Van, Lake salt l. Turkey **85** C2
Van Buren U.S.A. **123** G1
Vancouver Can. **112** C3
Vancouver Island Can. **112** C3
Vandalia U.S.A. **122** C3
Vanderhoof Can. **112** C2
Vändra Estonia **36** C2
Vänern l. Sweden **41** C4
Vänersborg Sweden **41** C4
Vangaindrano Madag. **97** [inset]
  D2
Van Gölü salt l. Turkey see
  Van, Lake
Van Horn U.S.A. **126** D2
Vanimo P.N.G. **63** D3
Vanino Rus. Fed. **73** F1
Vannes France **52** B2
Van Rees, Pegunungan mts
  Indon. **63** D3
Vanrhynsdorp S. Africa **98** A3
Vantaa Fin. **41** E3
Vanua Levu i. Fiji **142** E6
Vanuatu country S. Pacific Ocean
  100
Van Wert U.S.A. **122** D2
Vanwyksvlei S. Africa **98** B3
Van Zylsrus S. Africa **98** B2
Varanasi India **79** C2
Varangerfjorden sea chan.
  Norway **40** F1

Varangerhalvøya *pen.* Norway 40 F1
Varaždin Croatia 57 C1
Varberg Sweden 41 C4
Vardar *r.* Macedonia 59 B2
Varde Denmark 41 B4
Vardø Norway 40 G1
Varel Ger. 48 D1
Varèna Lith. 36 B3
Varese Italy 56 A1
Varginha Brazil 139 C2
Varkaus Fin. 41 F3
Varna Bulg. 58 C2
Värnamo Sweden 41 C4
Várzea da Palma Brazil 139 D1
Varzino Rus. Fed. 34 C2
Vasknarva Estonia 36 D2
Vaslui Romania 38 C2
Västerås Sweden 41 D4
Västerdalälven *r.* Sweden 41 D3
Västerhaninge Sweden 36 A2
Västervik Sweden 41 D4
Vasto Italy 56 B2
Vasyl'kiv Ukr. 39 E1
Vatan France 52 C2
Vatican City Europe 56 B2
Vatnajökull *ice cap* Iceland 40 [inset]
Vatra Dornei Romania 38 C2
Vättern *r.* Sweden 41 C4
Vaughn U.S.A. 126 C2
Vauvert France 53 C3
Vava'u Group *is* Tonga 111
Växjö Sweden 41 C4
Vaygach, Ostrov *i.* Rus. Fed. 34 E1
Vechta Ger. 49 D1
Vedea *r.* Romania 38 C3
Veendam Neth. 48 C1
Veenendaal Neth. 48 B1
Vegreville Can. 113 D2
Vejer de la Frontera Spain 54 B2
Vejle Denmark 41 B4
Velbüzhdki Prohhod *pass* Bulg./Macedonia 58 B2
Veldhoven Neth. 48 B2
Velebit *mts* Croatia 56 B2
Velenje Slovenia 56 C1
Veles Macedonia 57 D2
Vélez-Málaga Spain 54 C2
Velhas *r.* Brazil 139 D1
Velika Plana S.M. 58 B2
Velikaya *r.* Rus. Fed. 36 C2
Velikiye Luki Rus. Fed. 37 D2
Velikiy Novgorod Rus. Fed. 34 C2
Velikiy Ustyug Rus. Fed. 34 D2
Veliko Türnovo Bulg. 58 C2
Velikšiy Loshii Croatia 56 B2
Velizh Rus. Fed. 37 D2
Vellberg Ger. 49 D3
Vel'sk Rus. Fed. 34 D2
Velykyy Burluk Ukr. 39 E1
Venceslau Bráz Brazil 138 C2

Vendôme France 52 C2
Venev Rus. Fed. 37 E3
Venezia Italy *see* Venice
Venezuela *country* S. America 134 C2
Venezuela, Golfo de *g.* Venez. 134 B1
Venice Italy 56 B1
Venice U.S.A. 125 D3
Venice, Gulf of Europe 56 B1
Venray Neth. 48 B2
Venta *r.* Latvia/Lith. 36 B2
Ventnor U.K. 47 C4
Ventspils Latvia 36 B2
Ventura U.S.A. 119 C4
Venustiano Carranza, Presa *resr* Mex. 127 D3
Vera Spain 55 C2
Veracruz Mex. 129 C3
Veraval India 78 B2
Verbania Italy 56 A1
Vercelli Italy 56 A1
Vercors *reg.* France 53 D3
Verdalsøra Norway 40 C3
Verde *r. Goiás* Brazil 138 B1
Verde *r. Mato Grosso do Sul* Brazil 138 B2
Verde *r.* Mex. 128 B2
Verde *r.* U.S.A. 126 B2
Verde, Cape Senegal 96
Verde Grande *r.* Brazil 139 D1
Verden (Aller) Ger. 49 D1
Verdinho, Serra do *mts* Brazil 138 B1
Verdun France 53 D2
Vereeniging S. Africa 99 C2
Verín Spain 54 B1
Verkhnebakanskiy Rus. Fed. 39 E3
Verkhneimbatsk Rus. Fed.
Verkhniy Mamon Rus. Fed. 39 F1
Verkhov'ye Rus. Fed. 37 E3
Verkhoyansk Rus. Fed. 87 K2
Verkhoyanskiy Khrebet *mts* Rus. Fed. 87 K2
Vermilion U.S.A. 121 D2
Vermont *state* U.S.A. 123 F2
Vernal U.S.A. 118 E2
Vernon Can. 112 D2
Vernon U.S.A. 127 E2
Vero Beach U.S.A. 125 D3
Veroia Greece 59 B2
Verona Italy 56 B1
Versailles France 52 C2
Vert, Cape Senegal 96
Vertou France 52 B2
Verviers Belgium 48 B2
Verzy France 48 B3
Vescovato France 53 D3
Veselaya, Gora *mt.* Rus. Fed. 35 E3
Vesele Ukr. 39 E2
Veselovskoye Vodokhranilishche *resr* Rus. Fed. 39 F2

Veselyy Rus. Fed. 39 F2
Veshenskaya Rus. Fed. 39 F2
Vesoul France 53 D2
Vesterålen *is* Norway 40 C2
Vestfjorden *sea chan.* Norway 40 C2
Vestmannaeyjar *is* Iceland 36
Vesuvius *vol.* Italy 56 B2
Ves'yegonsk Rus. Fed. 37 E2
Vetlanda Sweden 41 D4
Veurne Belgium 48 A2
Vevey Switz. 53 D2
Veydelevka Rus. Fed. 39 E1
Vezirköprü Turkey 84 B1
Viana Brazil 135 E3
Viana do Castelo Port. 54 B1
Viangchan Laos *see* Vientiane
Vianópolis Brazil 138 C1
Viareggio Italy 56 B2
Viborg Denmark 41 B4
Vibo Valentia Italy 57 C3
Vic Spain 55 D1
Vicente Guerrero Mex. 128 A1
Vicenza Italy 56 B1
Vichuga Rus. Fed. 37 F2
Vichy France 53 C2
Vicksburg U.S.A. 124 B2
Viçosa Brazil 139 D2
Victor Harbor Austr. 104 B3
Victoria *r.* Austr. 102 C1
Victoria *state* Austr. 104 C3
Victoria Can. 112 C3
Victoria Chile 137 A4
Victoria Seychelles 95
Victoria U.S.A. 127 E3
Victoria, Lake Africa 95 D3
Victoria, Lake Austr. 104 C2
Victoria, Mount Myanmar 66 A1
Victoria, Mount P.N.G. 63 D3
Victoria Falls Zambia/Zimbabwe 98 B1
Victoria Island Can. 110 E2
Victoria West S. Africa 98 B3
Victorville U.S.A. 119 C4
Videle Romania 38 C3
Vídalsá Iceland 40 [inset]
Viedma Arg. 137 B5
Viedma, Lago *l.* Arg. 137 A5
Vienenburg Ger. 49 E2
Vienna Austria 51 D3
Vienne France 53 C2
Vienne *r.* France 52 C2
Vientiane Laos 66 B2
Viersen Ger. 48 C2
Vierzon France 52 C2
Vieste Italy 57 C2
Vietnam *country* Asia 66 B2
Việt Trì Vietnam 66 B1
Vigan Phil. 68 B2
Vigevano Italy 56 A1
Vigo Spain 54 B1
Vijayawada India 77 C3
Vík Iceland 40 [inset]

ikøyri Norway **42** E1
ila Franca de Xira Port. **54** B2
lagarcía de Arousa Spain
54 B1
ilaíba Spain **54** B1
ila Nova de Gaia Port. **54** B1
ilanova i la Geltrú Spain **55** D1
ila Real Port. **54** B1
ilar Formoso Port. **54** B1
ila Velha Brazil **139** D2
ilcabamba, Cordillera *mts* Peru
134 B4
il'cheka, Zemlya *i.* Rus. Fed.
86 G1
ilhelmina Sweden **40** D3
ilhena Brazil **134** C4
ilandi Estonia **36** F2
ilkaviškis Lith. **36** B3
illa Ahumada Mex. **128** B1
illablino Spain **54** B1
illach Austria **50** C3
illa Flores Mex. **129** C2
illagrán Mex. **129** C2
ilahermosa Mex. **129** C3
illa Insurgentes Mex. **128** A2
illa María Arg. **136** B4
illa Montes Bol. **136** B3
illanueva de la Serena Spain
54 B2
illa Ocampo Arg. **136** C3
illarrica Para. **136** C4
illarrobledo Spain **54** C2
illa Unión Arg. **136** B3
illa Unión *Durango* Mex. **128** B2
illa Unión *Sinaloa* Mex. **128** B2
illavicencio Col. **134** B2
illazon Bol. **136** B3
illefranche-sur-Saône France
50 A3
illena Spain **55** C2
illenueve-sur-Lot France **52** C3
ille Platte U.S.A. **124** B2
illers-Cotterêts France **48** A3
illeurbanne France **53** C2
ilnius Lith. **36** C3
il'nohirs'k Ukr. **39** D2
il'nyans'k Ukr. **39** E2
ilvoorde Belgium **48** B2
ilyeyka Belarus **36** C3
immerby Sweden **41** D4
iña del Mar Chile **137** A4
iñaroŝ Spain **55** C1
incennes U.S.A. **122** C3
ineland U.S.A. **123** E3
inh Vietnam **66** B2
inh Long Vietnam **67** B2
inita U.S.A. **127** E1
innytsya Ukr. **38** C2
inson Massif *mt.* Antarctica
107 K2
instra Norway **41** B3
irac Phil. **68** B2
irden Can. **113** E3
ire France **52** B2

Virei Angola **96** A1
Virgem da Lapa Brazil **139** D1
Virgin *r.* U.S.A. **126** B1
Virgin Is. S. Africa **99** C2
Virginia U.S.A. **121** E1
Virginia *state* U.S.A. **123** E3
Virginia Beach U.S.A. **123** E3
Virginia City U.S.A. **119** C3
Virgin Islands (U.K.) *terr.*
West Indies **131** D3
Virgin Islands (U.S.A.) *terr.*
West Indies **131** D3
Virovitica Croatia **57** C1
Virton Belgium **48** B3
Virtsu Estonia **36** B2
Viru *i.* Croatia **57** C2
Visaginas Lith. **36** C2
Visalia U.S.A. **119** C3
Visayan Sea Phil. **68** B2
Visby Sweden **41** D4
Viscount Melville Sound
sea chan. Can. **110** E2
Viseu Brazil **135** I3
Viseu Port. **54** B1
Vishakhapatnam India **77** C3
Viški Latvia **36** C2
Visoko Bos.-Herz. **57** C2
Vistula *r.* Pol. **51** D2
Viterbo Italy **56** B2
Viti Levu *i.* Fiji **142** E6
Vitim *r.* Rus. Fed. **87** J3
Vitória Brazil **139** D2
Vitória da Conquista Brazil
135 E4
Vitoria-Gasteiz Spain **54** C1
Vitré France **52** B2
Vitry-le-François France **53** C2
Vitsyebsk Belarus **37** D2
Vittoria Italy **56** B3
Viveiro Spain **54** B1
Vizcaíno, Sierra *mts* Mex.
128 A2
Vize Turkey **58** C2
Vizianagaram India **77** C3
Vlaardingen Neth. **48** B2
Vladikavkaz Rus. Fed. **35** D4
Vladimir Rus. Fed. **37** F2
Vladivostok Rus. Fed. **70** B2
Vlieland *i.* Neth. **48** B1
Vlissingen Neth. **48** A2
Vlorë Albania **59** A2
Vöcklabruck Austria **50** C3
Vogelsberg *hills* Ger. **49** D2
Vohimena, Tanjona *c.* Madag.
97
Voi Kenya **95** D3
Voiron France **53** D2
Voisey Bay Can. **115** D1
Vojens Denmark **50** B1
Vojvodina *prov.* S.M. **58** A1
Voknavolok Rus. Fed. **40** G3
Volcano Bay Japan *see*
Uchiura-wan
Volda Norway **42** E1

Volga Rus. Fed. **37** E2
Volga *r.* Rus. Fed. **37** E2
Volgodonsk Rus. Fed. **35** D4
Volgograd Rus. Fed. **35** D4
Volkhov Rus. Fed. **37** D2
Volkhov *r.* Rus. Fed. **37** D1
Volnovakha Ukr. **39** E2
Volochys'k Ukr. **38** C2
Volodarsk Rus. Fed. **37** F2
Volodars'ke Ukr. **39** E2
Volodars'k-Volyns'kyy Ukr. **38** C1
Volodymyrets' Ukr. **38** C1
Volodymyr-Volyns'kyy Ukr. **38** B1
Vologda Rus. Fed. **37** E2
Volokolamsk Rus. Fed. **37** E2
Volokonovka Rus. Fed. **39** E1
Volos Greece **59** B3
Volosovo Rus. Fed. **36** C2
Volot Rus. Fed. **37** D2
Vol'sk Rus. Fed. **35** D3
Volta, Lake *resr* Ghana **90** C4
Volta Redonda Brazil **139** D2
Volzhskiy Rus. Fed. **35** D4
Vopnafjörður Iceland **40** [inset]
Voranava Belarus **36** C3
Voreioi Sporades *is* Greece
84 A2
Vorkuta Rus. Fed. **34** F2
Vormsi *i.* Estonia **36** B2
Vorona *r.* Rus. Fed. **39** F1
Voronezh Rus. Fed. **37** E3
Voronezh *r.* Rus. Fed. **37** E3
Vorontsovka Rus. Fed. **39** F1
Vorskla *r.* Rus. Fed. **39** D2
Võrtsjärv *l.* Estonia **36** C2
Võru Estonia **36** C2
Vosburg S. Africa **98** B3
Vosges *mts* France **53** D2
Voskresensk Rus. Fed. **37** E2
Voss Norway **41** B3
Vostochno-Sibirskoye More *sea*
Rus. Fed. *see* East Siberian Sea
Vostochnyy Sayan *mts* Rus. Fed.
87 I3
Vostok Rus. Fed. **70** C1
Votkinsk Rus. Fed. **34** E3
Votuporanga Brazil **138** C2
Vouziers France **48** B3
Voynitsa Rus. Fed. **40** G2
Voznesens'k Ukr. **39** D2
Voznesenskoye Rus. Fed. **37** F2
Vrangel' Rus. Fed. **70** B2
Vrangelya, Ostrov *i.* Rus. Fed. *see*
Wrangel Island
Vranje S.M. **58** B2
Vratnik *pass* Bulg. **58** C2
Vratsa Bulg. **58** B2
Vrbas *r.* Bos.-Herz. **57** C1
Vrbas S.M. **58** A1
Vredenburg S. Africa **98** A3
Vredendal S. Africa **98** A3
Vršac S.M. **58** B1
Vryburg S. Africa **98** B2
Vryheid S. Africa **99** D2

Vsevolozhsk Rus. Fed. **37** D1
Vučitrn S.M. **58** B2
Vukovar Croatia **57** C1
Vuktyl' Rus. Fed. **34** E2
Vukuzakhe S. Africa **99** C2
Vulcano, Isola i. Italy **56** B3
Vung Tau Vietnam **67** B2
Vyatka Rus. Fed. see Kirov
Vyaz'ma Rus. Fed. **37** D2
Vyazniki Rus. Fed. **37** F2
Vyerkhnyadzvinsk Belarus **36** C2
Vyksa Rus. Fed. **37** F2
Vylkove Ukr. **38** C2
Vynohradiv Ukr. **38** B2
Vypolzovo Rus. Fed. **37** D2
Vyritsa Rus. Fed. **37** D2
Vyselki Rus. Fed. **39** E2
Vyshhorod Ukr. **38** D1
Vyshniy-Volochek Rus. Fed. **37** D2
Vyškov Czech Rep. **51** D3
Vytegra Rus. Fed. **34** C2

W

Wa Ghana **90** B3
Waal r. Neth. **48** B2
Waalwijk Neth. **48** B1
Wabasca r. Can. **112** D2
Wabasca-Desmarais Can. **112** D2
Wabash r. U.S.A. **122** C3
Wabē Gestro r. Eth. **93** C4
Wabē Shebelē Wenz r. Eth. **93** C4
Wabowden Can. **113** F2
Waccasassa Bay U.S.A. **125** D3
Wächtersbach Ger. **49** D2
Waco U.S.A. **127** E2
Wad Pak. **78** A2
Waddān Libya **91** D2
Waddenzee sea chan. Neth. **48** B1
Waddington, Mount Can. **112** D2
Waddinxveen Neth. **48** B1
Wadena Can. **113** E2
Wadena U.S.A. **121** D1
Wadgassen Ger. **48** C3
Wadi Halfa Sudan **92** B3
Wad Medani Sudan **92** B3
Wafangdian China **74** C2
Wageningen Neth. **48** B2
Wagga Wagga Austr. **105** D3
Wahoo U.S.A. **121** D2
Wahpeton U.S.A. **121** D1
Waiau r. N.Z. **106** B3
Waigeo i. Indon. **63** C3
Waikabubak Indon. **65** C2
Waikerie Austr. **104** B2
Waimate N.Z. **106** B3
Wainganga r. India **79** B3
Waingapu Indon. **65** D2

Wainwright Can. **113** D2
Wainwright U.S.A. **110** B2
Waiouru N.Z. **106** C2
Waipara N.Z. **106** B3
Waipawa N.Z. **106** C2
Wairau r. N.Z. **106** B3
Wairoa N.Z. **106** C2
Waitaki r. N.Z. **106** B3
Waitara N.Z. **106** B2
Waiuku N.Z. **106** B2
Wajir Kenya **95** E2
Wakasa-wan b. Japan **71** C3
Wakatipu, Lake N.Z. **106** A4
Wakayama Japan **71** C4
WaKeeney U.S.A. **120** D3
Wakefield N.Z. **106** B3
Wakefield U.K. **46** C3
Wake Island terr. N. Pacific Ocean **100**
Wakkanai Japan **70** D1
Wałbrzych Pol. **51** D2
Walcha Austr. **105** E2
Walchum Ger. **48** C1
Wałcz Pol. **51** D2
Wales admin. div. U.K. **47** B3
Walgett Austr. **105** D2
Walker Lake U.S.A. **119** C3
Walla Walla U.S.A. **118** C1
Walldürn Ger. **49** D3
Wallendbeen Austr. **105** D2
Wallis, Îles is Wallis and Futuna Is **111**
Wallis and Futuna Islands terr. S. Pacific Ocean **101**
Walney, Isle of i. U.K. **46** B2
Walsall U.K. **47** C3
Walsenburg U.S.A. **120** C3
Walsrode Ger. **49** D1
Walterboro U.S.A. **125** D2
Walvis Bay Namibia **96** A2
Wamba Dem. Rep. Congo **95** C2
Wanaaring Austr. **104** C1
Wanaka N.Z. **106** A3
Wanaka, Lake N.Z. **106** A3
Wanapitei Lake Can. **114** B2
Wanda Arg. **138** B3
Wanda Shan mts China **70** B1
Wanding China **66** A1
Wanganui N.Z. **106** C2
Wangaratta Austr. **105** D3
Wangqing China **69** B1
Wan Hsa-la Myanmar **66** A1
Wanning China **75** B4
Wanxian China **74** A2
Wanyuan China **74** A2
Warangal India **77** B3
Warburg Ger. **49** D2
Warburton Austr. **102** B2
Warburton watercourse Austr. **104** B1
Wardha India **79** B2
Ward Hill U.K. **44** C1
Ware Can. **112** C2
Waren Ger. **49** F1

Warendorf Ger. **48** C2
Warialda Austr. **105** E1
Warmbad Namibia **98** A2
Warm Springs U.S.A. **119** C3
Warner Lakes U.S.A. **118** C2
Warner Robins U.S.A. **125** D2
Warracknabeal Austr. **104** C3
Warrego r. Austr. **105** D2
Warren Austr. **105** D2
Warren AR U.S.A. **124** B2
Warren OH U.S.A. **123** D2
Warren PA U.S.A. **123** E2
Warrenpoint U.K. **45** C1
Warrensburg U.S.A. **121** E3
Warrenton S. Africa **98** B2
Warri Nigeria **91** C4
Warrington U.K. **46** B3
Warrnambool Austr. **104** C3
Warsaw Pol. **51** E2
Warszawa Pol. see Warsaw
Warta r. Pol. **51** C2
Warwick Austr. **105** E1
Warwick U.K. **47** C3
Wasco U.S.A. **119** C3
Washburn U.S.A. **120** C1
Washington DC U.S.A. **123** E3
Washington IA U.S.A. **121** E2
Washington IN U.S.A. **122** C3
Washington MO U.S.A. **121** E3
Washington NC U.S.A. **125** E1
Washington PA U.S.A. **123** D2
Washington state U.S.A. **118** B1
Washington, Mount U.S.A. **123** F2
Washuk Pak. **78** A2
Waskaganish Can. **114** C1
Waskaiowaka Lake Can. **113** F2
Waswanipi, Lac l. Can. **114** C2
Watampone Indon. **65** D2
Waterbury U.S.A. **123** F2
Waterbury Lake Can. **113** E2
Waterford Rep. of Ireland **45** C2
Waterford Harbour Rep. of Ireland **45** C2
Waterloo U.S.A. **121** E2
Waterpoort S. Africa **99** C1
Watertown NY U.S.A. **123** E2
Watertown SD U.S.A. **121** D2
Watertown WI U.S.A. **122** C2
Waterville U.S.A. **123** G2
Watford U.K. **47** C4
Watford City U.S.A. **120** C1
Wathaman r. Can. **113** E2
Watonga U.S.A. **127** E1
Watsa Dem. Rep. Congo **95** C2
Watsi Kengo Dem. Rep. Congo **94** C3
Watson Lake Can. **112** C1
Watsonville U.S.A. **119** B3
Wau Sudan **93** A4
Wauchope Austr. **105** E2
Waukegan U.S.A. **122** C2
Wausau U.S.A. **122** C2
Waveney r. U.K. **47** D3

averly U.S.A. **121** E2
aycross U.S.A. **125** D2
ayne U.S.A. **121** D2
aynesboro *GA* U.S.A. **125** C2
aynesboro *VA* U.S.A. **123** E3
azirabad Pak. **78** B1
ear *i.* U.K. **46** C2
eatherford U.S.A. **127** E2
ebequie Can. **114** B1
ebi Shabeelle *r.* Somalia **93** C4
ebster U.S.A. **121** D1
ee Waa Austr. **105** E2
egorzewo Pol. **51** E2
eiden in der Oberpfalz Ger.
49 F3
eifang China **74** B2
eihai China **74** C2
eilmoringle Austr. **105** U1
eimar Ger. **49** E2
einan China **74** A2
einsberg Ger. **48** D3
eipa Austr. **103** D1
eir *r.* Austr. **105** F1
eishan China **66** B1
eißenburg in Bayern Ger.
49 E3
eißenfels Ger. **49** E2
eißkugel *mt.* Austria/Italy **50** C3
ejherowo Pol. **51** D2
ekweti Can. **112** D1
eldiya Eth. **93** B3
elkom S. Africa **99** C2
elland *r.* U.K. **47** C3
ellesley Islands Austr. **103** C1
ellington Austr. **105** D2
ellington N.Z. **106** B3
ellington China **121** D3
ellington, Isla *i.* Chile **137** A5
ellington, Lake Austr. **105** D3
ells U.K. **47** B4
ells U.S.A. **118** D2
ells, Lake *salt flat* Austr.
102 B2
ellsford N.Z. **106** B2
ells-next-the-Sea U.K. **46** D3
els Austria **50** D2
elshpool U.K. **47** B3
emindji Can. **114** C1
enatchee U.S.A. **118** B1
enchang China **75** B4
endelstein Ger. **49** E3
endeng China **74** C2
engyuan China **75** B3
enling China **75** C3
enshan China **75** A3
entworth Austr. **104** C2
enzhou China **75** C3
epener S. Africa **99** C2
erda Botswana **98** B2
erdau Ger. **49** F2
erder Ger. **49** F1
ernberg-Köblitz Ger. **49** F3
ernigerode Ger. **49** F2
erra *r.* Ger. **49** D2

Werris Creek Austr. **105** E2
Wertheim Ger. **49** D3
Wesel Ger. **48** C2
Wesendorf Ger. **49** E1
Weser *sea chan.* Ger. **49** D1
Wessel Islands Austr. **103** C1
Wesselton S. Africa **99** C2
West Antarctica *reg.* Antarctica
107 I2
West Bank *terr.* Asia **80** B2
West Bromwich U.K. **47** C3
Westerbury Ger. **48** C2
Western Australia *state* Austr.
102 B2
Western Cape *prov.* S. Africa
98 B3
Western Desert Egypt **92** A2
Western Ghats *mts* India **77** B3
Western Sahara *terr.* Africa
90 A2
Westerschelde *est.* Neth. **48** A2
Westerstede Ger. **48** C1
West Falkland *i.* Falkland Is
137 B6
West Frankfort U.S.A. **122** C3
West Frisian Islands Neth. **48** B1
West Indies *is* Caribbean Sea
131 D2
Westlock Can. **112** D2
Westmalle Belgium **48** B2
West Memphis U.S.A. **124** F1
Weston-super-Mare U.K. **47** B4
West Palm Beach U.S.A. **125** D3
West Plains U.S.A. **121** E3
West Point U.S.A. **121** E3
Westport Rep. of Ireland **45** B2
Westport N.Z. **106** B3
Westray Can. **113** E2
Westray *i.* U.K. **44** C1
West Siberian Plain Rus. Fed.
see Zapadno Sibirskaya Ravnina
West-Terschelling Neth. **48** B1
West Town Rep. of Ireland **45** B1
West Virginia *state* U.S.A.
123 D3
West Wyalong Austr. **105** D2
West Yellowstone U.S.A. **118** D2
Wetaskiwin Can. **112** D2
Wetzlar Ger. **49** D2
Wewak P.N.G. **63** D3
Wexford Rep. of Ireland **45** C2
Weyburn Can. **110** F3
Weyhe Ger. **49** D1
Weymouth U.K. **47** B4
Whakatane N.Z. **106** C2
Whale Cove Can. **113** F1
Whalsay *i.* U.K. **44** [inset]
Whangarei N.Z. **106** B2
Wharfe *r.* U.K. **46** C3
Wha Ti Can. **112** D1
Wheatland U.S.A. **120** B2
Wheeler Peak *NM* U.S.A. **126** C1
Wheeler Peak *NV* U.S.A. **119** D3

Wheeling U.S.A. **123** D2
Whernside *h.* U.K. **46** B2
Whistler Can. **112** C2
Whitby U.K. **46** C2
White *r.* Can./U.S.A. **112** B1
White *r.* U.S.A. **124** B2
White, Lake *salt flat* Austr.
102 B2
White Bay Can. **115** E2
White Butte *mt.* U.S.A. **120** C1
White Cliffs Austr. **104** C2
Whitecourt Can. **112** D2
Whitefish U.S.A. **118** D1
Whitehaven U.K. **46** B2
Whitehorse Can. **112** B1
White Lake U.S.A. **124** B3
White Mountain U.S.A.
118 C0
White Nile *r.* Sudan/Uganda
93 B3
White Sea Rus. Fed. **34** C2
White Sulphur Springs U.S.A.
118 D1
Whiteville U.S.A. **125** E2
Whitewater Baldy *mt.* U.S.A.
126 C2
Whitewater Lake Can. **114** B1
Whithorn U.K. **44** B3
Whitianga N.Z. **106** C2
Whitney, Mount U.S.A. **119** C3
Whitsunday Island Austr. **103** D2
Whyalla Austr. **104** B2
Wichita U.S.A. **121** D3
Wichita Falls U.S.A. **127** E2
Wick U.K. **44** C2
Wickenburg U.S.A. **126** D2
Wicklow Rep. of Ireland **45** C2
Wicklow Head Rep. of Ireland
45 D2
Wicklow Mountains
Rep. of Ireland **45** C2
Widnes U.K. **46** B3
Wiehengebirge *hills* Ger. **49** D1
Wiehl Ger. **48** C2
Wieluń Pol. **51** D2
Wien Austria *see* Vienna
Wiener Neustadt Austria **51** D3
Wieringerwerf Neth. **48** B1
Wiesbaden Ger. **48** D2
Wiesloch Ger. **49** D3
Wiesmoor Ger. **48** C1
Więżyca *h.* Pol. **51** C2
Wight, Isle of *i.* U.K. **47** C4
Wijchen Neth. **48** B2
Wilcannia Austr. **104** C2
Wild Coast S. Africa **99** C3
Wilge *r.* S. Africa **99** C2
Wilhelm, Mount P.N.G. **110**
Wilhelmshaven Ger. **48** D1
Wilkes-Barre U.S.A. **123** E2
Wilkes Land *reg.* Antarctica
107 G2
Willcox U.S.A. **126** C2
Willebroek Belgium **48** B2

Willemstad Neth. Antilles **131** D3
William, Mount Austr. **104** C3
William Creek Austr. **104** B1
Williams U.S.A. **126** B1
Williamsburg U.S.A. **123** E3
Williams Lake Can. **112** C2
Williamston U.S.A. **122** D3
Williamsport U.S.A. **123** E2
Williamston U.S.A. **125** E1
Williston S. Africa **98** B3
Williston U.S.A. **120** C1
Williston Lake Can. **112** C2
Willits U.S.A. **119** B3
Willmar U.S.A. **121** D1
Willowmore S. Africa **98** B3
Willowvale S. Africa **99** C3
Wills, Lake *salt flat* Austr. **102** B2
Willunga Austr. **104** B3
Wilmington Austr. **104** B2
Wilmington *DE* U.S.A. **123** E3
Wilmington *NC* U.S.A. **125** E2
Wilnsdorf Ger. **48** D2
Wilson U.S.A. **125** E1
Wilson's Promontory *pen.* Austr.
105 D3
Wiluna Austr. **102** B2
Winchester U.K. **47** C4
Winchester *KY* U.S.A. **122** D3
Winchester *VA* U.S.A. **123** E3
Wind *r.* Can. **112** B1
Windermere *l.* U.K. **46** B2
Windhoek Namibia **98** A1
Windorah Austr. **103** D2
Wind River Range *mts* U.S.A.
120 B2
Windsor Austr. **105** E2
Windsor Can. **114** D2
Windward Islands Caribbean Sea
131 D3
Windward Passage Cuba/Haiti
131 C3
Winfield U.S.A. **121** D3
Winisk Can. **114** B1
Winisk *r.* Can. **114** B1
Winisk Lake Can. **114** B1
Winnebago, Lake U.S.A. **122** C2
Winnemucca U.S.A. **118** C3
Winner U.S.A. **120** C2
Winnfield U.S.A. **124** B2
Winnibigoshish, Lake U.S.A.
121 E1
Winnipeg Can. **113** F3
Winnipeg *r.* Can. **113** F2
Winnipeg, Lake Can. **113** F2
Winnipegosis, Lake Can. **113** E2
Winnipesaukee, Lake U.S.A.
123 F2
Winnsboro U.S.A. **124** B2
Winona *MN* U.S.A. **121** E2
Winona *MS* U.S.A. **124** C2
Winschoten Neth. **48** D1
Winsen (Aller) Ger. **49** D1
Winsen (Luhe) Ger. **49** E1

Winslow U.S.A. **126** B1
Winston-Salem U.S.A. **125** D1
Winterberg Ger. **49** D2
Winter Haven U.S.A. **125** D3
Winterswijk Neth. **48** C2
Winterthur Switz. **53** D2
Winton Austr. **103** D2
Winton N.Z. **106** A4
Wirrabara Austr. **104** B2
Wisbech U.K. **47** D3
Wisconsin *r.* U.S.A. **122** B2
Wisconsin *state* U.S.A. **122** C2
Wisconsin Rapids U.S.A. **122** C2
Wisła *r.* Pol. *see* Vistula
Wismar Ger. **50** C2
Witbank S. Africa **99** C2
Witney U.K. **47** C4
Wittenberge Ger. **49** E1
Wittingen Ger. **49** E1
Wittlich Ger. **48** C1
Wittmund Ger. **48** C1
Wittstock Ger. **49** F1
Witvlei Namibia **98** A1
Witzenhausen Ger. **49** D2
Władysławowo Pol. **51** D2
Włocławek Pol. **51** D2
Wodonga Austr. **105** D3
Woippy France **48** C3
Wokam *i.* Indon. **63** C3
Woking U.K. **47** C4
Woldegk Ger. **49** F1
Wolfen Ger. **49** F2
Wolfenbüttel Ger. **49** E1
Wolfhagen Ger. **49** D2
Wolf Point U.S.A. **120** B1
Wolfsburg Ger. **49** E1
Wolfville Can. **115** D2
Wolgast Ger. **50** C2
Wolin Pol. **50** C2
Wollaston Lake Can. **113** E2
Wollaston Lake *l.* Can. **113** E2
Wollaston Peninsula Can.
110 E2
Wollongong Austr. **105** E2
Wolmirstedt Ger. **49** E1
Wolvega Neth. **48** C1
Wolverhampton U.K. **47** B3
Wŏnju S. Korea **69** B2
Wonowon Can. **112** C2
Wŏnsan N. Korea **69** B2
Wonthaggi Austr. **105** D3
Woocalla Austr. **104** B2
Woodah, Isle *i.* Austr. **103** C1
Woodbridge U.K. **47** D3
Woodroffe, Mount Austr. **102** C2
Woods, Lake *salt flat* Austr.
102 C1
Woods, Lake of the Can./U.S.A.
121 E1
Woods Point Austr. **105** D3
Woodstock Can. **123** G1
Woodville N.Z. **106** C3
Woodward U.S.A. **127** E1
Woolgoolga Austr. **105** E2

Woomera Austr. **104** B2
Worcester S. Africa **98** A3
Worcester U.K. **47** B3
Worcester U.S.A. **123** F2
Wörgl Austria **50** C3
Workington U.K. **46** B2
Worksop U.K. **46** C3
Worland U.S.A. **120** B2
Worms Ger. **49** D3
Wörth am Rhein Ger. **49** D3
Worthing U.K. **47** C4
Worthington U.S.A. **121** D2
Wotu Indon. **65** D2
Wowoni *i.* Indon. **65** D2
Wrangel Island Rus. Fed.
87 O2
Wrangell U.S.A. **112** B2
Wrangell Mountains U.S.A.
110 B3
Wrath, Cape U.K. **44** B1
Wray U.S.A. **120** C2
Wreck Point S. Africa **98** A2
Wrexham U.K. **46** B3
Wrightmyo India **67** A2
Wrigley Can. **112** C1
Wrocław Pol. **51** D2
Września Pol. **51** D2
Wudu China **74** A2
Wuhai China **74** A2
Wuhan China **75** B2
Wuhu China **74** B2
Wukari Nigeria **91** C4
Wuli China **79** D1
Wuliang Shan *mts* China
66 B1
Wuliaru *i.* Indon. **63** C3
Wumeng Shan *mts* China
75 A3
Wunnummin Lake Can. **114** B1
Wunsiedel Ger. **49** F2
Wunstorf Ger. **49** D1
Wuntho Myanmar **66** A1
Wuppertal Ger. **48** C2
Würzburg Ger. **49** D3
Wurzen Ger. **49** F2
Wuwei China **74** A2
Wuxi *Chongqing* China **74** A2
Wuxi *Jiangsu* China **74** C2
Wuxing China *see* Huzhou
Wuyishan China **75** B3
Wuyi Shan *mts* China **75** B3
Wuyuan China **74** A1
Wuzhishan China **75** A4
Wuzhong China **74** A2
Wuzhou China **75** B3
Wyangala Reservoir Austr.
105 D2
Wycheproof Austr. **104** C3
Wye *r.* U.K. **47** B4
Wyndham Austr. **102** B1
Wynne U.S.A. **124** B1
Wynyard Can. **113** E2
Wyoming *state* U.S.A. **120** B2
Wyszków Pol. **51** E2

X	Xuanwei China 75 A3	Yangzhou China 74 B2
	Xuchang China 74 B2	Yanji China 69 B1
aafuun Somalia 93 D3	Xuddur Somalia 93 C4	Yankton U.S.A. 121 D2
aignabouli Laos 66 B2	Xun Jiang r. China 75 B3	Yanskiy Zaliv g. Rus. Fed. 87 L2
ai-Xai Moz. 97 C2	Xuwen China 75 B3	Yantai China 74 C2
amba China 74 A1	Xuyong China 75 A3	Yaoundé Cameroon 94 B2
a Nua Laos 66 B1		Yap i. Micronesia 63 D2
anagas Botswana 98 B1	**Y**	Yapen i. Indon. 63 D3
angongo Angola 96 A1		Yapen, Selat sea chan. Indon. 63 D3
ankändi Azer. 85 C2	Ya'an China 75 A2	Yaqui r. Mex. 128 A2
anthi Greece 59 B2	Yabëlo Eth. 93 B4	Yaransk Rus. Fed. 34 D3
anxerê Brazil 138 B3	Yablonovyy Khrebet mts Rus. Fed. 73 D1	Yaren Nauru 100
apuri Brazil 134 C4	Yadkin r. U.S.A. 125 D1	Yarim Yemen 82 B3
ativa Spain 55 C2	Yagnitsa Rus. Fed. 37 E2	Yarlung Zangbo r. China 72 C3
iamen China 75 B3	Yahk Can. 112 D3	Yarmouth Can. 115 D2
i'an China 74 A2	Yahualica Mex. 128 B2	Yaroslavl' Rus. Fed. 37 E2
ianfeng China 75 A3	Yahyalı Turkey 84 B2	Yaroslavskiy Rus. Fed. 70 B2
iangfan China 74 B2	Yaizu Japan 71 C4	Yarram Austr. 105 D3
ianggelila China 66 A1	Yakima U.S.A. 118 B1	Yartsevo Rus. Fed. 37 D2
ianghuang Qi China see Xin Bulag	Yakumo Japan 70 D2	Yasnogorsk Rus. Fed. 37 E3
iangkhoang Laos 66 B2	Yakutat U.S.A. 112 B2	Yasothon Thai. 67 B2
iantan China 75 B3	Yakutat Bay U.S.A. 112 A2	Yass Austr. 105 D2
iantao China 75 B2	Yakutsk Rus. Fed. 87 K2	Yatağan Turkey 59 C3
ianyang China 74 A2	Yakymivka Ukr. 39 E1	Yathkyed Lake Can. 113 F1
iaogan China 74 B2	Yala Thai. 67 B3	Yatsushiro Japan 71 B4
iao Hinggan Ling mts China 73 E1	Yallourn Austr. 105 D3	Yavari r. Brazil/Peru 134 C3
iaoshan China 75 C2	Yalova Turkey 59 C2	Yavatmal India 79 B2
ichang China 66 B1	Yalta Ukr. 39 D3	Yavi, Cerro mt. Venez. 146
feng Gansu China 74 A2	Yalu Jiang r. China/N. Korea 69 A1	Yavoriv Ukr. 38 B2
ilinhot China 74 B1	Yamagata Japan 70 D3	Yawatahama Japan 71 B4
in Bulag China 73 D3	Yamaguchi Japan 71 B4	Yazd Iran 85 D2
inghai China 72 C2	Yamal, Poluostrov pen. Rus. Fed. see Yamal Peninsula	Yazoo City U.S.A. 124 B2
inghua China 74 B2	Yamal Peninsula Rus. Fed. 34 F1	Ydra i. Greece 59 B3
ingning China 66 B1	Yamba Austr. 105 E1	Ye Myanmar 67 A2
ingtai China 74 A2	Yambio Sudan 93 A4	Yecheng China 81 E3
ingu r. Brazil 135 D3	Yambol Bulg. 58 C2	Yécora Mex. 128 B2
ingyi China 75 A3	Yamburg Rus. Fed. 34 G2	Yefremov Rus. Fed. 37 E3
ining China 72 C2	Yamethin Myanmar 66 A1	Yegorlyk r. Rus. Fed. 39 F2
injiang Uygur Zizhiqu aut. reg. China 79 C1	Yamoussoukro Côte d'Ivoire 90 B4	Yegorlykskaya Rus. Fed. 39 F2
inmin China 69 A1	Yampil' Ukr. 38 C2	Yegor'yevsk Rus. Fed. 37 E2
inning China 75 B3	Yamuna r. India 79 C2	Yei Sudan 93 B4
intai China 74 B2	Yamzho Yumco r. China 79 D2	Yekaterinburg Rus. Fed. 34 F3
inxiang China 74 B2	Yana r. Rus. Fed. 87 L2	Yelets Rus. Fed. 37 E3
inyang China 74 B2	Yan'an China 74 A2	Yell i. U.K. 44 [inset]
inyu China 75 B3	Yanbu' al Bahr Saudi Arabia 82 A2	Yellowknife Can. 112 D1
inzhou Shanxi China 74 B2	Yancheng China 74 B2	Yellow Sea N. Pacific Ocean 73 E2
inzhou Shanxi China 73 D2	Yanchep Austr. 102 A3	Yellowstone r. U.S.A. 118 E1
inzho de Limia Spain 54 B1	Yangchun China 75 B3	Yellowstone Lake U.S.A. 120 A2
iqing Shan mts China 72 C2	Yangdok N. Korea 69 B2	Yel'sk Belarus 36 C3
i Ujimqin Qi China see Bayan Ul Hot	Yangjiang China 75 B3	Yemen country Asia 82 B3
iujing China 75 B3	Yangquan China 74 B2	Yemva Rus. Fed. 34 E2
izang Zizhiqu aut. reg. China 72 B2	Yangtze r. Qinghai China 72 C2	Yenakiyeve Ukr. 39 E2
o'jayli Uzbek. 80 C2	Yangtze r. China 75 C2	Yenangyaung Myanmar 66 A1
uancheng China 74 B2	Yangtze r. China 66 B1	Yên Bai Vietnam 66 B1
	Yangtze, Mouth of the China 74 C2	Yendi Ghana 90 B4
		Yeovil U.K. 47 B4
		Yerevan Armenia 85 C1
		Yereymentau Kazakh. 81 E1
		Yermish' Rus. Fed. 37 F3
		Yershov Rus. Fed. 35 D3
		Yesil' Kazakh. 81 D1
		Yeşilova Turkey 59 C3
		Yetman Austr. 105 E1

Ye-U Myanmar **66** A1
Yeu, Île d' i. France **52** B2
Yevlax Azer. **35** D4
Yevpatoriya Ukr. **39** D2
Yeysk Rus. Fed. **39** E2
Yezyaryshcha Belarus **36** C2
Yibin China **75** A3
Yichang China **74** B2
Yichun *Heilong.* China **73** E1
Yichun *Jiangxi* China **75** B3
Yilan China **70** A1
Yıldız Dağları *mts* Turkey **58** C2
Yıldızeli Turkey **84** B2
Yinchuan China **74** A2
Yingde China **75** B3
Yingkou China **74** C1
Yingshan *Sichuan* China **74** A2
Yingtan China **75** B3
Yining China **81** F2
Yirga Alem Eth. **93** B4
Yitong China **69** B1
Yiwu China **72** C2
Yixing China **74** B2
Yiyang China **75** B3
Yizhou China **75** A3
Yli-Kitka *l.* Fin. **40** F2
Ylitornio Fin. **40** E2
Ylivieska Fin. **40** E3
Yogyakarta Indon. **65** C3
Yokohama Japan **71** D3
Yola Nigeria **91** D4
Yonezawa Japan **71** D3
Yong'an China **75** B3
Yongchun China **75** B3
Yongdeng China **74** A2
Yongsheng China **66** B1
Yongzhou China **75** B3
Yopal Col. **134** B2
York Austr. **102** A3
York U.K. **46** C3
York *NE* U.S.A. **121** D2
York *PA* U.S.A. **123** E3
York, Cape Austr. **63** D3
Yorke Peninsula Austr. **104** B3
Yorketown Austr. **104** B3
Yorkshire Wolds *hills* U.K. **46** C3
Yorkton Can. **110** F3
Yoshkar-Ola Rus. Fed. **35** D3
Youghal Rep. of Ireland **45** D3
Young Austr. **105** D2
Younghusband Peninsula Austr.
104 B3
Youngstown U.S.A. **123** D2
Youvarou Mali **90** B3
Yozgat Turkey **84** B2
Ypé-Jhú Para. **138** A2
Yreka U.S.A. **118** C2
Yr Wyddfa *mt.* U.K. *see* Snowdon
Ystad Sweden **41** C4
Ysyk-Köl *salt l.* Kyrg. **81** E2
Ytri-Rangá *r.* Iceland **40** [inset]
Yuan Jiang *r.* China **66** B1
Yuba City U.S.A. **119** B3
Yucatán *pen.* Mex. **129** C3

Yucatan Channel Cuba/Mex.
130 B2
Yuendumu Austr. **102** C2
Yueyang China **75** B3
Yugorsk Rus. Fed. **34** F2
Yukagirskoye Ploskogor'ye *plat.*
Rus. Fed. **87** M2
Yukon *r.* Can./U.S.A. **112** B1
Yukon Territory *admin. div.* Can.
110 C2
Yulin *Guangxi* China **75** B3
Yulin *Shaanxi* China **74** A2
Yulong Xueshan *mt.* China **66** B1
Yuma *AZ* U.S.A. **126** B2
Yuma *CO* U.S.A. **120** C2
Yumen China **72** C1
Yunak Turkey **84** B2
Yuncheng China **74** B2
Yungas *reg.* Bol. **146**
Yunnan *prov.* China **75** A3
Yunta Austr. **104** B2
Yunyang China **74** B2
Yurungkax He *r.* China **79** C1
Yur'yevets Rus. Fed. **37** F2
Yü Shan *mt.* Taiwan **75** C3
Yushkozero Rus. Fed. **40** G3
Yutian China **79** C1
Yuxi China **66** B2
Yuzha Rus. Fed. **37** F2
Yuzhno-Kuril'sk Rus. Fed. **70** E2
Yuzhno-Sakhalinsk Rus. Fed.
70 D1
Yuzhnoukrayinsk Ukr. **39** D2
Yuzhou China **74** B2
Yvetot France **52** C2

Z

Zaandam Neth. **48** B1
Zabīd Yemen **82** B3
Zābol Iran **83** D2
Zābolī Iran **83** D2
Zacapa Guat. **129** D3
Zacapu Mex. **128** B3
Zacatecas Mex. **128** B2
Zacatlán Mex. **129** C3
Zacharo Greece **59** B3
Zacoalco Mex. **128** B2
Zadar Croatia **56** C2
Zadetkyi Kyun *i.* Myanmar **67** A3
Zadonsk Rus. Fed. **37** E3
Za'farānah Egypt **84** B3
Zafra Spain **54** B2
Zagreb Croatia **57** C1
Zagros Mountains Iran **85** C2
Zagros, Kūhhā-ye *mts* Iran *see*
  Zagros Mountains
Zagros Mountains Iran **85** C2
Zāhedān Iran **83** D2
Zahlé Lebanon **84** B2
Zaḥrān Saudi Arabia **82** B3
Zahrez Chergui *salt pan* Alg.
55 D2

Zaječar S.M. **58** B2
Zākhō Iraq **85** C2
Zakynthos Greece **59** B3
Zakynthos *i.* Greece **59** B3
Zalaegerszeg Hungary **51** D3
Zalău Romania **38** B2
Zalim Saudi Arabia **82** B2
Žalma, Jabal az *mt.* Saudi Arabia
82 A2
Zama City Can. **112** D2
Zambeze *r.* Angola *see* Zambezi
Zambezi *r.* Angola **97** B1
Zambezi Zambia **96** B1
Zambia *country* Africa **96** B1
Zamboanga Phil. **68** B3
Zamboanga Peninsula Phil. **68** B3
Zamora Spain **54** B1
Zamora de Hidalgo Mex. **128** B3
Zamość Pol. **51** E2
Zanda China **79** C1
Zandvliet Belgium **48** B2
Zanesville U.S.A. **122** D3
Zanjān Iran **85** C2
Zanskar Mountains India **79** B1
Zante *i.* Greece *see* Zakynthos
Zanzibar Tanz. **95** D3
Zanzibar Island Tanz. **95** D3
Zaokskiy Rus. Fed. **37** E3
Zaouatallaz Alg. **91** C2
Zaozhuang China **74** B2
Zapadnaya Dvina *r.* Europe **37** D1
Zapadnaya Dvina Rus. Fed.
37 D2
Zapadno Sibirskaya Ravnina
  plain Rus. Fed. **34** H2
Zapadnyy Sayan *reg.* Rus. Fed.
72 B1
Zapata U.S.A. **127** E3
Zapolyarnyy Rus. Fed. **40** G2
Zaporizhzhya Ukr. **39** E2
Zara Turkey **84** B2
Zaragoza Spain **55** C1
Zarand Iran **83** C1
Zaranj Afgh. **78** A1
Zarasai Lith. **36** C2
Zaraysk Rus. Fed. **37** E3
Zaraza Venez. **134** C2
Zaria Nigeria **91** C3
Zarichne Ukr. **38** C1
Zarqān Iran **85** D3
Zarubino Rus. Fed. **70** B2
Żary Pol. **50** D2
Zastron S. Africa **99** C3
Žatec Czech Rep. **49** F2
Zavitinsk Rus. Fed. **73** E1
Zawiercie Pol. **51** D2
Zaysan, Lake Kazakh. **81** F2
Zdolbuniv Ukr. **38** C1
Zealand *i.* Denmark **41** C4
Zeebrugge Belgium **48** A2
Zeerust S. Africa **99** C2
Zeil, Mount Austr. **102** C2
Zeitz Ger. **49** F2
Zelenogorsk Rus. Fed. **41** F3

lenogradsk Rus. Fed. **36** B3
ammora Alg. **55** D2
mpel'tepetl, Nudo de *mt.*
Mex. **129** C3
ngfeng Shan *mt.* China **69** B1
nzach Alg. **55** D2
reh, Gowd-e *depr.* Afgh. **78** A2
rrmatt Switz. **53** D2
nograd Rus. Fed. **39** F2
ulenroda Ger. **49** E2
ven Ger. **49** D1
venaar Neth. **48** C2
ya Rus. Fed. **87** K3
ydābād Iran **85** D3
yskoye Vodokhranilishche
esr Rus. Fed. **87** K3
ierz Pol. **51** D2
abinka Belarus **36** B3
altyr Kazakh. **81** D1
anaozen Kazakh. **80** C2
angjiajie China **75** B3
angjiakou China **74** B1
angping China **75** B3
angshu China **75** B3
angwu China **69** A1
angye China **72** C2
angzhou China **75** B3
anibek Kazakh. **80** D2
an'an China **75** B3
aoqing China **75** B3
aotong China **75** A3
ari Namco *salt l.* China **79** C1
arkent Kazakh. **81** F2
arkovskiy Rus. Fed. **37** D2
ashkiv Ukr. **38** D2
ejiang *prov.* China **75** C3
ielaniya, Mys c. Rus. Fed. **86** C1
eleznogorsk Rus. Fed. **37** E3
en'an China **74** A2
engzhou China **74** B2
enyuan China **75** A3

Zherdevka Rus. Fed. **37** F3
Zheshart Rus. Fed. **34** D2
Zhezkazgan *Karagandinskaya
Oblast'* Kazakh. **81** D2
Zhezkazgan *Karagandinskaya
Oblast'* Kazakh. **81** D2
Zhicheng China *see* Qingzhou
Zhigansk Rus. Fed. **87** K2
Zhitikara Kazakh. **80** D1
Zhlobin Belarus **36** D3
Zhmerynka Ukr. **38** C2
Zhob Pak. **78** A1
Zhongba China **79** C2
Zhongning China **74** A2
Zhongshan China **75** B3
Zhongwei China **74** A2
Zhoukou China **74** B2
Zhoushan China **75** C2
Zhovti Vody Ukr. **39** D2
Zhuanghe China **73** A2
Zhukovka Rus. Fed. **37** D3
Zhukovskiy Rus. Fed. **37** E2
Zhumadian China **74** B2
Zhuzhou *Hunan* China **75** B3
Zhuzhou *Hunan* China **75** B3
Zhydachiv Ukr. **38** B2
Zhytkavichy Belarus **36** C3
Zhytomyr Ukr. **38** C1
Žiar nad Hronom Slovakia
51 D3
Zibo China **74** B2
Zielona Góra Pol. **51** D3
Zigaing Myanmar **66** A1
Zigong China **75** A3
Ziguinchor Senegal **90** A3
Žilina Slovakia **51** D3
Zillah Libya **91** D2
Zima Rus. Fed. **87** I3
Zimapán Mex. **129** C2
Zimbabwe *country* Africa **97** C2
Zimmi Sierra Leone **90** A4
Zimnicea Romania **38** C3
Zinder Niger **91** C3

Zitácuaro Mex. **129** B3
Zittau Ger. **50** C2
Zlatoust Rus. Fed. **35** E3
Zlín Czech Rep. **51** D3
Zmiyevka Rus. Fed. **37** E3
Zmiyiv Ukr. **39** E2
Znamenka *Orlovskaya Oblast'*
Rus. Fed. **37** E3
Znam"yanka Ukr. **39** D2
Znojmo Czech Rep. **51** D3
Zolochiv *Kharkivs'ka Oblast'* Ukr.
39 E1
Zolochiv *L'vivs'ka Oblast'* Ukr.
38 B2
Zolotonosha Ukr. **39** D2
Zolotukhino Rus. Fed. **37** E3
Zomba Malawi **97** C1
Zonguldak Turkey **84** B1
Zossen Ger. **49** F1
Zouar Chad **91** D2
Zouérat Maur. **90** A2
Zrenjanin S.M. **58** B1
Zubtsov Rus. Fed. **37** D2
Zug Switz. **53** D2
Zugdidi Georgia **85** C1
Zumbo Moz. **97** C2
Zumpango Mex. **129** C3
Zuni Mountains U.S.A.
126 C1
Zunyi China **75** A3
Županja Croatia **57** C1
Zürich Switz. **53** D2
Zutphen Neth. **48** C1
Zuwārah Libya **91** D1
Zvenyhorodka Ukr. **38** D2
Zvishavane Zimbabwe **97** C2
Zvolen Slovakia **51** D3
Zwedru Liberia **90** B4
Zweibrücken Ger. **48** B3
Zwettl Austria **50** C3
Zwickau Ger. **49** F2
Zwolle Neth. **48** C1
Zyryanka Rus. Fed. **87** M2

If you have enjoyed this atlas, why not expand your geographical knowledge with other Collins titles?

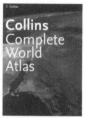

This fully revised atlas presents a complete view of the world, bringing it to life through innovative maps, stunning images and detailed content.

336pp £40.00

HB   0 00 720666 6

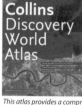

This atlas provides a comprehensive and topical view of today's world and the issues facing it.

240pp   £17.99

HB   0 00 719089 1

All the maps and facts you need to know in today's world.

64pp   £7.99

PB   0 00 719831 0

An up-to-date guide to the flags of over 200 countries including origins, history and relevance of colours for each flag.

256pp   £4.99

PB   0 00 716526 9

To order any of these titles please telephone **0870 787 1732**
For further information about Collins books visit our website:
www.collins.co.uk